Our Common Journey

a transition toward

SUSTAINABILITY

Board on Sustainable Development

Policy Division

National Research Council

D1007464

NATIONAL ACADEMY PRESS
Washington, D.C.

NATIONAL ACADEMY PRESS • 2101 Constitution Avenue, N.W. • Washington, D.C. 20418

NOTICE: The project that is the subject of this report was approved by the Governing Board of the National Research Council, whose members are drawn from the councils of the National Academy of Sciences, the National Academy of Engineering, and the Institute of Medicine. The members of the committee responsible for the report were chosen for their special competences and with regard for appropriate balance.

This study was supported by grants from Mitchell Energy and Development Corporation, the George and Cynthia Mitchell Foundation, and the National Research Council. Additional support for the Summer Study, 1996 was provided by Contract No. 56-DKNA-5-31000 between the National Academy of Sciences and the National Oceanic and Atmospheric Administration. Any opinions, findings, conclusions, or recommendations expressed in this publication are those of the authors and do not necessarily reflect the views of the organizations or agencies that provided support for the project.

Additional copies of this report are available from the National Academy Press, 2101 Constitution Avenue, N.W., Lockbox 285, Washington, D.C. 20055; (800) 624-6242 or (202) 334-3313 (in the Washington metropolitan area); http://www.nap.edu

Library of Congress Catalog Card Number 99-50619

International Standard Book Number 0-309-06783-9

Printed on Recycled Paper ♻

Printed in the United States of America

THE NATIONAL ACADEMIES

National Academy of Sciences
National Academy of Engineering
Institute of Medicine
National Research Council

The **National Academy of Sciences** is a private, nonprofit, self-perpetuating society of distinguished scholars engaged in scientific and engineering research, dedicated to the furtherance of science and technology and to their use for the general welfare. Upon the authority of the charter granted to it by the Congress in 1863, the Academy has a mandate that requires it to advise the federal government on scientific and technical matters. Dr. Bruce M. Alberts is president of the National Academy of Sciences.

The **National Academy of Engineering** was established in 1964, under the charter of the National Academy of Sciences, as a parallel organization of outstanding engineers. It is autonomous in its administration and in the selection of its members, sharing with the National Academy of Sciences the responsibility for advising the federal government. The National Academy of Engineering also sponsors engineering programs aimed at meeting national needs, encourages education and research, and recognizes the superior achievements of engineers. Dr. William A. Wulf is president of the National Academy of Engineering.

The **Institute of Medicine** was established in 1970 by the National Academy of Sciences to secure the services of eminent members of appropriate professions in the examination of policy matters pertaining to the health of the public. The Institute acts under the responsibility given to the National Academy of Sciences by its congressional charter to be an adviser to the federal government and, upon its own initiative, to identify issues of medical care, research, and education. Dr. Kenneth I. Shine is president of the Institute of Medicine.

The **National Research Council** was organized by the National Academy of Sciences in 1916 to associate the broad community of science and technology with the Academy's purposes of furthering knowledge and advising the federal government. Functioning in accordance with general policies determined by the Academy, the Council has become the principal operating agency of both the National Academy of Sciences and the National Academy of Engineering in providing services to the government, the public, and the scientific and engineering communities. The Council is administered jointly by both Academies and the Institute of Medicine. Dr. Bruce M. Alberts and Dr. William A. Wulf are chairman and vice chairman, respectively, of the National Research Council.

Acknowledgments

Many individuals assisted the board in its task by participating in summer studies and workshops, developing background papers, and providing critical reviews of chapters. The board is especially grateful to Tony Patt, Harvard University, Darby Jack, Williams College, and Garren Bird, Williams College, for assisting in preparing background materials; C. Ford Runge, University of Minnesota, for contributing a thoughtful paper on globalization of the economy and sustainability; Eric Kemp-Benedict, Charlie Heaps, and Jack Sieber, Stockholm Environment Institute-Boston/Tellus Institute, Boston, Massachusetts, for preparing the scenarios found in the appendix to Chapter 3; and Professor Harvey Brooks, Harvard University, who provided critical analyses of the strategic approach to navigation and illuminated various terms.

The board would also like to express appreciation to individuals, other than members of the board, National Research Council staff, or individuals serving in a staff role, who participated in summer studies and workshops. They are:

1996 Summer Study: "Scouting the Rapids"
Bar Harbor, Maine
July 20-26, 1996

Bruce Alberts, National Academy of Sciences, Washington, D.C.
Richard Balzhiser, Electric Power Research Institute, Palo Alto,
     California
Robert W. Corell, National Science Foundation, Arlington, Virginia
Arthur J. Hanson, International Institute for Sustainable Development,
     Winnipeg, Manitoba, Canada
H. Theodore Heintz, Jr., Department of Interior, Washington, D.C.
Steve Katona, College of the Atlantic, Bar Harbor, Maine
Mary Hope Katsouros, The H. John Heinz III Center for Science,
     Economics and the Environment, Washington, D.C.
Nancy Maynard, National Aeronautics and Space Administration,
     Washington, D.C.
Donella H. Meadows, Dartmouth College, Durham, New Hampshire
Nebojsa Nakicenovic, International Institute for Applied Systems
     Analysis, Laxenburg, Austria
Robert C. Repetto, World Resources Institute, Washington, D.C.
Roberto Sanchez, Commission for Environmental Cooperation,
     Montreal, Canada
Jurgen Schmandt, Houston Advanced Research Center, The Woodlands,
     Texas
Billie L. Turner, II, Clark University, Worcester, Massachusetts
Robert Watson, World Bank, Washington, D.C.

Workshop on Environmental Barriers to Sustainable Development
Stanford University, Stanford, California
December 12, 1996

Miguel Altieri, University of California, Berkeley, California
Gretchen C. Daily, Stanford University, Stanford, California
Anne H. Ehrlich, Stanford University, Stanford, California
Paul R. Ehrlich, Stanford University, Stanford, California
Walter P. Falcon, Stanford University, Stanford, California
Rosamond Naylor, Stanford University, Stanford, California
Peter M. Vitousek, Stanford University, Stanford, California

Workshop on Decomposition of Complex Issues in Sustainable Development
Washington, D.C.
February 27-28, 1997

Jesse Ausubel, The Rockefeller University, New York, New York
William Bender, Independent Scholar, Groton, Massachusetts
Cabell Brand, Recovery Systems Inc., Salem, Virginia
Thomas Dietz, George Mason University, Fairfax, Virginia
Kenneth Frederick, Resources for the Future, Washington, D.C.
Peter H. Gleick, Pacific Institute for Studies in Development, Environment, and Security, Oakland, California
Mark Rosegrant, International Food, Policy & Research Institute, Washington, D.C.
Lee Schipper, International Energy Agency, Paris, France
Iddo Wernick, Columbia University, New York, New York

Workshop on Food Security: Sustaining the Potential
Minneapolis, Minnesota
May 28-31, 1997

Robert Evenson, Yale University, New Haven, Connecticut
Robert Goodman, University of Wisconsin, Madison, Wisconsin
Anne R. Kupuscinski, University of Minnesota, St. Paul, Minnesota
John Mellor, John Mellor Associates, Inc., Washington, D.C.
Ronald L. Phillips, University of Minnesota, St. Paul, Minnesota
Terry Roe, University of Minnesota, St. Paul, Minnesota
C. Ford Runge, University of Minnesota, St. Paul, Minnesota
G. Edward Schuh, Hubert Humphrey Institute, Minneapolis, Minnesota
Benjamin Senauer, University of Minnesota, St. Paul, Minnesota
Paul Waggoner, Connecticut Agricultural Experiment Station, New Haven, Connecticut

1997 Summer Study: "Science for a Sustainability Transition"
Woods Hole, Massachusetts
July 7-12, 1997

Bruce Alberts, National Academy of Sciences, Washington, D.C.

Jesse H. Ausubel, The Rockefeller University, New York, New York

Richard Balzhiser, Electric Power Research Institute, Palo Alto, California

Eric Davidson, Woods Hole Research Center, Woods Hole, Massachusetts

Paul R. Epstein, Harvard University Medical School, Cambridge, Massachusetts

Christopher Field, Stanford University, Stanford, California

Genevieve Giuliano, University of Southern California, Los Angeles, California

Susan Hanson, Clark University, Worcester, Massachusetts

Gary S. Hartshorn, Organization for Tropical Studies, Durham, North Carolina

Robert W. Lake, Rutgers University, New Brunswick, New Jersey

Jerry M. Melillo, The Ecosystems Center, Woods Hole, Massachusetts

Vicki Norberg-Bohm, Massachusetts Institute of Technology, Cambridge, Massachusetts

Rick Piltz, U.S. Global Change Research Program Office, Washington, D.C.

Robert C. Repetto, World Resource Institute, Washington, D.C.

F. Sherwood Rowland, University of California at Irvine, Irvine, California

Ambuj Sagar, Center for Science and International Affairs, Cambridge, Massachusetts

Jurgen Schmandt, Houston Advanced Research Center, The Woodlands, Texas

Robert H. Socolow, Princeton University, Princeton, New Jersey

H. Guyford Stever, National Research Council, Washington, D.C.

Henry J. Vaux, University of California, Riverside, California

Thomas J. Wilbanks, Oak Ridge National Laboratory, Oak Ridge, Tennessee

William A. Wulf, National Academy of Engineering, Washington, D.C.

Reviewers

This report has been reviewed by individuals chosen for their diverse perspectives and technical expertise in accordance with procedures approved by the National Research Council's Report Review Committee. The purpose of this independent review is to provide candid and critical comments that will assist the authors and the NRC in making the published report as sound as possible and to ensure that the report meets institutional standards for objectivity, evidence, and responsiveness to the study charge. The content of the review comments and draft manuscript remains confidential to protect the integrity of the deliberative process. We thank the following individuals for their participation in the review of this report:

Brian J.L. Berry, University of Texas at Dallas, Richardson, Texas
John S. Chipman, University of Minnesota, Minneapolis, Minnesota
Elisabeth M. Drake, Massachusetts Institute of Technology, Cambridge, Massachusetts
Christopher Field, Stanford University, Stanford, California
Harold K. Forsen, National Academy of Engineering, Washington, D.C.
Peter H. Gleick, Pacific Institute for Studies in Development, Environment, and Security, Oakland, California
Thomas Graedel, Yale University, New Haven, Connecticut
Robert Harriss, Texas A&M University, College Station, Texas
Geoffrey Heal, Columbia University, New York, New York
Brian Heap, Royal Society of London, United Kingdom
Donald F. Hornig, Harvard University, Boston, Massachusetts
Ronald Lee, University of California, Berkeley, California
Daniel P. Loucks, Cornell University, Ithaca, New York
Akin Mabogunje, Development Policy Centre, Ibadan, Nigeria
Harold A. Mooney, Stanford University, Stanford, California
Tarla Rai Peterson, Texas A&M University, College Station, Texas
M.S. Swaminathan, Centre for Research on Sustainable Agriculture, Madras, India
Gilbert E. White, University of Colorado, Denver, Colorado
Robert M. White, Washington Advisory Group, Washington, D.C.

While the individuals listed above provided many constructive comments and suggestions, responsibility for the final content of this report rests solely with the authoring committee and the NRC.

Preface

This report is a work of moderate length, considerable effort, and large ambition. In seeking to reinvigorate the strategic connections between scientific research, technological development, and societies' efforts to achieve environmentally sustainable improvements in human well-being, it has drawn upon nearly 375 reports of the National Research Council and hundreds of other works cited in the text. In the course of its four-year effort, the board held eight meetings, two summer studies, three workshops, and a public symposium, and commissioned two studies. We benefited enormously from the voluntary efforts of the participants in these studies and workshops and their willingness to share with us their knowledge and experience and provide the critical analysis, perspectives, and questions the board needed to sharpen its understanding and judgments.

Most of all, this report is the work of the 25 members of the Board on Sustainable Development, its executive director, Shere Abbott, and her associate, Laura Sigman. The board is extremely large and diverse, as is the nature of our topic, with a heady mix of the natural and social sciences and engineering, seasoned by a few members with considerable experience in both industry and government, and from north and south of the United States. With mutual respect, careful listening, deep thought, and much hard work, they came together with the set of unanimous findings, judgments, and priorities for knowledge and action. Early on, the board benefited from the experience of its first director, John Perry, and the guidance of our chairman, Edward Frieman. Laura Sigman filled in the blanks of memory, intention, and citation with great research and good humor. But in the crucial years of preparation of this report, Shere Abbott piloted us on the board's journey, drafted significant parts of the report, and shared with us the pains of understanding and the pleasures of discovery. On behalf of our colleagues on the board and all who benefit from this report, we acknowledge her central contribution and offer her our heartfelt thanks.

Unlike most NRC reports, this one does not originate in a request from government for scientific advice. Rather it is a product of the desire of a major benefactor, George P. Mitchell, to address the research needs for the global commons of atmosphere, land, and water. Equally, it is a product of the desire of the Academies to reinvigorate the role of science and technology in sustainable development, and to contribute to the meeting of 80 international academies in 2000, co-chaired by the National Academy of Sciences' Foreign Secretary Sherwood Rowland, on the topic of a transition toward sustainability. Mr. Mitchell and the National Research Council have shared the cost of the study and the sometimes anxious awaiting of its outcome. In a special sense, however, the report is the product of Bruce Alberts, the president of the National Academy of Sciences, ably assisted by William Colglazier, who saw in the idea of a sustainability transition the great challenge of the coming century and consistently urged the board to explore and articulate how the science and technology enterprise could provide the knowledge and know-how to help enable that transition.

Finally, we acknowledge all of our children and grandchildren who, by their very presence, anchor us in the vague and uncertain future of the next two generations and make real our common journey. They, and their contemporaries, are the thinkers and doers and movers and shakers of the first half of the next century. And to them this report is dedicated with our hopes for a successful journey.

Robert W. Kates and William C. Clark, *Co-Chairs*
Sustainability Transition Study

Contents

 # Executive Summary

A transition is under way to a world in which human populations are more crowded, more consuming, more connected, and in many parts, more diverse, than at any time in history. Current projections envisage population reaching around 9 billion people in 2050 and leveling off at 10 to 11 billion by the end of the next century—approaching nearly double that of today's 6 billion. Most of this future growth will be concentrated in the developing countries of Africa, Asia, and Latin America, where the need to reduce poverty without harming the environment will be particularly acute. Meeting even the most basic needs of a stabilizing population at least half again as large as today's implies greater production and consumption of goods and services, increased demand for land, energy, and materials, and intensified pressures on the environment and living resources. These challenges will be compounded to the extent that the resource-intensive, consumptive lifestyles currently enjoyed by many in the industrialized nations are retained by them and attained by the rest of humanity.

Can the transition to a stabilizing human population also be a transition to sustainability, in which the people living on earth over the next half-century meet their needs while nurturing and restoring the planet's life support systems? The toll of human development over the last half-century on the environment suggests that the answer may well be negative. However, there is reason for optimism. People have begun to secure more goods and services from activities ranging from agriculture to manufacturing while creating less environmental damage. In addition, efforts

1

have grown up around the world over the last decade that have succeeded in putting sustainability issues on the global political agenda and
in beginning the difficult process of translating this global interest into
practices that will actually work in local and regional circumstances.
Although humanity's common journey toward sustainability has not been
charted with a discernible endpoint, the journey has already begun.

The reconciliation of society's developmental goals with the planet's
environmental limits over the long term is the foundation of an idea
known as *sustainable development*. This idea emerged in the early 1980s
from scientific perspectives on the interdependence of society and environment, and has evolved since in tandem with significant advances in
our understanding of this interdependence. During the concept's first
decade, it garnered increasing political attention and acceptance around
the world—most notably through the activities of the Brundtland Commission (1983-1987) and the United Nations Conference on Environment
and Development, held in Rio de Janeiro in 1992.

As the 20th century draws to a close, however, the difficulties of actually delivering on the hopes that people around the world have attached
to the idea of sustainable development have become increasingly evident.
In part, these difficulties reflect political problems, grounded in questions
of financial resources, equity, and the competition of other issues for the
attention of decision makers. In part, they reflect differing views about
what should be developed, what should be sustained, and over what
period. Additionally, however, the political impetus that carried the idea
of sustainable development so far and so quickly in public forums has
also increasingly distanced it from its scientific and technological base.
As a result, even when the political will necessary for sustainable development has been present, the knowledge and know-how to make some
headway often have not.

This study, conducted by the National Research Council's Board on
Sustainable Development, is an attempt to reinvigorate the essential strategic connections between scientific research, technological development,
and societies' efforts to achieve environmentally sustainable improvements in human well-being. To that end, the Board seeks to illuminate
critical challenges and opportunities that might be encountered in serious
efforts to pursue goals of sustainable development.

Of course, *which* goals should be pursued is a normative question, not
a scientific one. Our analysis, therefore, is based on goals for human well-
being and environmental preservation that have been defined through
recent extensive and iterative processes of international political debate
and action, and sanctioned at intergovernmental conferences over the last
several decades. (These goals are reviewed in some detail below.) Our
choice of goals could have been different, and the goals actually pursued

by society in the future will surely depart from those espoused by its diplomats in the past. Nonetheless, the Board believes that an explicit articulation of goals is necessary if the journey toward sustainability is to be more than a drifting with the powerful currents now shaping interactions between human development and the environment. Less obviously, explicit sustainability goals are required if research and development are to be focused on the most important threats and opportunities that humanity is likely to confront along the way.

This report presents a scientific exploration of the "transition toward sustainability" that would be constituted by successful efforts to attain internationally sanctioned goals for human welfare and environmental protection over the next two generations. This time horizon of analysis, a period of two generations, is necessarily somewhat arbitrary, and it inevitably de-emphasizes obstacles that become severe only over the longer run. However, in our judgment, it is over the next two generations that many of the stresses between human development and the environment will become acute. It is over this period that serious progress in a transition toward sustainability will need to take place if interactions between the earth's human population and life support systems are not to significantly damage both. Additionally, two generations is a realistic time frame for scientific and technological analysis that can provide direction, assess plausible futures, measure success—or the lack of it—along the way, and identify levers for changing course.

The metaphors of "journey" and "navigation" in the work reported here were adopted with serious intent. They reflect the Board's view that any successful quest for sustainability will be a collective, uncertain and adaptive endeavor in which society's discovering of where it wants to go is intertwined with how it might try to get there. Also, they reflect the view that the pathways of a transition to sustainability cannot be charted fully in advance. Instead, they will have to be navigated adaptively at many scales and in many places. Intelligent adjustments in view of the unfolding results of our research and policies, and of the overall course of development, can be made through the process of social learning. Such learning requires some clearly articulated goals for the journey toward sustainability, better understanding of the past and persistent trends of social and environmental change, improved tools for looking along alternative pathways, and clearer understanding of the possible environmental and social threats and opportunities ahead. Ultimately, success in achieving a sustainability transition will be determined not by the possession of knowledge, but by using it, and using it intelligently in setting goals, providing needed indicators and incentives, capturing and diffusing innovation, carefully examining alternatives, establishing effective institutions, and, most generally, encouraging good decisions and taking appropriate actions.

GOALS FOR THE TRANSITION TO SUSTAINABILITY

In the Board's judgment, the primary goals of a transition toward sustainability over the next two generations should be to meet the needs of a much larger but stabilizing human population, to sustain the life support systems of the planet, and to substantially reduce hunger and poverty. For each of these dimensions of a successful sustainability transition, international conventions and agreements reflect a broad consensus about minimal goals and targets, though there is seldom analysis of these goals' implications, their potential interactions with one another, or their competing claims on scarce resources. Our analysis documents these goals and the uneven progress that has been made in meeting them.

In particular, in the area of human needs, internationally agreed-on targets exist for providing food and nutrition, nurturing children, finding shelter, and providing an education, but not for finding employment. There is an implicit hierarchy of needs that favors children and people in disasters and that favors feeding and nurturing first, followed by education, housing, and employment.

Compared to targets for meeting human needs, quantitative targets for preserving life support systems are fewer, more modest, and more contested. Global targets now exist for ozone-depleting substances and greenhouse gases, and regional targets exist for some air pollutants. Absolute prohibitions (zero targets) exist for ocean dumping of radioactive wastes and some toxics, for the taking and/or sale of a few large mammals (whales, elephants, seals), migratory birds when breeding or endangered, and certain regional fishing stocks. Water, land resources, and ecosystems such as arid lands and forests have, at best, qualitative targets for the achievement of sustainable management or restoration. International standards exist for many toxic materials, organic pollutants, and heavy metals that threaten human health, but not for ecosystem health.

TRENDS AND TRANSITIONS

Certain current trends of population and habitation, wealth and consumption, technology and work, connectedness and diversity, and environmental change are likely to persist well into the coming century and could significantly undermine the prospects for sustainability. If they do persist, many human needs will not be met, life support systems will be dangerously degraded, and the numbers of hungry and poor will increase. Among the social trends reviewed by the Board that merit particular attention are expanding urbanization, growing disparities of wealth, wasteful consumption, increasing connectedness, and shifts in the distribution of power. Environmental trends of special concern include the buildup of long-lived greenhouse gases in the atmosphere and associated climate changes, the decline of valued marine fisheries; increasing regional shortfalls in the quality and quantity of fresh water; expanding tropical deforestation; the continuing loss of species, ecosystems, and their services; the emergence and reemergence of serious diseases; and more generally, the increasing human dominance of natural systems. Some of these current trends present significant opportunities for advancing a transition toward sustainability, as well as threats to that transition. All, however, bear watching.

Even the most alarming current trends, however, may experience transitions that enhance the prospects for sustainability. Trends are rarely constant. Breaks or inflections in long-term trends mark periods of transition. Some transitions relevant to the prospects for sustainability are already under way to varying degrees in specific places and regions around the globe: the demographic transition from high to low birth and death rates; the health transition from early death by infectious diseases to late death by cancer, heart disease, and stroke; the economic transition from state to market control; the civil society transition from single-party, military, or state-run institutions to multiparty politics and a rich mix of governmental and nongovernmental institutions. Environmentally, some significant positive transitions have occurred in specific regions. These include shifts from increasing to decreasing rates of emissions for specific pollutants, from deforestation to reforestation, and from shrinking to expanding ranges for certain endangered species. Individual, local trend reversals such as these clearly do not make a sustainability transition. But they do show that efforts to catalyze or accelerate relevant shifts can have significant implications for meeting human needs in ways that sustain the life support systems of the planet.

EXPLORING THE FUTURE

The Board evaluated various tools (integrated assessment models, scenarios, regional information systems) that could be used to explore what the future may hold and to test the likelihood of achieving the goals it set, under varied assumptions about human development and the environment. The purpose of these tools is not to predict the future, but rather to structure and discipline thinking about future possibilities in the light of present knowledge and intentions. They can be used to explore what contingencies society may face, assess how well society is prepared to deal with those contingencies, and identify indicators for which society should be watchful.

Integrated assessment models seek to link in a consistent fashion formal models of the environment and society. The accumulating experience suggests that the models can make a difference in society's ability to address complex interactions between environment and development by providing analytic insight through problem redefinition and by directly informing policy making through supporting international environmental negotiations (e.g., whaling and stratospheric ozone depletion). Models can also be useful probes of uncertainties and their significance in exploring the possible future implications of current decisions. Deliberate simplification of such complex models can be an important part of strategies for exploring the future. But the art of providing useful simplifications remains demanding and underdeveloped.

Long-range development scenarios are summary stories of how the world might unfold. They are useful for organizing scientific insight, gauging emerging risks, and challenging the imagination. Scenarios are told in the language of words as well as numbers, because some critical dimensions—assumptions about culture, values, lifestyles, and social institutions—require qualitative description. Scenarios do not predict the future; they provide insight into the present. Experience suggests that scenarios to support the study of global futures and the requirements for a transition to sustainability should be rigorous, reflecting the insights of science and modeling. But scenario building must also recognize that the story of the future is not a mere projection of current trends and understanding. The spectrum of scenarios to consider should contrast long-range visions that reflect the uncertainty about how the global system might unfold, the possibility of surprise, and a range of pathways to a sustainable future.

Regional information systems constitute a third tool. These systems harness scientific knowledge to support policy decisions affecting the long-term interactions of development and environment, and often contain elements of scenario development and integrated modeling. Experience in developing such information systems shows that a regional scale approach grounded in ecosystem knowledge and cooperative and adaptive management constitutes an infrastructure for social learning—a way to lay out scientific knowledge in a form that can be accessible to nonspecialists. As such, these systems provide a mode of communication and negotiation that can draw opponents together for learning as well as conflict resolution, allowing learning to continue as action proceeds. Work at the regional scale shows that the way human and natural systems interact can be studied and acted upon within an integrated framework.

Although the future is unknowable, **based on our analysis of**

persistent trends and plausible futures, the Board believes that a successful transition toward sustainability is possible over the next two generations. This transition could be achieved without miraculous technologies or drastic transformations of human societies. What will be required, however, are significant advances in basic knowledge, in the social capacity and technological capabilities to utilize it, and in the political will to turn this knowledge and know-how into action. There is ample evidence from attitudinal surveys and grassroots activities that the public supports and demands such progress.

ENVIRONMENTAL THREATS AND OPPORTUNITIES

Knowledge about the most significant potential obstacles to sustainability is needed along with an awareness of the opportunities for deflecting, adapting to, or mitigating the threats. The most serious threats are those that affect the ability of multiple sectors of society to move ahead toward the normative goals for sustainability; have cumulative or delayed consequences, with effects felt over a long time; are irreversible or difficult to change; or have a notable potential to interact with each other to damage earth's life support systems. The Board attempted several approaches to identify significant environmental threats, including (1) a review of comparative rankings of the severity of environmental hazards for particular times and places; (2) expert assessment of the challenges and opportunities of human activities in several developmental sectors that the Brundtland Commission identified as critical (human population and well-being, urban systems, agricultural production, industry, energy, and living resources); and finally, (3) evaluation of how these threats and opportunities may change when multiple activities from different sectors interact with complex environmental systems (e.g. freshwater systems, atmosphere and climate, and species and ecosystems).

Overall, hazard rankings suggest that, for most nations of the world, water and air pollution are the top priority issues; for most of the more industrialized nations, ozone depletion and climate change are also ranked highly; while for many of the less-industrialized countries, droughts or floods, disease epidemics, and the availability of local living resources are crucial. The rankings, however, tend to depend on the circumstances of the assessed region, focus on the problem rather than the cause, and do not address interactions. The analysis of common challenges to development showed that while some progress had been made in each sector (e.g., lowering fertility to improve the balance between population and resources; increasing opportunities for health and education; providing water, air, and sanitation services in urban centers; expanding food production; reducing and reusing materials; using energy more efficiently; and implementing conservation measures for living resources), many of the remaining challenges are at least as serious as they were 10 years ago.

In addition, our review of hazards and sectors showed that most decision making and much research about threats has chosen to treat environmental perturbations and associated human activities in relatively discrete categories such as "soil erosion," "fisheries depletion," and "acid rain." Such categorization is also apparent in the organization of ministries, regulation, and research administration around the world. Both understanding and management have benefited substantially from these approaches. However, much has been missed, and many of the challenges in seeking a sustainability transition lie in the interactions among environmental and human activities that were previously treated as separate and distinct.

The Board concludes that most of the individual environmental problems that have occupied most of the world's attention to date are unlikely in themselves to prevent substantial progress in a transition toward sustainability over the next two generations. Over longer time periods, unmitigated expansion of even these individual problems could certainly pose serious threats to people and the planet's life support systems. Even more troubling in the medium term, however, are the environmental threats arising from multiple, cumulative, and interactive stresses, driven by a variety of human activities. These stresses or syndromes, which result in severe environmental degradation, can be difficult to untangle from one another, and complex to manage. Though often aggravated by global changes, they are shaped by the physical, ecological, and social interactions at particular places, that is, locales or regions. **Developing an integrated and place-based understanding of such threats and the options for dealing with them is a central challenge for promoting a transition toward sustainability.**

REPORTING ON THE TRANSITION

Indicators are essential to inform society over the coming decades how, and to what extent, progress is being made in navigating a transition toward sustainability. Regularly repeated observations of natural and social phenomena facilitate the provision of systematic feedback. They provide both quantitative and qualitative descriptions of human well-being, the economy, and impacts of human activities upon the natural world.

Numerous efforts are now underway to collect, analyze, and aggregate the information needed to form sets of indicators of environmental, societal, and technological change. On an ecological scale, these efforts range in coverage from watersheds to the whole planet, and on a political scale from municipal to international institutions and activities. **Nonetheless, the Board finds that there is no consensus on the appropriateness of the current sets of indicators or the scientific basis for choosing among them.** Their effectiveness is limited by the lack of agreement on the meaning of sustainable development, on the appropriate level of specificity or aggregation for optimal indicators, and on the preferred use of existing as opposed to desired data sets.

For reporting on a sustainability transition, however, it is clear that multiple indicators are needed to chart progress toward the goals for meeting human needs and preserving life support systems, and to evaluate the efficacy of actions taken to attain these goals. Thus, specific indicators of human welfare will be required on global and regional scales. Many of these indicators are already available. Selecting indicators of life support systems will be more difficult. In this report, the Board suggests three levels of indicators: planetary circulatory systems, regional zones of critical vulnerability, and local inventories of productive landscapes and ecosystems. Monitoring planetary circulatory systems captures changes in the Earth's biogeochemical cycles and its networks of human communication, technology, trade, and travel. Critical zones of human-environment vulnerability are characterized in ways that capture the regional interactions of specific ecosystems, human activities, social and economic capacity to respond and adapt, and the feasibility of reversing damage. Local inventories assist conservation by capturing the effects of human settlements on environmental services and resources, and on the prospects for sustaining species, habitats, and ecosystems.

To characterize the effectiveness of actions undertaken to reach the goals, at least four approaches seem promising and deserving of further study: maintaining national capital accounts; conducting policy assessments; monitoring essential trends and transitions; and surprise diagnosis. One approach to national capital accounts uses economic accounting to assess the value of three types of national resources—natural, human, and produced capital. This analytical framework draws attention to transformations among forms of wealth, and acknowledges and highlights the importance of undervalued natural capital. The second approach, policy assessment, supports adaptive management by attending to the details of policy implementation (e.g., data gathering) such that lessons can be learned from any policies instituted—even those that fail. The third approach measures progress that has been made by monitoring essential trends and transitions—such as those in demographics, consumption patterns, and energy-intensity and pollution per unit of economic output. Finally, surprise diagnoses—the search for and evaluation of unanticipated indicator patterns such as the stratospheric ozone hole—are essential for identifying mistakes and omissions of analysis.

INTEGRATING KNOWLEDGE AND ACTION

Because the pathway to sustainability cannot be charted in advance, it will have to be navigated through trial and error and conscious experimentation. The urgent need is to design strategies and institutions that can better integrate incomplete knowledge with experimental action into programs of adaptive management and social learning. A capacity for long-term, intelligent investment in the production of relevant knowledge, know-how, and the use of both must be a component of any strategy for the transition to sustainability. In short, this strategy must be one not just of thinking but also of doing. Our explorations suggest that this strategy should include a spectrum of initiatives, from curiosity-driven research addressing fundamental processes of environmental and social change, to focused policy experiments designed to promote specific sustainability goals.

Tensions exist between broadly based and highly focused research strategies; between integrative, problem-driven research and research firmly grounded in particular disciplines; and between the quest for generalizable scientific understanding of sustainability issues and the localized knowledge of environment-society interactions that give rise to those issues and generate the options for dealing with them. These understandable tensions must be addressed.

Priorities for Research: Sustainability Science

From the Board's efforts to address these tensions, three priority tasks emerged for advancing the research agenda of what might be called "sustainability science."

• **Develop a research framework that integrates global and local perspectives to shape a "place-based" understanding of the interactions between environment and society.** The framework should build on the intellectual foundations of the geophysical, biological, social, and technological sciences, and on their interdisciplinary research programs, such as earth systems science and industrial ecology. It will need to integrate across geographic scales to combine global, regional, and local perspectives as needed in understanding what is going on in the particular places where people live, work, and govern. Establishing a place-based sustainability science will also provide a conceptual and operational approach for monitoring progress in integrated understanding and management.

• **Initiate focused research programs on a small set of understudied** questions that are central to a deeper understanding of interactions between society and the environment. The concepts of critical loads and carrying capacities have proven sufficiently problematical that further efforts are needed to determine whether scientifically meaningful "limits" can be established beyond which the life support systems of the planet cannot safely be pushed. Improving the understanding and documentation of transitions will be necessary as these transitions unfold (e.g., changes in population growth patterns, globalization of the economy, energy and materials intensity in human activities, and governance). In addition, more exploration will be needed of the determinants of and alternatives to consumption patterns; the incentives (in markets, remedies for market failure, and information) for technical innovation that produces more of human value with less environmental damage; and the institutions, indicator systems, and assessment tools for navigating a sustainablity transition.

• **Promote better utilization of existing tools and processes for linking knowledge to action in pursuit of a transition to sustainability.** A great deal of knowledge, know-how, and capacity for learning about sustainable development is already assembled in various observational systems, laboratories, and management regimes around the world—but these resources are not widely known or used. The successful production and use of the knowledge needed for a sustainability transition will require significant strengthening of institutional capacity in at least four areas: the linking of long-term research programs to societal goals; coupling global, national, and local institutions into effective research systems; linking academia, government, and the private sector in collaborative research partnerships; and integrating disciplinary knowledge in place-based, problem-driven research efforts.

Priorities for Action: Knowledge-Action Collaboratives

Developing the knowledge, assessment tools and methods, and institutional understanding needed for a sustainability transition is a central task for science and technology. But enough is already known to undertake early priorities for action. For the challenges in the core sectoral areas of sustainable development identified more than a decade ago by the Brundtland Commission —human population and well-being, cities, agriculture, energy and materials, and living resources— the Board has identified appropriate next steps by integrating what is known about a sector with what can be done. This means integrating both the lessons learned from the last decade and the projected needs and know-how over the coming decades with both the policy actions that can move society along a positive pathway and the indicators that can monitor our progress.

It also means creating new and strengthening existing "knowledge-action collaboratives" that bring together the many diverse and sector-specific groups that have the knowledge and know-how and the means to implement it.

Priorities for action include the following:

• **Accelerate current trends in fertility reduction.** After reviewing the continuing trends of reduction in fertility and the potential for accelerated reductions, the Board believes that achieving a 10 percent reduction in the population now projected for 2050 is a desirable and attainable goal. While growth rates are declining, because the current growth rate (still higher than replacement level) is applied to a fast-increasing population base, absolute population growth will continue to have tremendous momentum over the next two decades. World population size is expected to increase by 3 billion people by 2050. This number can be reduced by meeting the large unmet need for contraceptives worldwide, by postponing having children through education and job opportunities, and by reducing desired family size while increasing the care and education of smaller numbers of children. Moreover, the lack of access to family planning contributes significantly to maternal and infant mortality, an additional burden on human well-being. Allowing families to avoid the unwanted births, enhancing the status of women to delay childbearing, and nurturing children would result in a billion fewer people and substantially ease the transition toward sustainability.

• **Accommodate an expected doubling to tripling of the urban system in a habitable, efficient, and environmentally friendly manner.** The urban proportion of the world's population is projected to grow from 50 percent to 80 percent or more over the next two generations, with 4 billion people added to the 3 billion people living in cities today. The cities emerging from this unprecedented growth in urban populations must meet the needs for housing, nurturing, educating and employing these 4 billion new urban dwellers. Providing them with adequate water, sanitation, and clean air may be one of the most daunting and underappreciated challenges of the first half of the 21st century. Nonetheless, by learning how to utilize the potential efficiencies provided by increasing population densities and the opportunity to build anew, these cities could meet human needs while reducing their relative "ecological footprint" and providing more environmentally friendly engines of development.

• **Reverse declining trends in agricultural production in Africa; sustain historic trends elsewhere.** The most critical near-term aspect of this goal is to reverse the decline in agricultural production capability in Sub-Saharan Africa, the only region where population growth has outpaced growth in agricultural production. A collaborative effort involving

African governments, the African scientific community, African farmers, and nongovernmental organizations will be needed to address the causes and the responsive actions to achieve the technical capacity and implementation needed. At the same time, over the two generations to come, meeting the challenge of feeding the burgeoning world population as a whole and reducing hunger while sustaining life support systems will require a dramatic overall advance in food production, distribution, and access. Sustainable increases in output per hectare of two to three times present levels will be required by 2050. Productivity must be increased on robust areas and restored to degraded lands, while damage to fragile land areas is reduced. New biology-based technologies and implementation will be needed to meet these challenges, renewing yield increases and diminishing negative environmental and social consequences.

• **Accelerate improvements in the use of energy and materials.** A reasonable goal for the sustainability transition is to double the historical rate of improvements in energy and materials use. These improvements include both the long-term reduction in the amount of carbon produced per unit of energy ("decarbonization") and, more generally, in the amount of energy or material used per unit of product (efficiency or intensity). Research and development should continue on the many efforts under way to improve household energy-efficiency, build low-polluting, energy-efficient automobiles, and reduce waste, as well as to minimize the throughput of energy and materials from industrial processes through reuse, recycling, and the substitution of services for products. In designing and evaluating institutions and incentives to encourage sustainable energy technologies, it will be important to carefully examine system implications for these technologies over their full life cycles, using such strategies as material balance modeling and economic input-output analysis together with consideration of environmental loadings. Without such systematic assessment, policies that appear to promote better solutions may in the long run have serious undesirable consequences, such as creating difficult problems for the recycling and disposal of materials.

• **Restore degraded ecosystems while conserving biodiversity elsewhere.** For the human-dominated ecosystems (forests, grasslands, agricultural, urban, and coastal environments) undergoing degradation from multiple demands and stresses, the goal should be to work toward restoring and maintaining these systems' functions and integrity. Their services, including genetic diversity, and their human uses both need to be sustained over the long term. Greater understanding is needed of how biological systems work, how to stem the continued loss of habitats, and how ecosystems can be restored and managed at the landscape or regional scale. This will require knowledge of the socioeconomic determinants of overexploitation, the appropriate valuation of ecosystem services, and sustainable management and harvesting techniques. Those ecosystems that have been the least influenced by human activities represent the last reserves of the earth's biodiversity. For future generations, these systems provide a treasure of stored biodiversity and of ethical, aesthetic, and spiritual qualities. For these systems, the goal should be to protect and conserve biological diversity, both by dramatically reducing current rates of land conversion and by more rigorously identifying and selecting protected areas.

Achievements in one sector do not imply improvements in other sectors or in the situation overall. For example, efforts to preserve natural ecosystems for ethical or aesthetic reasons, or for the goods and services they provide to humans, may ultimately fail if they do not account for the longer-term changes likely to be introduced by atmospheric pollution, climate change, water shortages, or human population enchroachment. **The Board therefore also proposes integrated approaches to research and actions at the regional scale related to water, atmosphere and climate, and species and ecosystems.** The need is to develop both a thorough understanding of the most critical interactions and an integrated strategy for planning and management. This will require evaluation of ongoing experiments in integrative research, more focused effort on such research at all spatial scales, and new frameworks for improving interactions among partners in industry, academia, foundations, and other organizations.

There is no precedent for the ambitious enterprise of mobilizing science and technology to ensure a transition to sustainability. Nevertheless, the United States has a special obligation to join and help guide the journey. In addition to having a robust scientific and technological capacity, the United States is a major consumer of global resources. Moreover, sustainable communities have not been realized across the U.S. landscape. Carrying out this enterprise successfully will require collaborative efforts across many dimensions of science and society.

Implementation of the recommendations in this report will be a task not only for the National Research Council and its U.S. partners in science, but also for the international science community, governments, foundations, voluntary organizations, and the private sector working together through innovative knowledge-action collaboratives. Our goal here has not been to preempt any broader endeavors involving these national and international partners, but rather to encourage them and to suggest some initial directions for our common journey toward sustainability.

 # Introduction

We are in the midst of a transition to a world in which human populations are more crowded, more consuming, more connected, and in many parts of the world, more diverse, than at any time in history. Current projections envisage population reaching around 9 billion people in 2050 and leveling off at 10 to 11 billion by the end of the next century—close to double that of today's 6 billion.[1] Most of this future growth will be concentrated in the developing countries of Africa, Asia, and Latin America, where the need to reduce poverty without harm to the environment will be particularly acute. Meeting even the most basic needs of a stabilized population at least half again as large as today's implies greater production and consumption of goods and services, increased demand for land, energy, and materials, and intensified pressures on the environment and living resources. These challenges will be compounded to the extent that the resource-intensive, consumptive lifestyles currently enjoyed by many in the industrialized nations are retained by them and attained by the rest of humanity.

Can the transition to a stable human population also be a transition to sustainability, in which the people living on earth over the next half-century meet their needs while nurturing and restoring the planet's life support systems? The toll of human development over the last half-century on the environment suggests that the answer may well be "no." The examples of Appalachian coal country, the Aral Sea, or the Southeast Asian forest fires serve as vivid reminders of how devastating to both society and the environment the implications of heedless development can be. On a more optimistic note, people have begun learning how to secure more social "goods" while creating fewer environmental "bads" in activities ranging from agriculture to manufacturing to recreation. A remarkable number of efforts have grown up around the world over the last decade that have succeeded in putting sustainability issues on the global political agenda—and in beginning the actual search for specific pathways toward sustainability in many local contexts. If, at the close of the 20th century, the end of our common voyage toward sustainability has not yet been charted, much less brought into sight, the journey has at least begun.

In recent years, the science and technology community has not been a particularly prominent participant on this journey. This has not always been the case. Early thinking on sustainability issues—for example, the World Conservation Strategy[2]—was firmly grounded in a scientific understanding of the workings and limits of resources and environmental systems. But, with the possible exception of the ozone protocols, the central thrusts of many recent sustainability initiatives have been shaped more by political than scientific ideas. Major recent innovations have come in the realm of policies and institutions, rather than knowledge and know-how. Relatively little progress has been made in developing a scientific understanding of the obstacles facing any transition to sustainability, the technological opportunities for pursuing this goal, or the use of modern sensing and information systems for providing navigational aids along the way.

The principal national and international reports have thus tended to address science and technology as necessary, potentially expensive, but otherwise unproblematic inputs to the process of sustainable development. As inputs, science and technology have been addressed either as highly specific requirements (e.g., methods for the safe disposal of nuclear wastes) or as the most general needs (e.g., enhanced scientific understanding, better technology transfer, more useful policy assessments, improved environmental prediction, more complete monitoring and reporting, or strengthened capacity). Moreover, overall investments in research and development have been declining in recent years for a variety of reasons. Thus, we approach the 21st century with less than might be hoped for in the way of a useful strategic appraisal of how the knowledge and know-how most crucial to successfully navigating the transition toward sustainability is to be identified or of how the capacity to create the needed science and technology is to be developed and sustained.

This report and the processes involved in its preparation and dissemination seek to help reengage the science and technology community as a committed partner in the ongoing global effort to achieve sustainable development. This report is the result of a nearly four-year study of the

National Research Council's Board on Sustainable Development. The Board is composed of 25 members with expertise in diverse topics relating to sustainability, including population demographics, agronomy, agriculture, geography, meteorology, atmospheric chemistry, oceanography, ecology, integrative biology, modeling, hydrology, economics, industry, international finance, energy research, engineering, political science, anthropology, health, and public policy. Since its formation in 1994, the Board has held three workshops (Environmental Barriers to Sustainable Development, December 1996; Decomposition of Complex Issues in Sustainable Development, February 1997; Food Security: Sustaining the Potential, May 1997), two week-long summer studies (Scouting the Rapids, Bar Harbor, Maine, August 1996; Science for the Sustainability Transition, Woods Hole, Massachusetts, July 1997) and other meetings; and the Board has commissioned several papers. The concepts and broad findings of this study were presented at a Symposium on The Transition to Sustainability, which was held at the 135th Annual Meeting of the National Academy of Sciences, in April 1998.

The Board has an ambitious plan for disseminating the messages of the report both within the United States and to the international science and technology communities. In particular, we have suggested that the InterAcademy Panel on International Issues (IAP)—an informal network of academies of science—take up the issue of sustainability as a major thrust of its program over the next several years. In pursuit of this goal, the Board will present its report as a contribution to an IAP Conference on the Transition to Sustainability, being held in Tokyo on May 15-19, 2000. It is hoped that this conference will set in motion a number of international initiatives that reengage the scientific and technical communities in the dialog on sustainability.

We adopted the metaphors of "journey" and "navigation" in the work reported here with serious intent. They reflect our conviction that any successful quest for sustainability will necessarily be a collective, uncertain, and adaptive endeavor in which society's discovering of where it wants to go and how it might try to get there will be inextricably intertwined. Humanity is no more master of its fate in interactions with the environment than is a canoeist shooting the rapids of a turbulent river— a vivid image used to suggest the challenges to policy in seeking sustainable development.[3] But if we do not suffer the delusion of having total control of the future, neither are we fatalists who believe that the skills of the canoeist, boat builder, and mapmaker are irrelevant to the journey's outcome. Instead, as evidenced by many successful explorations from the Beagle to the Hubble, science and technology, we believe, are the necessary complements to inspired leadership, creative imagination, and good luck. The objective of this report is to suggest how the science and technology enterprise can increase society's chances of undertaking and achieving our common journey of a transition toward sustainability.

We are too aware of the host of shortcomings in the present study. Despite our commitment to international perspectives, except for members from Canada and Mexico, the Board has been essentially a group of U.S. nationals examining a global issue with regard to which local conditions, traditions, and perceptions matter very much. Despite our understanding of how greatly the prospects for any transition to sustainability depend on substantial international political stability and effective domestic governance, we have not explored the political threats or all possible social threats (e.g., terrorism, violence) to such conditions or how they might be mitigated. Despite our belief that poverty alleviation is central to the challenges of sustainability, we have not focused on the economic programs needed to increase productivity of the abjectly poor segments of the world's population. And despite our conviction that taking on the challenges of sustainability is an inherently interdisciplinary activity, we have been better at mobilizing the insights of some disciplines than others in our work. Finally, we are aware that the questions posed and issues addressed in this report are hardly new. Much is known about population, cities, land transformation, agriculture, ecology, and other phenomena that we discuss here only in the most general of terms. We are equally aware that much of what is known is not applied—for a variety of political, economic, and cultural reasons.

Thus, in this report we have found ourselves both emphasizing the necessity of better applying what is known and arguing that the capacity to produce new knowledge will become increasingly important as pressures on societies and the life support systems of the planet become more intense. More of the same in science and technology or in politics is unlikely to meet the reasonable aspirations of people throughout the globe. But we believe that the scientific and technical community must play an important role in helping societies to realize these aspirations. We believe there are no ready answers to questions of whether or how billions of people in societies all over the globe can achieve their hopes for a better quality of life without severely degrading life support systems. At the same time, we also believe that failure to engage the issues in a truly serious way is shirking both our technical responsibilities and our public duties. Nevertheless, we sit at the Board's table as experts in particular fields, not as advocates of particular causes. This study represents our attempt to seriously engage the issues and to offer a few suggestions for next steps in what appears to be the right direction.

To this end, Chapter 1 develops the Board's concept of a transition to sustainability and the roles of science, technology, and values in outfitting and navigating the journey toward it. Chapter 2 provides an historically based map of the persistent, large-scale currents of social and environmental change into which the voyage is launched, and with which it will have to contend. Chapter 3 reviews the range of modeling, assessment, and scenario methods available for looking ahead at possible development pathways and their implications for sustainability. Chapter 4 draws on current scientific understanding to outline some of the most significant environmental threats and opportunities that the voyage might encounter. Chapter 5 explores the contributions that appropriate monitoring and indicator systems might make for our abilities to proceed in a turbulent world of surprise and inevitable policy failures. Chapter 6 presents a vision of how knowledge and action could be better integrated in a strategy for navigating toward sustainability, and priorities for research and action to promote the life and livelihood goals of our common journey.

ENDNOTES

[1]   UN (United Nations). 1999 (forthcoming). *Word population prospects: The 1998 revision.* New York: United National Population Division.
[2]   IUCN (The World Conservation Union), UNEP (United Nations Environment Programme), WWF (World Wildlife Fund), FAO (Food and Agriculture Organization of the United Nations), and UNESCO (United Nations Educational, Scientific, and Cultural Organization). 1980. *World conservation strategy: Living resource conservation for sustainable development.* Gland, Switzerland: IUCN.
[3]   William Ruckelshaus, former Administrator of the U.S. Environmental Protection Agency and member of the World Commission on Environment and Development, the well-known "Brundtland Commission," 1989. Toward a sustainable world. Scientific American 261, No. 3:166-74.

 **Our Common Journey**

The test of our progress is not whether we add more to the abundance of those who have much; it is whether we provide enough for those who have too little.
Franklin Delano Roosevelt (Second Inaugural Address, January 20, 1937)

Over the last two decades, as appreciation of the challenge of "sustainable development" has very rapidly grown, the term has been used with diverse and evolving meanings in public debate and the scholarly literature. At the outset of our analysis, we therefore look at these various uses of the term. Next, we review action that has been taken in pursuit of sustainability goals since the 1987 publication of the World Commission on Environment and Development's report (often called "the Brundtland report") *Our Common Future.* In the heart of this chapter, we develop our concept of a "transition toward sustainability"—a transition over the early decades of the 21st century in which a stabilizing world population comes to meet its needs by moving away from actions that degrade the planet's life support systems and living resources, while moving toward those that sustain and restore these systems and resources. Moreover, this transition would move away from actions that widen disparities in human welfare and toward measures that reduce hunger and poverty. Ours is a normative vision of sustainability, which in our view is defined by the joint objectives of meeting human needs while preserving life support systems and reducing hunger and poverty. This vision is firmly anchored in the goals and aspirations of the world community as expressed through major international conventions and commissions of the past decade. Finally, in this chapter, we close with a brief exposition of the role of science and technology in this transition—a role that we see above all as one of fostering rapid and effective social learning.

SUSTAINABLE DEVELOPMENT:
COMMON CONCERNS, DIFFERING EMPHASES

"Sustainable development"—the reconciliation of society's developmental goals with its environmental limits over the long term—is the most recent conceptual focus linking the collective aspirations of the world's peoples for peace, freedom, improved living conditions, and a healthy environment. These four conditions frequently emerge as key ideals of the last half of the 20th century. Peace, the first, was thought to be secured in the postwar world of 1945. It was thereafter complicated by the nuclear arms race, then maintained globally but still fought locally in the long cold war, and is now sought again in places as diverse as Bosnia, Central Africa, the Middle East, and Ireland. Freedom proclaimed itself in the struggle to end imperialism, to extend human rights, and to end totalitarian oppression. Now, in the wake of establishing widespread national independence, development is the primary ideal that captures the hopes of the poorest two-thirds of the world, who aspire to both the basic necessities and the material well-being of the wealthy third. The most recently emphasized ideal has concerned the earth itself, initially focusing on natural resources, later extending to the human environment, and finally to the complex systems that support life on earth. Characteristic of the last quarter of a century is the effort to link all these aspirations of humankind—particularly through the realization of how often the pursuit of one condition requires pursuit of the others. International high-level commissions (such as the Independent Commission on International Development Issues 1980 [Brandt], the Independent Commission on Disarmament and Security Issues 1982 [Palme], and the World Commission on Environment and Development 1987 [Brundtland]), often followed by great international conferences, have attempted to make a case, moral and pragmatic, for such links. A specific recent focus has thus been on the critical relationships between development and the environment.

Many notions now incorporated within the concept of sustainable development can be traced back through the 1980 World Conservation Strategy and the 1972 Stockholm Conference on the Human Environment to the early days of the international conservation movement.[1] Today's understanding of the links between environment and development, however, is little more than a decade old, stemming from the Brundtland report, *Our Common Future*.[2] The idea of sustainable development was given additional impetus at the 1992 United Nations Conference on Environment and Development (UNCED) in Rio de Janeiro. It has rapidly spread and is now a central theme in the missions of countless international organizations, national institutions, "sustainable cities," and locales.

The genius of the idea of sustainable development lies in its attempt to reconcile the real conflicts between economy and environment and between the present and the future. Thus, the Brundtland Commission, in its widely accepted statement, defines sustainable development as the ability of humanity "to ensure that it meets the needs of the present without compromising the ability of future generations to meet their own needs."[3] Within this general framework, an extraordinarily diverse set of groups and institutions have taken the concept of sustainable development and projected upon it their own hopes and goals. There have been extensive reviews of these diverse concepts and definitions.[4] From these reviews, four types of key differences emerge. While sharing a common concern for the fate of the earth, proponents of sustainable development differ in their emphases on (1) what is to be sustained, (2) what is to be developed, (3) the types of links that should hold between the entities to be sustained and the entities to be developed, and (4) the extent of the future envisioned. (See Figure 1.1.)

What Is To Be Sustained

The emphases on what is to be sustained fall within three major areas: nature, life support systems, and community. The most common emphases concern *life support systems*, where the life to be supported first is human. Subsumed within this group are emphases on the classic *natural resources*—which, while found in nature, are particularly useful for people. Classified as either renewable or nonrenewable, flow or stock, these resources have preoccupied many generations seeking to exploit, conserve, or preserve them. In the last quarter of a century, the concept of natural resources has expanded, from a focus on primary products and production inputs to include the values of aesthetics, recreation, and the absorption and cleansing of pollution and waste.[5] This extended view of natural resources becomes popularly associated with *environment* and the many features are defined by ecologists as *ecosystem services*.[6] A recent study catalogued and valued 17 ecosystem services, ranging from atmospheric gas regulation to cultural opportunities.[7]

A less anthropocentric view of life and values is found in the emphases on sustaining *nature* itself for its own intrinsic value. The earth's assemblages of life forms, whether described as *biodiversity* in general, or as *species* or *ecosystems* in particular, are to be sustained not only for their utilitarian service to humans, but also because of humanity's moral obligations. These obligations are characterized as "stewardship"—acknowledging the primacy of humans—or as the proper response to a form of "natural rights" in which earth and its other living things have equal claims to existence and sustenance. Additionally, not only are biological species seen as endangered, but cultural species are as well. Thus, the

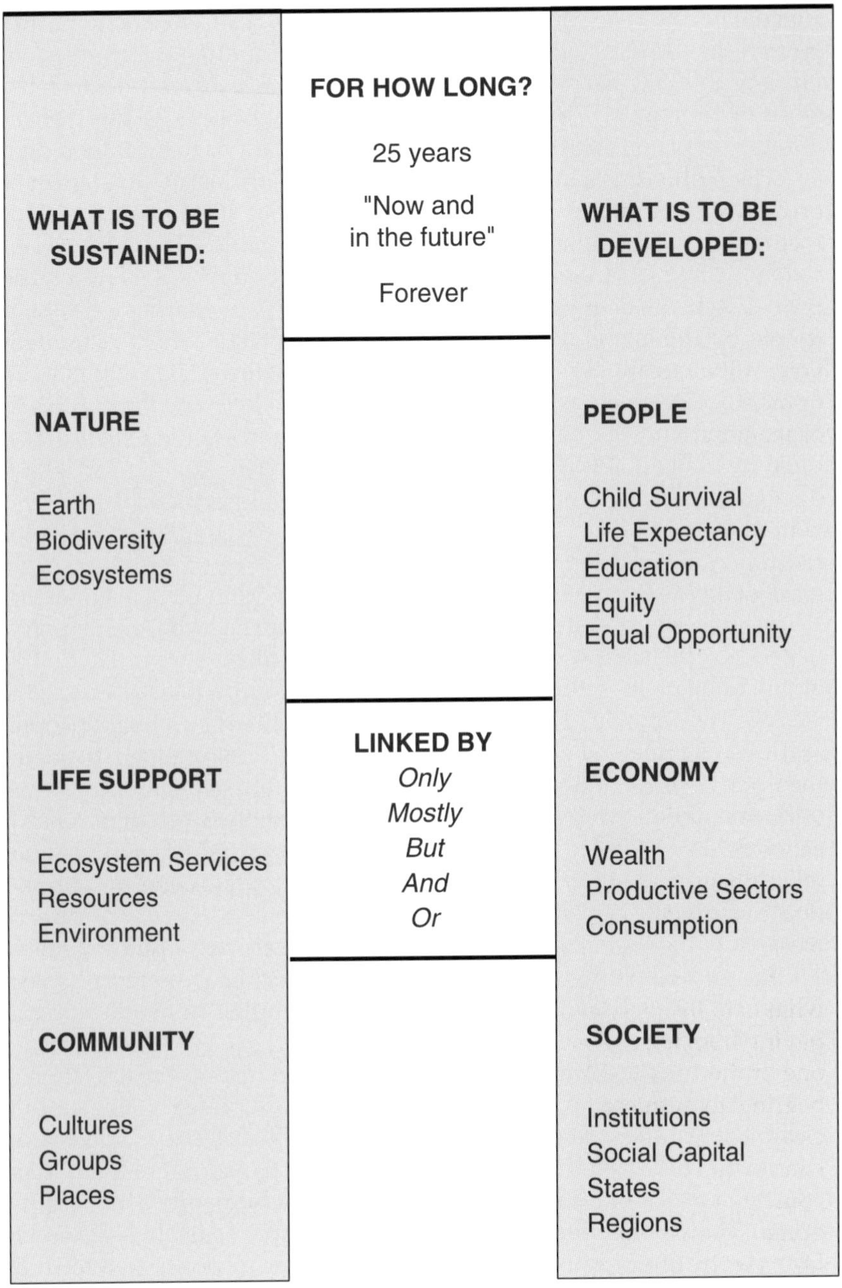

WHAT IS TO BE SUSTAINED:	FOR HOW LONG? 25 years "Now and in the future" Forever	WHAT IS TO BE DEVELOPED:
NATURE Earth Biodiversity Ecosystems		**PEOPLE** Child Survival Life Expectancy Education Equity Equal Opportunity
LIFE SUPPORT Ecosystem Services Resources Environment	**LINKED BY** *Only* *Mostly* *But* *And* *Or*	**ECONOMY** Wealth Productive Sectors Consumption
COMMUNITY Cultures Groups Places		**SOCIETY** Institutions Social Capital States Regions

FIGURE 1.1 Sustainable development: common concerns, differing emphases.

concept of *communities* to be sustained covers distinctive *cultures*, particular *groups* of people, and specific *places*.

What Is To Be Developed

The emphases on what is to be developed also fall within three major areas: people, economy, and society. More often than not, when development is discussed, the emphasis is on the *economy*, with its *productive sectors* providing both employment and desired *consumption*, and *wealth* providing the incentives and the means for investment as well as funds for environmental maintenance and restoration. Yet another form of development stressed is human development. Such *people*-centered development focuses on the "quantity" of life as seen in the *survival of children* or increased *life expectancy*, and on the quality of life in terms of *education, equity,* and *equal opportunity*. Finally, some discussions of what is to be developed adopt a broader conception of *society*, emphasizing the well-being and security of national *states, regions,* and *institutions* and, more recently, the valued social ties and community organizations known as *social capital*.

The Links Between

The concept of sustainable development links what is to be sustained and what is to be developed. The emphases differ according to whether the links are stated or implied. For example, the U.S. President's Council on Sustainable Development believes in "mutually reinforcing goals of economic growth, environmental protection, and social equity."[8] It sees these goals as equal in importance and linked together. *And* is the operative conjunction between what is to be sustained, namely, the environment, and what is to be developed, namely the economy and society.

But this is just one of many ways of envisioning the links between what is to be sustained and what is to be developed. Some views, while paying homage to sustainable development, focus almost entirely on just one of the two desiderata, the sustaining or the developing (thereby appearing to suggest "sustain *only*" or "develop *mostly*"). Others, while clearly emphasizing one or the other, subject this choice to a conditional constraint. For example, a Brundtland Commission member, noted "Sustainability is the nascent doctrine that economic growth and development must take place, and be maintained over time, *[but]* within the limits set by ecology in the broadest sense."[9] Other views tend to leave to some set of publics or decision makers with determining the exact nature of and tradeoffs between what is to be sustained *or* what is to be developed.

For How Long?

It is widely thought that sustainable development is meaningful only if it is intergenerational. Thus, there is general acceptance of the loosely stated time horizon of the World Conference on Environment and Development as *now and in the future*. The time horizons considered in specific contexts for future sustainable development, however, range from a single generation of *25 years* or so, to several generations, as in the Intergovernmental Panel on Climate Change (IPCC) assessments that extend until 2100, to an unstated, but implicit, *forever*. Each of these time periods presents very different prospects and obstacles for sustainable development. Over the space of a single generation, almost any development appears sustainable. Over forever, almost none do, as even the smallest growth in numbers, resource use, or economy extended indefinitely creates situations that seem surely unsustainable. Over the century encompassed by many energy-environment assessments (e.g., those of the IPCC), the large-scale and the long-term dimensions of the future are both remote and uncertain. The sustainability of development in any usefully concrete sense is even more so.

SUSTAINABLE DEVELOPMENT:
THE FIRST DECADE

The vision of the interdependence of development and environmental protection, first sketched in the Brundtland report, was fleshed out at the 1992 Rio Conference on Environment and Development (UNCED), oftentimes referred to as the "Earth Summit." The summit's "Rio Declaration" and "Agenda 21" together set forth detailed principles, action programs, and resource needs for achieving sustainable development in the 21st century.[10] Following the Earth Summit, international conventions on biological diversity, climate change, desertification, and the law of the sea have entered into force. Ongoing negotiations are evaluating the implementation of these agreements and of other treaties adopted before the summit. A number of additional international conferences on sustainable development have been held, including conferences on small island developing states, population and development, social development, straddling and migratory fish stocks, women, human settlements, and food.[11] Intergovernmental panels and forums are also considering problems of chemical safety, forests, and climate change. Finally, an uncounted number of regional, national, and local sustainable development initiatives have been undertaken in every corner of the world.

A UN Commission on Sustainable Development (UNCSD) was established in the wake of the Earth Summit to monitor and report on implementation of the agreements reached in Rio. The commission's first review was tabled and discussed at a UN General Assembly Special Session in June 1997. The resulting UN resolution on the "programme for the further implementation of Agenda 21," supplemented by the assessments of other organizations and by analyses undertaken by the Board on Sustainable Development, suggests a sobering appraisal of the successes, failures, and unfinished business of the first decade of efforts to realize sustainable development. Many participants and observers at the UN special session concluded, with some justification, that efforts to implement the Brundtland and Rio agendas on sustainable development have failed. While Brundtland and Rio had been hailed as great successes, the leaders of the UN's 1997 special session could only make note of their countries' efforts to hold themselves accountable without implying that substantial progress had been made on previous commitments. Moreover, media and political attention to the environment have plummeted from their post–Brundtland report peak. Many participants in the special session have observed that the drive and optimism that characterized Rio seem to have given way to resignation and cynicism.

Environment and Development

Sustainability initiatives must ultimately be evaluated in terms of their impacts on patterns of environmental degradation and human development. The disappointing conclusion of the 1997 UN special session was that the impacts of sustainability initiatives on global trends in development and environment have been few, small, and slow. Backed by the UN Environment Program's recently published *Global Environmental Outlook 2000*,[12] the special session noted:

• While population growth rates continue to decline globally, the number of people living in absolute poverty has increased.

• While globalization has presented new opportunities for sustainable development, many countries have been unable to take advantage of those opportunities; the extent of income inequality within and among nations, and the technology gap between the richest and poorest countries have all increased.

• While a number of countries have significantly reduced some levels of pollution and slowed or reversed resource depletion, the state of the global environment has continued to deteriorate, with generally increasing trends of pollution threatening to exceed the capacity of the global environment to absorb them.

Funds and Financing

Questions of resources and financing for sustainable development were problematic in the Brundtland report, contentious at Rio, and unresolved at the 1997 UN special session. The Global Environment Facility, an institutional product of the Earth Summit, was created to provide a funding mechanism for supporting the incremental costs of integrating global environmental goals into the development process. Its establishment, restructuring, funding, and replenishment are major accomplishments, but the total resources involved remain inadequate to the tasks at hand. More broadly, even the modest financial pledges made by governments at Rio have generally failed to materialize, substantially limiting the ability and willingness of developing countries to undertake important sustainability initiatives. These shortfalls in governmental assistance are to some extent compensated for by increased private investment flows into developing economies. But the volume of these flows, their ultimate destinations, and their implications for sustainability are not fully understood. Likewise, the relationships between financing sustainable development and regulating international trade and multinational corporate activities remain underdeveloped and poorly understood.

The View from Below

Despite these global concerns and disappointments, there is a more encouraging version of the story about sustainable development's first decades. This version holds that significant policy change of the sort sought by sustainability initiatives commonly requires a decade or more to come to fruition.[13] With the Brundtland Commission's *Our Common Future* barely 10 years old, and the Rio "Agenda 21" only half that, it is then not surprising that most of these proposals' tangible impacts on people and the environment lie in the future. To see this view of the story, in short, requires a shift in perspective from a short-term, globally averaged vision of international diplomacy and the media to a longer term and more local view of sustainable development as it is happening on the ground.

The abundant examples of local successes in sustainable development are not detailed in any one collection, although the submissions of individual countries and organizations to the UN Commission on Sustainable Development in preparation for the 1997 special session are a good place to begin.[14] These local pictures are, of course, complete with their own share of environmental horrors, economic greed, and program failures. But compared with 20, 10, or even 5 years ago, the degree to which notions of sustainability have entered mainstream thinking is astounding. Nongovernmental organizations (NGOs) and private corporations have been central to this transformation. Together with local and regional communities, they are carrying forward much of the ongoing work on sustainable development. Governments and international organizations have crucial roles to play in facilitating this work and in making sure that it does not leave pressing concerns unaddressed. The international scientific and engineering communities can make very significant contributions to sustainable development in particular sectors, areas, societies, and regions. Educators in early and continuing education can inform the general public about sustainability issues and make these issues an integral part of the university curricula relating to science, technology, and business. Whether these groups can in fact move beyond the verbal and political stalemate evident at the UN special session and learn to play their new roles effectively may be one of the most important questions in the next century, when the world's people begin their next appraisal of progress towards sustainability.

Knowledge* and Know-How†

As noted earlier, discussions of the role of science and technology have not been central to the last decade's debates on sustainable development. Few have denied the importance of mobilizing knowledge and know-how, but fewer still have applied themselves seriously to what this task might entail and how it might be done. Even Rio's "Agenda 21," drawing on the proceedings of the International Council for Science's (ICSU) International Conference on an Agenda of Science for Environment and Development into the 21st Century[15] known as "ASCEND 21," devotes only 3 out of 40 chapters to science and technology and has little to say about priorities or their implementation. With so little to aim at, the 1997 UN special session did not even try to appraise the implementation of Rio's vague intentions for science and technology. Instead, it confined itself to a reiteration of general needs. In consequence, societies approach the 21st century with little in the way of a useful strategic appraisal of how to identify and create the knowledge and know-how most crucial to achievements in sustainable development.

---

* *Knowledge* here refers to the *Webster's Ninth New Collegiate Dictionary* definition, "… the fact or condition of knowing something with familiarity gained through experience or association…or the acquaintance with or understanding of a science, art, or technique."

† *Know-how* here refers to the *Webster's Ninth New Collegiate Dictionary* definition, "knowledge [conveyed by expertise] of how to do something smoothly and efficiently."

GOALS FOR A SUSTAINABILITY TRANSITION

If the genius of sustainable development is to allow all in the common tent to project their hopes and goals, one limit of this valuable concept then is that it encompasses too much to provide a framework to map research and policy in the years ahead. Even if there were consensus on what specifically to sustain and what specifically to develop, and for how long, societies would not know how to arrive at these goals. The experience of efforts to adaptively manage natural resources and to cope with natural hazards is instructive—an experience partly captured in the metaphor of *Compass and Gyroscope*.[16] In such situations, scientific understanding is incomplete, past policies have often failed, new policies are untested, and the unexpected is a recurrent truth. At best, science can provide compass direction, while the gyroscope of politics can maintain some steadiness of course across often-uncharted seas. In light of the trends of population growth, increased consumption, global connectedness and diversity, and environmental stress (see Chapter 2), a transition to sustainability appears necessary, but remote and difficult.

Such a transition will entail meeting the needs and coping with the desires of many more people than there are today in the space of two human generations—which is just a few decades ahead. By 2050, UN demographers project a population of about 8.9 billion, with a range from 7.3 to 10.7 billion.[17] Meeting the needs of that many people implies much greater consumption of energy and materials and the environmental and ecological problems that result from their extraction, consumption, and disposal. These problems will be compounded as more people adopt the materials-intensive, consumption-oriented lifestyle now enjoyed by industrialized nations.

The increasing connectedness of economies, peoples, and technologies will fuel growth in some parts of the world, diminish it in others, and amplify the forces that drive increased consumption (see Chapter 2). Some environmental problems of the industrialized world will be exported to the developing and recently industrializing countries, and also, with some delay, the institutions and technologies to address them. In a more connected but still diverse world, differences in human experience will offer opportunities for alternative lifestyles and new possibilities for addressing our common future. Yet at the same time, increasingly widespread divisiveness may well make common tasks much more difficult. War, the ultimate expression of conflict, remains the greatest threat to human development, life support systems, and the environment.

Driven by population growth and increasing consumption, past and current practices of energy and material transformation have led to the large-scale introduction of pollutants, the widespread destruction of biota, and human-induced climate change—which are already threatening the life support systems of many local areas and a few regions. In the future, with large increases in total population and consumption, these environmental threats, cumulative and linked, could threaten the life support systems of entire regions and the globe.

For a successful transition to sustainability, the world must provide the energy, materials, and information to feed, house, nurture, educate, and employ many more people than are alive today—while preserving the basic life support systems of the planet and reducing hunger and poverty. The Board has adopted this framework of a "transition toward sustainability" to help encourage movement over the next few decades toward meeting human needs in ways that do less damage to the physical and biological support systems for life, and more to sustain or restore them, along with movement toward development paths that do less to widen disparities in human welfare and more to reduce or eliminate hunger and poverty. In short, in the Board's judgment, **the primary goals of a transition toward sustainability over the next two generations should be to meet the needs of a much larger but stabilizing human population, to sustain the life support systems of the planet, and to substantially reduce hunger and poverty.** Using goals outlined in international conventions, we define meeting human needs as providing food and nutrition, nurturing children, finding shelter, providing an education, and finding employment. We define preserving life support systems as ensuring the quality and supply of fresh water, controlling emissions into the atmosphere, protecting the oceans, and maintaining species and ecosystems. We define reducing hunger and poverty as ensuring income growth, employment opportunities, and essential safety net services. Although the conventions and agreements we looked to for our definitions each have their own limitations, we believe that altogether they constitute a well-founded set of values and objectives on which to base discussions of sustainability. Their international input and endorsement ensures that the goals, which guide our transition toward sustainability, are relevant to and supported by governments and citizens worldwide.

The Board's interest in focusing on the prospects for a global transition toward sustainability over the coming decades flows from our scientific understanding of trends in the environment, development, and associated problems. It is over the lifetimes of the next two generations of the world's citizens that we anticipate the greatest stresses arising through growing numbers and concentrations of people, extraordinary increases in energy and material throughput, and institutions just learning to cope with the barriers and opportunities of globalization. But if our scale of concern is based on technical understanding, our threefold conceptualization of a successful transition—meeting human needs, preserving life

support systems, reducing hunger and poverty—is a normative judgment, both scientific and moral.

Our knowledge tells us much about what is needed to feed, nurture,
house, educate, and employ; what imperils life support systems; and how
to reduce hunger and poverty. But to accept the responsibility of meeting
the human development needs of generations yet to come, of providing
the minimal necessities to reduce hunger and poverty, and of sustaining
the natural world that in turn sustains us is a choice for which we have no
special aptitude beyond our common humanity. Fortunately for science,
it is not a choice we make alone, but is widely confirmed by the conference proceedings and statements representing the world's peoples and
nations' consensual choice of goals to meet human needs. Unfortunately
for humanity, societies have not begun to meet most of the targets established by international consensus. However, analysis of trends in human
development (see Chapter 2) shows substantial improvements in the overall well-being of people over the past two generations. In our review and
analysis, we have not attempted to determine closely how achieving any
one of these international goals may affect the realization of others. To do
so is a central challenge for any transition to sustainability.

Meeting Human Needs

Providing Food and Nutrition

To feed the increased population of the next two generations is to
meet both the basic need for food and the desire for varied diets. The
former has been reasonably well defined by the sciences of human physiology and nutrition—that is, what food is needed to avoid hunger. The
desire for the varied diets is evident in the behavior of people—they
choose diets of increasing variety, often in the form of animal consumption, when income and opportunity permit. The basic need for food and
the avoidance of hunger have been the focus of repeated international
meetings. Based on these meetings, and the recent World Food Summit
held in Rome in 1996, we can derive minimal goals in the area of nutrition
for a transition toward sustainability.

Chronic hunger and nutrient deficiencies are part of the daily experience of more than a billion people. For them, hunger is a dietary intake
that does not provide the kind and quantity of food required for growth,
activity, or the maintenance of good health. Such biologically defined
hunger comes in many guises, four of which are globally estimated on a
regular basis. Starvation, the near absence of dietary intake suffered in the
course of famines, can be contrasted with undernutrition, the chronic or
seasonal absence of needed food proteins and caloric energy. There is also

the hidden hunger of micronutrient deficiencies, among which three predominate: dietary shortages of iron, iodine, and vitamin A. Also, there are the nutrient-depleting diseases, in which dietary intake may not be absorbed or is wasted by fever or parasites.

Because famines are such dramatic events, they are often equated with hunger by the media and the public, yet they actually constitute a very small fraction of world hunger.[18] Despite the widespread attention focused on recent famines, only about 15 to 35 million people have been at risk of famine in recent years. Indeed, there has been a consistent decline in the numbers at risk of famine over time, and today famine only occurs where there is war or civil unrest. The major hunger problem of the world is undernutrition, in which needed food proteins and caloric energy are chronically or seasonally absent. (Micronutrient deficiencies and wasting diseases are addressed further in the next section.)

The extent of undernutrition is estimated indirectly as the number of persons in households that cannot provide food sufficient for health, moderate activity, and children's growth. The most recent United Nations estimate found 828 million people in developing countries resided in such households in 1994 to 1996, representing about 19 percent of the population of developing countries.[19] By this measure, hungry people in developing countries decreased by 80 million over the last two decades, and the proportion of hungry people almost halved (from 35 to 19 percent), despite the increase in global population of well over a billion people. The decline in numbers of hungry people has taken place primarily in China and South and Southeast Asia; some of these improvements may have reversed recently with the massive economic decline in Southeast Asia. Additionally, during the 1980s, the numbers of hungry people rose in Africa and Latin America, and they continued to rise in the 1990s in Africa.

The current international consensus, as evidenced in the Rome Declaration on World Food Security calls for a rapid acceleration in worldwide hunger reduction efforts. The declaration calls for a "common and national commitment to achieving food security for all and to an ongoing effort to eradicate hunger in all countries, with an immediate view to reducing the number of undernourished people to half their present level no later than 2015."[20] By the year 2015, then, the declaration thus calls for the number of undernourished people to drop by half—from 800 million to 400 million—and thereafter for the maintenance of this trend for the eventual elimination of hunger. Assuming that population grows significantly during the first target period, the rate of undernourishment would need to be reduced by more than half in the following decades.

Nurturing Children

To nurture the children of this and the coming two generations is also to provide the gift of life itself, in the form of health and nourishment for growth, protection from harm or abuse, and a caring environment that furnishes the necessary stimuli for physical and mental development. International concern has focused on the critical years of vulnerability, (i.e., infant and under-five mortality), on health and nourishment (i.e., low birth weight, wasting, stunting, and disease), on children's rights, and on later years of education.

In 1990, some 12.5 million children under the age of five died, mostly (in descending order of impact) from diarrhea, pneumonia, birth-related causes, measles, malaria, tetanus, whooping cough, tuberculosis, and diphtheria—though many died from multiple causes.[21] Some 142 million children were also born in that year, 88 percent in developing countries. If prevailing trends continue, for every 100 children, 17 will be born with low birth weights, 94 will live to age one, and 91 to age five, yet of these surviving 91, 28 will be malnourished.[22] Similar indices of morbidity and mortality can be found in pockets of poverty within some industrialized countries, such as the United States, that have high levels of child nurture overall.

Even when children recover from such diseases, there are lasting effects on their development. Low birth weight can prevent a child from realizing his or her full potential mental and physical development. Nutrient-depleting diseases contribute to the pronounced wasting and stunting of children (low weight and height for age), the characteristic measure of children's undernutrition. For example, diarrhea inhibits the absorption of dietary intake; measles and malaria waste the intake by fever; and parasites, such as worms, rob the intake. In all, 184 million children under five years of age, over a third of the world's children, were estimated to be underweight in 1990—a number that had risen because of increased population growth, even though the proportion of children underweight had actually declined since 1975. Over half of these underweight children lived in Bangladesh, India, and Pakistan.[23] A lively debate persists over whether such numbers are overestimates.

Children also suffer from dietary shortages of iron, iodine, and vitamin A, in the hidden hunger of micronutrient deficiencies. Severe anemia leads to death, while moderate iron deficiency causes lethargy, low work potential, and severe learning disabilities that can persist lifelong. Upward of 12 percent of the world population suffers from iodine-deficient goiter, and more severe deficiencies lead to the dwarfism and idiocy of cretinism, deaf-mutism, and impaired fetal growth and development. Vitamin A deficiency leads to eye diseases, blindness, and death in small children, and is also linked to increased risk of infection and overall mortality in children.

In October 1990, the World Summit for Children[24] brought together representatives of 150 countries and 71 heads of state to formally adopt a series of goals for the year 2000. These included a one-third reduction in child deaths, halving of child malnutrition, immunization levels of 90 percent, control of major childhood diseases, eradication of polio, elimination of micronutrient deficiencies, halving of maternal mortality rates, provision of primary school education for at least 80 percent of children, provision of clean water and safe sanitation for all communities, and ratification of the 1989 Convention on the Rights of the Child.

Finding Shelter

To house the many more people of the next two generations, in the words of one international agreement, is to ensure "shelter and basic services which are financially affordable and adequate in terms of space, quality, health, design, durability, livability, and accessibility."[25] There is greater variety of interpretation in these standards than in requirements for food and nurture, but international concern focuses on an end to homelessness, with basic shelter that is affordable, secure in tenure and location, and healthy, with access to clean and safe drinking water, sewage and refuse disposal, and living and working quarters that are free of indoor air pollution.

The lives and health of at least 600 million urban dwellers in Africa, Asia, and Latin America are continually at risk because they occupy housing that is overcrowded and of poor quality, and that inadequately provides for water, sanitation, drainage, and garbage collection. A billion more rural dwellers live in similar conditions, largely because of inadequate water and sanitation. An estimated 100 million people have no home and sleep outside or in public buildings or, where available, in night shelters. Several million more homeless people are found in Europe and North America. Most low-income households are particularly vulnerable to eviction, as they have no legal tenure of the house they occupy. Several million urban dwellers are forcibly evicted from their housing each year. In fact, most new housing in the cities of developing countries has been built on illegally occupied or subdivided land.[26]

In 1996, the Second UN Conference on Human Settlements, Habitat II, took place in Istanbul, Turkey. While avoiding the proposal of quantitative goals, representatives of the 171 nations assembled adopted "the goal of ensuring an adequate supply of shelter and basic services for all and improving living and working conditions on a sustainable basis so that everyone, including people living in poverty, the vulnerable and the disadvantaged, will have access to shelter and basic services which is financially affordable and adequate in terms of space, quality, health, design, durability, livability and accessibility."[27] In addition, the participants committed themselves to "make special efforts to eradicate homelessness by promoting the availability of affordable low-cost, decent housing, targeting subsidies to the most needy and providing emergency shelter where needed."[28] More specific than general statements on shelter was the commitment made in 1990 to provide clean water and sanitation to all, both rural and urban dwellers, by the year 2000. These commitments were necessary to build on the poor progress and partial achievements of the International Drinking Water Supply and Sanitation Decade (1981–1990), which was coordinated by the World Health Organization.

Providing an Education

To educate the current and coming two generations is to help them develop their skills, knowledge, and capacity for learning such that they become literate members of their communities, acquire the necessary skills for work, and have access to the cumulative storehouse of human culture. Such education is both formal and informal, but international attention has focused on a single competency—literacy—and on the formal requirements of primary, secondary, and post-secondary schooling.

In 1995, world adult literacy was estimated at 74 percent for men and 56 percent for women, down from the 1990 figures of 81 percent for men and 66 percent for women; primary school enrollment (as percentage of age group) was 88 percent for boys and 84 percent for girls, and successful completion of fifth grade stood at 78 percent, roughly the same as the figures for 1990.[29] For every 100 children born in 1990, given then-current trends, 85 would start primary school, 55 would finish, and 32 would complete secondary school.[30] Thus, approximately 100 million six to eleven year olds were not attending schools (60 percent of whom were girls), and one in four adults (two-thirds of them women)—or almost a billion people—could not read or write.

In 1990, the World Conference on Education for All was held in Jomtien, Thailand, followed by the World Summit for Children.[31] At Jomtien, three commitments were made to basic education for all. The first was to bring literacy, numeracy, and essential life skills to the great majority of children during the 1990s. The second was to reduce the adult illiteracy rate to half its 1990 level. And the third was to end the great disparities in education between boys and girls. The World Summit for Children reinforced these goals by making specific commitments to complete by the year 2000: universal access to basic education, primary education completed by at least 80 percent of primary age school children, and reduction of the adult illiteracy rate (though it varies from country to country) to at least half its 1990 level, with emphasis on reducing female illiteracy.[32] Since the conference in Jomtien, basic education has gained a higher profile in policy discourse within the donor community than it had in the 1980s. Yet as of the mid-1990s, an increase in the number of educated girls had not been realized,[33] and among the majority of bilateral donors, the level of funding for basic education projects and programs in developing countries was inadequate to meet the goals for education set out in Jomtien.[34]

Finding Employment

To employ the present unemployed or underemployed and the emerging labor force of the next two generations is to provide the opportunity for meaningful work, to fulfill a need to engage the mind and body in productive activity, and to receive in turn a level of material security and sustenance. International concerns have focused on job creation, both formal and informal, conditions of work, and remuneration sufficient to maintain households above the poverty level.[35] The Copenhagen Declaration, a nonbinding agreement adopted at the World Summit for Social Development in 1995, and the following report,[36] set out the commitment by governments to promote the goal of full employment. In the industrialized countries, the main worry is that increasing unemployment has become a permanent feature of the economy. In Europe, for instance, the rate of unemployment exceeds 10 percent in many countries, although many countries are adopting measures to bring more labor into the workforce (e.g., by creating more flexible labor markets and work rules, and reducing the costs of benefits for permanent workers and the number of hours in the work week) in an effort to meet targets agreed upon for European integration. In the United States, Norway, and Japan, the unemployment rates are lower and stable, although in the case of Japan, the unemployment rate has risen sharply and is of concern.[37] Finally, there is great disparity in unemployment across divisions of age and wage, with high numbers of the young entering the workforce, and with laid-off middle-aged, and ethnic minorities being unemployed. In some developing countries, unemployment rates are loosely estimated to be as high as 50 percent, although data for unemployment in most developing countries, particularly in Africa, are scarce.[38] Equally problematic, especially for rural areas, is underemployment, both seasonal and sustained, that is, working substantially less than full time and wishing to work longer, or earning less than a living wage. Underemployment rates are estimated to be about 25 to 30 percent of the world's labor force.[39]

With much of developing countries' labor forces in the agricultural sector, growing rural populations and increased agricultural productivity often create fewer per capita opportunities for agricultural employment. The problem is not that people have no work; rather they do not have enough work or work at a wage too low to earn an adequate amount of money.

While there are excellent data on paid employment for industrialized countries, no equivalent data exist for developing countries.[40] In the latter countries, much employment is self-employment or farm labor, or is seen in the very large, so-called informal sectors of the economy—none of which have regular reporting systems for numbers of people employed, wages, or earnings. These data shortages are mirrored by the lack of specific good intentions normally articulated in legally binding conventions and international agreements. Unlike the other human needs reviewed here, the need for work for all has received little serious international attention or commitment (except through general economic development programs) beyond the concerns of the industrialized countries.

Targets for Meeting Human Needs

Internationally agreed-on targets for meeting human needs exist for four of the five major needs of providing food and nutrition, nurturing children, finding shelter, providing an education, and finding employment. These are summarized in Table 1.1. A comparative review of these needs and aspirations in meeting the targets suggests two important conclusions. First, there is an implicit hierarchy of needs that favors children and people in disasters, and the activities of feeding and nurturing first, followed by education, housing, and employment. This hierarchy is demonstrated by the specific goals adopted, the ambition of their targets, the emphases of the conferences that adopt the targets, the information systems that monitor progress, and the international agencies that coordinate implementation. For example, it was the World Summit for Children, which had the highest attendance of heads of state, that adopted the most numerous and ambitious targets for feeding, nurturing, educating, and even housing children and their families. UNICEF (the United Nations Children's Fund), a strong, partly independent, single-purpose UN agency, provides leadership for implementing this agenda and regularly collects data on progress in meeting those goals.

Second, although in general the overall well being of people has substantially improved (see the discussion of trends in human development in Chapter 2), the periodic revising of unmet targets demonstrates the difficulties in acting in sustained ways over large scales and over long time horizons. Even the most desired goals for the betterment of children, as societies stand today two years away from the deadline for meeting

TABLE 1.1   International Targets for Meeting Human Needs

Needs/ Problem Areas	Year: Target Goal [Adopted By]	Number of People at Risk	
		At Adoption of Target	More Recently
Providing food and nutrition			
Undernourishment	1996: Reduce by 30% by 2015 [WFS]	840 million	828 million (1996)
Nurturing children			
Under 5 mortality	1990: Reduce by 33% by 2000 [WSC]	14 million	11.7 million (1996)
Malnourished	1990: Reduce by 50% by 2000 [WSC]	177 million	184 million (1996)
Micronutrient deficiencies	1990: Virtual elimination by 2000 [WSC]	Iodine: 1.6 billion Vitamin A: 190 million preschool children Iron: 2.15 billion	N/A
Finding shelter			
Water	1990: Provide to all by 2000 [WSC]	1,230 million	1,115 million (1994)
Sanitation	1990: Provide to all by 2000 [WSC]	1,740 million	2,873 million (1994)
Housing	1996: Provide [UNCHS]	600 million	N/A
Providing an education			
Adult literacy	1990: Reduce by 50% by 2000 [WCE][WSC]	900 million	877 million (1995)
Primary school	1990: 80% complete 4 years by 2000 [WSC]	100 million not in school only 55% complete	71% complete (1993)
Male/Female (M/F) disparities	1990: Reduce [WCE]	Illiterate: 66% F; of those not in school: 60% F	Illiterate: 62% F; of those not in school: 62.6% F (1996)
Finding employment	1995: Full employment [WSSD]	N/A	N/A

Sources: For target goals: [WFS] World Food Summit, (Rome, 1996); [WSC] World Summit for Children, (New York, 1990); [WHO] World Health Organization (1996); [UNCHS] United Nations Conference on Human Settlements, Istanbul, (1996a); [WCE] World Conference on Education for All, (Jomtien, Thailand, 1990); [WSSD] World Summit for Social Development, (Copenhagen, 1995). For number of people at risk: FAO (1998); UNICEF (1999); Uvin (1993); WHO (1996); UNCHS (1996b); UNESCO (1998).

these targets, appear overly ambitious and not likely to be attained. Only the targets for immunization, eradication of Guinea worm, iodine deficiency disorders, vitamin A deficiency (with increased awareness of supplement needs), and acute respiratory infections (with expanded home care) might be met by the year 2000, while the numbers of people who are malnourished or in need of rehydration from diarrheal diseases may be even higher by that date than when the target was originally adopted.[41]

There is also social learning in evidence as shown by the recently agreed-upon target of reducing household hunger by half by the year 2015. The international consensus to give hunger a "half-life" was initiated in November 1989 as a nongovernmental initiative[42] that proposed four goals: (1) to eliminate deaths from famine; (2) to end hunger in half of the world's poorest households; (3) to cut malnutrition in half for mothers and small children; and (4) to eradicate iodine and vitamin A deficiencies. Together, these goals made up a comprehensive yet practical program to end half of world hunger in a decade by building on the better and best of existing programs and policies for overcoming hunger. Over the next seven years, this declaration became in one form or another the hunger reduction agenda for the decade. Its key elements were found in the declarations of the 71 heads of state attending the 1990 World Summit for Children, in the resolutions of the 159 nations participating in the 1992 International Conference on Nutrition, in the deliberations of the 1993 World Bank Conference on Overcoming Global Hunger, in a mid-course nongovernmental review in Salaya, Thailand, in 1994, and finally, in the focus of the 1996 World Food Summit. Over this period of consensus building and discussion, the time required for a "half-life" for hunger grew from a decade (year 2000) to almost a generation (year 2015); in retrospect, a more achievable target.

For scientists, there is an elemental appeal to the concept of the half-life for reducing the great disparities of human development. This appeal is reflected in the approach of several of the world conferences mentioned above that provide the consensus targets upon which we draw. Thus, we suggest that a defensible overarching initial target to meeting human needs would be to halve the current unmet needs in a generation and halve them again in the second generation of a transition to sustainability.

Preserving Life Support Systems

Ensuring the Quality and Supply of Fresh Water

An objective for maintaining freshwater systems is "to make certain that adequate supplies of water of good quality are maintained for the entire population of this planet, while preserving the hydrological, biological and chemical functions of ecosystems, adapting human activities within the capacity limits of nature and combating vectors of water-related diseases."[43] Without specifying quantitative goals, "Agenda 21" emphasizes the need to protect fresh water in an integrated manner, with a call for national activities for the conservation of water resources, prevention and control of water pollution, and protection of groundwater by the year 2000. The 1992 Convention on the Protection and Use of Transboundary Watercourses and International Lakes mandates measures to protect transboundary waters against pollution from point sources by calling for the use of low- and non-waste technologies.

Controlling Emissions into the Atmosphere

Goals for controlling emissions into the atmosphere are to prevent changes in the composition of the atmosphere, according to the Convention on Long-Range Transboundary Air Pollution 1979, or in the earth's climate that harm human or natural systems, according to the Framework Convention on Climate Change 1992 and its Kyoto Protocol 1997. The Convention on Long-Range Transboundary Air Pollution, which applies only to several European countries, sets out "to limit and, as far as possible, gradually reduce and prevent air pollution including long-range transboundary air pollution."[44] This convention defines specific goals for maintaining the integrity of the atmosphere through the control of potentially harmful emissions and fluxes of sulfur, nitrogen oxides (NO_x), and volatile organic compounds (VOC). The 1994 Sulfur Protocol commits parties to "control and reduce their sulfur emissions in order to protect human health and the environment from adverse effects, in particular acidifying effects, and to ensure, as far as possible, without entailing excessive costs, that depositions of oxidized sulfur compounds in the long term do not exceed critical loads for sulfur...."[45*]

The Vienna Convention for the Protection of the Ozone Layer of 1985, its 1987 Montreal Protocol on Substances that Deplete the Ozone Layer, and amendments to this protocol were formulated to halt human-induced depletion of the ozone layer. As the convention states, these treaties aim "to protect human health and the environment against adverse effects resulting or likely to result from human activities that modify or are likely to modify the ozone layer."[46] To accomplish these goals, the protocol commits to the phase-out of a specified list of chlorofluorocarbons (CFCs)

---

* "Critical loads" are defined as the rates of sulfur deposition that receptors (e.g., organisms or ecosystems) can tolerate in the long term. These rates are presented in an annex to the protocol.

and halons and to the full phase-out of carbon tetrachloride by the year 2000; this phase-out date was brought forward four years by a subsequent amendment. In addition, the protocol stipulates the phase-out of methyl chloroform by 2005 and reductions in other chemicals in upcoming years. But methyl bromide, a potent ozone depleter, has proved to be a much more difficult compound to deal with in the protocol, despite widespread scientific agreement concerning its negative effects on human health and the ozone shield. There are several reasons for this difficulty. Methyl bromide impacts are scientifically complex; the substance is present from both natural and human sources; and, unlike CFCs, it is used widely in applications for which no readily available and economically viable substitute has been identified.

Maintaining the earth's climate system means preventing anthropogenic interference with climate processes when this interference would have dangerous implications for life. The 1992 Framework Convention on Climate Change, which was ratified internationally in 1994, set a goal of stabilizing "atmospheric concentrations of greenhouse gases at a level which would prevent dangerous human interference in the climate system."[47] The not-yet-ratified Kyoto Protocol set initial binding targets for greenhouse gas emission reductions by industrial nations only for the 2008–2012 time period, specifying reductions in overall emissions of six greenhouse gases by at least 5 percent below 1990 levels. Because of natural variability in climate, scientists have yet to discern with confidence whether they are seeing a slow or rapid rate of climate change. If the world is on a slow path, societies may only have to adjust modestly. The Kyoto Protocol represents only a first step, and much more drastic reductions might be needed if the world is on a rapid climate change path. In this latter scenario, industrial nations would have to decrease emissions even more, and developing countries also would have to curb growth rates of fossil fuel use.

Protecting the Oceans

To maintain the world's oceans, according to the 1982 UN Convention on the Law of the Sea (UNCLOS), is to prevent pollution of the marine environment "which results or is likely to result in such deleterious effects as harm to living resources and marine life, hazards to human health, [and] hindrance to marine activities."[48] UNCLOS calls for protection of the marine environment through "the prevention, reduction and control of pollution and other hazards to the marine environment, including the coastline, and of interference with the ecological balance of the marine environment, particular attention being paid to the need for protection from harmful effects of such activities as drilling, dredging, excavation, disposal of waste, construction and operation or maintenance of installations, pipelines and other devices related to human activities."[49] The dumping of specified wastes, including radioactive wastes, or other matter, into marine environments is limited or prohibited without permission of identified authority by the 1972 Convention on the Prevention of Marine Pollution by Dumping of Wastes and Other Matter.[50] Dumping of substances including mercury, cadmium, and organohalogen compounds is prohibited with certain exceptions by the Convention for the Prevention of Marine Pollution by Dumping from Ships and Aircraft, 1972.[51]

Maintaining Species and Ecosystems

Maintaining the species and ecosystems of the earth means preventing further exploitation and the ultimate extinction of overharvested or otherwise threatened wildlife; protecting areas or types of ecosystems on which species' survival depends; and maintaining the earth's biological diversity of species and ecosystems.

The most comprehensive agreements to protect marine wildlife worldwide set limits on the harvesting of whales and fish. The International Convention for the Regulation of Whaling 1946, and its amendments, enable the designation of protected species of whales, specific ocean areas such as sanctuaries, open and closed seasons for harvesting, and regulations on whaling methods.[52] For fish and other living marine resources, Article 2 of the 1958 Convention on Fishing and Conservation of the Living Resources of the High Seas sets targets for resource conservation programs at levels that ensure "the optimum sustainable yield from those resources so as to secure a maximum supply of food and other marine products."[53]

Goals for the protection of birds are outlined in the 1950 International Convention for the Protection of Birds (Paris), which prohibits actions that would lead to the destruction of indigenous or migratory species.[54] It establishes protection of all birds during their breeding seasons, and of endangered species year-round, and it restricts the trade of bird and bird components, the removal or destruction of nests, and the mass killing or capture of birds. Protecting other forms of migratory animals in addition to birds, as outlined in the 1979 Convention on the Conservation of Migratory Species of Wild Animals, involves prohibiting the taking of species listed as endangered by the convention, conserving and restoring habitats, removing obstacles to migration, and preventing factors that endanger these species.[55]

Addressing the protection of endangered species globally, the 1973 Convention on International Trade in Endangered Species of Wild Fauna and Flora (CITES) establishes the need to limit or prohibit trafficking in these species and their products to the extent that trade threatens their existence.[56] It mandates the protection of a total of 30,043 species, 821 of which are considered to be threatened with extinction. Other attempts to protect flora and nonmigratory fauna are often regionally based and focus more on habitat preservation than do agreements that address marine or migratory species.

Efforts to conserve specific types of ecosystems ensure the maintenance of the life support systems that provide essential goods and services for human needs. The 1971 Convention on Wetlands of International Importance Especially as Waterfowl Habitat (Ramsar) mandates that each of its parties protect at least one wetland of international importance within its borders.[57] In December 1996, 858 sites totaling more than 54 million acres of wetland worldwide were listed for protection.[58] UNCLOS enables the designation of marine sanctuaries, but does not determine a minimum amount of area that needs to be protected. Preventing desertification and drought is an objective of the 1994 UN Convention to Combat Desertification in those Countries Experiencing Serious Drought and/or Desertification, Particularly in Africa. As stated in Article 3, "improved productivity of land, and the rehabilitation, conservation and sustainable management of land and water resources, leading to improved living conditions, in particular at the community level" are critical to maintaining the integrity of land for human use.[59]

To conserve the diversity of the world's species and ecosystems, the 1992 Convention on Biological Diversity outlines broad international objectives. The maintenance of species and ecosystems, according to the convention's first article, entails provisions for "the conservation of biological diversity, the sustainable use of its components and the fair and equitable sharing of the benefits arising out of the utilization of genetic resources." The convention has no protocols to date, but it requires parties to develop national strategies, plans, or programs to conserve biological diversity and, as stated in Article 6, to integrate "the conservation and sustainable use of biological diversity into relevant sectoral or cross-sectoral plans, programmes and policies."[60]

Targets for Preserving Life Support Systems

Compared to targets for meeting human needs, quantitative targets for preserving life support systems are fewer, more modest, and more contested. Global targets now exist for ozone-depleting substances and greenhouse gases, and regional targets for some air pollutants (see Table 1.2). Absolute prohibitions (zero targets) exist for ocean dumping of radioactive wastes and some toxics, for the taking and/or sale of a few large mammals (whales, elephants, seals), migratory birds when breeding or endangered, and certain regional fishing stocks. Water, land resources, and ecosystems such as arid lands and forests have at best qualitative targets to achieve sustainable management or restoration. For example, the Forest Principles set forth at the 1992 World Conference on Environment and Development do not set quantitative targets for forest protection; but they establish in Article 2b that "forest resources and forest lands should be sustainably managed to meet the social, economic, ecological, cultural and spiritual needs of present and future generations" for forest products and services. International standards exist for many toxic materials, organic pollutants, and heavy metals that threaten human health, but not for ecosystem health.

Reducing Hunger and Poverty

In spite of the numerous statistics compiled by the United Nations and the World Bank,[61] no definitive determination exists of the number of hungry and poor people worldwide. Part of the problem is conceptual (e.g., how to draw poverty lines); part of it is practical or motivational (e.g., countries with many poor people invest little to document the fact). Poverty lines that enable analysts to separate the poor from the less needy are difficult to create, though there is a large literature to guide the creation of these lines.[62] An important analytical distinction is between absolute measures, those based on the adequacy of resources and income to provide for minimal necessities of households, and relative measures, those that designate the poor as represented by the lower end of a national or regional distribution of resources and income (e.g., the lowest quintile). Addressing hunger rather than overall poverty further complicates the making of distinctions. Sometimes hunger is measured in ways similar to absolute poverty, such as the inability of a household to obtain food sufficient to meet nutritional requirements (see section on "Providing food and nutrition" above); at other times, it is measured by anthropometric measurements of people, particularly children. These absolute and relative distinctions blur when societal comparisons are made: the income line below which households are considered hungry shifts upward with overall average national income (see sheet 4 of appendix, Chapter 3). Despite these analytical problems, two recent attempts to estimate absolute poverty and hunger are shown in Table 1.3. Between one fifth and one sixth of the world population is poor or hungry, with the largest part of these people in Africa and South Asia.

TABLE 1.2   International Targets for Preserving Life Support Systems

System	Goals and Targets	Target Year	Sources
Water	Give to the satisfaction of basic needs and the safeguarding of ecosystems. National water conservation activities to prevent and control water pollution and protect groundwater	2000	UNCED (1992) (See Agenda 21, chapter 18)
Atmosphere and Climate			
Sulfur	Reduce depositions of oxidized sulfur to below critical loads	N/A	Sulfur Protocol (1994)
Nitrogen oxides (NO_x)	Reduce emissions to, at most, 1987 levels	1994	NO_x Protocol (1988)
Volatile organic compounds (VOC)	Reduce emissions by 30-100% of 1988 levels	1999	VOC Protocol (1991)
Chlorofluoro-carbons (CFCs)	Complete phase-out of specified forms of CFCs and halocarbons	1992	Montreal Protocol (1987, amended 1990, 1991, 1992)
Greenhouse gases (specified forms)	Prevent dangerous human interference in the climate system; Reduce emissions by at least 5% below 1990 levels for industrial nations	2008-2012	Framework Convention on Climate Change (1992); Kyoto Protocol (1997)
Oceans	Prevent, reduce, and control pollution and other hazards to the marine environment	N/A	UN Convention on the Law of the Sea (1982)
Species and Ecosystems			
Whales	Moratorium on harvesting of commercially exploited stocks	1986	International Whaling Commission
Fish	Ensure the optimum sustainable yield of fish and living resources	N/A	Convention on Fishing and Conservation of the Living Resources of the High Seas (1958)

continued

TABLE 1.2 Continued

System	Goals and Targets	Target Year	Sources
Birds	Prevent destruction of indigenous or migratory species	N/A	International Convention for the Protection of Birds (1950)
Biodiversity	Conserve biological diversity	N/A	Convention on Biological Diversity (1992)

TABLE 1.3 Estimates of Population, Poor and Hungry (millions of people)

Region	Hunger (1995)*	Region	Poverty (1993)
Africa	241	Sub-Saharan Africa	218.6
China	210	China	372.3
Eastern Europe and Central Asia	6.3	Eastern Europe and Central Asia	14.5
Latin America and the Caribbean	65	Latin America and the Caribbean	109.6
Middle East	29	Middle East and North Africa	10.7
South and Southeast Asia	337	South Asia	514.7
North America	7	North America	0[†]
Pacific OECD	1	Pacific OECD	0[†]
Western Europe	3	Western Europe	0[†]
World	889	World	1313.9

Source: For data on hunger, Raskin et al. (1998); for data on poverty, World Bank (1999).

* Data for hunger are taken from the Reference Scenario in Raskin et al. (1998). See also Chapter 3.
[†] A different measure of poverty is used for OECD countries.

Targets for Reducing Hunger and Poverty

Meeting human needs for food, nurture, housing, education, and employment may help but does not ensure a reduction in hunger and poverty. If the target for feeding the world populations is to halve the number of hungry people in each of the next two generations, then by definition hunger would be reduced. This feeding of people would imply a reduction in poverty, since the world's poor spend some 85 percent of their income on food. Nurturing, education, and housing are less closely linked to alleviation of poverty. In general, the poor are less healthy, educated, and housed, but some poor countries have shown that it is possible to make dramatic increases in longevity, education, or access to clean water despite the large numbers of poor people. Even employment does not necessarily eliminate poverty: most of the world's poor work—indeed work very hard—but they receive little or no income from their labor. Thus, for a transition to sustainability, reducing hunger and poverty (as shown in the example of the "Hunger and Climate Change Reduction scenario" in the appendix to Chapter 3) requires conscious and simultaneous efforts in three directions: encouraging overall growth in income and employment opportunities, increasing the share of the increased income that accrues to poor and hungry people, and providing the crucial public services of nurturing, education, and housing. With evidence mounting that a substantial surge in the poverty rate in East Asia has followed the financial crises there, these efforts will be more difficult to achieve.[63]

THE TRANSITION TO SUSTAINABILITY AS SOCIAL LEARNING

A transition toward sustainability would be unprecedented; it has no charted course. The evidence from the first decade of efforts to achieve sustainable development shows that, in general, societies do not know how to do it. But the widespread experience of local efforts and successes is instructive and suggests an ability of societies to learn on the relevant scales. Hope for successfully navigating the transition in the future lies in conceptualizing sustainable development not as a knowable destination or computable trajectory, but rather as a process of social learning and adaptive response amid turbulence and surprise.

What would it mean for society to learn how to better navigate a transition to sustainability? Scholarly studies of social learning over the large spatial and temporal scales of relevance are few but suggestive.[64] On the social side, they include work on the shaping of social policy in Britain and Sweden, study of the long-term development of the international capacity to manage the spread of infectious diseases, analysis of the spread and influence of Keynesian ideas in economic policy, and examination of the evolution of democratic norms and practices in Europe.[65] In the environmental realm, there is a substantial body of scholarship on social responses to natural hazards, work on the Mediterranean, analysis of the Columbia Basin experience, studies on ecosystem management, review of policy learning in regional environmental management, and a forthcoming collaborative study on how societies around the world learned to deal with the risks of acid rain, ozone depletion, and climate change.[66] While a coherent theory of social learning has not emerged from these works, several common themes stand out and we have drawn on them to guide the present study.

Central to social learning in this context are many individual and group actions in response to change. But significant changes in societal responses to issues as complex as those involved in sustainable development generally require slow, interactive accumulations of scientific knowledge, technical capacity, management institutions, and public concern over periods of a decade or more. Moreover, while some adaptive learning can accrue throughout such extended periods, the more fundamental and important learning of changes in deeply held beliefs or perceptions of problems is rare and seems to require the impetus of crisis or surprise.[67] A successful effort to promote social learning for a sustainability transition must therefore be expected to require patience and persistence over generations, while at the same time retaining enough flexibility to seize the moment when opportunities arise.

The serious pursuit of social learning entails efforts to make sense of what is happening, to shape interventions informed by that awareness, and to interpret the consequences of the interventions against expectations of what might otherwise have occurred. All of these actions require a strategic perspective. For learning how to navigate the transition toward sustainability, such a strategic perspective will need to encompass large intervals of time and space, and facilitate an appreciation of the complex interactions of natural, economic, and social forces at work over those intervals. In short, societies must understand the long-term, large-scale trends and transitions that have shaped past and present interactions of environment and development. We attempt to sketch such historical perspectives on the transition to sustainability in Chapter 2. Looking forward, a strategic perspective on sustainable development does not mean a feckless quest to predict the future. Rather, it means thinking in an organized way about possible futures and the possible implications of present choices for them. Chapter 3 of this report summarizes recent work on the use of integrated assessment models, structured scenarios, and regional information systems to inform the strategic perspectives needed for learning how to achieve sustainable development.

If societies' efforts to navigate the transition cannot count on predictions of the future, neither are they condemned to simply steer into the darkness without an understanding of what lies ahead. If the scientific community does not know enough to say with confidence how the interactions of environment and development will work out over the relevant long-term and global scales, it can nonetheless do a good deal to heighten awareness of and preparations for the sorts of obstacles and opportunities that might be encountered along the way. This report attempts such a strategic reconnaissance in Chapter 4, employing past development experience and present scientific understanding to identify some of the most problematic environmental obstacles to human development that may be met in the transition to sustainability. The chapter then seeks to evaluate the potential social, technical, and environmental opportunities for circumventing or mitigating such obstacles, employing integrated strategies for the management of water, the atmospheric environment, and species and ecosystems.

A fundamental requirement of social learning is feedback. In the report's analysis of efforts in social learning, the development, measurement, and reporting of appropriate indicators has been repeatedly singled out as one of the most important factors contributing to improved performance. Indicators can serve a variety of functions, from monitoring progress toward goals, through providing early warning of approaching hazards and detecting surprises, to assessing the effectiveness of particular interventions. The difficulty of designing indicators for use in promoting a transition to sustainability is to articulate what is needed and how the need for continued learning and response to surprise may be made part of the system for navigation. In Chapter 5 of this report, we develop a framework for indicators. One set of indicators is aimed at catching signals on different spatial scales to inform societies if they are on the right course in meeting goals for human needs and reducing hunger and poverty. These include monitoring biophysical circulatory systems,[68] identifying critical regions, conserving productive landscapes, and preserving ecosystems. Another set of indicators evaluate the efficacy of actions taken to attain the goals. These include creating national capital accounts, analyzing policies, monitoring ongoing transitions, and conducting "surprise" diagnostics. Chapter 5 also discusses how to design, build, and maintain measurement and monitoring capacity, how to include the end users of the information, and how to use the scales of relevance.

Social learning is a knowledge-intensive endeavor. It involves not only making use of and testing existing knowledge in new circumstances, but also the creation of new knowledge and know-how. The difficulty of creating knowledge and know-how to support the transition to sustainability transcends not only national boundaries but also the individual human life span and the customary planning horizons of human enterprises. Developing a useful "sustainability science" will require novel approaches for research linking the natural and social sciences, and studying adaptive management and policy; for technology development and diffusion, to provide the most useful and needed tools for navigating the choices; and for institutions, to overcome barriers and find new funding mechanisms. Perhaps most challenging, sustainability science will require the design of new ways for learning from the uniquely large-scale, long-term experiments created every time a new technology, management scheme, or policy is tried out in the real world. The barriers to such learning are immense, but so are the potential rewards for overcoming them. Chapter 6 of this report provides a strategy for setting priorities for action to promote the life and livelihood goals described here, in navigating our common journey toward sustainability.

REFERENCES AND BIBLIOGRAPHY

Adams, W. M. 1990. *Green development: Environment and sustainability in the Third World.* London: Routledge.

Agenda 21. See UNCED 1992.

Baskin, Yvonne. 1997. *The work of nature: How the diversity of life sustains us.* Washington: Island Press.

Bean, Michael J. 1983. *The evolution of national wildlife law.* New York: Praeger Publishers.

Bellagio Declaration. 1989. *Overcoming hunger in the 1990s.* Bellagio, Italy.

Bennell, P., and Furlong, D. 1998. Has Jomtien made any difference? Trends in donor funding for education and basic education since the late 1980s. *World Development* 26, no. 1: 45-59.

Bergesen, Helge Ole, and Georg Parmann. 1997. *Green globe yearbook of international cooperation on environment and development.* New York: Oxford University Press.

Brandt Report. See Independent Commission on International Development Issues, 1980.

Brown, B. J., M. E. Hanson, D. M. Liverman, and R. W. Merideth, Jr. 1987. Global sustainability: Toward definition. *Environmental Management* 11, no. 6:713-719.

Brundtland Report. See WCED 1987.

Burton, Ian, Robert W. Kates and Gilbert F. White. 1993. *The environment as hazard.* New York: Guilford Press.

Caldwell, Lynton Keith. 1990. *International environmental policy: emergence and dimensions.* 2d ed. Durham: Duke University Press.

Carincross, S., J. E. Hardoy, and D. Sattherwaite. 1990. The urban context. In *The poor die young: Housing and health in Third World cities,* eds. J.E. Hardoy, S. Cairncross, and D. Sattherwaite. London: Earthscan Publications.

Chen, Robert S., and Robert W. Kates. 1996. Towards a food-secure world: Prospects and trends. In *Global Environmental Change,* 27-32. NATO ASI Series, vol. 37. London: Springer.

Clark, W. C., and R. E. Munn, eds. 1986. *Sustainable development of the biosphere.* Cambridge, UK: Cambridge University Press.

Clark, W. C. 1990. Visions of the 21st century: Conventional wisdom and other surprises in the global interactions of population, technology and the environment. In *Perspective 2000: Proceedings of a conference sponsored by the Economic Council of Canada*, eds. K. Newton, T. Schweitaer, and J-P. Voyer, 7-32. Ottawa: Canadian Government Publishing Center.

Clark, W. C., J. Jaeger, J. van Eijndhoven, and N. Dickinson, eds. 1999. *Learning to manage global environmental risks: A comparative history of social responses to climate change, ozone depletion and acid rain*. Cambridge: MIT Press.

Cohen, Joel C. 1995. *How many people can the earth support?* New York: Norton.

Cooper, Richard N. 1989. International cooperation in public health as a prologue to macroeconomic cooperation. In *Can Nations Agree? Issues in International Economic Cooperation*. Washington, D.C.: Brookings Institution.

Convention on the Rights of the Child. 1989. General Assembly Resolution 44/25, annex. UN Document A/44/49. New York: United Nations.

Cooper, Richard N. 1989. International cooperation in public health as a prologue to macroeconomic cooperation. pp. 178-254 in Richard N. Cooper, Barry Eichengreen, C. Randall Henning, Gerald Holtham and Robert D. Putnam, eds. *Can nations agree? Issues in international economic cooperation*. Washington, D.C.: The Brookings Institution.

Costanza, R., R. d'Arge, R. de Groot, S. Farber, M. Grasso, B. Hannon, K. Limburg, S. Naeem, R.V. O'Neill, J. Paruelo, R.G. Raskin, P. Sutton, and M. van der Belt. 1997. The value of the world's ecosystem services and natural capital. *Nature* 387, no. 6630: 253-260.

Daily, Gretchen C, ed. 1997. *Nature's services: Societal dependence on natural ecosystems*. Washington, D.C.: Island Press.

Daly, H. 1990. Toward some operational principles of sustainable development. *Ecological Economics* 2:1-6

Dasgupta, Partha. 1993. *An inquiry into well-being and destitution*. Oxford: Oxford University Press.

Dooge, J.C.I., G.T. Goodman, J.W.M. La Rivière, J. Marin-Lefèvre, T. O'Riodran, F. Praderie, eds. 1992. *An agenda of science for environment and development into the 21st century*. Cambridge, UK: Cambridge University Press.

Dryzek, John. 1997. *The politics of the earth*. London: Oxford University Press.

Earth System Sciences Committee. 1986. *Earth system science: Overview: A program for global change*. Washington: National Aeronautics and Space Administration.

Eder, Klaus. 1987. Learning and the evolution of social systems: An epigenetic perspective. In *Evolutionary theory in social science*, eds. M. Schmid and F. M. Wuketits. Dordrecht: Reidel.

FAO (Food and Agricultural Organization of the United Nations). 1998. *The state of food and agriculture 1998*. Rome: FAO.

Forest Principles. See UN 1992.

Gillies, A.M. 1993. *Economic prosperity in the 21st century: The win-win benefits of managing our economy in harmony with the environment*. Winnipeg, Canada: International Institute for Sustainable Development.

Grubb, M., M. Koch, A. Munson, F. Sullivan, and K. Thomson. 1993. *The Earth Summit agreements: A guide and assessment*. London: The Royal Institute of International Affairs.

Gunderson, L. H., Holling, C. S., and Light, S. L., eds. 1995. *Barriers and bridges to the renewal of ecosystems and institutions*. New York: Columbia University Press.

Haas, Peter M. 1990. *Saving the Mediterranean: The politics of international environmental cooperation*. New York: Columbia University Press.

Hall, Peter. 1989. *The political power of economic ideas: Keynesianism across nations*. Princeton, NJ: Princeton University Press.

Heclo, Hugh. 1974. *Modern social politics in Britain and Sweden: From relief to income mainte-nance.* New Haven: Yale University Press.

Holling, C.S., ed. 1978. *Adaptive environmental assessment and management.* London: John Wiley.

ILO (International Labour Organization). 1998. *World employment report 1998-1999.* Geneva: International Labour Office.

IUCN (The World Conservation Union), UNEP (United Nations Environment Programme), WWF (World Wildlife Fund), FAO (Food and Agriculture Organization of the United Nations), and UNESCO (United Nations Educational, Scientific, and Cultural Organi-zation). 1980. *World conservation strategy: Living resource conservation for sustainable de-velopment.* Gland, Switzerland: IUCN.

IUCN (The World Conservation Union), UNEP (United Nations Environment Programme), and WWF (World Wide Fund For Nature). 1991. *Caring for the earth: A strategy for sustainable living (World Conservation Strategy II).* Gland, Switzerland: IUCN, UNEP, and WWF.

Independent Commission on Disarmament and Security Issues. 1982. *Common security: A blueprint for survival.* New York: Simon and Schuster. (Palme Report)

Independent Commission on International Development Issues. 1980. *North-South: A pro-gram for survival.* Cambridge, MA: MIT Press. (Brandt Report)

Kates, R. W., and W. C. Clark. 1996. Environmental surprise: Expecting the unexpected? *Environment* 38, no. 2: 6-11, 28-35.

de Klemm, Cyrille, with Clare Shine. 1993. *Biological diversity conservation and the law: Legal mechanisms for conserving species and ecosystems.* Gland: World Conservation Union (IUCN).

Lee, K. N. 1993. *Compass and gyroscope: Integrating science and politics for the environment.* Washington: Island Press.

Lipton, M. 1988. *The poor and the poorest.* Washington: The World Bank.

Lubchenco, J., A. M. Olson, L. B. Brubaker, S. R. Carpenter, M. M. Holland, S. P. Hubbell, S. A. Levin, H. A. MacMahon, P. A. Matson, J. M. Melillo, H. A. Mooney, C. H. Peterson, H. R. Pulliam, L. A. Real, P. J. Regal, and P. G. Risser. 1991. The sustainable biosphere initiative: An ecological research agenda. *Ecology* 72, no. 2: 371.

Mooney, H. A., and P. R. Ehrlich. 1997. Ecosystem services: A fragmentary history. In *Nature's Services: Societal Dependence on Natural Ecosystems,* ed. Gretchen C. Daily. Washington: Island Press.

Morita, T., Kawashima, Y., and Inohara, I. 1993. Sustainable development: Its definitions and goals. *Mita Gakkai Zasshi (Mita Journal of Economics)* 85, no. 4. Translated from Japanese.

Murcott, S. 1995. *Sustainable systems: Definitions, principles, criteria and indicators.* Paper pre-pared for a IIASA (International Institute for Applied Systems Analysis) workshop on Sustainable Development: Criteria and Indicators, 25 July.

NRC (National Research Council). 1986. *Global change in the geosphere-biosphere: Initial priori-ties for an IGBP.* US Committee for an International Geosphere-Biosphere Program. Washington, D.C.: National Academy Press.

_____. 1996. *Upstream: Salmon and society in the Pacific Northwest.* Committee on Protection and Management of Pacific Northwest Anadromous Salmonids. Washington, D.C.: National Academy Press.

_____. 1994. *The role of terrestrial ecosystems in global change: A plan for action.* Board on Global Change. Washington, D.C.: National Academy Press.

O'Riordan, T. 1988. The politics of sustainability. In *Sustainable environmental management: Principles and practice,* ed. R. K. Turner, 29-50. Boulder, CO: Westview.

OECD (Organization for Economic Cooperation and Development). 1998. *Employment Outlook: 1998.* Paris: OECD.

Palme Report, see Independent Commission on Disarmament and Security Issues, 1982.

Parson, E. R. and Clark, W. C. 1995. Sustainable development as social learning: Theoretical perspectives and practical challenges for the design of a research program. In *Barriers and bridges to the renewal of ecosystems and institutions.*, eds. L. H. Gunderson, C. S. Holling, and S. L. Light, 428-460. New York: Columbia University Press.

PCSD (President's Council on Sustainable Development). 1996. *Sustainable America: A new consensus for prosperity, opportunity, and a healthy environment for the future.* Washington: US Government Printing Office.

Raskin, P., Chadwick, M., Jackson, T., and Leach, G. 1995. *The transition toward sustainability: Beyond conventional development.* Boston: Stockholm Environmental Institute.

Raskin, P., G. Gallopin, P. Gutman, A. Hammond, and R. Swart. 1998. *Bending the curve: Toward global sustainability.* A report of the Global Scenario Group. PoleStar Series Report no. 8. Boston: Stockholm Environment Institute.

Redclift, Michael. 1987. *Sustainable development: Exploring the contradictions.* London: Methuen.

Ruckelshaus, William D. 1989. Toward a sustainable world. *Scientific American* 261, no. 3: 166-74. Reprinted in *Managing planet earth: Readings from* Scientific American *Magazine.* New York: W.H. Freeman, 1990.

Sabatier, Paul, and Matthew Zafonte. 1997. *Policy-oriented learning between coalitions: Characteristics of successful professional/scientific fora.* Paper presented at the 1997 Annual Meeting of the American Association for the Advancement of Science, Seattle, February 9.

Sen, Amartya. 1981. *Poverty and entitlements.* Oxford: Pergamon Press for the International Labor Organization.

US Environment Protection Agency (EPA). 1995. *The President's Council on Sustainable Development: Principles, goals, and definition task force, background papers.* EPA 230K-95-001. Washington, D.C.: EPA.

UN (United Nations). 1950. International Convention for the Protection of Birds, Paris, 638 UN Treaty Series 185. New York: United Nations.

_____. 1958. Convention on Fishing and Conservation of the Living Resources of the High Seas, Geneva. 17 US Treaties and other International Agreements 138. New York: United Nations.

_____. 1972. *The Stockholm Declaration.* In *In defence of the earth: The basic texts on environment,* UNEP (United Nations Environment Programme), 1981. Nairobi: UNEP.

_____. 1979. Convention on Long-Range Transboundary Air Pollution, Geneva. US Treaties and Other Acts Series 1054. New York: United Nations.

_____. 1982. UN Convention on the Law of the Sea, Montego Bay. UN certified true copy XI.6, March 1983. New York: United Nations.

_____. 1985. Vienna Convention for the Protection of the Ozone Layer, Vienna. UN Document TIAS 1097. New York: United Nations.

_____. 1990. *The world summit for children.* New York: UNICEF.

_____. 1992. *Non-legally binding authoritative statement of principles for a global consensus on the management, conservation and sustainable development of all types of forests.* (Forest Principles). From the UN Conference on Environment and Development, Rio de Janeiro, June 1992. New York: United Nations.

_____. 1992a. UN Framework Convention on Climate Change, New York. Senate Treaty Document 102-38, 102nd COngress, 2nd Session. Washington, D.C.: U.S. Government Printing Office.

_____. 1992b. Convention on Biological Diversity, Rio de Janeiro. New York: United Nations.

_____. 1994a. Protocol to the 1979 Convention on Long-Range Transboundary Air Pollution on Further Reduction of Sulfur Emissions, 0510. UN certified True Copy XXVII. 1(e). New York: United Nations.

_____. 1994b. UN Convention to Combat Desertification in those Countries Experiencing Serious Drought and/or Desertication, Particularly in Africa. UN Certified True Copy. XXVII.10. New York: United Nations.

_____. 1995a. *The Copenhagen declaration and programme of action.* Adopted at the World Summit for Social Development, Copenhagen, 6-12 March, 1995. New York: United Nations.

_____. 1995b. *Report of the World Summit for Social Development, Copenhagen, 6-12 March 1995.* New York: United Nations.

_____. 1997. *Report on the world social situation 1997.* New York: United Nations.

_____. 1999 (forthcoming). *World population prospects: The 1998 revision.* New York: United Nations Population Division.

UNCED (United Nations Conference on Environment and Development). 1992. *Report of the United Nations Conference on Environment and Development, Rio de Janeiro, 3-14 June 1992.* Rio de Janeiro: UN. (Annex I: Rio Declaration; Annex II: Agenda 21)

UNCHS (United Nations Conference on Human Settlements). 1996a. *Habitat action plan.* Global Plan of Action from the Second UN Conference on Human Settlements, 1996. Istanbul: United Nations. Available at http://habitat.unchs.org/unchs/english/hagenda/index.htm.

UNCHS (United Nations Center for Human Settlements). 1996b. *An urbanizing world: Global report on human settlements 1996.* Oxford: Oxford University Press.

UNCSD (United Nations Commission on Sustainable Development). 1997. *Overall progress achieved since the UN Conference on Environment and Development.* Addendum on international institutional arrangements. UN E/CN.17/1997/2/Add.28. New York: United Nations.

UNDP (United Nations Development Programme). 1998. *Human development report 1998.* Oxford: Oxford University Press.

UNEP (United Nations Environment Programme). 1999. *Global environmental outlook 2000.* London: Earthscan.

UNESCO (United Nations Educational, Scientific and Cultural Organization). 1971. Convention as Wetlands of International Importance Especially as Waterfowl Habitat, Ramsar. Paris, France: UNESCO.

_____. 1998. UNESCO Statistical Yearbook. Paris, France: UNESCO. Available http://unescostat. unesco.org/yearbook/ybindexnew.htm. Visited 8/13/99.

UNICEF (United Nations Children's Fund). 1991. *The state of the world's children 1991.* Oxford: Oxford University Press.

_____. 1993. *The state of the world's children 1993.* Oxford: Oxford University Press.

_____. 1995. *The state of the world's children 1995.* Oxford: Oxford University Press.

_____. 1998. *The progress of nations 1998.* New York: UNICEF.

_____. 1999. *The state of the world's children 1999.* Oxford: Oxford University Press.

Uvin, Peter. 1993. The state of world hunger. In *The hunger report 1993,* Peter Uvin, ed., 1-42. Langhorne, PA: Gordon and Breach.

Vitousek, P., P. Ehrlich, A. Ehrlich, and P. Matson. 1986. Human appropriation of the products of photosynthesis. *Bioscience* 36: 368-373.

WCE (World Conference on Education for All). 1990. *World Declaration on Education for All and Framework for action to meet basic learning needs.* No. 86290. Paris, France: UNESCO,

WCED (World Commission on Environment and Development). 1987. *Our common future.* New York: Oxford University Press. (Brundtland Report)

WFS (World Food Summit). 1996. *Rome declaration on world food security and world food summit plan of action*. Rome: FAO. Available http://www.fao.org/wfs/final/rd-e.htm. Visited 7/8/99.

WHO (World Health Organization). 1996. *Water supply and sanitation sector monitoring report 1996 (Sector status as of 1994)*. New York: Water Supply and Sanitation Collaborative Council and UNICEF.

WRI (World Resources Institute). 1992. *World resources 1992-93: A guide to the global environment*. A joint publication by the World Resources Institute, the United Nations Environment Programme, the United Nations Development Programme, and the World Bank. New York: Oxford University Press.

WSC (World Summit for Children). 1990. *The world summit for children*. New York: UNICEF.

WSSD (World Summit for Social Development). 1995. *Copenhagen declaration on social development and programme of action*. Copenhagen: UN.

Walter, H.S. 1998. Land use conflicts in California. In *Landscape degradation in Mediterranean-type ecosystems*, eds. P.W. Rundel, G. Montenegro, and F. Jaksic. *Ecological Studies* 136: 107-126. Berlin: Springer-Verlag.

Walters, C.J. 1986. *Adaptive management of renewable resources*. New York: MacMillan.

Weiss, Thomas G., David P. Forsythe, and Roger A. Coate. 1997. *The United Nations and changing world politics*. 2d ed. New York: Westview Press.

Wilbanks, T. J. 1994. "Sustainable Development" in geographic perspective. *Annals of the Association of American Geographers* 84: 541-556.

Windham, D., M. Lakin, M. Sutton, N. Colletta, N. Fisher, and W. Haddad. 1990. *Meeting basic learning needs: A vision for the 1990s*. Background document, World Conference on Education for All, Jomtien, Thailand, 5-9 March 1990. New York: Inter-Agency Commission for the World Conference on Education for All (UNICEF, UNDP, UNESCO, World Bank).

World Bank. 1997. *World development indicators 1997*. Washington: The World Bank.

_____. 1999. *World Bank poverty update: Trends in poverty*. Washington: The World Bank. Available http://www.worldbank.org. Visited 6/4/99.

ENDNOTES

1 World Conservation Strategy, IUCN et al. (1980); Stockholm Conference, UN (1972); conservation movement, Adams (1990).

2 WCED (1987), p. 8.

3 WCED (1987).

4 Clark and Munn (1986), Brown et al. (1987), Redclift (1987), O'Riordan (1988), Adams (1990), Daly (1990), Morita et al. (1993), Wilbanks (1994), Murcott (1995), PCSD (1996), WRI (1992), Gillies (1993), Dryzek (1997).

5 Daily (1997).

6 Mooney and Ehrlich (1997).

7 Costanza et. al. (1997).

8 PCSD (1996), p. v.

9 Ruckelshaus (1989), p. 166.

10 UNCED (1992).

11 Small island developing states, UN Global Conference on the Sustainable Development of Small Island Developing States, Bridgetown, Barbados, April 25-May 6, 1994; population and development, United Nations International Conference on Population and Development, Cairo, September 5-13, 1994; social development, World Summit for Social Development, Copenhagen, March 5-12, 1995; straddling and migratory fish stocks, United Nations Conference on Straddling Fish Stocks and Highly Migratory Fish Stocks, New

York, March 27-April 12, 1995; women, United Nations Fourth World Conference on Women, Beijing, September 4-15, 1995; human settlements, United Nations Conference on Human Settlements, Istanbul, June 3-14, 1996; and food, World Food Summit, Rome, November 13-17, 1996.

[12] UNEP (1999).

[13] Weiss et al. (1997).

[14] UNCSD (1997).

[15] Dooge et al. (1992).

[16] Lee (1993).

[17] UN (1999).

[18] Chen and Kates (1996).

[19] FAO (1998). Although there is some hunger in industrialized or transitional economies, no international estimates exist.

[20] WFS (1996), p. 1.

[21] UNICEF (1993), p. 6.

[22] UNICEF (1991), p. 35.

[23] Dasgupta (1993).

[24] WSC (1990).

[25] UNCHS (1996a), para. 45.

[26] UNCHS (1996b), pp. xxviii-xxix.

[27] UNCHS (1996a), para. 45.

[28] Op cit., para. 48a.

[29] UNICEF (1999).

[30] UNICEF (1991), p. 35.

[31] World Declaration on Education for All, UNESCO (1990); World Summit for Children, UN (1990).

[32] UNICEF (1991), p. 26.

[33] UNICEF (1999).

[34] Bennell and Furlong (1998).

[35] UN (1995a,b).

[36] UN (1995b).

[37] OECD (1998).

[38] Unemployment rates, UNDP (1998); unemployment data, ILO (1998).

[39] ILO (1998).

[40] UN (1997), Ch. VII, p. 18; ILO (1998).

[41] UNICEF (1998).

[42] Bellagio Declaration (1989).

[43] "Agenda 21" of UNCED (1992), Ch. 19.

[44] UN (1979), Article 2.

[45] UN (1994a), Article 2.

[46] UN (1985), Preamble.

[47] UN (1992a), Article 2.

[48] UN (1982), Article 1:1(4).

[49] Op cit., Article 145.

[50] Convention on the Preservation of Marine Pollution by Dumping of Wastes and Other Matter, London, Mexico City, Moscow, and Washington. 26 US Treaties and Other International Agreements 2403. Washington, D.C.

[51] Convention for the Prevention of Marine Pollution by Dumping from Ships and Aircraft, Oslo. 11 International Legal Materials 262. Norway.

[52] Inernational Convention for the Regulation of Whaling, Washington, 1946. 4 Bevans 248, US Treaties and other International Acts Series 1849. Washington, D.C.

53 UN (1958), Article 2.

54 UN (1950), Article 3.

55 Convention of the Conservation of Migratory Species of Wild Animals, Bonn. 1979. 19 International Legal Materials 15. Germany. Article 2.

56 Convention on International Trade in Endangered Species of Wild Fauna and Flora, Washington, 1973. US Treaties and Other International Acts Series 8249, Article 2.

57 UNESCO (1971), Article 2.

58 Bergesen and Parmann (1997).

59 UN (1994b), Article 3.

60 UN (1992b), Article 6.

61 E.g., World Bank (1999).

62 Sen (1981); Lipton (1988); Dasgupta (1993).

63 World Bank (1999); World Bank News Release (1999), No. 99/2214/S.

64 Parson and Clark (1995).

65 Social policy, Heclo (1974); infectious diseases, Cooper (1989); economic policy, Hall (1989); democracy, Eder (1987).

66 Natural hazards, Burton et al. (1993); Mediterranean, Haas (1990); Columbia Basin, Lee (1993) and NRC (1996); ecosystem management, Holling et al. (1978), Gunderson et al. (1995), Walter (1998); regional environmental management, Sabatier and Zafonte (1997); acid rain, ozone depletion, land, and climate change, Clark et al. (1999).

67 Clark (1990); Kates and Clark (1996).

68 As Chapter 5 explains, biophysical circulatory systems include rapid circulation in atmosphere and oceans, driven by solar energy and slower changes in the lithosphere as tectonic plates move, and in the biosphere as migration patterns shift and species radiate.

 **Trends and Transitions**

T his chapter explores some major historical trends and transitions
that might significantly affect the prospects for sustainability over
the next half-century. It addresses trends in human development
and the earth's environment, and also the interactions between them. In
the first part of this chapter, we look at directions in human development,
especially the increasing connectedness of economies, peoples, and technologies; the persisting and even growing human diversity in modern
cities; the changing patterns of consumption; the emergence of human
development as a significant biogeochemical force; and the basic trends in
population, economy, resource use, and pollution. In the second part, the
chapter traces trends in the transformation of life support systems at local
and regional scales, through trends in human-induced changes of atmosphere and climate, oceans, freshwater, land, species and ecosystems, and
disease organisms and their vectors.

The trends discussed here are not always constant over time. Instead,
long periods of relative constancy are sometimes interspersed with shorter
episodes of rapid change. Early in these episodes, changes are often
accelerating and may appear exponential. Later, as the episode runs its
course or feedbacks cut in, these changes tend to decelerate and may even
reverse direction. In between come periods of transition, marked by
breaks or inflections in the long-term trends.[1] In its examination of critical trends in global change, the United Nations' Department for Policy
Coordination and Sustainable Development defines transitions as gradual
and continuous shifts in society from one state to another.[2]

We live in an era of such transitions, which are under way to varying degrees in specific places and regions around the globe. In the social realm, the transitions that seem most relevant to sustainability include the demographic transitions from high to low birth and death rates; the health transition from early death by infectious diseases to late death by cancer, heart attack, and stroke; the economic transition from state to market control; the civil society transition from single-party, military, or state-run institutions to multiparty politics and a rich mix of nongovernmental institutions. Environmentally, some of the more significant transitions or breaks in trends in specific regions include shifts from the dominance of particular biogeochemical cycles by natural forces to their dominance by human releases, from increasing to decreasing rates of emissions for specific pollutants, and from deforestation to reforestation.

How should societies think of the relationship between major trends or transitions and sustainability? A series of seven interlinked transitions to a more sustainable world has been identified.[3] These were later elaborated and amplified[4] as demographic, technological, economic, social, institutional, ideological, and informational transitions. For the most part, the researchers present these transitions as *requirements* for a more sustainable world: if each individual transition is completed successfully the result will constitute a transition to sustainability.

We take a different tack in this study. In Chapter 1 we argued that the path for a transition toward sustainability could not be charted in advance. Instead, we suggested that it would have to be navigated adaptively through trial-and-error experimentation. We remain unconvinced that any specific set of trends or transitions constitutes necessary or sufficient conditions for sustainability. Yet we think that the triad of goals set out in Chapter 1—meeting human needs, preserving life support systems, reducing hunger and poverty—would guide the successful navigation of a transition toward sustainability over the next two generations. Knowledge of trends and emerging transitions may well prove helpful in attaining these goals; societies must first know the directions of present trajectories in the environment and development. Thus, we begin with trends in human development, then turn to the environmental transformations that have been influenced by human actions, emphasizing the interconnectedness of human development and the environment and the needed shifts in trends for attaining a sustainable future. Specialized studies, named in the text that follows, have addressed trends and transitions for particular aspects of environmental change and particular regions of the world. National Research Council studies related to each developmental sector or environmental issue are provided in endnotes keyed to each section. Our purpose is not to duplicate these extensive treatments found throughout the environmental science literature. Rather, we cite recent studies that present authoritative findings on these topics.

HUMAN DEVELOPMENT

Population Growth, Urbanization, and Well-Being

Slowing Growth

The global human population at the end of the 20th century will reach about 6 billion people. With an annual growth rate of 1.33 percent between 1995 and 2000, about 80 million people were added to the planet each year. Current growth rates are falling and have been doing so since the peak global growth rate in the early 1960s of about 2.04 percent per year. Because this slowly declining growth rate is applied to an increasing population base, absolute population growth will remain high for the next few decades. Thus, population size is expected to increase by almost 2 billion between 2000 and 2025, the same amount as in the last quarter of this century.[5]

Changes in birth rates and death rates over time, a process referred to as the demographic transition, were first studied in Europe. Within two centuries, trends in Europe went from conditions of high birth and death rates to the current conditions of low birth and death rates. In such a transition, deaths first decline more rapidly than births. During that time, population grows rapidly, but eventually it stabilizes as the decline in birth rates matches or even exceeds the decline in death rates. While the general description of the demographic transition is widely accepted, there is much that is debated as to cause and details. Humanity is now in the midst of a global demographic transition that is more rapid than the European transition. Birth and death rates in developing countries have dropped unexpectedly rapidly. The transition in fertility rates in the developing world has declined to 3 births per woman compared to 6 births per woman at the post World War II peak of population growth and is more than halfway towards the level of 2.1 births per woman required to achieve eventual zero population growth. The average number of births for each woman of reproductive age has declined to 3 compared to 6 at the post World War II peak of population growth. The mortality transition in developing countries has also proceeded very rapidly, with life expectancy at birth having increased from 40 years in 1950 to about 64 years today—though this is still well below the 75 years of life expectancy in the industrialized countries.

Today's population growth has immense momentum because large new generations of young people are reaching reproductive age. How much population will grow depends on their choices of family size and their ability to implement these choices. Policies designed to encourage such implementation can slow growth considerably.[6] In fact, the recent rates of decline in fertility outpaced earlier projections of demographers, such that the United Nations reduced its mid-range forecast of global population for 2050 from almost 9.8 billion in the 1994 projection to 8.9 billion in the 1998 projection.[7] By the end of the 21st century, the world's human population is now projected to reach 9.5 billion.[8] Nearly all of this increase—about 97 percent—will occur in the less developed areas of the world.[9] (Figure 2.1).

Expanding Urbanization[10]

Changes in distribution of the world's population over the last 50 years have been relatively small at the global scale (that is, between continents), but relatively large at the intranational scale. Currently, more than half of the world's population lives in Asia, as was the case at the end of the Second World War. The percentage of the world's population residing in Europe and North America has steadily declined, from about

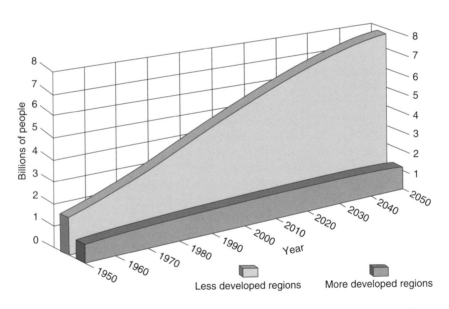

FIGURE 2.1 Historical and projected human population growth in billions for less developed and more developed regions, 1950-2050.
Source: UN (1999). Courtesy of the United Nations.

30 percent in 1950 to closer to 20 percent at the century's end. The largest proportional gains have been in Africa, which today has nearly 22 percent of the world's population, almost three times its share at mid-century.[11]

At the beginning of the 21st century, more people will live and work in the urban centers of the world than in rural areas for the first time in history. In 1999, the intranational changes in distribution are mostly related to past and current trends in urbanization. Urban populations are currently growing substantially faster than the population as a whole. The urban proportion of the world's population is thus projected to grow from 45 to about 60 percent in a generation.[12] It could well grow to upwards of the 80 percent that now characterizes Europe and Japan in two generations.[13] Combined with the rates of overall population growth cited earlier, this means accommodating on the order of 80 million new urban dwellers a year, every year, throughout the transition to sustainability, a feat equivalent to building almost 20 great cities or 10 megacities each year.*

Cities grow because people desire the infrastructure and opportunities that urban areas offer. Jobs, culture, schools, health care, and social services are generally more concentrated and accessible in cities than they are in rural areas. On average, people who live in urban areas receive more income, have fewer children, have better access to education, and live longer than their rural counterparts. But cities are also places of extreme contrast in wealth and opportunity. In some rapidly growing urban areas, it is harder to establish a sense of local community and shared responsibility for the well-being of the poor and hungry; thus in many cities, for the poor, urban life is more difficult, less healthy, and less safe than life in the countryside.[14]

The global transition to urban life is reflected in increases in both the proportion of urban dwellers and the size of cities. Within these constraints, the growth in the proportion of the population that is urban seems to follow an "s" shaped logistic, leveling off at 80 to 90 percent in industrialized countries.[15] The overall percentage of people worldwide living in urban areas increased from 37 percent in 1970 to 45 percent in 1994, and is projected to reach 60 percent in 2025.[16] The number of large cities has also grown significantly. In 1950, there were 81 "million cities" (cities with populations between 1 and 10 million); by 1990 there were 270 cities of this size. The number of megacities is increasing rapidly; while in 1950 there were only two megacities, New York and London, by 1990 there were 21 cities of this size, 15 in less developed regions. By 2015,

---

*A "megacity" is defined as an urban aggregation of 8 million or more inhabitants. A "great city" is a city of 5 million inhabitants.

these numbers are projected to increase to 516 "million cities" and 33 megacities. But while the number of megacities has increased, their growth has slowed, suggesting that there may be some ceilings for city size. Twenty-three of these megacities will be located in less developed countries, a dramatic increase over the complete absence of cities of this size in these regions in the 1950s. By 2015, 378 million persons, or 12 percent of the urban population of these areas, will live in megacities.[17]

Improved Well-Being

As population has doubled and urbanized over the past two generations, the overall well-being of people has substantially improved. Life expectancy has been rapidly extended; lifestyle has been enriched by literacy and education and made more secure economically. The Human Development Index (HDI), reported by the UN Development Program in its annual *Human Development Report*, provides a convenient and graphic indicator of these changes in the human condition, combining four indicators of well-being in the population of a nation: life expectancy at birth, adult literacy, school enrollment ratio, and real gross domestic product (GDP) per capita. The measures of lifespan, education, and economic welfare are transformed into index values, and the HDI is the simple average of the three index values.[18] Figure 2.2 compares the distribution of the world's population on the HDI scale in 1960 and 1992.

The evolving distribution of the human population on the HDI scale reflects the dramatic improvement in the material conditions of human life since the Second World War, particularly in developing countries. Since 1960 life expectancy in the developing world has increased by 17 years, and infant mortality has been cut in half. Access to safe drinking water has roughly doubled to more than two-thirds of all people. Primary school enrollment has increased by nearly two-thirds, reaching 77 percent by 1991. Per capita income has more than tripled. In sum, the developing world has covered as much ground in a generation, in a material sense, as the developed economies did in a century.[19] Yet despite these gains, over one-sixth of the population still lives in poverty; and while the percentage of people living below the absolute poverty line of US$1/day in developing countries declined slightly from 30.1 percent in 1987 to 29.4 percent in 1993, the actual number of people living in poverty rose from 1.2 billion in 1987 to 1.3 billion in 1993.[20] *

Progress has been social as well as material. Women have made im-

---

*The absolute poverty line of US$1/day is measured as purchasing power parity (PPP) dollars in 1985. World Bank (1999).

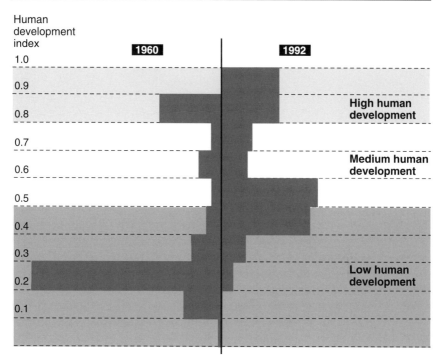

FIGURE 2.2 Distribution of the world's population by decile of the Human Development Index (HDI), 1960 versus 1992. The HDI provides a convenient and graphic indicator of changes in the human condition by combining four indicators of well-being in the population of a nation: life expectancy at birth, adult literacy, school enrollment ratio, and real GDP per capita. Source: UNDP (1995). Courtesy of Oxford University Press.

portant gains over the past generation in ways that go beyond economic measures, including through narrowing gender gaps in education, increased literacy, and decreased female child labor rates.[21] The available measures, however, show clearly that no society treats its women as well as its men. In addition, the relative well-being of different groups in societies remains contentious, as demonstrated by the persistence of underclasses of race, ethnicity, and poverty, and increasing disparities among groups in most societies.

Transitions are also taking place in many other aspects of human development. They include the health transition underlying increasing longevity, with movement away from the infectious diseases characteristic of developing countries to the chronic diseases of industrialized countries. Yet despite these trends, there has been a surprising reemergence of infectious disease even in industrialized countries, with human immunodeficiency virus (HIV) being the most prominent example. A number of diseases have been connected to technological and environmental changes, such as Legionnaire's disease (air conditioning), toxic shock syndrome (super-absorbent tampons), Lyme disease (changing suburban ecology), and Hanta virus (desert ecology). There may be a transition in education as well—from predominantly informal to formal learning and now to lifelong learning. Educational institutions, especially in the developed countries, are now addressing the needs for lifelong learning. And with the continued development and use of the Internet, especially in the developing countries, education and access to information are both expected to increase rapidly. Development itself was once thought to be a progression of stages.[22] But if this is true, it is highly irregular and punctuated by regional differences and periods of economic stagnation and decline (Figure 2.3), by reversals of longevity, such as that of young people in AIDS-affected countries and of men in Russia, and by educational requirements outpacing of educational offerings.

For a Sustainable Future

The persistent trends of growing population numbers but slowing rates of population increase have two major implications. There will be an enormous challenge in meeting the needs of almost twice as many people as there are today in the space of a few decades. But if met successfully, this challenge is not likely to be repeated within the next century or two. Housing and employing the additional people of the equivalent of a thousand additional cities over the next two generations is one part of today's challenge. The 600 million homeless and overcrowded in today's cities suggest the magnitude of the future task. At the same time, building these equivalent cities provides a needed opportunity to replace the current infrastructure and to build anew in an energy- and water-efficient manner.[23]

The rapid improvements in human well-being over the last two generations make more realistic the prospects of attaining the social goals of a sustainability transition. But the absolute numbers to be fed, nurtured, and educated will be almost twice those of the past two generations. Recent reversals in longevity and sustained periods of economic stagnation in Africa, Latin America, and perhaps Asia argue for caution in the simple projection of trends of improvement into the future. Thus, meeting human needs in ways that provide for future generations is at the heart of the transition to sustainability.

Wealth and Consumption[24]

Growing Wealth—Growing Disparities

Dramatic changes in human well-being are reflected substantially in changes in economic output (Figure 2.3). Trends in GDP—a measure of the total economic activity in a nation's markets—reflect a nation's production and income per capita, and hence give an indication of a country's poverty levels. GDP has been tracked back to 1820 (shown in Figure 2.3 on a logarithmic scale), a date at which the modern era of economic growth began in the view of an economic historian.[25]

There has been an average worldwide gain in GDP per person by a factor of 7.9 between 1820 and 1992; in the four "Western offshoots," Australia, Canada, New Zealand, and the United States, economic growth has brought about a gain of more than 17-fold over this span of roughly six generations—doubling economic output within each human lifespan. Even in Africa, the region with the weakest record, economic output per capita almost tripled between 1820 and 1980.

Despite recent gains in GDP per capita, however, economic statistics do not provide a complete measure of societal production. A society that measures its economic attainments only by market transactions misses important activities. For example, family work in households, which is usually done by women, is not counted unless it generates market transactions; and home appliance use is not accounted for in GDP, while appliance repair is incorporated into this measure of economic activity. Pollution, which diminishes the value of ecosystem services and other valued activities and assets, is excluded from conventional GDP accounts as a liability, but appears as a valued economic good as effort, money, and materials are used to respond to it (such as for the repair of a pollution-damaged building façade or the restoration of habitat).

Favorable trends in GDP also fail to account for disparities in the distribution of income. These disparities are widening and are likely to continue to do so in the absence of strong remedial actions.[26] The gap is growing between rich and poor countries as a whole and between the rich and poor within many countries. On a global basis, the ratio of the income share of the richest 20 percent to the poorest 20 percent doubled over the past 30 years from 30:1 to 60:1.[27] Among the rich countries (OECD countries), there has been a tendency over the last half-century toward convergence of productivity and income levels and a narrowing of disparities in wealth. Between the OECD and the poor or less developed countries, however, there has not been a general trend toward convergence, with the exception of a small but very important subset of developing countries primarily from east and Southeast Asia.[28]

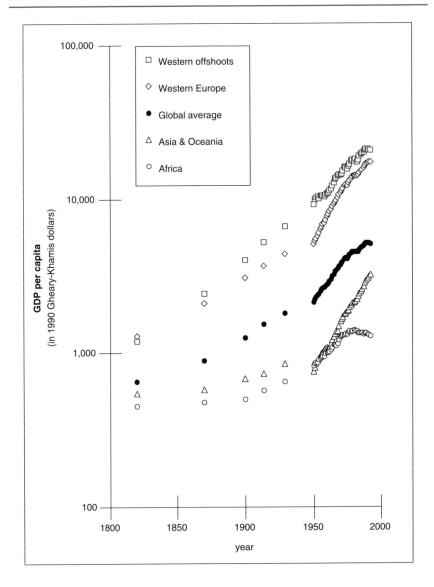

FIGURE 2.3 Gross Domestic Product (GDP) per capita, by geographic region. "Western offshoots" are the United States, Canada, Australia, and New Zealand. GDP is converted to a common standard, 1990 Geary-Khamis dollars, a method that uses estimates of purchasing power parity to compare national economies. Source: Maddison (1995).* Courtesy of the Organisation for Economic Cooperation and Development (OECD).

*See Maddison (1995) Table G-3, p. 228. Appendix B describes treatment of changes in GDP over time.

The relationship between economic growth and income distribution remains controversial among economists.[29] Within countries, developing countries have historically had higher levels of income inequality than more developed countries. There is evidence in some countries that increasing development has not contributed to the worsening of disparities in income distribution.[30] But in some poor countries that have experienced rapid growth, disparities in earnings and income level have widened. In the developed world—and particularly in the United States—the gap in incomes between the highest 20 percent and the lowest 20 percent of workers has tended to increase since the late 1960s.[31]

Greater Consumption

Trends toward increasing population and income have also meant trends towards increasing consumption worldwide. In general, extraction, production, and use of energy and materials have increased at rates exceeding the rate of population growth but more slowly than growth in GDP. At the same time, as consumption has increased, use of energy and materials has become more efficient on average.

Varying views of consumption on the part of scientists from different disciplines[32] have led to differing interpretations of consumption and its importance. For physicists, matter and energy are conserved, so consumption must be regarded as transformations of matter and energy that produce entropy or disorder. For economists, consumption is spending on consumer goods and services and is distinguished from the production and distribution of those goods. For ecologists, consumption is the process by which living species obtain energy and nutrients by eating green plants, which produce energy, or other consumers of green plants. And for some sociologists, consumption is a status symbol in that individuals and households use their income to improve their social status through certain kinds of purchases.

To further understanding of human consumption and encourage effective actions toward sustainability, the officers of the U.S. National Academy of Sciences and the Royal Society of London have issued a joint statement on consumption. They choose a variant of the physicist's definition, stating: "Consumption is the human transformation of materials and energy." Their statement goes on to note that "consumption is of concern to the extent that it makes the transformed materials or energy less available for future use, or negatively impacts biophysical systems in such a way as to threaten human health, welfare, or other things people value."[33]

For consumption as the transformation of energy and materials, data recording trends are limited. Yet there is relatively good global knowledge of energy transformations due in part to the common units of conversion between different technologies. Between 1970 and 1997, for example, the global consumption of energy increased from 207 to 380 quadrillion British thermal units (Btu).[34] For material transformations, on the other hand, globally aggregated data exist only for some specific classes of materials, including materials for energy production, construction, industrial minerals and metals, agricultural crops, and water.[35] At the national level, however, aggregate analyses are beginning to appear. In the United States, for example, it has been estimated that the mass of current material production and consumption averages well over 50 kilos per person per day (excluding water and extractive waste). Three-quarters of the material flow is split between energy and related feedstock conversion (38 percent) and minerals for construction (37 percent), with the remainder as industrial minerals (5 percent), metals (2 percent), and products of fields (12 percent) and forests (5 percent).[36] Of the 50 kilos, about half goes into the air and onto the land as waste. Adding in wastewater and materials associated with extraction may double the total mass of material consumption per person per day.[37]

In the absence of globally aggregated data, trends and projections in agriculture, energy, and economy can serve as surrogates for more detailed data on energy and material transformation, as suggested in Table 2.1. These data show that over the second half of the 20th century, while world population more than doubled, food production (as measured by grain production) almost tripled, energy use more than quadrupled, and the overall level of economic activity quintupled. Scenarios of current trends show these rapid growth rates of the last 50 years slowing somewhat over the coming 50 years. For example, in one such scenario of current forces and trends (see appendix, Chapter 3), over the next 50 years world population would less than double (1.6×), food and energy consumption would almost double (1.8× and 2.4× respectively) and the economy quadruple (4.3×).

TABLE 2.1 Actual and Projected Changes in World Population, Food, Energy, and Economy

	Actual 1950-1993	Reference Scenario 1995-2050
Population	2.2 ×	1.6 ×
Food (Grain)	2.7 ×	1.8 ×
Energy	4.4 ×	2.4 ×
Economy (GDP)	5.1 ×	4.3 ×

Sources: For actual, Brown et al. (1994), courtesy of Worldwatch Institute. For scenarios, Raskin et al. (1998) (see Chapter 3 of this report).

Thus, while future growth in population and consumption is projected to increase less than in the past, both history and future scenarios would predict consumption rate increases at well beyond the rates of population increase. Such scenarios build on a postulated "energy and materials transition" somewhat parallel to that of the demographic transition described above. In such a transition, societies will use increasing amounts of energy and materials as consumption rises, but over time the energy and materials inputs per unit of consumption will decrease.

For a Sustainable Future

Overall, the growth of wealth is as persistent as the growth of population. Like the leveling of population, growth in wealth is perhaps slowing, but barring severe disruptions to the global economy, growth should continue at rates well above that of population. Recent increases in wealth could be seen as leading to a world characterized both by the popular economics maxim—a rising tide raises all boats big and small—and by the increasing division between rich and poor in absolute as well as relative terms. It is difficult to foresee a sustainable future if the latter trend prevails. Regardless of distribution, increased wealth and income imply increased consumption. Sustaining the supply of energy and materials needed to support this level of consumption, making them available where most needed, and addressing the environmental problems resulting from their extraction, consumption and disposal may be the most significant challenges to a sustainability transition, especially as more people adopt the materials-intensive, consumptive lifestyle now enjoyed by most people in industrialized nations.

Technology and Work[38]

Changing Technologies

On the scale of generations, within the current scientific-industrial revolution, four 60- to 70-year periods of technologically driven economic development have taken place, marked by characteristic sectors of growth, emerging technologies, and concepts of management and industrial organization (Table 2.2). These emerging technologies provoke technological transitions, generally emerging slowly and growing rapidly toward saturation (in logistic growth curve) in the following period. While economists and technology historians differ on the details of period characteristics and timing, and may differ greatly in their explanations of the relationships of these phenomena to large-scale fluctuations in economic growth and recession, there is wide acceptance of the historical sequence of changing and emerging technologies. Most speculative of course is the fifth cycle, of which we are in the early stages and which coincides with the desired transition toward sustainability.

In the current transition, several major technological trends since World War II have combined to change the nature of industry, consumption, and the world. Fossil fuels, including the liquid fuels used in transportation, have been cheap, and in real terms have become cheaper.[39] The availability of inexpensive fuel, the rise of the long-range electric distribution grid, the development and widespread commercialization of jet aircraft, and the proliferation of automobiles and long-range diesel trucks, along with the building of major road networks, have all revolutionized the availability of electricity and widespread transportation.

Experience with complex systems and processes of all kinds has led to increased understanding of their management and control, built in part on the research and development of national defense and weapons systems during the post–World War II period. [40] These advances include the control of process chemistry, material synthesis, robotics, telecommunications (including power systems, nets, and grids), structural design and construction at all scales, and, most recently, biological technology (both medical and agricultural) and design.

Smaller, More Efficient, and More Mobile

The rise of global communication systems, combining radio, satellite, and fiber systems, has come along more or less in parallel with the rise in transportation. The development of digital computing and the microchip, with continually decreasing size, energy requirements, and cost per digital transaction, have made computation, memory, word, logic, and number processing easily available worldwide. Combined with communications systems, transactions can not only be done at long distances, but computing chores can be divided among sites. Thus, it is no longer necessary for data gathering, analysis, and control to be in the same place. Engineers in different parts of the world can work simultaneously on designs, and a machine can be controlled remotely from any distance.

These technological changes have enabled the improved and systematic pursuit of greater efficiency in the use of energy,[41] materials, and money at all scales in large and complex systems. Efficiency in the use of materials has resulted not only from control over materials' properties, but from improvements in their design, which result in more efficiency in their use. [42] In addition, reuse of materials through the recycling of old products has become an important and more efficient source of materials.[43]

TABLE 2.2 Characteristics of Major Technological Complexes

	1770-1830	1820-1890	1880-1945	1935-1995	1985-2050
Growth sectors	Water power Ships Canals	Coal Railroads Steam power Mechanical equipment	Cars Trucks Trolleys Chemical Industry Metallurgical processes	Electric power Oil Airplanes Radio and TV Instruments and controls	Gas Nuclear Information Telecommunications Satellite communications Laser communications
Emerging technologies	Mechanical equipment Coal Stationary steam power	Electricity Internal combustion Telegraphy Steam shipping	Electronics Jet engine Air transport	Nuclear Computers Gas Telecommunications	Biotechnology Artificial intelligence Space communication and transport
Management		Economy of scale Interchangeable parts	Administrative management	Professional management	Participatory and interconnected systems management
Industrial organization	Concept of the industrial firm Division of labor	Concept of mass production Interchangeable parts	Concept of management structure and delegation	Concept of decentralization	Concept of systems structure

Source: Grübler and Nowotny (1990). Courtesy of Inderscience Enterprises Ltd.

Lessened Work

For those who toil, the great technological revolutions of agriculture and industry initially meant longer hours and harder work. The industrial revolution led to a painful restructuring of agricultural societies, but much later, it led to great improvements in health, longevity, and living and working conditions. For the industrialized world, there has been a dramatic and consistent drop in hours worked over the 150 years of increasingly reliable records. Within the long-term trend, however, there is much variation by age, sex, and education—a reflection of the growing divisions of income and opportunity. For example, while average hours worked have also declined in the United States from 40.2 to 39.2 hours per week over the last 35 years, hours worked (compensated) have risen for college educated men and have dramatically increased for women.[44] Indeed, the stresses of the two-worker household and the second job have led to concern about overworked Americans.[45]

Currently, knowledge of the control and management of complex systems, along with computers and communications, has propelled the use of the robot and automatic control into new and increasingly pervasive forms. This advance has made possible the economic replacement of labor by controllable, semi-intelligent and, perhaps, intelligent machines, first for physical labor, increasingly for routine bureaucratic work, and eventually, perhaps, for most or all routine intelligent work. In addition, societies are beginning to separate the control of processes from the location of the processes themselves. This arrangement enables the separation of the people in control from the entity being controlled, and more generally enables the separation of people from their work. Ultimately, this capability may allow the production of the required goods and services for a very large population by a small number of people who may be in scattered locations.

We are not sure how to organize such a radically changed economic and social system. In most industrialized countries (other than the United States), endemic unemployment has become a way of life and a matter of high concern. Also, mechanization tends to displace lower skilled workers, so unless displaced workers are retrained and new jobs are created, this trend will increase problems for the already poor. Whether such unemployment is only temporary and part of a restructuring between periods of growth or represents a new and long-term result of technological change and globalization is of continuing concern and speculation in the industrialized world.[46]

For a Sustainable Future

Periodically, industrialized countries replace their lead technologies in a process of early adoption, rapid diffusion, and saturation. Industrial history suggests that humanity is in the early stages of still another such transition. The emerging technologies of this transition, for the most part, augur well for needed technological changes as they include evolving energy sources and transmissions, new materials, and the substitution of information for energy and materials. The characteristics of these technologies and the move away from the production of commodities to the provision of services offers the potential for skipping over the dirty (more polluting), intermediate stages of economic development. Trends toward using fewer materials, or "dematerialization," will be furthered by research in molecular and submolecular technologies: microelectronics, biotechnology, and nanotechnology materials. Such technological transitions have always been accompanied by changes and disruptions in the nature of work, even if they lead to an overall reduction in working hours and an increase in unobligated time. Such disruptions may make more difficult the employment of many workers in the next two generations.

Connectedness and Diversity

Increasing Connectedness

The larger population of the future will be closely connected through ties of economic production and consumption, migration, communication, transportation, and interlinking technologies, together often described as "globalization." The expansion of major regional common markets, free-trade blocs, and the ensuing flows of goods, capital, and technology will likely be accompanied by flows of people between countries. New information technologies and mass communication techniques will continue to penetrate many different geographic, temporal, linguistic, cultural, and political barriers.

Since 1950, trade between nations has grown at more than twice the rate of the economy (GNP), and as of this decade, 20 percent of the world's goods and services pass over a border on the road from production to consumption.[47] This pace will accelerate as the two current free-trade blocs in North America and Europe are joined by others in Latin America and Asia and global free-trade efforts continue. Prevailing economic opinion sees these rapid increases in trade as the engine of development; in the long run, most participants in such trade will be better off. Yet many in industrialized countries see increased trade as a continuing threat to their own standards of living, imperiling their welfare systems and leading to large unemployment. For the developing countries that are capable of combining their prevailing low wages with flexible and efficient production, the opportunity exists for rapid growth and perhaps a long-term redistribution of the world's wealth with increased trade.

Trade in money and capital now moves quickly with electronic movement of funds, worldwide currency markets, and a 24-hour sequence of open financial markets. Private currency traders set exchange rates, once the purview of governments, and trade $1.3 trillion a day, nearly 100 times the volume of world trade. Private capital flows grow twice as fast as trade, and for U.S. investors, international portfolio transactions exceed 1.5 times U.S. GDP.[48]

The exchange of words, images, and ideas has also accelerated substantially during the past 50 years. Globally, the exchange of words, as measured by minutes of international telephone calls, quadrupled in the last decade.[49] The number of televisions per 1,000 persons worldwide has increased from 153 in 1988 to 228 in 1995.[50] The number of Internet users worldwide has increased from 26 million in 1995 to 205 million in 1999 and is expected to reach 350 million by 2005.[51] With the exchange of words and images comes the transfer of ideas and culture, which in current technology is dominated by English words and images of industrialized countries' lifestyles and their consumer products.

The spread of cultural ideas about the desirability of consumption into distant places enlarges markets and fuels energy and materials transformations at rates far exceeding population growth. While modern technology enables communication that may be freighted with these values, it also distributes a culture of environmental concern that builds on universal concerns for the fate of the earth. Increased communication links those who have environmental concerns to common international efforts, to shared information, and to growing numbers of environmental NGOs (nongovernmental organizations). Such links have had a large impact on shaping public attitudes and opinions, and ultimately on influencing public policy and political will. Changes in attitudes and beliefs, influenced by the proliferation of communication, seem under way in at least three important sets of ideas: (1) that cohabitation with the natural world is necessary, (2) that there are limits to human activity, and (3) that the benefits of human activity need to be more widely shared.[52]

Flows of people—temporary, permanent, and forced—have also increased, although most of these movements are poorly measured. According to the most recent worldwide estimates of the number of international migrants, dating from 1990, perhaps as many as 120 million people cross a border annually, or about 2 percent of the world's population. This figure represents a growth rate in migration of 1.9 percent per year since 1965, when the global estimate of cross-border migration was 75 million persons per year. The percentage of people who migrate with the intention of becoming permanent or long-term residents of a foreign country remained relatively stable at between 2.1 and 2.3 percent of the world's population from 1965 to 1990; but the number of countries hosting a significant proportion of migrants (e.g., more than 300,000 migrants or more than 15 percent of population 1965-1990) has increased.[53] Within countries, massive migrations continue, often from countryside to city, from places of limited to greater opportunity. Between 40 and 60 percent of urban growth is attributed to internal migrants from the countryside.[54] Increasingly, some movements of populations are forced, with about 20 million refugees in 1997 seeking asylum in other countries and more forced to move within their own.[55] The rate of increase in refugees is more rapid than the rate of increase in world trade.

The rise of the global transportation network has made the location of most material goods nearly irrelevant (though this does not equate with access); generally, products are easily transportable and only land and ecosystems stay put. Fresh fruit and vegetables, fish and meat, as well as furniture, vehicles, building materials and other products may reach their consumers from anywhere in the world. Because the rise of the computer and the global communication network have made knowledge widely available, worldwide distribution has been greatly facilitated, though inaccessibility of material goods continues to be a serious problem for many countries with mostly lower income populations.

The increasing connectedness of the world population also presents environmental threats.[56] The rapid movement of peoples and products makes possible the rapid transmission of infectious diseases that affect people, crops, and livestock and of biological invasions that destroy native biota as well as crops.[57] Environmental changes related to extractive processes for mines, fields, forests, and the sea are accelerated, as tropical forests are exploited for industrialized country consumption and as coastal forests and farmlands are destroyed in shrimp aquaculture. Environmental problems associated with manufacturing are exported to countries with weak environmental regulations or where rapid industrialization uses older technologies that do not incorporate recent advances in energy efficiency or industrial ecology. Most feared of all may be the rapid increases in consumption fueled by aggressive marketing and rooted in cultural change as well as economic growth. Often these changes combine to bring about destructive effects, such as the recent fires in Southeast Asia, where drought from El Niño, fires to clear land for palm oil production, and massive urban air pollution combined to shroud portions of four countries in health-impairing, accident-causing smog.

Persistent Diversity

Although the exchange of words, ideas, and cultures will increase in the next half-century, the increasing connectedness of the human population will not make all people alike. New opportunities for human development may increase personal and societal diversity as well as the availability of material things. Places of wealth or opportunity toward which people and products gravitate become more diverse by drawing people from different regions and cultures.[58] In response to such increased connectedness of diverse peoples, and the corresponding infiltration of outside values into societies, strong ethnic, nationalistic, and religious movements can emerge to counteract homogenization and reassert traditional cultural values.

Trends in urban centers, which hold wealth or opportunities toward which migrants are drawn, show that diversity is increasing in cities: there are 20 or more languages available to schoolchildren for bilingual education in some countries, and the shelves of supermarkets are laden with foods from many parts of the world. With the collapse of the Soviet Union came a dramatic increase in nationhood, but this was only the latest in a process of decolonization seen since the end of World War II, with the number of nations more than doubling from the 73 countries at that time to the 190 today. In these newer nations, old claims persist and new claims arise for regional autonomy or national independence. The much-reported resurgence of Islamic religious vitality and conflict tends to obscure equally tense religious differences between and within the majority of the world's religions.[59]

Are these differences among people and nations—in wealth, ethnicity, religion, and opportunities, differences that divide people, create inequities, and encourage conflicts—likely to persist and perhaps grow? Current trends in some measures of human development, such as the earlier-discussed trends in health and human rights, show decreasing inequity; wealth measures are indicating stable or growing disparities; and either despite or because of the Cold War's end, conflicts remain and emerge, and may be increasing. Some observers also see trends in the diminution of social capital—in the common bonds, activities and organizations that create community and mutual support.[60] In addition, it is not apparent whether increasing divisiveness is a persistent trend, similar to trends in connectedness, or an artifact of communication in which news of conflict and division is selectively and rapidly disseminated, or has been constant and is only more readily revealed as greater global divisions diminish.

Changing Institutions, Shifting Power

Connectedness and diversity are reflected in institutional innovations and shifts in power.[61] At a global level, new institutions of governance have emerged, transnational corporations and financial institutions have grown and consolidated, and NGO networks have collaborated and expanded. At the subnational level, government has devolved, privatization is common, and civic society in many places has been strengthened. Power has shifted from the central, national state both upwards to the global and downward to the local as well as to civic society and private enterprise.

The power shift from central government is paralleled by an expansion of private property rights and market relationships. In less-developed countries, such shifts have been marked by declines in shared common-property resources and increases in individually held and marketed resources.[62] Labor relationships have similarly shifted through various institutions from labor tied to place or person to labor free to circulate, for example, in China.[63] In the former socialist economies of Europe and Asia, and in the social democracies of Europe, once centrally held property is increasingly privatized.

For a Sustainable Future

Increasing connectedness will fuel growth in some parts of the world, diminish it in others, and amplify the forces that drive increased consumption. In addition, it will export to some developing and recently industrializing countries many of the environmental problems of the industrialized world and, with some delay, the institutions and technologies to control them. Connectedness, while creating common elements of culture in most places and increasing the similarity of places, can also increase diversity, particularly in urban areas that attract migrants. The diversity of the human experience offers possibilities for alternative lifestyles and new possibilities of addressing our common future, but divisiveness between diverse communities makes common tasks much more difficult. Ultimately, divisiveness may lead to war—the greatest threat to human development and the environment.

HUMAN ACTION AND ENVIRONMENTAL
TRANSFORMATIONS

Rates, Scales, and Multiple Stresses[64]

Rapid Global Change

The world has experienced human-induced changes in local, regional, and global environments for much of the past 10,000 years, but most of that change has occurred during our lifetime.[65] Recent analyses comparing modifications in the environment over the last 300 years to changes over the last 10,000 years demonstrate the unprecedented nature, scale, and rate of human-induced changes in the earth's environment.[66] In the last 300 years, humankind has demonstrated the capacity to change the environment on a scale that equals or exceeds the rate of natural environmental changes, as human population, economic growth, and technological capability have combined to create human-influenced ecosystems on much of the land and coastal areas of the earth.

Human actions have significantly altered biogeochemical cycles, of both land and water, along with biotic diversity. In 13 worldwide measures reconstructed by the *Earth Transformed*[67] project— including carbon, carbon tetrachloride, lead, nitrogen, phosphorus and sulfur; deforested area, sediment flows, soil area loss, and water withdrawal; and flora, marine mammals, and terrestrial vertebrates—most of the change has been extraordinarily recent. For 10 of the 13 measures, half of all the change over the last 10,000 years took place within our lifetime (Table 2.3). Overall, since the dawn of agriculture roughly 100 centuries ago, an area the size of the continental United States has been deforested by human actions. In addition, half of the ecosystems of the ice-free lands of the earth have been modified, managed, or utilized by people. Water in an amount greater than the contents of Lake Huron is withdrawn each year for human use. As a whole, many flows of materials and energy that are removed from their natural settings or synthesized now rival the flows of such materials within nature itself.

Other related studies by biologists and systems analysts have assessed the degree to which humans dominate ecosystems.[68] For example, researchers[69] analyzed sunlight as the basic source of energy for nearly all life on earth. Using three different definitions of the proportion of the net primary productivity that should be assigned to human "appropriation," the study suggested that as much as 40 percent of the photosynthesis on land, in the form of plant biomass, is being used by humans. Using the same framework, researchers[70] estimated the fraction of fresh water "co-opted" by humans; while this estimate depends on assumptions that de-

TABLE 2.3 Magnitude, Recency, and Rate of Change in Human-Induced Transformation of Environmental Components

Rates	Magnitude of Change Since 10,000 Years Before Present	
Changes Since 1950	50% Total Change Reached in the 19th Century	50% Total Change Reached in the 20th Century
Rates Decelerating	Terrestrial vertebrate diversity	Carbon tetrachloride releases Lead releases Sulfur releases Human population Marine mammals
Rates Accelerating	Deforested area loss	Carbon releases Nitrogen releases Phosphorus releases Floral diversity Sediment flows Water withdrawals

Source: Turner et al. (1990b). Courtesy of Cambridge University Press.

fine how various flows of water are to be counted, their estimates range upward from 23 percent of the annual flow accessible to humans. A related estimate of water needs[71] suggests that growing food to feed the existing human population a vegetarian diet already claims half the water used by humans. The most recent of these studies[72] summarizes the body of work on human dominance of ecosystems.

The central thrust of these analyses is that humans are now recruiting significant fractions of sunlight, fresh water, and life forms to their purposes, with the fraction rising to over half in some instances. These estimates, while inexact, portend that expansions in the human claim on the planet's life support systems cannot be indefinitely extended, especially as human numbers rise through the remainder of the demographic transition.

Taken together, do these massive and recent human-induced environmental changes threaten the life support systems of the earth for human life? Although for the earth as a whole the entire system has not likely been irreparably damaged, in some regions, according to available studies, environmental threats from human activities loom. In a recent comparative study, six of nine regions—located in Brazil, China, Europe, Indonesia, Kenya, and the United States—were found to have "current human uses and levels of well-being [that] appear to be environmentally unsustainable over the middle-to long-term future."[73] Two regions—one in Nepal and one in Mexico—appear environmentally unsustainable in the near-term future, and the Aral Sea region in Central Asia is already unsustainable.

In addition to regional and global indications of unsustainability, the intensity of human use of the natural world makes it virtually certain that environmental threats will continue and that surprises are inevitable, for example, in the form of new and reemergent plant and animal diseases. By definition, environmental surprises cannot be foreseen, but the structural conditions that encourage their emergence and proliferation can be described. Environmental surprises should be expected as trade continues to expand, with the accompanying movement of peoples, life forms, and goods; as new molecular-level technologies in biology and materials are deployed; as older technologies are applied in new, untried settings; and as humans respond to existing environmental problems, in responses that have sometimes produced unexpected and unwanted consequences.[74]

Shifting Problems and Policies

In the upcoming decades, there may also be shifts in the nature of environmental problems, their scales, and the societal policies to reduce or ameliorate them. Since the 1950s, 6 of the 13 indicators shown in Table 2.3 have changed at a decelerating rate, while the remainder still seem to be accelerating in change.[75] The deceleration occurs for those environmental components most subject to government regulation, suggesting increased efficacy of environmental policies.

The idea of environmental transitions was framed in an analysis[76] that identified three different trajectories that environmental problems may follow with a rise in per capita income. Characteristic problems of developing countries such as inadequate water supply and sanitation decline with rising income. Air and water pollution increase and then decrease (an inverted U-curve) as governments with seemingly greater resources have regulated and taxed enough facilities to bring down pollutant concentrations. But as income increases, so apparently does material consumption, which leads to increased trash production and carbon dioxide emissions. These activities show no signs as yet of abating.

These curious irregularities[77] have stirred a great deal of debate by suggesting that, in some cases, environmental quality can improve with prosperity. The inverted U-curves have come to be called "Kuznets" curves by analogy with a pattern noticed by economist Simon Kuznets in the 1950s—income inequality appeared first to rise and then to fall in the course of early industrialization.

These findings suggest that a transition toward sustainability may be characterized by a change in the relative importance of environmental problems, with the most serious concerns perhaps shifting from dirty water and lack of sanitation, to air and water pollution, and then to climate change. The scale of concern may increasingly shift from household, neighborhood, and village, to urban area and region, and finally, to region and the world. Policy emphases should correspondingly shift, whether in the areas of public health, pollution abatement, source reduction, or efficiencies in reducing consumption and reusing and recycling materials.

For a Sustainable Future

Human domination of natural systems is already so extensive in many places, however, and our dependence on natural resources so deep, that permanent management of ecosystems appears to be the only practicable alternative for a sizable fraction of the natural world. Instituting and sustaining management on large scales to serve so many partially competing ends is a feat achieved in only a few places for relatively brief periods. At smaller spatial scales, however, and for some significant problems, including safe drinking water and industrial air pollution, there are encouraging signs of effective control as societies marshal the social will and economic capabilities to address these problems. Transitions in the relationships between humans and nature are inevitable; whether they will result in a sustainable economy and ecology cannot be discerned from the trends themselves.

Global Atmosphere and Climate[78]

Declining but Stabilizing Stratospheric Ozone

Human activities have altered the chemical composition of the atmosphere locally, regionally, and globally. Although these changes are small in terms of percentage changes, even a small amount of change in the composition of the atmosphere can have noticeable and serious environmental impacts. These effects result in part from the high reactivity of compounds such as ozone and oxides of sulfur and nitrogen, and in part from the fact that the greenhouse gases and stratospheric ozone play crucial gatekeeper roles for the earth's life support systems.

Human use of chlorofluorocarbon gases (CFCs), beginning in the 1930s, has released a small but potent quantity of these industrial chemicals into the atmosphere. As CFC molecules drift to the upper atmosphere, they are broken down by solar ultraviolet radiation and release chlorine atoms. These atoms interact catalytically with the layer of ozone (O_3) in the stratosphere, with each chlorine atom on average destroying a large number of ozone molecules before reacting to form relatively inert compounds that are subsequently transported down to Earth's surface and removed in precipitation and on land and water surfaces. For this reason, a small quantity of CFC gases can have a substantial effect on the stratospheric ozone layer. This layer is an important component in the life support systems of the planet in that it screens all life forms from harmful solar ultraviolet radiation.

The discovery of the atmospheric chemistry of the chlorofluorocarbons, followed just over a decade later by the discovery of the seasonal ozone hole over the Antarctic and its chemical explanation, spurred governments all over the world to enter into a treaty to reduce CFC emissions.[79] In response, the Montreal Protocol of 1987 and its subsequent amendments have led to sharply decreased emissions of CFCs and other ozone-destroying compounds, including brominated chemicals such as halons. Atmospheric amounts of several of these key compounds are now observed to be decreasing.[80] However, data on total stratospheric ozone amounts do not yet clearly demonstrate recovery of the ozone layer.

Increasing Greenhouse Gases—A Warmer Climate

Greenhouse gases, which include carbon dioxide (CO_2), nitrous oxide (N_2O), methane (CH_4), and halocarbons (CFCs, HFCs, PFCs), are expected to modify the earth's climate, with effects unfolding over time scales of decades to centuries.[81] These gases have increased steadily with the use of fossil fuels over the course of industrialization, with a total increase in CO_2 of more than 30 percent over preindustrial levels in the past century and a half. Ninety percent of energy sold today comes from fossil fuels.[82] Total energy use has tripled in the past 50 years, with the share from nonfossil fuel sources slowly rising as the use of nuclear generators and hydropower has increased.

While carbon dioxide and methane increases are expected to have the biggest impact on climate, some of the most uncertain aspects of climate change are the direct and indirect radiative effects of sulfate and carbonaceous aerosols (particles) in the climate system and their related impacts on tropospheric chemistry and human health. These particles enter into the processes forming clouds, which result in more reflection of solar radiation and more absorption of the infrared radiation. The magnitude of this effect is uncertain but is believed to be substantial. The increase in global average surface air temperature from 1860 until the present is shown in Figure 2.4. Recent decades are the warmest in the instrumental record. The global temperature increase is generally consistent with

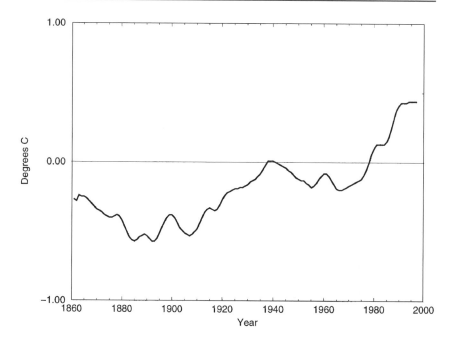

FIGURE 2.4   Annual global mean temperature for land areas from 1861 to 1997. The curve shows anomalies with respect to the mean temperature for the 30 years 1961-1990.
Source: Global Historical Climatology Network (GHCN); Peterson and Vose (1997). Courtesy of the National Climatic Data Center.

climate model calculations of the combined effects of the observed increases of greenhouse gases and aerosols. Because of the long atmospheric lifetimes of most greenhouse gases and the thermal inertia of the oceans, it is widely acknowledged that even rapid reductions in contemporary greenhouse gas emissions would still leave the world committed to significant climate change at an average rate of warming greater than any seen in the last 10,000 years. Of course, most places on earth would not experience the global average. Rather, they would likely experience more extreme weather patterns of variation due to the regionality of climate and sea level change and the impacts of natural variability at the annual to decadal scale. These changing finer scale patterns cannot now be predicted with confidence, but could eventually entail significant changes in the frequency of heat stress episodes, the severity of droughts, and the competitive balance among species.[83]

Increasing and Decreasing Regional and Local Air Pollutants

Industrialization has been accompanied by increases in air pollution, mainly from the combustion of fossil fuels. These pollutants are mostly redeposited locally, although there are important cases of long-distance transport of pollutants by horizontal and vertical winds. Tropospheric ozone—the ozone in the lowest and densest part of the atmosphere where humans live—is produced by the oxidation of many precursor gases, including carbon monoxide, nitrogen oxides, and hydrocarbons. Other important pollutants, including oxides of sulfur and aerosols such as soot, result from the burning of coal and oil. As noted above, some of these pollutants have been successfully managed regionally as income levels have risen.

Over the past century, as industrialization has spread from the OECD countries into the developing world, measured amounts of ozone at the earth's surface and throughout the troposphere have increased and then stabilized, as pollution-control technology has been developed and adopted. These trends slowed and/or vanished in North America and Western Europe during the 1980s and 1990s.[84] By contrast, tropospheric ozone amounts continue to increase over Japan. The likely cause is increasing emissions of ozone precursors, principally nitrogen oxides and carbon monoxide from combustion in China, Taiwan, Korea, and Japan.[85]

Similar patterns have been observed in sulfur and nitrogen compounds, the principal pollutants in acid rain.[86] In at least one advanced country, data show that reduced sulfur dioxide emissions have led to decreased amounts of sulfate in atmospheric aerosols (and presumably to decreased precipitation of sulfuric acid). Researchers[87] reported that aerosol sulfate measurements from 1979 to 1996 at Whiteface Mountain and Mayville in New York declined about 45 percent and 30 percent respectively, from corresponding amounts averaged over the period from 1981 to 1991. During this time, upwind emissions of SO_2 from the U. S. Midwest declined by about 35 percent.

The data records are less clearly interpreted for carbon monoxide in the troposphere.[88] Measurements of CO in surface air show decreases in the early 1990s, and globally averaged amounts have decreased by 2 to 5 percent per year.[89] The cause of this decrease is not clear.

For a Sustainable Future

It has been possible in some instances to manage pollution of the atmosphere so that damage is stabilized or even reversed. This is taking place at the global scale with stratospheric ozone, at the regional level for acid rain in Europe, and in numerous urban areas via regulation and pollution control technology. That pollution control has been possible in these instances does not, of course, assure sustainable future conditions in the atmosphere, but clearly shows the direction of what is possible. In the short run, however, air quality conditions continue to worsen in a large number of areas, especially in Latin America and Asia.

There is a large international research and monitoring effort to study the atmosphere and its modification by humans. Most of the expertise is concentrated in the developed countries, however, and an important element of a transition toward sustainability will be continued effective transfer of scientific and technical resources to developing countries.

Managing climate change in a sustainability transition will have to account for the trend of rising energy consumption, together with the predominant role played by fossil fuels up to now. Large-scale departures from that trend will entail far more than a new technology, including global markets and infrastructures to handle new means of generating energy and to integrate them into existing technological systems and markets. In response to the 1992 Framework Convention on Climate Change goal (see Chapter 1) of stabilizing "atmospheric concentrations of greenhouse gases at a level which would prevent dangerous human interference in the climate system," governments have so far only adopted the near-term objective of stabilizing emission rates. This means that the atmospheric concentrations of greenhouse gases will continue to grow. While scientists cannot predict exactly the impacts of such trends, persistent addition of greenhouse gases to the atmosphere is very likely to make achieving a sustainability transition harder. The changes in energy use required to substantially mitigate the risk of global climate change will require considerable changes in existing infrastructure and institutions. Comparably significant changes may be required to reduce the vulnerability of societies to such climate changes that do occur.

Oceans[90]

Stable Oceans, Changing Coastal Zones

Although humans have intensively exploited fish and other living resources, mined minerals, and released pollutants, the open seas have so far been relatively less affected by human activities.[91] This fact is a reflection of the size of the world ocean, which covers 71 percent of the earth's surface, and the relatively modest presence of humans on the seas so far. An important exception is the status of some high seas fisheries (e.g., swordfish and orange roughy) which are harvested at unsustainable rates; and many estuaries, coastal zones, and confined seas have been degraded or extensively modified, with few instances of successful recovery. Also, the effect of long-term changes in atmospheric forcing on oceans, as perhaps may be seen in the recent greater extremes of El Niño and the widespread environmental consequences, is increasingly of concern.

Humans have extensively altered coastal zones, largely as an indirect effect of developing adjoining land and littoral areas.[92] As the near-coastal human population, including the residents of most of the world's megacities, continues to increase, these effects will increase. In addition to residents of the coastal zone, many additional people flock to the coast for recreation and tourism, increasing the environmental pressures from roads, commercial development, waste disposal, marinas, and other recreational facilities. The resources of coastal ecosystems are very often intensively exploited for seafood and energy resources.

Coastal ecosystems are often affected by activities that occur far inland, through changes in the delivery of water, nutrients, and chemical contaminants from rivers and atmospheric deposition.[93] Large areas of important coastal waters such as the Chesapeake Bay, the northern Gulf of Mexico, Long Island Sound, and Lake Erie, in the United States and the North Sea and the northern Adriatic Sea, in Europe have experienced increased plankton blooms and depletion of dissolved oxygen as a result of nutrient overenrichment from both point-source (sewage discharges) and diffuse inputs (agricultural and urban runoff and atmospheric inputs) during the latter half of this century. At present, coasts are affected by the continued rise in sea level worldwide, at about 1.8 mm per year for over a century. These values are an order of magnitude greater than the average experienced over the last few millennia.[94] This worldwide rise, if combined with local land subsidence, results in a large local rise in relative sea level, flooding of coastal areas, and increases in beach erosion. Also, coastal environments are among the areas most susceptible to the consequences of global climate change that could affect sea level, freshwater runoff, frequency and intensity of storms, and temperature patterns.[95]

Other longer term physical and biological responses of the oceans to climate change are possible, including the disruption of North Atlantic deepwater formation, a condition that has been associated with significant climate variability in the past, and the effect of warming polar oceans on sea-ice melting, which can alter ecosystem processes including primary production.

Declining Valued Marine Fisheries

The human impact on marine life was long assumed to be small because of the great numbers of species in the oceans and their large populations. This view has been proven wrong as fisheries around the world have been overexploited during the last 40 years.[96] In the United States, approximately one-third of those species whose status is known are over-fished.[97] Studies in marine ecology and fisheries demonstrate that humans have caused at least local extinctions, together with many other ecosystem modifications that are difficult or impossible to reverse.[98] Along with the declines in catch, it is likely that ecosystem impacts caused by humans are increasing in severity.

Current levels of fisheries overexploitation are associated with the failure of fishery management to contain human fishing pressures within sustainable limits.[99] Fishery failures are usually attributable to direct causes, including a lack of political will, scientific uncertainty, destructive fishing practices, and excessive levels of fishing capacity that create pressure to abandon conservative levels of exploitation. The 1996 passage of the Magnuson-Stevens Fishery Conservation and Management Act in the United States introduced a number of more conservative elements into the U.S. federal fisheries management system, including a requirement to eliminate overfishing, to define and protect essential fish habitat, and to reduce bycatch.[100] The next reauthorization, due in 2000, is likely to further broaden the precautionary approach to fisheries management and to strengthen coordination with other statutes that protect marine species.

Human activities affect marine species indirectly as well, notably through the degradation or modification of habitats used by marine species at some point in their life cycles. Pacific salmon, for example, a migratory species that spawns in freshwater, has been substantially affected by logging, grazing, farming, urbanization, and dams in the U.S. Pacific Northwest.[101] More generally, sedimentation and pollution resulting from the large-scale conversion of land and coastal regions to human purposes (e.g., conversion of mangroves to rice farming) have affected coastal areas and the composition of river waters (e.g., runoff from poultry farms as in Chesapeake Bay) flowing to the sea. These actions have affected the abundance and diversity of marine life through changes in the quantity of coastal wetlands and the quality of estuarine waters, a primary source of marine productivity.[102]

Fishing itself can affect marine ecosystems, especially the habitats of fish and other marine species, by changing bottom topography and associated benthic communities. Large-scale changes in coral reef ecosystems in the Caribbean and in community structure in the Bering, Barents, and Baltic seas, on Georges Bank, and in other regions have been attributed to fishing. Together with increasing introductions of exotics and increasing pollution, fishing and other human activities will continue to effect the loss of goods and services from marine ecosystems.[103]

For a Sustainable Future

Although the open seas have been modified comparatively little by human activity, there are serious problems that need to be addressed for a successful transition to sustainability, including the unsustainable harvest of some marine fisheries. There is no indication that humans will moderate their transformation of the nearshore marine environment. Coastal zones, along with tropical forests, are the regions of the earth currently undergoing maximum human transformation. The trend of the marine environment is, in sum, one of continuing human modification, much of it inadvertent.

Despite serious attempts at conservation and management[104] the unsustainable use of fisheries persists, sometimes until the fishery collapses economically. For decades, scientists have called for managing fisheries from an ecosystem perspective, and some steps have been taken in this direction that appear to be feasible in some fisheries.[105] In many other instances, the appropriate application of ecosystem concepts remains difficult or impossible under current institutional conditions.[106] Sustainability of the oceans will above all require an integrated and adaptive ecosystem-based approach to management, incorporating such elements as conservative single-species management, reductions of excess fishing capacity and assignment of fishing rights, establishment of marine protected areas and appropriate institutions, consideration of bycatch and discards in fishing mortality estimates, and other information needs.[107] Such an approach may help to ensure the production of goods and services from marine ecosystems, and, at the same time continue to provide food, revenue, and recreation for humans.[108]

Fresh Water[109]

Slowing Global Withdrawals, Regional and Local Scarcity

From 1940 to 1990, withdrawals of water for human use (i.e., removals from a natural source for storage or use) increased by more than a factor of four, reflecting a long-term trend of increasing withdrawals per capita.[110] The rate of withdrawal, an average of 2.5 percent per year, has been more rapid than population growth. Per capita availability of fresh water on a global basis fell from 17,000 m^3 in 1950 to 7,300 m^3 in 1995,[111] while per capita freshwater demand rose until the mid-1980s.[112] One result was a large global investment in and construction of dams and transport systems. However, since the mid-1980s, absolute water withdrawals have slowed and per capita water withdrawals have declined worldwide.[113] In the United States, water withdrawals in 1995 had declined nearly 10 percent from their highest level in 1980. In fact, actual global water withdrawals have been consistently less than estimates of withdrawals predicted between 1967 and 1996.[114] Nevertheless, with increasing population growth, there is no reason to be complacent about water withdrawals.

Although fresh water is a renewable resource (through groundwater recharge, surface runoff from local rainfall, in-flow from nearby regions) and global water supplies are abundant, regional water resources are unevenly distributed among countries, and local supplies or stocks are finite. In some areas with low supply, the continued high withdrawal causes serious local water shortages and harm to aquatic ecosystems.[115] Nearly one-third of the world's population is found in countries stressed by pressure on the availability of water resources (i.e., consumption levels that exceed 20 percent of available supply).[116] The unmet demand in developing countries for household water use remains high—nearly 1.2 billion people do not have access to safe and reliable water.[117] Developing countries that have both high water stress and low per capita income have the greatest potential problem of unmet demand, because they use most of the available water for intensive farm irrigation, have few financial resources to shift investment from irrigation to other sectors, and have few pollution controls.[118] Thus, most of the nations especially vulnerable to water scarcity are located in the arid or semiarid regions of Africa and Asia and the Middle East.[119] Altogether, 26 countries—approximately 232 million people—are considered "water scarce."[120]

While water is a renewable resource because of the characteristics of the hydrologic cycle, various human actions can lead to nonrenewable or unsustainable water use. Groundwater aquifers can be pumped faster than the rate of recharge,[121] leading to declining aquifer levels, land subsidence, or, in coastal areas, contamination from salt water intrusion. Similarly, land use and landscape modifications can affect both the quality and quantity of water in a watershed that is available on a renewable basis.

If treated properly, water can be reused so that withdrawals alone do not accurately measure the degree of human pressure on water resources.[122] As the quality of water declines because of increasing water contamination (e.g., from human settlements, industry, and agriculture) and land use changes (e.g., from practices that enhance water runoff from the surface, such as clearing forests or paving roads), however, water supply declines. Competition for scarce water resources, especially between rural and urban users, is increasing, with potentially serious implications for food production as urban areas with greater political strength will tend to out-compete local farmers.[123]

Where water is abundant, economic growth has been accompanied by the expansion of infrastructure to transport fresh water and waste-water. Methods of treating wastewater to render it clean enough for reuse by human settlements downstream have also been developed, usu-ally after a delay of decades.[124] Water is expensive to transport, and the large capital investments required to move water usually dictate wells and recycling when there is not enough surface water at hand. Meeting the needs of development in such regions of surface water scarcity re-quires that water come from wells, sometimes from nonrenewable aqui-fers, from distant rivers and, more recently, from careful husbanding and recycling.[125]

Shifting Usage, Declining Quality, Increasing Efficiency of Use

As countries have industrialized, there has been a shift in water usage from agriculture to industry, commercial activity, and households, with domestic consumption increasing greatly with increasing affluence.[126] This trend is expected to continue with the share of agricultural use of water declining, though the amount of water use in agriculture is ex-pected to increase with increasing worldwide demand for food, espe-cially in developing countries.[127]

Water use per person appears to rise with income to a point beyond which additional income per capita leads to declining per capita water use in households and industry. But water use per capita is not in direct proportion to national income, because increased use in one sector (in-dustry) may be offset by decreases in another (agriculture) in the course of development. Increased efficiency in water use can play an important role. In recent years, rising per capita income in higher-income develop-ing countries is correlated with lower per capita consumption of water in industry and households.[128]

Water quality has steadily improved in most of the developed coun-tries because of regulatory controls and investments in water treatment and sanitation. However, water quality in developing countries is declin-ing, especially in urban areas, because of rapid industrialization and in-creased contamination by toxics.[129] In many areas of the world, water withdrawn for human use is groundwater from wells and natural outlets. Industrial toxins, if not carefully controlled, can spill and enter aquifers, contaminating groundwater. Where groundwater reserves are a major source of water supply (e.g., 50 percent of domestic supplies in Asia), expanding mining or industrial development can lead to problems of contamination.[130]

Water is a basic human need and the failure to provide clean drinking water and sanitation services to all is one of the most fundamental failures of development in the 20th century. As of 1994, according to the UN, 1.2

billion people lacked access to clean drinking water, while nearly 3 billion lacked access to sanitation services. This failure to meet basic human needs for water causes between 5 and 10 million deaths a year, mostly of small children and the elderly, from water-related diseases. Some efforts to eradicate water-related diseases have been successful. For example, guinea worm (dracunculiasis), which is a parasitic disease that can be eliminated through providing clean drinking water, is on the verge of elimination in Africa and Asia where it used to be prevalent.[131] Cholera is not as easily eradicated with improved water supply, but it can be prevented by removing the bacterium with sewage and water treatment and treated by oral hydration therapy. However, fatality rates are often high in parts of Africa and Asia because of the lack of treatment facilities and preparedness.[132] In 1991, an extraordinary spread of cholera in Latin America has been linked to dumping of contaminated bilge water from a ship in the harbor in Lima, Peru, the lack of adequate facilities for providing clean water and sanitation, and the increase in algal blooms resulting from the warmer water, heavier rain and higher nutrient runoff associated with El Niño.[133]

For a Sustainable Future

In a transition to sustainability, water use seems likely to rely increasingly on efficiency in use and supply, closed cycles, more effective means of preventing and controlling water pollution, and more appropriate water pricing.[134] These trends also imply more efficient use of energy, the continuing decline in the construction of large projects, and increasing innovation and use of water-saving technologies. Thus, the stresses on water accessibility and use will require that water use must grow ever-more efficient and that balances must be struck to achieve a successful sustainability transition. For example, water could increasingly be a source of conflict between users (agriculture, industry, households), between ecosystems and regions (uplands, flood plains, dam sites, cities), and nations (Middle East, Nile valley, South Asia) in places of potential regional and local scarcity. Where hydrological systems match regions rather than national boundaries—for example, in the Middle East—efforts are needed to forge regional plans for water resources.[135]

Land[136]

Increasing Intensification of Agriculture

Over the past 300 years, land planted with agricultural crops has increased nearly fivefold, to about 15 million km^2.[137] This net increase in cropland has been accompanied by a net decrease of forested land of similar magnitude. Another vast area of land has been lost to productive use since the emergence of agriculture 10,000 years ago, as a result of erosion, salinization of irrigated lands, desertification, and permanent conversions of arable land to cities, roads, and reservoirs. During the 20th century, the rate of loss of productive land has accelerated sharply, to a rate of 70,000 km^2 per year, an annual loss the size of Sierra Leone.[138] An underlying factor in the acceleration of farmland conversion to nonagricultural use is that, with a rapidly growing economy, the market value of land for alternative use is growing at a far faster pace than its value for agricultural productivity. Except for a very elite set of crops, the value of land for photosynthesis will be less than for most alternative uses, considering the cash and energy flows through most nonagricultural enterprises per unit of land.

The discussion of hunger earlier in this chapter records an extraordinary achievement of the 20th century rising agricultural outputs that have outpaced human population growth and dramatically reduced the incidence of famine. This advance has been accomplished over the last 50 years by the large-scale application of scientific and practical knowledge to farming, with dramatic results in many poor nations such as India and economically impressive rises in agricultural production in rich countries such as Australia and the United States. The intensification of agriculture has been rooted in the identification, development, and widespread adoption of high-yielding varieties of cereal crops, the use of fertilizers and mechanized equipment in developing countries, and irrigation. High-yield varieties and fertilizers form the foundation of the Green Revolution in Asia and Latin America.[139] The declining real cost of food for the past several decades, associated with more efficient agricultural production, has increased food accessibility, thus reducing the incidence of famine.[140] An additional benefit of the increasing intensification of agriculture may be that, by lifting global yields by 1.5 percent per year over the period of a transition to sustainability, approximately one-quarter of the 1.4 billion hectares of cropland can be spared for nature.[141]

However, although the world has come to depend on these enhancements in food production, it is unclear whether they are sustainable.[142] In future decades, the food supply must continue to expand within a range set by basic needs, expanded incomes, and dietary preferences, and at the same time, it must do so with reduced environmental consequences. High-productivity agriculture is built on the use of monocultures, often of genetically identical plants, nourished by irrigation water and fertilizers, protected by pesticides, all delivered by technological and market mechanisms managed and paid for by humans.[143] Many such ecosystems are difficult to sustain because of several factors. The low species diversity and high concentration of nutrients provides a setting that favors specialized predators and weed species. Biological regulation by soil organisms is altered, so that decomposition is interrupted and additional nutrients must be supplied. And the application of water and fertilizer during times when growing crops cannot use them leads to waste and pollution.[144] Technologies that minimize erosion, water use, salinization, chemical pollution, and other environmental damage are available, but have not been broadly utilized.[145]

Clearing of Tropical Forests, Regrowing Temperate Zone Forests

Forests currently cover approximately 40 million km², about three-quarters of their area before the emergence of agriculture.[146] They occupy more than twice as much land area as agriculture and harbor two-thirds of all plant species.[147] Traditional agro-ecological economies remain both widespread and significant in the tropics; forests are home to millions of people who combine subsistence agriculture on small plots with hunting, gathering, and commercial harvest of materials from the surrounding forest. In temperate zone countries, including parts of China, Russia, and the United States, many forests have regrown during the 20th century, both through deliberate replanting and as agricultural lands have become uneconomical to farm. However, these increases are more than offset, in terms of area cleared or wood cut, by deforestation in tropical countries and land clearing in response to the prices of land for nonforest uses.[148]

Forest land is cleared for many reasons—for timber, during mining, and to make land available for agriculture. Data on rates of deforestation are sometimes controversial because of the difficulties in obtaining data in many regions of the world, but the estimated gross global deforestation rate is roughly 100,000 km² per year, yielding 5 billion m³ of wood and fuel.[149] Forest soils and standing timber are major storehouses of carbon, and the steady removal of carbon dioxide from the atmosphere by long-lived forest plants is a substantial counterweight to the burning of fossil fuels.[150] Forests also provide countless other goods and services; some of these goods, like cacao, play important roles in world markets, while others, including watershed services and medicinals, are valued only by localized human populations. If the rainforests were, for example, an extremely rich and valuable source of pharmaceutical precursor opportunities as many believe, their preservation should be assured by market forces which would not allow their destruction. Unfortunately, to date, they have been only occasionally such a resource.[151] Thus, while the management of forests for specific goods or services ranges from tightly regulated in some instances to uncontrolled in others, it is evident that managing for sustainable, multiple-purpose use of forestlands remains elusive.[152]

For a Sustainable Future

Over the past 50 years humans have altered the earth's lands substantially. To the benefit of our species, agricultural output has been raised dramatically and the regrowth of cleared forests has dominated landscapes in some regions. Much of the increased agricultural output takes place on existing cropland through intensification of production, thus releasing more marginal land for forest and grassland regrowth and reducing further land conversion. But these gains must be seen against the risks and losses of the past half-century. Decreases in tropical forest area and the intensification of agriculture both result in stresses on biodiversity and on ecological systems. Some of these stresses—for example the loss of soil organic matter and of pollinator species, and the changes in biogeochemical and hydrological cycles—are not visible to the casual observer, but their long-term consequences for life support systems warn that a sustainability transition is likely to require wide-ranging shifts in the values ascribed to land and the way people manage its living resources.

Species and Ecosystems[153]

Decreasing Diversity, Increasing Invasions

In the geologic record, paleontologists have found five mass extinction events, each of which drastically reduced the number of species on earth. Each time, enough life forms survived to repopulate the earth's waters and lands. The impact of human activities on the planet has now accelerated the loss of species and ecosystems to a level comparable to a sixth mass extinction.[154] This loss of species diversity is the first driven by a living species.

Rates of species extinction have been estimated to be 100 to 1,000 times as high as before large-scale human dominance of ecosystems.[155] Today, 11 percent of birds, 18 percent of mammals, 5 percent of fish, and 8 percent of plant species are threatened by extinction.[156] These rates of loss are driven primarily by the alteration of natural habitats. In a given region, the loss of species can be much higher than the proportional loss of land area if habitats are fragmented by roads or other human clearings that isolate patches of unconverted land. Depletion of species in these remaining patches can be delayed, but is still inevitable in the absence of human intervention.

In addition to causing extinctions, human activities also introduce species into ecosystems in which they have not been present. In some situations, these so-called exotic species proliferate, and the introduction of a new species can transform the ecological relationships of habitats and further stress endangered species. For example, an estimated 20 percent of the world's endangered land vertebrates are threatened by invading exotic species.[157] Biological invasions of this kind are usually inadvertent, but their frequency can be high. Introduction of exotic aquatic species by human action, often accidentally, such as transporting a species to a distant location in the ballast water of ships, has affected the species composition of heavily traveled coastal areas and bays.[158] For example, in San Francisco Bay, California, an average of one new species has been introduced every 36 weeks since 1850, a rate rising to every 12 weeks over the past decade.[159] As a result, the life-forms visible to humans in that bay are predominantly nonnative.

Efforts to prevent or control the transfer of exotic species across marine ecosystems are rudimentary, although there has been some progress since the problem came to light more than a decade ago.[160] Such accelerating rates of depletion and change will not continue for long: habitats are finite and the loss of species is irreversible. Efforts to slow rates of depletion and change require recognition of the value of the system or what is lost when replaced by exotics, whether in terms of provision of resources and services or on aesthetic or ethical grounds, as well as recognition of the potential economic and environmental costs of invasive species. Yet the value placed on species and ecosystems has been historically uneven. A very small suite of edible and useful species has been valued, conserved, and propagated by humans. These number in the thousands out of tens of millions of species. The far larger ecological assemblages within which these well-known, valuable species live have been neither understood nor managed.

In a small number of cases, endangered species have recovered when protected by human efforts. For example, the bald eagle and marine mammals in North America have rapidly rebuilt their numbers and many populations of marine mammals worldwide are recovering. These recoveries have taken place under conditions where habitats required by the species were either intact or readily protected and where there the public will to preserve or conserve them was strong. Such circumstances do not currently apply to most regions of the world where species are threatened.

Losses of Ecosystems and Ecosystem Services

Just as land conversions and land degradation can lead to losses of species, these trends affecting species can result in degradation or loss of ecosystems and ecosystem services. On a global basis, freshwater, coral reef, and forest ecosystems (the latter just discussed under "Land" above) have suffered enormous assault from human activities.

Covering less than 1 percent of the earth's surface, freshwater ecosystems have lost the largest proportion of species and habitat when compared with other ecosystems on land or with the oceans.[161] Increasing trends of overfishing, dam building, river development, and contamination, as human activities expand, will continue to place greater threats on freshwater ecosystems.[162] Many estuaries and bays have deteriorated because of activities associated with land development as well as fishing pressure, with resulting declines in ecosystem services. For example, the depletion of the oyster population in Chesapeake Bay through over-exploitation has had a profound effect on the Bay—the oysters once filtered a volume of water equal to that of the entire bay about once a week; they now filter that volume in about one year's time. This circumstance has adversely affected the water quality of the estuary and has impacted many species that live in it, including those consumed by humans.[163] Similar human development along coasts, together with associated pollution from agriculture and other land-based sources and harmful fishing practices, has caused 58 percent of the world's coral reefs to be in jeopardy of loss, changes in species composition, or other major ecosystem effects.[164] These losses challenge the livelihood of local communities that depend on the reef for food, tourism, and protection against damaging storms. For global forests, expanding populations, together with the increasing need for fuelwood and land for agriculture, have resulted in a net loss of some 180 million hectares between 1980 and 1995. Despite reforestation efforts, the rates of deforestation remain high in many areas of the world.

The decrease and decline of freshwater ecosystems, coral reefs, and forests represents incalculable losses of ecological services, including the recycling of nutrients, water, and wastes; the mitigation of climate and temperature extremes; the management of watersheds; and the support of local communities and cultures.[165]

For a Sustainable Future

Without active efforts to conserve biodiversity, pinpoint the vectors of and control bioinvasions, and protect natural ecosystems, the trends of increasing loss of species, ecosystems, and ecosystem services will continue and threaten both the long-term stability of ecosystems and the quality of life for humans that depend on those systems for their livelihood. For a sustainable future, efforts will be needed to strengthen the barriers to the free flow of species given growing global trading, to avoid intentional introductions of exotics, to protect and preserve ecosystems as well as endangered or threatened species, to improve mechanisms and information systems for detecting changes and assessing threats, and to promote science for conservation.

Though people have been motivated by aesthetic and cultural considerations to preserve special natural places for millennia, the scientific understanding of conservation biology has taken clear form only in the past decade and a half.[166]   As these two currents of human activity converge, there has been growing awareness of the need to conserve ecosystem processes.   It is therefore necessary to work at the scale of whole landscapes, with explicit attention both to the preservation of critical ecosystems and to the interactions between human activities and the managed and unmanaged ecosystems among them.[167]   An open question for a transition toward sustainability is whether a reformulated idea of conservation of this kind will prove workable in enough places to salvage the biological richness of the planet. Moreover, the ability to assess and monitor the well-being of the earth's living resources and the services they provide is far from proven, yet efforts in those areas will be essential to understand the roles of species and ecosystems for a sustainable future.

Disease Organisms and Vectors[168]

Emerging and Reemerging Diseases

The 1980s and 1990s have seen the emergence of 30 new diseases,[169] the resurgence of "old" diseases (e.g., tuberculosis), and the redistribution of old diseases on a global scale (e.g., cholera). These trends are in large part related to human activities associated with land use, especially agricultural practices; water storage and use (see Fresh Water section for a discussion of cholera), including irrigation; and urbanization. The intensification of agricultural production has not only increased crop yields, but the related practices of irrigation, land conversion, and habitat disturbance have also increased the risk of infectious diseases such as malaria and schistosomiasis. Some 30 diseases have been linked to irrigation practices (e.g., malaria and Japanese encephalitis with Asian paddy-rice agriculture, mosquito-borne diseases with farming in Central and South America). [170] The incidence of schistosomiasis is believed to have risen over the last 50 years because of the expansion in irrigation systems in hot climates. [171] A tripling of the prevalence of schistosomiasis in Ghana in the late 1950s and early 1960s is believed to be related to the construction of agricultural impoundments which provide habitat for the intermediate host organism.[172]

Forest land conversions have been associated with higher incidences of malaria and leishmaniasis, through habitat creation conducive to tick and other insect vector breeding. The forest fringes are places where contact between disease organisms and human populations are most efficient in disease transmission. [173] Rising surface temperatures associated with deforestation in Africa are believed to be responsible for accelerating the life cycle of the mosquitoes.[174]

Although commonly believed to be a disease of the past, nearly 3 million people died from tuberculosis in 1995, an indication of the continuing influence of the disease with increasing poverty and homelessness in urban areas, and the importance of multidrug resistance.[175] With an apparent leveling off in 1996, the TB epidemic is expected to continue to pose human health problems for developing countries.[176]

In addition to infectious diseases, a series of new diseases of chemical origin have emerged worldwide in recent decades. There have been dramatic episodes of such disease, for example, the disaster at Bhopal where several thousand persons were killed by acute exposure to the pesticide intermediate toluene diisocyanate (TDI). Also, there are chronic lower level exposures of populations to chemical toxins such as organic mercury, which has the power to damage the nervous system; benzene, which causes cancer; and polychlorinated biphenyls (PCBs), which can impair infant development. New diseases of chemical origin are often first seen in populations occupationally exposed to toxic chemicals, inasmuch as exposures in these groups are typically heavier than in the general population and occur earlier than in the population at large.

For a Sustainable Future

The emergence and reemergence of infectious diseases have important implications for sustainability, especially with expanding populations in areas where diseases are expanding. There will be an enormous challenge to containing the spread of disease while transportation and trading systems grow and while human populations grow and expand into new ecological settings, thereby establishing contact with previously isolated microbes and other infectious agents. Clearly, better systems of surveillance and recognition of emerging diseases are needed, coupled with integrated modeling and the use of geographically based data systems, and also measures for intervention (vaccine and drug development, vector control, and education) to manage future outbreaks.[177] These approaches will enable the medical community to take more anticipatory approaches and help optimize preventive strategies.[178] Also, better management of the interactions between humans and the environment, especially changes in agricultural practices and water management, will be needed to ensure a sustainable future.

CONCLUSIONS

Based on our analysis of persistent trends and transitions, the Board concludes that **certain current trends of population and habitation, wealth and consumption, technology and work, connectedness and diversity, and environmental change are likely to persist well into the coming century and could significantly undermine the prospects for sustainability. If they do persist, many human needs will not be met, life support systems will be dangerously degraded, and the numbers of hungry and poor will increase.** Some of these current trends present significant opportunities for advancing a transition toward sustainability, as well as threats to that transition. All, however, bear watching. Among social trends the Board reviewed that may merit particular attention in efforts to navigate a transition to sustainability are expanding urbanization, growing disparities of wealth, wasteful consumption, increasing connectedness, and shifts in the distribution of power. Environmental trends of special concern include the buildup of long-lived greenhouse gases in the atmosphere and associated climate changes, the decline of valued marine fisheries, increasing regional shortfalls in the quality and quantity of fresh water, expanding tropical deforestation, continuing losses of species, ecosystems, and their services, the emergence and reemergence of serious diseases, and more generally, the increasing human dominance of natural systems.

Even the most alarming current trends, however, may experience transitions that enhance the prospects for sustainability. Trends are rarely constant over time. Breaks or inflections in the long-term trends mark periods of transition. Transitions relevant to the prospects for sustainability are already underway to varying degrees in specific places and regions around the globe: the demographic transition from high to low birth and death rates; the health transition from early death by infectious diseases to late death by cancer, heart disease, and stroke; the economic transition from state to market control; the civil society transition from single-party, military, or state-run institutions to multiparty politics and a rich mix of governmental and nongovernmental institutions. Environmentally, some significant positive transitions have occurred in specific regions. These include shifts from increasing to decreasing rates of emissions for specific pollutants, from deforestation to reforestation, and from shrinking to expanding ranges for certain endangered species.

Individual, local trend reversals such as these clearly do not make a sustainability transition. But they do show that efforts to catalyze or accelerate relevant shifts can have significant implications for meeting human needs in ways that sustain the life support systems of the planet.

REFERENCES AND BIBLIOGRAPHY

Adelman, I., and S. Robinson. 1989. Income distribution and development. In *Handbook of development economics,* vol. 2, ed. H. Chenery and T. N. Srinivasan, 949-103. Amsterdam: North Holland.

API (American Petroleum Institute). 1998. *How much we pay for gasoline.* API Publication No. R26903, 1997 Annual Review.

Anderson, C. 1991. "Cholera epidemic traced to risk miscalculation." *Nature,* Vol. 354, p. 255.

Anderson, J.L., W.H. Brune, S.A. Lloyd, W.L. Starr, M. Lowenstein, and J.R. Podolske. 1989. Kinetics of ozone destruction by ClO and BrO within the Antarctic vortex: an analysis based on in-situ ER-2 data. *Journal of Geophysical Research* 94: 11480.

Arrow, K., B. Bolin, R. Costanza, P. Dasgupta, C. Folke, C.S. Holling, B.O. Jansson, S. Levin, K.G. Maeler, C. Perrings, and D. Dimentel. 1995. Economic growth, carrying capacity, and the environment. *Science* 268, no. 5210: 520-521.

Ausubel, J.H., and R. Herman eds. 1988. *Cities and their vital systems: Infrastructure past, present, and future.* Washington, D.C.: National Academy Press.

Ausubel, J.H. 1996a. Can technology spare the earth? *American Scientist* 84: 166.

Ausubel, J.H. 1996b. The liberation of the environment. *Deadalus* 125, no. 3: 1-17.

Ausubel, J.H., and A. Grübler. 1995. Working less and living longer: Long-term trends in working time and time budgets. *Technological Forecasting and Social Change* 50, no. 3: 113-131.

Bacha, E. L. 1978. The Kuznets curve and beyond: Growth and Change in Inequalities. In *Economic growth and resources* vol. 1, ed. E. Malinvaud, 52-81. New York: St. Martins Press.

Barbault, R., and S.D. Sastrapradja. 1995. Generation, maintenance and loss of biodiversity. In *Global biodiversity assessment,* ed. V. H. Heywood. Published for the United Nations Environment Programme. New York: Cambridge University Press.

Bartone, Carl, Janis Bernstein, Josef Leitman, Jochen Eigen. 1994. *Toward Environmental Strategies for Cities: Policy Considerations for Urban Environmental management in Developing Countries.* Urban Management Programme Series 18. Washington, D.C.: The World Bank.

Baumol, W.J., R.B. Nelson, and E.N. Wolff, eds. 1994. *Convergence and productivity: Cross-national studies and historical evidence.* Oxford: Oxford University Press.

Beckmann, M.J. 1988. An economic model of urban growth. in *Cities and their Vital Systems: Infrastructure Past, Present, and Future.,* eds. J. H. Ausubel and R. Herman. Washington, D.C.: National Academy Press.

Benedick, Richard Elliot. 1991. *Ozone diplomacy: New directions in safeguarding the planet.* Cambridge, MA: Harvard University Press.

BLS (Bureau of Labor Statistics). 1998. Unpublished data from the *Current population survey.* Washington, D.C.: BLS.

_____. 1999. BLS Current Population Survey. Washington, D.C.: BLS.

Bongaarts, J. 1994. Population policy options in the developing world. *Science* 263: 771-776.

Bongaarts, J., and J. Bruce. 1997. What can be done to address population growth? Unpublished background paper for *High hopes: The United States, global population and our common future.* Washington, D.C.: Resources for the Future.

Bos, E., M.T. Vu, E. Masiah, and R.A. Bulatao. 1994. *World Population Projections 1994-95 Edition.* Baltimore: Johns Hopkins University Press.

Botsford, Louis W., Juan Carlos Castilla, and Charles H. Peterson. 1997. The management of fisheries and marine ecosystems. *Science* 277, no. 5325: 509-515.

Bouwer, Herman. 1992. Agricultural and municipal use of wastewater. Proceedings of the 16th biennial conference of the International Association on Water Pollution Research and Control. *Water Science and Technology* 26, nos. 7-8: 1583-1591.

Bradley, D. 1994. Institutional capacity to monitor the interactions of agricultural and health change. In *Agriculture, environment, and health: Sustainable development in the 21st century,* ed. V. W. Ruttan, 308-338. Minneapolis: University of Minnesota Press.

Brandt Report. See Independent Commission on International Development Issues, 1980.

Brown, L.R., Kane, H. and Roodman, D.M. 1994. *Vital signs 1994: The trends that are shaping our future.* New York: W. W. Norton and Co.

Brown, L.R., M. Renner, C. Flavin. 1998. *Vital signs: The environmental trends that are shaping our future.* New York: W.W. Norton and Co.

Brundtland Report. See World Commission on Environment and Development, 1987.

Bruno, Michael, Martin Ravallion, and Lyn Squire. 1995. *Equity and growth in developing countries: Old and new perspectives in the policy issues.* Prepared for the IMF Conference on Income Distribution and Sustainable Growth, June 1-2, 1995. Washington, D.C.: The World Bank.

Burke, Lauretta, et al. 1998. *Reefs at Risk: A Map-Based Indicator of Potential Threats to the World's Coral Reefs.* World Resources Institute, Washington, D.C.

Carlton, J.T. 1993. Neoextinctions of marine invertebrates. *American Zoologist* 33, no. 6: 499-409.

Cernea, Michael M. 1993. *Urban Environment and Population Relocation.* Discussion Paper 152. Washington, D.C.: The World Bank.

Chant, Sylvia H., and Alan Greig. 1996. Gender, urban development, and housing. Publication series for Habitat II, Vol. 2. New York: UNDP.

Chapin, F.S., B.H. Walker, R.J. Hobbs, D.U. Hooper, J.H. Lawton, E. Sala, and D. Tilman. 1997. Biotic control over the functioning of ecosystems. *Science* 277: 500-505.

Ciais, P., P.P. Tans, M. Trolier, J.W.C. White, and R.J. Francey. 1995. A large northern hemisphere terrestrial CO_2 sink as indicated by the $^{13}C/^{12}C$ Ratio of Atmospheric CO_2. *Science* 269, no. 5227: 1098-1102.

Clark, W.C. 1985. Scales of climate impacts. *Climate Change* 7: 5-27.

Cohen, A.N., and J.T. Carlton. 1995. *Biological study: Nonindigenous aquatic species in a United States estuary: A case study of the biological invasions of the San Francisco Bay and Delta.* Washington, D.C.: US Fish and Wildlife Service.

Cohen, Joel E. 1995. *How many people can the earth support?* New York: W.W. Norton.

Costanza, R., F. Andrade, P. Antunes, M. van den Belt, D. Boersma, D.F. Boesch, F. Catarino, S. Hanna, K. Limburg, B. Low, M. Molitor, J.G. Pereira, S. Rayner, R. Santos, J. Wilson, M. Young. 1998. Principles for sustainable governance of the oceans. *Science* 281, no. 5374: 198-199.

Councils of the Royal Society of London and the National Academy of Sciences. 1992. *Joint statement on population growth, resource consumption and a sustainable world.* Washington, D.C.: National Academy of Sciences.

Crutzen, P.J. 1992. On the potential importance of the gas phase reaction $CH_3O_2 + ClO \rightarrow ClOO + CH_3O$ and the heterogeneous reaction $HOCl + HCl \rightarrow H_2O + Cl_2$ in 'ozone hole' chemistry. *Geophysical Research Letters* 19, no. 11: 1113-1116.

Crutzen, P.J., and F. Arnold. 1986. Nitric acid cloud formation in the cold Antarctic stratosphere: A major cause for the springtime "ozone hole." *Nature* 324: 651-655.

Daily, Gretchen C., ed. 1997. *Nature's services: Societal dependence on natural ecosystems.* Washington, D.C.: Island Press.

Daily, Gretchen C., Pamela A. Matson, and Peter M. Vitousek. 1997. Ecosystem services supplied by soil. In *Nature's services*, ed. Daily. Washington, D.C.: Island Press.

Dakan, Zuo, and Zhang Peiyuan. 1990. The Huang-Huai-Hai Plain. Chap. 28 in *The earth as transformed by human action: Global and regional changes in the biosphere over the past 300 years*, eds. Turner et al. Cambridge, UK: Cambridge University Press.

Davey, Kenneth J. 1993. *Elements of Urban Management.* Urban Management Program Papers No. 11 and 11S. Washington, D.C.: The World Bank.

Deevey, Edward. 1960. The human population. *Scientific American* 203: 194-204.

DoE/EIA (Department of Energy/Energy Information Administration). 1998a. *International energy outlook.* DoE/EIA-0484, April 1998. Washington, D.C.: US Government Printing Office.

_____. 1998b. *Annual energy review.* DoE/EIA-0384, July 1998. Washington, D.C.: US Government Printing Office.

_____. 1999. World Primary Energy Consumption (Btu), 1988-1997. Available http://www.eia.doe.gov/emeu/iea/table1.html. Last updated 3/25/99.

Dobson, A.P., M.S. Campbell, and J. Bell. 1997. Fatal Synergisms: Interactions between infectious diseases, human population growth and loss of biodiversity. Pages 87-110 in *Biodiversity and human health,* F. Grifo and J. Rosenthal, eds. Washington, D.C.: Island Press.

Douglas, B.C. 1995. Global sea level change: Determination and interpretation. *Reviews of Geophysics* 33: 1425-1432.

Dunlap, Riley E. 1997. International opinion at the century's end: public attitudes toward environmental issues. In *Environmental policy: Transnational issues and national trends,* eds. L.K. Caldwell and R.V. Bartlett, 201-224. Westport, CT: Quorum Books.

Ecological Society of America, Committee on the Scientific Basis for Ecosystem Management. 1996. *The report of the Ecological Society of America Committee on the scientific basis for ecosystem management.* Washington, D.C.: The Ecological Society of America.

Farman, J.C., B.G. Gardiner, and J.D. Shanklin. 1985. Large losses of total ozone in Antarctica reveal seasonal chlorine oxide-nitrogen oxide interaction. *Nature* 315, no. 6016: 207-210.

Farvacque-Vitkovic, Catherine, and Lucien Goldin. 1998. *The Future of African Cities: Challenges and Priorities in Urban Development.* Washington, D.C.: The World Bank.

FAO (United Nations Food and Agriculture Organization). 1997. *The state of world fisheries and aquaculture 1996.* Rome: FAO.

Freeman, C., and L. Soete. 1987. *Technical change and full employment.* London: Pinter.

Friedenburg, L.K. 1997. Physical effects of habitat fragmentation. In *Conservation Biology,* 2d ed., eds. P.L. Fiedler and P.M. Kareiva, 66-79. New York: Chapman and Hall.

Frosch, R. 1994. Industrial ecology: Minimizing the impact of industrial waste. *Physics Today* 47, no. 11: 63-68.

Fox, William F. 1994. *Strategic Options for Urban Infrastructure Management.* Urban Management Programme Paper 17. Washington, D.C.: The World Bank.

Gell-Mann, M. 1994. *The quark and the jaguar: Adventures in the simple and complex.* New York: W. H. Freeman.

Gleick, Peter H. 1998. *The world's water: The biennial report on freshwater resources.* Washington, D.C.: Island Press.

Grossman, Gene M. and Alan B. Krueger. 1991. *Environmental impacts of a North American free trade agreement.* Discussion paper 158, November. Princeton, NJ: Woodrow Wilson School, Princeton University.

_____. 1995. Economic growth and the environment. *Quarterly Journal of Economics* 110, no. 2: 353-377.

Grübler, A. 1998. *Technology and global change.* Cambridge, UK: Cambridge University Press.

Grübler, A., and Nowotny, H. 1990. Towards the fifth Kondratiev upswing: Elements of an emerging new growth phase and possible development trajectories. *International Journal of Technology Management* 5, no. 4: 431-471.

Hayami, Yujiro, and V.W. Ruttan. 1985. *Agricultural development: An international perspective.* Baltimore: Johns Hopkins University Press. 73-93, 178-187, 264-298.

Hooper, D.U. and P.M. Vitousek. 1997. The effects of plant composition and diversity on ecosystem processes. *Science* 277: 1302-1305.

Hughes, Thomas P. 1998. *Rescuing Prometheus.* New York: Pantheon Books.

Husain, L., V.A. Dutkiewicz, and M. Das. 1998. Evidence for decrease in atmospheric sulfur burden in the Eastern United States caused by reduction in SO_2 emissions. *Geophysical Res. Letters* 25, no. 7: 967-970.

IOM (Institute of Medecine). 1992. *Emerging infections: Microbial threats to health in the United States.* J. Lederberg, R.E. Shope, S.C. Oaks, Jr., eds. Washington, D.C.: National Academy Press.

IPCC (Intergovernmental Panel on Climate Change). 1996. *Climate change 1995: The science of climate change.* Contribution of Working Group I to the Second Assessment Report of the Intergovernmental Panel on Climate Change. J.T. Houghton, L.G. Meira Filho, B.A. Callander, N. Harris, A. Kattenberg, and K. Maskell, eds. Cambridge, UK: Cambridge University Press.

IUCN (The World Conservation Union). 1996. *IUCN Red List of Threatened Animals.* Gland, Switzerland: IUCN.

Jickells, Timothy D., Roy Carpenter, and Peter S. Liss. 1990. Marine environment. Chap. 18 in Turner et al. 1990b.

Jodha, Narpat S. 1986. Common property resources and rural poor in dry regions of India. *Economic and Political Weekly* XXI, no. 27: 1169-81.

Jodha, Narpat S. 1987. A case study of the degradation of common property resources in India. In Piers Blaikie and Harold Brookfield, eds. *Land Degradation and Society.* London: Nethuen. pp. 196-207.

Kahrl, W.L. 1982. *Water and Power: The Conflict Over Los Angeles' Water Supply in the Owens Valley.* Berkeley: University of California Press.

Kasperson, Jeanne X., Roger E. Kasperson, B.L. Turner II, eds. 1995. *Regions at Risk: Comparisons of threatened environments.* Tokyo: United Nations University Press.

Kasperson, J.X., R.E. Kasperson, and B.L. Turner, II, eds. 1995. *Regions at risk: Comparisons of threatened environments.* Tokyo: United Nations University.

Kates, R.W. 1994. Sustaining life on earth. *Scientific American* 271, no. 4: 114-122.

Kates, Robert W. 1997. Population, technology, and the human environment: A thread through time. *Daedalus* 125, no. 3: 1-29. Also published in: Jesse H. Ausubel and H. Dale Langford eds. *Technological Trajectories and the Human Environment*, Washington, D.C.: National Academy Press. 33-55.

Kates, R.W. and W.C. Clark. 1996. Environmental surprise: Expecting the unexpected? *Environment* 38, no. 2: 6-11, 28-35.

Kates, R.W., B.L. Turner, and W.C. Clark 1990. The great transformation. Chap. 1 in *The earth as transformed by human action: Global and regional changes in the biosphere over the past 300 years*, eds. Turner et al. Cambridge, UK: Cambridge University Press.

Kempton, Willett, James S. Boster, and Jennifer A. Hartley. 1995. *Environmental values in American culture.* Cambridge, MA: MIT Press.

Khalil, M.A.K., and R.A. Rasmussen. 1994. Global decrease of atmospheric carbon monoxide concentration. *Nature* 370, no. 6491: 639-641.

Khush, G.S. 1995. Modern varieties and their real contributions to food supplies and equity. *GeoJournal* 35, no. 3: 275-284.

Kingsley, Thomas. 1994. *Managing Urban Environmental Quality in Asia.* World Bank Technical Paper 220. Washington, D.C.: The World Bank.

Knodel, J., and van de Walle, E. 1976. Lessons from the past: Policy implications of historical fertility studies. *Population and Development Review* 5:217-245.

Laurance, W.F., S.G. Laurance, L.V. Ferreira, J.M. Rankin-deMerona, C. Gascon, and T.E. Lovejoy. 1997. Biomass collapse in Amazonian forest fragments. *Science* 278, no. 5340: 1117-1118.

Lawton, J.H. and R.M. May, eds. 1995. *Extinction rates*. Oxford, UK: Oxford University Press.

Lee, K.N. 1993. *Compass and gyroscope: Integrating science and politics for the environment*. Washington, D.C.: Island Press.

Lee, S.H., H. Akimoto, H. Nakane, S. Kurnosenko, and Y. Kinjo. 1998. Lower tropospheric ozone trend observed in 1989-1998 at Okinawa, Japan. *Geophys. Res. Letters* 25, no. 10: 1637-1640.

Lindsay, S.W., and M.H. Birley. 1996. Climate change and malaria transmission. *Annals of Tropical Medicine and Parasitology* 90, no. 6: 573-588.

Logan, J.A. 1994. Trends in the vertical distribution of ozone: An analysis of ozone sonde data. *Journal of Geophysical Research* 99, no. 25: 553-525, 585.

Lovejoy, T.E. 1997. Biodiversity: What is it? In *Biodiversity II*, eds. M.L. Reaka-Kudla, D.E. Wilson, and E.O. Wilson, 7-14. Washington, D.C.: National Academy Press.

L'vovich, Mark I., and Gilbert F. White. 1990. Use and transformation of terrestrial water systems." Chapter 14 in *The earth as transformed by human action: Global and regional changes in the biosphere over the past 300 years*, eds. Turner et al. Cambridge, UK: Cambridge University Press.

MacDonald, I.A., L.L. Loope, M.B. Usher, and O. Hamann. 1989. Wildlife conservation and the invasion of nature reserves by introduced species: a global perspective. In *Biological Invasions: A Global Perspective*, eds. J.A. Drake, H.A. Mooney, F. di Castri, R.H. Groves, F.J. Kruger, M. Rejmánek, and M. Williamson. Chichester: John Wiley and Sons.

Maddison, Angus. 1995. *Monitoring the world economy, 1820-1992*. Paris: Development Centre of the Organisation for Economic Co-Operation and Development.

Margat, J. 1996. *Comprehensive assessment of the freshwater resources of the world: Groundwater component*. Contribution to Chapter 2 of the Comprehensive Global Freshwater Assessment, United Nations.

Mahlman, J.D. 1997. Uncertainties in projections of human-caused climate warming. *Science* 278: 1416-17.

Malakoff, D. 1997. Extinction on the high seas. *Science* 275, no. 5325: 486-488.

Marty, Martin E. and R. Scott Appleby, eds. 1991. *The fundamentalism project: A study conducted by the American Academy of Arts and Sciences*. Chicago: University of Chicago Press.

Mathews, J. 1997. Power shift. *Foreign Affairs* 76, no. 1: 50-66.

Matson, P.A., W.J. Parton, A.G. Power, and M.J. Swift. 1997. Agricultural intensification and ecosystem properties. *Science* 277: 504-509.

McAllister, Don E., Andrew L. Hamilton, and Brian Harvey. 1997. *Global freshwater biodiversity: Striving for the integrity of freshwater ecosystems*. Ottawa: Ocean Voice International.

McCrabb, G.J., K.T. Berger, T. Magner, C. May, and R.A. Hunter. 1997. Inhibiting methane production in Brahman cattle by dietary supplementation with a novel compound and the effects on growth. *Australian Journal of Agricultural Research* 48: 323-9.

McGrattan, E.R., and R. Rogerson. Changes in hours worked since 1950. *Federal Reserve Bank of Minneapolis Quarterly Review* 22, no. 1: 2-19.

Montzka, S.A., J.H. Butler, R.C. Myers, T.M. Thompson, T.H. Swanson, A.D. Clarke, L.T. Lock, and J.W. Elkins. 1996. Decline in the tropospheric abundance of halogen from halocarbons: Implications for stratospheric ozone depletion. *Science* 272, no. 5266: 1318-1322.

NAE (National Academy of Engineering). 1994. *The greening of industrial ecosystems.* B. Allenby and D. Richards, eds. Washington, D.C.: National Academy Press.

_____. 1997. *Technological trajectories and the human environment.* J.H. Ausubel and H.D. Langford, eds. Washington, D.C.: National Academy Press.

NMFS (National Marine Fisheries Service). 1996. *Magnuson-Stevens Fishery Conservation and Management Act, as amended through October 11, 1996.* Technical Memorandum NMFS-F/SPO-23, December 1996. Washington, D.C.: NOAA.

_____. 1997. *Report to Congress: Status of the fisheries of the United States, September 1997.* Washington, D.C.: National Oceanic and Atmospheric Administration (NOAA).

NRC (National Research Council). 1988. *Biodiversity.* E.O. Wilson, ed. Washington, D.C.: National Academy Press.

_____. 1986. *Acid deposition: Long-term trends.* Committee on Monitoring and Assessment of Trends in Acid Deposition. Washington, D.C.: National Academy Press.

_____. 1991. *Toward sustainability: A plan for collaborative research on agriculture and natural resource management.* Panel for Collaborative Research Support for AID's Sustainable Agriculture and Natural Resource Management. Washington, D.C.: National Academy Press.

_____. 1994. *Environmental science in the coastal zone: Issues for further research.* Washington, D.C.: National Academy Press.

_____. 1995a. *Science, policy, and the coast: Improving decision making.* Committee on Science and Policy for the Coastal Ocean. Washington, D.C.: National Academy Press.

_____. 1995b. *Understanding marine biodiversity.* Committee on Biological Diversity in Marine Systems. Washington, D.C.: National Academy Press.

_____. 1996. *Upstream: Salmon and society in the Pacific Northwest.* Committee on the Protection and Management of Pacific Northwest Anadromous Salmonids. Washington, D.C.: National Academy Press.

_____. 1997. *Environmentally significant consumption: Research directions.* Paul C. Stern, Thomas Dietz, Vernon W. Ruttan, Robert H. Socolow, and James L. Sweeney, eds. Committee on the Human Dimensions of Global Change. Washington, D.C.: National Academy Press.

_____. 1998a. *Issues in potable reuse: The viability of augmenting drinking water supplies with reclaimed water.* Committee to Evaluate the Viability of Augmenting Potable Water Supplies with Reclaimed Water. Washington, D.C.: National Academy Press.

_____. 1998b. *Opportunities in ocean sciences: Challenges on the horizon.* Ocean Studies Board. Washington, D.C.: National Academy Press.

_____. 1999a. *Sustaining marine fisheries.* Committee on Ecosystem Management for Sustainable Marine Fisheries. Washington, D.C.: National Academy Press.

_____. 1999b. *Water for the future: The West Bank and Gaza Strip, Israel, and Jordan.* Committee on Sustainable Water Supplies in the Middle East; Israel Academy of Sciences and Humanities; Palestine Academy for Science and Technology; Royal Scientific Society, Jordan; and the US National Academy of Sciences. Washington, D.C.: National Academy Press.

Nakicenovic, N. 1997. Freeing energy from carbon. In *Technological trajectories and the human environment,* eds. J.H. Ausubel and H.D. Langford. Washington, D.C.: National Academy Press.

Naylor, R.L. 1996. Energy and resource constraints on intensive agricultural production. *Annual Review of Energy and Environment* 21: 99-123.

Newell, R.I.E. 1988. Ecological changes in the Chesapeake Bay: Are they the results of over-harvesting the American oyster *Crassostrea virginica*? In *Understanding the estuary: Advances in Chesapeake Bay research.* Proceedings of a conference, 29-31 March 1988, Baltimore, MD. Solomons, MD: Chesapeake Research Consortium.

Noble, Ian R., and Rodolfo Dirzo. 1997. Forests and human-dominated ecosystems. *Science* 277: 522-525.

Novelli, P., K. Masarie, P. Tans, and P. Lang. 1994. Recent changes in atmospheric carbon monoxide. *Science* 263: 1587-1590.

NUA. 1998. NUA Internet Surverys. Available http://www.nua.ie/surveys/how_many_online/index.html.

Ostrom, Elinor. 1990. *Governing the commons. The evolution of institutions for collective action.* Cambridge, UK: Cambridge University Press.

PCAST (President's Committee of Advisers on Science and Technology). 1997. *Federal energy R&D for the challenges of the twenty-first century.* Report of the Energy R&D Panel of PCAST. Washington, D.C.: PCAST.

Patz, J.A., P.R. Epstein, T.A. Burke, and J.M. Balbus. 1996. Global climate change and emerging infectious diseases. *Journal of the American Medical Association* 275, no. 3: 217-23.

Pennisi, E. 1997. Brighter prospects for the world's coral reefs? *Science* 275, no. 5325: 491-493.

Peterson, T.C., and R.S. Vose. 1997. An overview of the Global Historical Climatology Network temperature data base. *Bulletin of the American Meteorological Society* 78: 2837-2849.

Pinstrup-Anderson, P., R. Pandya-Lorch, and M.W. Rosegrant. 1997. *The world food situation: Recent developments, emerging issues, and long-term prospects.* Washington, D.C.: International Food Policy Research Institute.

Population Reference Bureau. 1997. *1997 World population data sheet of the Population Reference Bureau.* Washington, D.C.: Population Reference Bureau.

Postel, Sandra, Gretchen C. Daily, and Paul Ehrlich. 1996. Human appropriation of renewable fresh water. *Science* 271, no. 5250: 785-788.

Postel, Sandra. 1997. *Last oasis: Facing water scarcity.* New York: W.W. Norton & Company.

Putnam, R. 1995. Tuning in, tuning out: The strange disappearance of social capital in America. *Political Science and Politics* 28, no. 4: 664-684.

Rakesh, Mohan. 1994. *Understanding the Developing Metropolis.* New York: Oxford University Press. Published for the World Bank.

Raskin, P. 1997. *Water futures: Assessment of long-range patterns and problems.* Background paper for UN/SEI Comprehensive Assessment of the Freshwater Resources of the World. Stockholm: Stockholm Environment Institute.

Raskin, P., M. Chadwick, T. Jackson, and G. Leach. 1995. *The transition toward sustainability: Beyond conventional development.* Boston: Stockholm Environmental Institute.

Raskin, P., H. Hansen, and R. Margolis. 1995. *Water and sustainability: A global outlook.* POLESTAR Series report no. 4. Stockholm: Stockholm Environment Institute.

Raskin, P., and R. Margolis. 1995. *Global energy in the 21st century: Patterns, projections, and problems.* POLESTAR Series report no. 3. Stockholm: Stockholm Environment Institute.

Raskin, P., G. Gallopin, P. Gutman, A. Hammond, and R. Swart. 1998. *Bending the curve: Toward global sustainability.* A report of the Global Scenario Group. PoleStar Series Report no. 8. Boston: Stockholm Environment Institute.

Rasmussen, Paul E., Keith W.T. Goulding, James R. Brown, Peter R. Grace, H. Henry Janzen, Martin Körschens. 1998. Long-eterm agroecosystem experiments: Assessing agricultural sustainability and global change. *Science* 282:893-896.

Reaka-Kudla, M.L. 1997. The global biodiversity of coral reefs: A comparison with rain forests. In *Biodiversity II: Understanding and Protecting Our Biological Resources,* eds. Marjorie L. Reaka-Kudla, Don E. Wilson, and Edward O. Wilson. Washington, D.C.: Joseph Henry Press.

Richards, John F. 1990. Land transformation. Chap. 10 in *The earth as transformed by human action: Global and regional changes in the biosphere over the past 300 years*, eds. Turner et al. Cambridge, UK: Cambridge University Press.

Rifkin, J. 1995. *The end of work: The decline of the global labor force and the dawn of the post-market era*. New York: G.P. Putnam.

Rogers, Peter P., Kazi F. Jalal, Bindu N. Lohani, Gene M. Owens, Chang-Ching Yu, Christian M. Dufournaud, and Jun Bi. 1997. *Measuring environmental quality in Asia*. Division of Engineering and Applied Sciences, Harvard University, Asian Development Bank. Cambridge, MA: Harvard University Press.

Rostow, W.W. 1961. *The stages of economic growth: A non-Communist manifesto*. Cambridge, UK: Cambridge University Press.

Rowland, F.S. and M. Molina. 1975. Chloromethane in the environment. *Reviews of Geophysics and Space Physics* 13: 1-35.

Rozanov, Boris G., Viktor Targulian, and D.S. Orlov. 1990. Soils. Chap. 12 in *The earth as transformed by human action: Global and regional changes in the biosphere over the past 300 years*, eds. Turner et al. Cambridge, UK: Cambridge University Press.

Runge, F. 1997. *Globalization and sustainability: The machine in the garden*. Unpublished paper prepared for the BSD.

Schmidt, K.F., and D. Malakoff. 1997. 'No-take' zones spark fisheries debate. *Science* 275, no. 5325: 489-491.

Schneider, S., and Turner, B.L., II. In preparation. *Report of the 1994 Aspen Global Change Institute: Summer session II on surprise and global environmental change*.

Schor, J. 1991. *The overworked American*. New York: Basic Books.

Schwarz, Harry E., Jacque Emel, William J. Dickens, Peter Rogers, and John Thompson. 1990. Water quality and flows. Chap. 15 in *The earth as transformed by human action: Global and regional changes in the biosphere over the past 300 years*, eds. Turner et al. Cambridge, UK: Cambridge University Press.

Sensenbrenner, Julia S. 1994. State enterprises tackle labor reform. *China Business Review* 21, no. 6.

Serageldin, Ismail, and Michael Cohen. 1995. *The Human Face of the Urban Environment: A Report ot the Development Community*. Environmentally Sustainable Development Proceedings Series Paper No. 5. Washington, D.C.: The World Bank.

Shiklomanov, Igor A. 1993. World fresh water resources. In *Water in crisis: A guide to the world's fresh water resources*, ed. P.H. Gleick. New York: Oxford University Press.

Simmonds, P.G., S. Seuring, G. Nickless, and R.G. Derwent. 1997. Segregation and interpretation of ozone and carbon monoxide measurements by air mass origin at the TOR station, Mace Head, Ireland from 1987 to 1995. *Journal of Atmospheric Chemistry* 28: 45-59.

Simpson, R. David, Roger A. Sedjo, and John W. Reid. 1996. Valuing biodiversity for use in pharmaceutical research. *Journal of Political Economy* 104:163-185,

Solley, W.B., R.R. Pierce, and H.A. Perlman. 1993. Estimated use of water in the United States in 1990. In *Trends 1950-1990*, 65, Table 31. Washington, D.C.: US Geological Survey circular (1081).

Solomon, S., R.R. Garcia, F.S. Rowland, and D.J. Wobbles. 1986. On the depletion of Antarctic ozone. *Nature* 321: 755.

Speth, J.G. 1992. The transition to a sustainable society. *Proceedings of the National Academy of Sciences* 89: 870-872.

Stephens, C. 1996. Healthy cities or unhealthy islands? The health and social implications of urban inequality. *Environment and Urbanization* 8, no. 2: 9-30.

Stern, P., T. Dietz, V. Ruttan, R.H. Socolow, and J.L. Sweeney., eds. 1997. *Environmentally significant consumption: Research directions.* Committee on the Human Dimensions of Global Change. Washington, D.C.: National Academy Press.

Thompson, Gary D., and Paul N. Wilson. 1994. Ejido reforms in Mexico: Conceptual issues and potential outcomes. *Land Economics* 70, no. 4: 448-465.

Turner, B.L., R.E. Kasperson, W.B. Meyer, K.M. Dow, D. Golding, J.X. Kasperson, R.C. Mitchell, and S.J. Ratick. 1990a. Two types of global environmental change: Definitional and spatial scale issues in their human dimensions. *Global Environmental Change* 1: 14-22.

Turner, B.L., W.C. Clark, R.W. Kates, J.F. Richards, J.T. Mathews, and W.B. Meyer. 1990b. *The Earth as transformed by human action: Global and regional changes in the biosphere over the past 300 years.* Cambridge, UK: Cambridge University Press.

UN (United Nations). 1980. *Patterns of urban and rural population growth.* New York: UN.

_____. 1992. Protection of the quality and supply of freshwater resources: Application of integrated approaches to the development, management and use of water resources. Chapter 18 of *Agenda 21.* New York: United Nations.

_____. 1993. *World population prospects: The 1992 revision.* New York: United Nations Department for Economic and Social Information and Policy Analysis.

_____. 1995a. *World urbanization prospects: The 1994 revision.* New York: United Nations.

_____. 1995b. The challenge of urbanization: The world's largest cities. Department for Economic and Social Information and Policy Analysis. Population Division. New York: United Nations.

_____. 1997a. *Critical trends: Global change and sustainable development.* New York: United Nations Department for Policy Coordination and Sustainable Development.

_____. 1997b. *Report of the Secretary-General on a comprehensive assessment of the freshwater resources of the world.* E/CN.17/1997/9. New York: United Nations.

_____. 1998. *World population prospects: The 1996 revision.* New York: United Nations Population Division.

_____. 1999 (forthcoming). *World population prospects: The 1998 revision.* New York: United Nations Population Division.

UNDP (UN Development Programme). 1992. *Human development report 1992.* New York: Oxford University Press.

_____. 1995. *Human development report 1995.* New York: Oxford University Press.

_____. 1996. *Human development report 1996.* New York: Oxford University Press.

_____. 1998. *Human development report 1998.* New York: Oxford University Press.

UNCHS (United Nations Centre for Human Settlements). 1996. *An urbanizing world: Global report on human settlements 1996.* Oxford: Oxford University Press.

UNEP (United Nations Environment Programme). Division of Environment Information and Assessment. 1996. *Characterization and assessment of groundwater quality concerns in Asia-Pacific region.* Nairobi: UNEP.

Vanderschueren, Franz, Emiel Wegelin and Kadmiel Wekwete. 1996. *Policy Programme Options for Urban Poverty Reduction: A Framework for Action at the Municipal Level.* Urban Management Program Paper No. 20. Washington, D.C.: The World Bank.

Vitousek, P., P. Ehrlich, A. Ehrlich, and P. Matson. 1986. Human appropriation of the products of photosynthesis. *Bioscience* 36: 368-373.

Vitousek, P.M., H.A. Mooney, J. Lubchenco, and J.M. Melillo. 1997. Human domination of earth's ecosystems. *Science* 277: 494-499.

WHO (World Health Organization). 1992. *Our planet, our health.* Geneva: WHO.

_____. 1996a. *The world health report 1996: Fighting disease and fostering development.* Geneva: World Health Organization.

_____. 1996b. *Groups at risk: WHO report on the Tuberculosis epidemic 1996.* Geneva, Switzerland: Global Tuberculosis Programme, WHO.

_____. 1996c. Water supply and sanitation sector monitoring report: 1996 (Sector Status as of 1994). Water Supply and Sanitation Collaborative Council and the United Nations Children's Fund. New York: UNICEF.

WRI (World Resources Institute). 1996. *World resources 1996-97: A guide to the global environment.* A joint publication by the World Resources Institute, the United Nations Environment Programme, the United Nations Development Programme, and the World Bank. New York: Oxford University Press.

_____. 1998. *World resources 1998-99: A guide to the global environment.* A joint publication by the World Resources Institute, the United Nations Environment Programme, the United Nations Development Programme, and the World Bank. New York: Oxford University Press.

Walker, H. Jesse. 1990. The coastal zone. Chapter 16 in *The earth as transformed by human action: Global and regional changes in the biosphere over the past 300 years,* eds. Turner et al. Cambridge, UK: Cambridge University Press.

Walsh, J. 1991. *Preserving the options: Food production and sustainability.* Working Papers on Issues of Agriculture. Washington, D.C.: Consultative Group on International Agricultural Research (CGIAR).

Wernick, I. 1996. Consuming Materials: The American way. *Technological Forecasting and Social Change* 53: 111-122.

Wernick, I. and J. Ausubel. 1995. National materials flow and the environment. *Annual Review of Energy and Environment* 20: 463-492.

Wernick, I., R. Herman, S. Govind, and J. Ausubel. 1997. Materialization and dematerialization: Measures and trends. In *Technological Trajectories and the Human Environment,* eds. J. Ausubel and H. Langford, 135-156. Washington, D.C.: National Academy Press.

White, R.M. and R.H. White. 1997. Technological advance and global work patterns. *Cosmos Journal* 7: 63-67.

Williams, Michael. 1990. Forests. Chap. 11 in *The earth as transformed by human action: Global and regional changes in the biosphere over the past 300 years,* eds. Turner et al. Cambridge, UK: Cambridge University Press.

Wilson, Edward O. 1993. *The Diversity of Life.* Cambridge, MA: Harvard University Press.

Wilson, Mary E. 1994. Disease in evolution: Introduction. In *Disease in evolution: Global changes and emergence of infectious diseases.* Annals of the New York Academy of Sciences, vol. 740. Eds. Mary E. Wilson, Richard Levins, and Andrew Spielman. New York: New York Academy of Sciences.

World Bank. 1992. *World development report 1992: Development and environment.* New York: Oxford University Press.

World Bank. 1995. *Better Urban Services: Finding the Right Incentives.* Washington, D.C.: The World Bank.

World Bank. 1996. *Livable Cities for the 21st Century.* Washington, D.C.: The World Bank.

World Bank. 1999. *World Bank poverty update: Trends in poverty.* Washington, D.C.: The World Bank. Available http://www.worldbank.org. Visited 6/4/99.

World Commission on Environment and Development. 1987. *Our common future.* New York: Oxford University Press. (Brundtland Report)

Zlotnick, Hania. 1998. International migration 1965-1996: An overview. In *Population and Development Review* 24, no. 3.

ENDNOTES

1 This discussion applies generally to both quantities and rates of change in quantities of interests (e.g., population size and population growth rates). Depending on circumstances, the transitions or breaks of interest may reflect either first or second derivatives for the quantity in question.

2 UN (1997a).

3 Speth (1992).

4 Gell-Mann (1994).

5 UN (1999).

6 Bongaarts (1994); Bongaarts and Bruce (1997).

7 See UN (1994a, 1999).

8 UN (1999).

9 UN (1999).

10 National Research Council reports (for most recent list and full texts, see http://www.nap.edu) related to trends in urbanization include:

> *Clean Air and Highway Transportation: Mandates, Challenges, and Research Opportunities.* Transportation Research Board. (1997).
>
> *Managing Wastewater in Coastal Urban Areas.* Committee on Wastewater Management for Coastal Urban Areas. (1993).
>
> *Meeting Megacity Challenges: A Role for Innovation and Technology.* Committee on Meeting Megacity Challenges. (1999).
>
> *Perspectives on Urban Infrastructure.* Committee on National Urban Policy. (1984).
>
> *Rethinking the Ozone Problem in Urban and Regional Air Pollution.* Committee on Tropospheric Ozone Formation and Measurement. (1991).
>
> *Rethinking Urban Policy: Urban Development in an Advanced Economy.* Committee on National Urban Policy. (1983).
>
> *The Costs of Sprawl—Revisited.* Transportation Research Board. (1998).
>
> *The Role of Transit in Creating Livable Metropolitan Communities.* Transportation Research Board. (1997).
>
> *Toward Infrastructure Improvement: An Agenda for Research.* Committee for an Infrastructure Technology Research Agenda. (1994).
>
> *Transit and Urban Form.* Transportation Research Board. (1997).
>
> *Transit-Focused Development.* Transportation Research Board. (1997).
>
> *Urban Change and Poverty.* Committee on National Urban Policy. (1988).
>
> *Urban Policy in a Changing Federal System.* Committee on National Urban Policy. (1985).

11 UN (1999).

12 UN (1998).

13 Beckman (1988); WRI (1996), p. 151.

14 WRI (1996).

15 Beckmann (1988).

16 UN (1995).

17 WRI (1996), pp. 8-9; UN (1995).

18 UNDP (1995), pp. 134-35.

19 UNDP (1995), Ch. 1.

20 World Bank (1999).

21 UNDP (1995), Ch. 3.

22 Rostow (1961).

23 Ausubel and Herman (1988).

24 National Research Council reports (for most recent list and full texts, see http://www.nap.edu) related to wealth and consumption include:

Environmentally Significant Consumption: Research Directions. Committee on the Human Dimensions of Global Change. Eds. Paul Stern, Thomas Dietz, Venon Ruttan, Robert Socolow, and James Sweeney. (1997).

Linking Science and Technology to Society's Environmental Goals. National Forum on Science and Technology Goals. (1996).

25 Maddison (1995).

26 UNDP (1996).

27 UNDP (1996), p. 13.

28 Baumol et al. (1994).

29 Bruno et al. (1995).

30 Bacha (1978); Adelman and Robinson (1989)

31 UNDP (1998).

32 NRC (1997).

33 Councils of the Royal Society of London and the National Academy of Sciences (1992). Not all growth in consumption is necessarily resource-depleting, or "less available for future use," or environmentally damaging in that it "negatively impacts biophysical systems in such a way as to threaten human health, welfare, or other things people value." However, there is no readily accepted methodology for separating out resource-depleting or environmentally damaging consumption from general consumption, or to identify harmful transformations from those that are benign. Increasingly, almost any human-induced transformation turns out to be either resource-depleting or damaging to some valued environmental component, or both. At best, there may be methods of separating consumption into more or less damaging and depleting classes.

34 DoE/EIA (1998a,b, 1999).

35 NAE (1997).

36 Wernick and Ausubel (1995).

37 Wernick (1996).

38 National Research Council reports (for most recent list and full texts, see http://www.nap.edu) related to technology and work include:

Automotive Fuel Economy: How Far Should We Go? Committee on Fuel Economy of Automobiles and Light Trucks. (1992).

Bridge Builders: African Experiences with Information and Communication Technology. Office of International Affairs. (1996).

Building an Effective Environmental Management Science Program: Final Assessment. Committee on Building an Environmental Management Science Program. (1997).

Building for Tomorrow: Global Enterprise and the U.S. Construction Industry. Committee on the International Construction Industry. (1988).

Clean Production in Rapidly Industrializing Countries: Challenges and Opportunities. National Academy of Engineering (NAE), Office of International Affairs. (1998).

Commercialization of New Materials for a Global Economy. National Materials Advisory Board. (1993).

Corporate Restructuring and Industrial Research and Development. Academy Industry Program. (1990).

Disposal of Industrial and Domestic Wastes: Land and Sea Alternatives. Panel on Land and Sea Alternatives for the Disposal of Industrial and Domestic Wastes. (1984).

Education for the Manufacturing World of the Future. Robert Frosch and Erich Bloch, Symposium on Education for the Manufacturing World of the Future. (1985).

Engineering and the Advancement of Human Welfare: Ten Outstanding Achievements 1964-1989. NAE. (1989).

Engineering Within Ecological Constraints. NAE. Ed. Peter Schulze. (1996).

In Situ Bioremediation: When Does it Work? Committee on In Situ Bioremediation. (1993).

Industrial Ecology: US-Japan Perspectives. NAE. Eds. Deanna Richards and Ann Fullerton. (1994).

Information Technologies and Social Transformation. NAE. Eds. Joseph V. Charyk and Bruce Guile. (1985).

Information Technology and the Conduct of Research: The User's View. Panel on Information Technology and the Conduct of Research. (1989).

Integrated Environmental and Economic Accounting. Committee on National Statistics. (1999).

Intrinsic Remediation of Contaminants in Subsurface Environments. Water Science and Technology Board. In progress.

Keeping Pace with Science and Engineering: Case Studies in Environmental Regulation. NAE. (1993).

Linking Science and Technology to Society's Environmental Goals. National Forum on Science and Technology Goals. (1996).

Marshaling Technology for Development: Proceedings of a Symposium. Technology and Development Steering Committee. Eds. Gerald Dineen and Jean-Françoise Rischard. Office of International Affairs. (1995).

Mastering a New Role: Shaping Technology Policy for National Economic Performances. NAE. Committee on Technology Policy Options in a Global Economy. (1993).

Measures of Environmental Performance and Ecosystem Conditions. NAE. Ed. Peter Schulze. (1999).

National Interests in an Age of Global Technology. NAE. Committee on Engineering as an International Enterprise. Eds. Thomas H. Lee and Proctor P. Reids. (1991).

Opportunities in Applied Environmental Research and Development. Committee on Opportunities in Applied Environmental Research and Development. (1991).

Putting Biotechnology to Work: Bioprocess Engineering. Committee on Bioprocess Engineering. (1992).

Realizing the Information Future: The Internet and Beyond. RENAISSANCE Committee. (1994).

Responding to Changes in Sea Level: Engineering Implications. Committee on Engineering Implications of Changes in Relative Mean Sea Level. (1987).

Restoring and Protecting Marine Habitat: The Role of Engineering and Technology. Committee on the Role of Technology in Marine Habitat. (1994).

Review of the Research Program of the Partnership for a New Generation of Vehicles (Phase 4). Standing Committee to Review the Research Program of the Partnership for a New Generation of Vehicles. (1998).

Review of the Research Program of the Partnership for a New Generation of Vehicles, Fifth Report. Board on Energy and Environmental Systems and the Transportation Research Board. (1999).

Technological Trajectories and the Human Environment. NAE. Eds. Jesse H. Ausubel and H. Dale Langford. (1997).

Technology and Environment. NAE. Eds. Jesse H. Ausubel and Hedy E. Sladovich. (1989).

The Ecology of Industry: Sectors and Linkages. NAE. Eds. Deanna Richards and Greg Pearson. (1998).

The Greening of Industrial Ecosystems. NAE. Eds. Braden Allenby and Deanna Richards. (1994).

The Industrial Green Game: Implications for Environmental Design and Management. NAE. Ed. Deanna Richards. (1997).

Tracking Toxic Substances at Industrial Facilities: Engineering Mass Balance Versus Materials Accounting. Committee to Evaluate Mass Balance Information for Facilities Handling Toxic Substances. (1990).

[39] API (1998).

[40] E.g., the experience of the Department of Defense and later NASA in the United States. See Hughes (1998).

[41] PCAST (1997); Grübler (1998).

[42] Grübler (1998), Fig. 6.17, p. 243.

[43] Grübler, A. (1998), Pages 644-247, Sec. 6.6.4, Table 6.5; NAE (1994).

[44] BLS (1998, 1999); McGrattan and Rogerson (1998).

[45] Schor (1991).

[46] Rifkin (1995); White and White (1997); Freeman and Soete (1987).

[47] Brown et al. (1994).

[48] Mathews (1997).

[49] See International Telecommunications Union Yearbook of Statistics (1999).

[50] 1988 figures, UNDP (1992); 1995 figures, UNDP (1998).

[51] NUA Internet Surveys (1998).

[52] Kempton et al. (1995); Dunlap (1997).

[53] Zlotnick (1998).

[54] WRI (1996).

[55] Brown et al. (1998, refugees, p. 105; trends, p. 77).

[56] Runge (1997).

[57] Rapid transmission of infectious diseases, WRI (1998); biological invasions, Vitousek et al. (1997).

[58] Zlotnick (1998).

[59] Marty and Appleby (1991).

[60] Putnam (1995).

[61] Mathews (1997).

[62] Jodha (1986); Jodha (1987); Ostrom (1990); Thompson and Wilson (1994).

[63] Sensenbrenner (1994).

[64] National Research Council reports (for most recent list and full texts, see http://www.nap.edu) related to rates, scales, and multiple stresses of global change include:

A Plan for a Research Program on Aerosol Radiative Forcing and Climate Change. Panel on Aerosol Radiative Forcing and Climate Change. Ed. John H. Seinfeld. (1996).

A Review of the U.S. Global Change Research Program and NASA's Mission to Planet Earth/Earth Observing System. Committee on Global Change Research. (1995).

China and Global Change: Opportunities for Collaboration. Panel on Global Climate Change Sciences in China. (1992).

Coastal Meteorology: A Review of the State of the Science. Committee on Meteorological Analysis, Prediction and Research. (1992).

Earth Observations From Space: History, Promise, and Reality. (1995).

Effects of Past Global Change on Life. Board on Earth Sciences and Resources. (1995).

Finding the Forest in the Trees: The Challenge of Combining Diverse Environmental Data. Committee for a Pilot Study on DAtabase Interfaces. (1995).

Four-Dimensional Model Assimilation of Data: A Strategy for the Earth System Sciences. Panel on Model-assimilated Data Sets for Atmospheric and Oceanic Research. (1991).

Global Change and Our Common Future: Papers from a Forum. Committee on Global Change. (1989).

Global Environmental Change: Research Pathways for the Next Decade. Committee on Global Change Research. (1998).

Global Environmental Change: Understanding the Human Dimensions. Committee on Human Dimensions of Global Change. (1991).

GOALS (Global Ocean-Atmosphere-Land System) for Predicting Seasonal-to-Interannual Climate: A Program of Observation, Modeling, and Analysis. Climate Research Committee. (1994).

Material Fluxes on the Surface of the Earth. Board on Earth Sciences and Resources. (1994).

National Science and Technology Strategies in a Global Context: Report of an International Symposium. Government-University-Industry Research Roundtable. (1998).

Oceanography in the Next Decade: Building New Partnerships. Ocean Studies Board. (1993).

One Earth, One Future: Our Changing Global Environment. Cheryl Silver and Ruth DeFries. (1992).

Opportunities and Priorities in Arctic Geoscience. Committee on Arctic Solid-Earth Geosciences. (1991).

Ozone Depletion, Greenhouse Gases, and Climate Change. Proceedings of a Joint Symposium by the Board on Atmospheric Sciences and Climate and the Committee on Global Change Research. (1989).

Policy Implications of Greenhouse Warming: Mitigation, Adaptation, and the Science Base. Committee on Science, Engineering, and Public Policy. (1992).

Research Strategies for the USGCRP. Committee on Global Change. (1990).

Research to Protect, Restore, and Manage the Environment. Committee on Environmental Research. (1993).

Review of EPA's Environmental Monitoring and Assessment Program: Overall Evaluation. Committee to Review the EPA's Environmental Monitoring and Assessment Program. (1995).

Science Policy and the Coast: Improving Decision-Making. Committee on Science and Policy for the Coastal Ocean. (1996).

Science Priorities for the Human Dimensions of Global Change. Committee on the Human Dimensions of Global Change. (1994).

Sea-Level Change. Geophysics Study Committee. (1990).

Solar Influences on Global Change. Board on Global Change. (1994).

Solid-Earth Sciences and Society. Committee on the Status and Research Opportunities in the Solid Earth Sciences: A Critical Assessment. (1993).

The Ocean's Role in Global Change: Progress of Major Research Programs. Ocean Studies Board. (1994).

The U.S. Global Change Research Program: An Assessment of FY 1991 Plans. Committee on Global Change. (1990).

Toward an Understanding of Global Change: Initial Priorities for U.S. Contributions to the International Geosphere-Biosphere Program. Committee on Global Change. (1989).

Understanding Risk: Informing Decisions in a Democratic Society. Committee on Risk Characterization. Eds. Paul C. Stern and Harvey V. Fineberg. (1996).

65 Kates et al. (1990).
66 Turner et al. (1990b).
67 Ibid.
68 Vitousek et al. (1986); Postel et al. (1996); Vitousek et al. (1997).
69 Vitousek et al. (1986).
70 Postel et al. (1996).
71 Cohen (1995), Ch. 14.

[72] Vitousek et al. (1997).

[73] Kasperson et al. (1995), p. 524.

[74] Kates and Clark (1996).

[75] Turner et al. (1990b).

[76] World Bank (1992).

[77] First discovered by Grossman and Krueger (1991); for review of debate, see e.g., Arrow et al. (1995).

[78] National Research Council reports (for most recent list and full texts, see http://www.nap.edu) related to atmosphere and climate include:

A Plan for a Research Program on Aerosol Radiative Forcing and Climate Change. Panel on Aerosol Radiative Forcing and Climate Change. (1996).

Acid Deposition: Atmospheric Processes in Eastern North America. Committee on Atmospheric Transport and Chemical Transformation in Acid Precipitation. (1983).

Acid Deposition: Long-Term Trends. Committee on Monitoring and Assessment of Trends in Acid Deposition. (1986).

Air Pollution, the Automobile, and Public Health. Eds. Ann Watson, Richard Bates, and Donald Kennedy. (1998).

Air Quality, Environment, and Energy. Transportation Research Board. (1992).

Atmosphere-Biosphere Interactions: Toward a Better Understanding of the Ecological Consequences of Fossil Fuel Combustion. Committee on the Atmosphere and Biosphere. (1981).

Carbon Dioxide and Climate Change. NAS Colloquium. Proceedings of the National Academy of Sciences. (1997).

China and Global Change: Opportunities for Collaboration. Panel on Global Climate and Sciences in China. (1992).

Clean Air and Highway Transportation: Mandates, Challenges, and Research Opportunities. Transportation Research Board. (1997).

Climate, Climatic Change, and Water Supply. Geophysics Research Board. (1977).

Coastal Meteorology: A Review of the State of the Science. Committee on Meteorological Analysis, Prediction and Research. (1992).

Confronting Climate Change: Strategies for Energy Research and Development. Committee on Alternative Energy Research and Development Strategies. (1990).

Decade-to-Century-Scale Climate Variability and Change: A Science Strategy. Panel on Climate Variability on Decade-to-Century Time Scales. (1998).

Expanding Metropolitan Highways: Implications for Air Quality and Energy Use. Transportation Research Board. (1995).

Global Change and Our Common Future: Papers from a Forum. Committee on Global Change. (1989).

Global Energy and Water Cycle Experiment (GEWEX) Continental-Scale International Project: A Review of Progress and Opportunities. GEWEX Panel. (1998).

Global Environmental Change: Research Pathways for the Next Decade. Committee on Global Change Research. (1999).

GOALS (Global Ocean-Atmosphere-Land System) for Predicting Seasonal-to-Interannual Climate: A Program of Observation, Modeling and Analysis. Climate Research Committee. (1994).

Haze in the Grand Canyon: An Evaluation of the Winter Haze Intensive Tracer Experiment. Committee on Haze in National Parks and Wilderness Areas. (1990).

Learning to Predict Climate Variations Associated with El Niño and the Southern Oscillation: Accomplishments and Legacies of the TOGA Program. Advisory Panel for the Tropical Oceans and Global Atmosphere Program. (1996).

Making Climate Forecasts Matter. Panel on the Human Dimensions of Seasonal-to-Interannual Climate Variation. Eds. Paul C. Stern and William E. Easterling. (1999).

Natural Climate Variability on Decade-to-Century Time Scales. Climate Research Committee. (1995).

Ozone Depletion, Greenhouse Gases, and Climate Change. Proceedings of a Joint Symposium by the Board on Atmospheric Sciences and Climate and the Committee on Global Change Research. (1989).

Policy Implications of Greenhouse Warming: Mitigation, Adaptation, and the Science Base. Committee on Science, Engineering and Public Policy. (1992).

Policy Implications of Greenhouse Warming—Synthesis Panel. Committee on Science, Engineering and Public Policy. (1991).

Research Priorities for Airborne Particulate Matter. Committee on Research Priorities for Airborne Particulate Matter. (1998).

Research Strategies for the U.S. Global Change Research Program. Committee on Global Change. (1990).

Rethinking the Ozone Problem in Urban and Regional Air Pollution. Committee on Tropospheric Ozone Formation and Measurement. (1991).

Review of the North American Research Strategy for Tropospheric Ozone (NARSTO) Program. (1998).

Solar Influences on Global Change. Board on Global Change. (1994).

The Atmospheric Effects of Stratospheric Aircraft Project: An Interim Review of Science and Progress. Panel on the Atmospheric Effects of Aviation. (1998).

The Atmospheric Sciences Entering the Twenty-First Century. Board on Atmospheric Sciences and Climate. (1998).

The U.S. Global Change Research Program: An Assessment of the FY 1991 Plans. Committee on Global Change. (1990).

The United States Antarctic Research Report to the Scientific Committee on Antarctic Research (SCAR): Number 32 - 1990. Polar Research Board. (1991).

Toward a Sustainable Future: Addressing the Long-Term Effects of Motor Vehicle Transportation on Climate and Ecology. Transportation Research Board. (1997).

79 Atmospheric chemistry of the chlorofluorocarbons, Rowland and Molina (1975); ozone hole over the Antarctic, Farman et al. (1985); chemical explanation, Crutzen et al. (1986); Solomon et al. (1986); Anderson et al. (1989); treaty background, Benedick (1991).

80 Montzka et al. (1996).

81 IPCC (1996); see Mahlman (1997).

82 WRI (1996).

83 IPCC (1996), pp. 6-7.

84 Logan (1994); Simmonds et al. (1997).

85 Lee et al. (1998).

86 Husain et al. (1998); NRC (1986).

87 Husain et al. (1998).

88 Khalil and Rasmussen (1994); Novelli et al. (1994); Simmonds et al. (1997).

89 Ibid.

90 National Research Council reports (for most recent list and full texts, see http://www.nap.edu) related to the oceans include:

A Plan for a Research Program on Aerosol Radiative Forcing and Climate Change. Panel on Aerosol Radiative Forcing and Climate Change. (1996).

A Scientific Strategy for U.S. Participation in the GOALS (Global Ocean-Atmosphere-Land System) Component of the CLIVAR (Climate Variability and Predictability) Programme. GOALS Panel, Climate Research Committee. (1998).

Alternatives for Inspecting Outer Continental Shelf Operations. Committee on Alternatives for Inspecting Outer Continental Shelf Operations. (1990).

An Assessment of Atlantic Bluefin Tuna. Committee to Review Atlantic Bluefin Tuna. (1994).

Applications of Analytical Chemistry to Oceanic Carbon Cycle Studies. Committee on Oceanic Carbon. (1993).

Assessment of the U.S. Outer Continental Shelf Environmental Studies Program I: Physical Oceanography. Committee to Review the Outer Continental Shelf Environmental Studies Program. (1990).

Assessment of the U.S. Outer Continental Shelf Environmental Studies Program II: Ecology. Committee to Review the Outer Continental Shelf Environmental Studies Program. (1992).

Assessment of the U.S. Outer Continental Shelf Environmental Studies Program III: Social and Economic Studies. Committee to Review the Outer Continental Shelf Environmental Studies Program. (1993).

Assessment of the U.S. Outer Continental Shelf Environmental Studies Program IV: Lessons and Opportunities. Committee to Review the Outer Continental Shelf Environmental Studies Program. (1993).

Beach Nourishment and Protection. Committee on Beach Nourishment and Protection. (1995).

Biodiversity. Ed. E. O. Wilson. (1988).

Building Ocean Science Partnerships: The U.S. and Mexico Working Together. Committee on U.S.-Mexico Collaboration for Ocean Science. (1998).

Causes and Management of Coastal Eutrophication. Ocean Studies Board, Water Science and Technology Board. (1999).

Clean Ships, Clean Ports, Clean Oceans: Controlling Garbage and Plastic Wastes at Sea. Committee on Shipborne Wastes. (1995).

Coastal Meteorology: A Review of the State of the Science. Committee on Meteorological Analysis, Prediction, and Research. (1992).

Contaminated Marine Sediments: Assessment and Remediation. Committee on Contaminated Marine Sediments. (1989).

Contaminated Sediments in Ports and Waterways: Cleanup Strategies and Technologies. Committee on Contaminated Marine Sediments. (1997).

Double-Hull Tanker Legislation: An Assessment of the Oil Pollution Act of 1990. Committee on Oil Pollution Act of 1990 (Section 4115) Implementation Review. (1998).

Dredging Coastal Ports: An Assessment of the Issues. Technical Panel on Ports, Harbors, and Navigational Channels. (1985).

Environmental Information for Alaskan Outer Continental Shelf Oil and Gas Decisions. Committee to Review Alaskan Outer Continental Shelf Environmental Information. (1994).

Environmental Science in the Coastal Zone: Issues for Further Research. Proceedings of a Retreat. (1994).

Four-Dimensional Model Assimilation of Data: A Strategy for the Earth System Sciences. Panel on Model-Assimilated Data Sets for Atmospheric and Oceanic Research. (1991).

Geodesy in the Year 2000. Committee on Geodesy. (1990).

Global Change and Our Common Future: Papers from a Forum. Committee on Global Change. (1989).

Global Energy and Water Cycle Experiment (GEWEX) Continental-Scale International Project: A Review of Progress and Opportunities. GEWEX Panel. (1998).

Global Ocean Science: Toward an Integrated Approach. Committee on Major U.S. Oceanographic Research Programs. (1998).

GOALS (Global Ocean-Atmosphere-Land System) for Predicting Seasonal-to-Interannual Climate: A Program of Observation, Modeling, and Analysis. GOALS Panel. Climate Research Committee. (1994).

International Network of Global Fiducial Stations: Science and Implementation Issues. Panel on Global Network of Fiducial Sites. (1991).

Managing Coastal Erosion. Committe on Coastal Erosion Zone Management. (1990).

Managing Troubled Waters: The Role of Marine Environmental Monitoring. Committe on a Systems Assessment of Marine Environmental Monitoring. (1990).

Managing Wastewater in Coastal Urban Areas. Committee on Wastewater Management for Coastal Urban Areas. (1993).

Marine Aquaculture: Opportunities for Growth. Committee on Assessment of Technology and Opportunities for Marine Aquaculture in the U.S. (1992).

Material Fluxes on the Surface of the Earth. Board on Earth Sciences and Resources. (1990).

Measuring and Understanding Coastal Processes. Committee on Coastal Engineering Measurement Systems. (1989).

Monitoring Southern California's Coastal Waters. Panel on the Southern California Bight. (1990).

National Collaboratories: Applying Information Technology for Scientific Research. Committee on a National Collaboratory: Establishing the User and Developer Partnership. (1993).

Natural Climate Variability on Decade-to-Century Time Scales. Climate Research Committee. (1995).

North American Continent-Ocean Transects Program. U.S. Geodynamics Committee. (1989).

Nutrient Requirements of Fish. Committee on Animal Nutrition, Subcommittee on Fish Nutrition. (1993).

Oceanography in the Next Decade: Building New Partnerships. Ocean Studies Board. (1993).

Opportunities and Needs in Coastal Engineering Research and Education. Committee on Opportunities in the Hydrologic Sciences. (1998).

Opportunities and Priorities in Arctic Geoscience. Committee on Arctic Solid-Earth Geosciences. (1991).

Opportunities in Ocean Sciences: Challenges on the Horizon. Ocean Studies Board. (1999).

Opportunities in the Hydrologic Sciences. Committee on Opportunities in the Hydrologic Sciences. (1990).

Opportunities to Improve Marine Forecasting. Committee on Opportunities to Improve Marine Observations and Forecasting. (1989).

Our Seabed Frontier: Challenges and Choices. Committee on Seabed Utilization in the Exclusive Economic Zone. (1989).

Priorities for Coastal Ecosystem Science. Committee to Identify High-Priority Science to Meet National Coastal Needs. (1995).

Reassessment of the Marine Salvage Posture of the United States. Committee on Marine Salvage Issues. (1994).

Responding to Changes in Sea Level: Engineering Implications. Committee on Engineering Implications of Changes in Relative Sea Level. (1987).

Restoring and Protecting Marine Habitat: The Role of Engineering and Technology. Committee on the Role of Technology in Marine Habitat. (1994).

Science and Stewardship in the Antarctic. Committee on Antarctic Policy and Science. (1993).

Science Policy and the Coast: Improving Decision-Making. Committee on Science and Policy for the Coastal Ocean. (1996).

Sea-Level Change. Geophysics Study Committee, Panel on Sea Level Change. (1990).

Solar Influences on Global Change. Board on Global Change. (1994).

Stemming the Tide: Controlling Introductions of Nonindigenous Species by Ships' Ballast Water. Committee on Ships' Ballast Operations. (1996).

Striking a Balance: Improving Stewardship of Marine Areas. Committee on Marine Area Governance and Management. (1997).

Sustaining Marine Fisheries. Committee on Ecosystem Management for Sustainable Marine Fisheries. (1998).

Tanker Spills: Prevention by Design. Committee on Tank Vessel Design. (1991).

The Bering Sea Ecosystem. Committee on the Bering Sea Ecosystem. (1996).

The Global Ocean Observing System: Users, Benefits, and Priorities. Committee to Review U.S. Planning for a Global Ocean Observing System. (1997).

The Ocean's Role in Global Change: Progress of Major Research Programs. Ocean Studies Board. (1994).

The United States Antarctic Research Report to the Scientific Committee on Antarctic Research (SCAR) Number 32 - 1990. Polar Research Board. (1991).

Understanding Marine Biodiversity. Committee on Biological Diversity in Marine Systems. (1995).

Upstream: Salmon and Society in the Pacific Northwest. Committee on Protection and Management of Pacific Northwest Anadromous Salmonids. (1996).

Using Oil Spill Dispersants on the Sea. Committee on the Effectiveness of Oil Spill Dispersants. (1989).

[91] Jickells et al. (1990).

[92] Walker (1990).

[93] NRC (1994).

[94] Douglas (1995).

[95] NRC (1995a).

[96] FAO (1997).

[97] NMFS (1997).

[98] NRC (1999a).

[99] NRC (1999a).

[100] NMFS (1996).

[101] NRC (1996).

[102] NRC (1995b).

[103] NRC (1998b).

[104] NRC (1996).

[105] NRC (1998b).

[106] E.g., NRC (1996), Ch. 13.

[107] NRC (1998b).

[108] Costanza et al. (1998); NRC (1998b).

[109] National Research Council reports (for most recent list and full texts, see http://www.nap.edu) related to fresh water include:

A New Era for Irrigation. Committee on the Future of Irrigation in the Face of Competing Demands. (1996).

A Review of the USGS National Water Quality Assessment Pilot Program. Committee to Review the USGS National Water Quality Assessment Pilot Program. (1990).

Alternatives for Ground Water Cleanup. Committee on Ground Water Cleanup Alternatives. (1994).

Assessment of Water Resources Project Planning Procedures. Water Science and Technology Board. (1999).

Climate, Climatic Change, and Water Supply. Panel on Water and Climate. (1977).

Colorado River Ecology and Dam Management: Proceedings of a Symposium, May 24-25, 1990, Santa Fe, New Mexico. Committee to Review the Glen Canyon Environmental Studies. (1991).

Drinking Water and Health. Volumes 5, 6, 7, 8, 9. Safe Drinking Water Committee. (1983-1989).

Drought Management and Its Impact on Public Water Systems. Report of a Symposium Sponsored by the Water Science and Technology Board. (1986).

Freshwater Ecosystems: Revitalizing Educational Programs in Limnology. Committee on Inland Aquatic Ecosystems. (1996).

Ground Water and Soil Contamination Remediation: Toward Compatible Science, Policy, and Public Perception: Report of a Colloquium. Sponsored by the Water Science and Technology Board. (1990).

Ground Water at Yucca Mountain: How High Can it Rise? Panel on Hydrologic/Tectonic/Hydrothermal Systems at Yucca Mountain. (1992).

Ground Water Models: Scientific and Regulatory Applications. Committee on Ground Water Modeling Assessment. (1990).

Ground Water Recharge Using Waters of Impaired Quality. Committee on Ground Water Recharge. (1994).

Ground Water Vulnerability Assessment: Predicting Relative Contamination Potential Under Conditions of Uncertainty. Committee on Techniques for Assessing Ground Water Vulnerability. (1993).

Hazardous Waste Site Management: Water Quality Issues. Report of a Colloquium. Water Science and Technology Board. (1988).

Hydrologic Sciences: Taking Stock and Looking Ahead. Proceedings of the 1997 Abel Wolman Distinguished Lecture and Symposium on the Hydrologic Sciences. Water Science and Technology Board. (1998).

Irrigation-Induced Water Quality Problems. Committee on Irrigation Induced Water Quality Problems. (1989).

Issues in Potable Reuse: The Viability of Augmenting Drinking Water Supplies with Reclaimed Water. Committee to Evaluate the Viability of Augmenting Potable Water Supplies with Reclaimed Water. (1998).

Managing Wastewater in Coastal Urban Areas. Committee on Wastewater Management for Coastal Urban Areas. (1993).

Managing Water Resources in the West Under Conditions of Climate Uncertainty: A Proceedings of a Colloquium. Committee on Climate Uncertainty and Water Resources Management. (1991).

Mexico City's Water Supply: Improving the Outlook for Sustainability. Joint Academies Committee on the Mexico City Water Supply. (1995).

Nature and Human Society: The Quest for a Sustainable World. Committee for the Second Forum on Biodiversity. Eds. Peter Raven and Tania Williams. (1999).

New Directions in Water Resources Planning for the U.S. Army Corps of Engineers. Committee to Assess the U.S. Army Corps of Engineers Water Resources Project Planning Procedures. (1999).

New Strategies for America's Watersheds. Committee on Watershed Management. (1999).

Opportunities in the Hydrologic Sciences. Committee on Opportunities in the Hydrologic Sciences. (1991).

Preparing for the Twenty-First Century: A Report to the USGS Water Resources Division. Committee on USGS Water Resources Research. (1991).

Proceedings of the 1997 Abel Wolman Distinguished Lecture and Symposium on the Hydrologic Sciences. Water Science and Technology Board. (1997).

Restoration of Aquatic Ecosystems: Science, Technology and Public Policy. Committee on Restoration of Aquatic Ecosystems. (1992).

Safe Water from Every Tap: Improving Water Service to Small Communities. Committee on Small Water Supply Systems. (1997).

Setting Priorities for Drinking Water Contaminants. Committee on Drinking Water Contaminants. (1998).

Soil and Water Quality: An Agenda for Agriculture. Committee on Long-Range Soil and Water Conservation. (1993).

Sustaining our Water Resources. Water Science and Technology Board. (1993).

Toward Sustainability: Soil and Water Research Priorities for Developing Countries. Committee on International Soil and Water Research and Development. (1991).

Upstream: Salmon and Society in the Pacific Northwest. Committee on Protection and Management of Pacific Northwest Anadromous Salmonids. (1996).

Use of Reclaimed Water and Sludge in Food Crop Production. Committee on the Use of Treated Municipal Wastewater Effluents and Sludge in the Production of Food Crops. (1996).

Valuing Ground Water: Economic Concepts and Approaches. Committee on Valuing Ground Water. (1997).

Water for the Future: The West Bank and Gaza Strip, Israel, and Jordan. Committee on Sustaining Water Supplies for the Middle East. (1999).

Water Transfers in the West: Efficiency, Equity and the Environment. Committee on Western Water Management. (1992).

Wetlands: Characteristics and Boundaries. Committee on Characterization of Wetlands. (1995).

[110] Increased water withdrawals, Shiklomanov (1993); reflecting-term trend of increasing withdrawals per capita (L'vovich and White (1990).

[111] UN (1997b).

[112] Gleick (1998).

[113] Gleick (1998), based on Shiklomanov (1993) and UN (1992).

[114] Gleick (1998).

[115] WRI (1998), NRC (1999b).

[116] UN (1997b).

[117] WHO (1996c).

[118] UN (1997a).

[119] Africa and Asia, Raskin (1997); Middle East, NRC (1999b).

[120] UN (1997b).

[121] Margat (1996).

[122] NRC (1998a).

[123] UN (1997a).

[124] L'vovich and White (1990).

[125] Nonrenewable aquifers, Schwarz et al. (1990); distant rivers, Kahrl (1982); husbanding and recycling, Bouwer (1992); NRC (1998a).

[126] Raskin, Hansen, and Margolis (1995).

[127] WRI (1998).

[128] UN (1997a).

129 WRI (1998).

130 UNEP (1996).

131 Gleick (1998).

132 Ibid.

133 Anderson (1991); the lack of adequate facilities, Gleick (1998); increase in algal blooms, Patz et al. (1996).

134 Gleick (1998); Raskin (1997).

135 NRC (1999b).

136 National Research Council reports (for most recent list and full texts, see http://www.nap.edu) related to land include:

A New Era for Irrigation. Committee on the Future of Irrigation in the Face of Competing Demands. (1996).

A Scientific Strategy for U.S. Participation in the GOALS (Global Ocean-Atmosphere-Land System) Component of CLIVAR (Climate Variability and Predictability) Programme. GOALS Panel, Climate Research Committee. (1998).

Agricultural Crop Issues and Policies. Committee on Managing Global Genetic Resources: Agricultural Imperatives. (1993).

Alternative Agriculture. Committee on the Role of Alternative Farming Methods in Modern Production Agriculture. (1989).

Biologic Markers of Air-Pollution Stress and Damage in Forests. Committee on Biologic Markers of Air Pollution Damage. (1989).

Biotechnology Unzipped: Promises and Realities. Eric S. Grace. Joseph Henry Press. (1997).

China and Global Change: Opportunities for Collaboration. Panel on Global Climate Change Sciences in China. (1992).

Colleges of Agriculture at the Land Grant Universities: A Profile. Committee on the Future of Land Grant Colleges of Agriculture. (1995).

Colleges of Agriculture at the Land Grant Universities: Public Service and Public Policy. Committee on the Future of Land Grant Colleges of Agriculture. (1996).

Cooperating With Nature: Confronting Natural Hazards with Land-Use Planning for Sustainable Communities. Ed. Raymond J. Burby. Joseph Henry Press. (1998).

Designing an Agricultural Genome Program. Board on Biology. (1998).

Ecological Risks: Perspectives from Poland and the United States. Eds. Wladyslaw Grodzinski, Ellis Cowling, Alicia Breymeyer and Anna Phillips. (1990).

Ecologically Based Pest Management: New Solutions for a New Century. Committee on Pest and Pathogen Control Through Management of Biological Control Agents. (1996).

Flood Risk Management and the American River Basin: An Evaluation. Committee on Flood Control Alternatives in the American River Basin. (1995).

Food Aid Projections for the Decade of the 1990s. Panel on Food Aid Requirements for the 1990s. (1989).

Forest Trees. Committee on Managing Global Genetic Resources: Agricultural Imperatives. (1991).

Forested Landscapes in Perspective: Prospects and Opportunities for Sustainable Management of America's Nonfederal Forests. Committee on Prospects and Opportunities for Sustainable Management of America's Nonfederal Forests. (1998).

Forestry Research: A Mandate for Change. Committee on Forestry Research. (1990).

Forests of the Pacific Northwest. Committee on Environmental Issues in Pacific Northwest Forest Management. (1998).

Future of Pesticides in Pest Management for U.S. Agriculture. Board on Environmental Studies and Toxicology. (1999).

Genetic Engineering of Plants: Agricultural Research Opportunities and Policy Concerns. Board on Agriculture. (1984).

Grasslands and Grassland Sciences in Northern China. Office of International Affairs. (1992).

Investing in Research: A Proposal to Strengthen the Agricultural, Food, and Environmental System. Board on Agriculture. (1989).

Irrigation-Induced Water Quality Problems: Planning for Remediation. Committee on Irrigation-Induced Water Quality Problems. (1996).

Land Use Planning and Oil and Gas Leasing on Onshore Federal Lands. Committee on Onshore Oil and Gas Leasing. (1989).

Livestock. Committee on Managing Global Genetic Resources: Agricultural Imperatives. (1993).

Lost Crops of Africa: Volume I: Grains. Board on Science and Technology for International Development. (1996).

Lost Crops of the Incas: Little-Known Plants of the Andes with Promise for Worldwide Cultivation. Panel on Lost Crops of the Incas. (1989).

Marine Aquaculture: Opportunities for Growth. Committee on Assessment of Technology and Opportunities for Marine Aquaculture in the U.S. (1992).

Microlivestock: Little-Known Small Animals with a Promising Future. Board on Science and Technology for International Development. (1991).

Mitigating Losses from Land Subsidence in the United States. Committee on Grand Failure Hazards Mitigation Panel on Land Subsidence. (1991).

Neem: A Tree for Solving Global Problems. Board on Science and Technology for International Development. (1992).

New Directions for Biosciences Research in Agriculture: High-Reward Opportunities. Committee on Biosciences Research in Agriculture. (1985).

Nutrient Requirements of Dairy Cattle. Committee on Animal Nutrition, Subcommittee on Dairy Cattle. (1989).

Nutrient Requirements of Fish. Committee on Animal Nutrition, Subcommittee on Fish Nutrition. (1993).

Nutrient Requirements of Horses. Committee on Animal Nutrition, Subcommittee on Horse Nutrition. (1989).

One Earth, One Future: Our Changing Global Environment. Cheryl Silver and Ruth DeFries. (1992).

Plant Biology Research and Training for the 21st Century. Committee on an Examination of Plant-Science Research Programs in the U.S. (1992).

Population and Land Use in Developing Countries: Report of a Workshop. Committee on Population. (1993).

Precision Agriculture in the 21st Century: Geospatial and Information Technologies in Crop Management. Committee on Assessing Crop Yield: Site-Specific Farming, Information Systems, and Research Opportunities. (1997).

Quality Protein Maize. Board on Science and Technology for International Development. (1988).

Rangeland Health: New Methods to Classify, Inventory, and Monitor Rangelands. Committee on Rangeland Classification. (1994).

Regenerating Agriculture: Policies and Practice for Sustainability and Self-Reliance. Jules N. Pretty. (1995).

Saline Agriculture: Salt Tolerant Plants for Developing Countries. Panel on Saline Agriculture for Developing Countries, Board on Science and Technology for International Development. (1990).

Setting Priorities for Land Conservation. Committee on Scientific and Technological Criteria for Federal Acquisition of Lands for Conservation. (1993).

Soil and Water Quality: An Agenda for Agriculture. Committee on Long-Range Soil Soil and Water Conservation. (1993).

Soil Conservation: An Assessment of the National Resources Inventory, Volume 1 and Volume 2. Committee on Conservation Needs and Opportunities. (1986).

Sustainable Agriculture and the Environment in the Humid Tropics. Committee on Sustainable Agriculture and the Environment in the Humid Tropics. (1993).

Sustainable Agriculture Research and Education in the Field: A Proceedings. Board on Agriculture. (1991).

Technological Trajectories and the Human Environment. Eds. Jesse Ausubel and H. Dale Langford. (1997).

The U.S. National Plant Germplasm System. Committee on Managing Global Genetic Resources: Agricultural Imperatives. (1991).

Toward Sustainability: A Plan for Collaborative Research on Agriculture and Natural Resource Management. Panel for Collaborative Research Support for AID's Sustainable Agriculture and Natural Resources Management Program. (1991).

Toward Sustainability: Integrated Pest Management as a Component of Sustainability Research. Subpanel on Integrated Pest Management, Panel for Collaborative Research Support for AID's Sustainable Agriculture and Natural Resources Management Program. (1992).

Toward Sustainability: Soil and Water Research Priorities for Developing Countries. Committee on International Soil and Water Research and Development. (1991).

Understanding Agriculture: New Directions for Education. Committee on Agricultural Education in Secondary Schools. (1998).

Use of Reclaimed Water and Sludge in Food Crop Production. Committee on the Use of Treated Municipal Wastewater Effluents and Sludge in Food Crop Production. (1996).

Vetiver Grass: A Thin Green Line Against Erosion. Board on Science and Technology for International Development. (1993).

Wood in Our Future: The Role of Life-Cycle Analysis: Proceedings of a Symposium. Board on Agriculture. (1997).

Xenotransplantation: Science, Ethics, and Public Policy. Institute of Medicine, Committee on Xenograft Transplantation: Ethical Issues and Public Policy. (1996).

[137] Richards (1990).
[138] Rozanov et al. (1990).
[139] Hayami and Ruttan (1985).
[140] Pinstrup-Anderson et al. (1997).
[141] Ausubel (1996b).
[142] Rasmussen et al. (1998).
[143] Khush (1995); Naylor (1996).
[144] Matson et al. (1997).
[145] Walsh (1991).
[146] Williams (1990).
[147] Noble and Dirizo (1997).
[148] Williams (1990).
[149] Noble and Dirizo (1997).
[150] Ciais et al. (1995).
[151] Simpson et al. (1996).
[152] Noble and Dirizo (1997).

153 National Research Council reports (for most recent list and full texts, see http://www.nap.edu) related to species and ecosystems include:

A Biological Survey for the Nation. Committee on the Formation of the National Biological Survey. (1993).

An Assessment of Atlantic Bluefin Tuna. Committee to Review Atlantic Bluefin Tuna. (1994).

An Evaluation of the U.S. Navy's Extremely Low Frequency Submarine Communications Ecological Monitoring Program. Committee to Evaluate the U.S. Navy's Exteremely Low Frequency Submarine Communications Ecological Monitoring Program. (1997).

Assessment of the U.S. Outer Continental Shelf Environmental Studies Program I: Ecology. Committee to Review the Outer Continental Shelf Environmental Studies Program. (1992).

Biodiversity. Ed. E. O. Wilson. (1988).

Biodiversity Conservation in Transboundary Protected Areas. Proceedings of an International Workshop, Bieszczady and Tatra National Parks, Poland. Eds. A. I. Breymeyer, R. D. Noble, and S. Deets. (1996).

Biodiversity II: Understanding and Protecting Our Biological Resources. Marjorie Reaka-Kudla, Don Wilson, and E. O. Wilson. Joseph Henry Press. (1995).

Building a Foundation for Sound Environmental Decisions. Committee on Research Opportunities and Priorities for EPA. (1997).

Chemical Ecology: The Chemistry of Biotic Interaction. Eds. Thomas Eisner and Jerrold Meinwald. (1995).

China and Global Change: Opportunities for Collaboration. Panel on Global Climate Change Sciences in China. (1992).

Colorado River Ecology and Dam Management: Proceedings of a Symposium May 24-25, 1990. Committee to Review the Glen Canyon Environmental Studies. (1991).

Conserving Biodiversity: A Research Agenda for Development Agencies. Panel on Biodiversity Research Priorities, Board on Science and Technology for International Development. (1992).

Contaminated Marine Sediments: Assessment and Remediation. Committee on Contaminated Marine Sediments. (1989).

Contaminated Sediments in Ports and Waterways: Cleanup Strategies and Technologies. Committee on Contaminated Marine Sediments. (1997).

Decline of the Sea Turtles: Causes and Prevention. Committee on Sea Turtle Conservation. (1990).

Dolphins and the Tuna Industry. Committee on Reducing Porpoise Mortality from Tuna Fishing. (1992).

Ecological Knowledge and Environmental Problem-Solving: Concepts and Case Studies. Committee on Applications of Ecological Theory to Environmental Problems. (1986).

Ecological Risks: Perspectives from Poland and the United States. Eds. Wladyslaw Grodzinski, Ellis Cowling, Alicia Breymeyer and Anna Phillips. (1990).

Ecologically-Based Pest Management: New Solutions for a New Century. Committee on Pest and Pathogen Control Through Management of Biological Control Agents. (1996).

Effects of Past Global Change on Life. Board on Earth Sciences and Resources. (1995).

Engineering Within Ecological Constraints. Ed. Peter C. Schulze. (1996).

Forest Trees. Committee on Managing Global Genetic Resources: Agricultural Imperatives. (1991).

Freshwater Ecosystems: Revitalizing Educational Programs in Limnology. Committee on Inland Aquatic Ecosystems. (1996).

Grasslands and Grassland Sciences in Northern China. Office of International Affairs. (1992).

Improving Fish Stock Assessments. Committee on Fish Stock Assessment Methods. (1998).

Land Use Planning and Oil and Gas Leasing on Onshore Federal Lands. Committee on Onshore Oil and Gas Leasing. (1989).

Linking Science and Technology to Society's Environmental Goals. National Forum on Science and Technology Goals. (1996).

Measures of Environmental Performance and Ecosystem Conditions. NAE. Ed. Peter Schulze. (1999).

Nature and Human Society: The Quest for a Sustainable World. Committee for the Second Forum on Biodiversity. Eds. Peter Raven and Tania Williams. (1999).

New Strategies for America's Watersheds. Committee on Watershed Management. (1999).

Perspectives on Biodiversity: Valuing Its Role in an Everchanging World. Committee on Economic and Noneconomic Value of Biodiversity. (1999).

Priorities for Coastal Ecosystem Science. Committee to Identify High-Priority Science to Meet National Coastal Needs. (1995).

Restoration of Aquatic Ecosystems: Science, Technology, and Public Policy. Committee on the Restoration of Aquatic Ecosystems. (1992).

River Resource Management in the Grand Canyon. Committee to Review the Glen Canyon Environmental Studies. (1996).

Science and the Endangered Species Act. Committee on Scientific Issues in the Endangered Species Act. (1995).

Shaping the Future: Biology and Human Values. Steve Olson. (1989).

Sharing the Fish: Toward a National Policy on Individual Fishing Quotas. Committee to Review Individual Fishing Quotas. (1999).

Soil and Water Quality: An Agenda for Agriculture. Committee on Long-Range Soil and Water Conservation. (1993).

Stemming the Tide: Controlling Introductions of Nonindigenous Species by Ships' Ballast Water. Committee on Ships' Ballast Operations. (1996).

Sustaining Marine Fisheries. Committee on Ecosystem Management for Sustainable Marine Fisheries. (1999).

Technological Trajectories and the Human Environment. NAE. Eds. Jesse H. Ausubel and H. Dale Langford. (1997).

The Bering Sea Ecosystem. Committee on the Bering Sea Ecosystem. (1996).

The Greening of Industrial Ecosystems. NAE. Eds. Braden Allenby and Deanna Richards. (1994).

The Mono Basin Ecosystem: Effects of Changing Lake Level. Mono Basin Ecosystem Study Committee. (1987).

The Ocean's Role in Global Change: Progress of Major Research Programs. Ocean Studies Board. (1994).

The Scientific Bases for Preservation of the Hawaiian Crow. Committee on the Scientific Bases for the Preservation of the Hawaiian Crow. (1992).

The Scientific Bases for Preservation of the Mariana Crow. Committee on the Scientific Bases for the Preservation of the Mariana Crow. (1997).

Toward a Sustainable Future: Addressing the Long-Term Effects of Motor Vehicle Transportation on Climate and Ecology. Transportation Research Board. (1997).

Understanding Marine Biodiversity: A Research Agenda for the Nation. Committee on Biological Diversity in Marine Systems. (1995).

Upstream: Salmon and Society in the Pacific Northwest. Committee on Protection and Management of Pacific Northwest Anadromous Salmonids. (1996).

Wetlands: Characteristics and Boundaries. Committee on Characterizations of Wetlands. (1995).

Wolves, Bears, and Their Prey in Alaska: Biological and Social Challenges in Wildlife Management. Committee on Management of Wolf and Bear Populations in Alaska. (1997).

154 The five commonly recognized mass extinctions of species were the Ordovician 440 million years ago, the Devonian 365 million years ago, the Permian 245 million years ago, the Triassic 210 million years ago, and the Cretaceaous 65 million years ago (see Wilson 1993, Ch. 3).

155 Lawton and May (1995).

156 Barbault and Sastrapradja (1995).

157 MacDonald et al. (1989).

158 NRC (1995b).

159 Cohen and Carlton (1995).

160 NRC (1995b).

161 IUCN (1996).

162 McAllister et al. (1997); NRC (1996).

163 Newell (1988); Lovejoy (1997).

164 Burke et al. (1998).

165 Daily (1997).

166 NRC (1988).

167 Ecological Society of America (1996); Daily (1997).

168 National Research Council reports (for most recent list and full texts, see http://www.nap.edu) related to disease organisms and vectors include:

Adverse Effects of Pertussis and Rubella Vaccines. Committee to Review the Adverse Consequences of Pertussis and Rubella Vaccines. (1991).

AIDS and Behavior: An Integrated Approach. Committee on Substance Abuse and Mental Health Issues in AIDS Research. (1994).

AIDS, Sexual Behavior, and Intravenous Drug Use. Committee on AIDS Research and the Behavioral, Social, and Statistical Sciences. (1989).

AIDS: The Second Decade. Committee on AIDS Research and the Behavioral, Social, and Statistical Sciences. (1990).

Antimicrobial Resistance: Issues and Options. Forum on Emerging Infections. Eds. Polly F. Harrison and Joshua Lederberg. (1998).

Assessing the Social and Behavioral Science Base for HIV/AIDS Prevention and Intervention: Workshop Summary. Committee on the Social and Behavioral Science Base for HIV/AIDS Prevention and Intervention. (1995).

Cattle Inspection. Committee on Evaluation of USDA Streamlined Inspection System for Cattle. (1990).

Companion Guide to Infectious Diseases of Mice and Rats. Committee on Infectious Diseases of Mice and Rats. (1991).

Conference on Human Health and Global Climate Change—Summary of the Proceedings. Eds. Valerie Setlow and Andrew Pope. (1996).

Confronting AIDS: Directions for Public Health, Health Care, and Research. Committee on a Naitonal Strategy for AIDS. (1986).

Confronting AIDS: Update 1988. Committee for the Oversight of AIDS Activities. (1988).

Ecologically Based Pest Management: New Solutions for a New Century. Committee on Pest and Pathogen Control Through Management of Biological Control Agents. (1996).

Effects of Health Programs on Child Mortality in Sub-Saharan Africa. Working Group on the Effects of Child Survival and General Health Programs on Mortality, Committee on Population. (1993).

Emerging Infections: Microbial Threats to Health in the United States. Committee on Microbial Threats to health in the United States. (1992).

Environmental Epidemiology, Volume I: Public Health and Hazardous Wastes. Committee on Environmental Epidemiology. (1991).

Environmental Medicine: Integrating a Missing Element into Medical Education. Committee on Curriculum Development in Environmental Medicine. (1995).

Evaluating AIDS Prevention Programs: Expanded Edition. Committee on AIDS Research and the Behavioral, Social, and Statistical Sciences. (1991).

Factors Affecting Contraceptive Use in Sub-Saharan Africa. Panel on Population Dynamics of Sub-Saharan Africa, Committee on Population. (1993).

Global Environmental Change: Understanding the Human Dimensions. Committee on Human Dimensions of Global Change. (1991).

Global Health in Transition: A Synthesis: Perspectives from International Organizations. Board on Internationl Health. Eds. John H. Bryant and Polly F. Harrison. (1996).

HIV and the Blood Supply: An Analysis of Crisis Decisionmaking. Committee to Study HIV Transmission through Blood and Blood Products. (1995).

In Her Lifetime: Female Morbidity and Mortality in Sub-Saharan Africa. Committee to Study Female Morbidity and Mortality in Sub-Saharan Africa. Ed. Christopher P. Howsen. (1996).

Infectious Diseases in an Age of Change: The Impact of Human Ecology and Behavior on Disease Transmission. Ed. Bernard Roizman. (1995).

Infectious Diseases of Mice and Rats. Committee on Infectious Diseases of Mice and Rats. (1991).

Issues in Potable Reuse: The Viability of Augmenting Drinking Water Supplies with Reclaimed Water. Committee to Evaluate the Viability of Augmenting Potable Water Supplies with Reclaimed Water. (1998).

Linking Research and Public Health Practice: A Review of CDC's Program of Centers for Research and Demonstration of Health Promotion and Disease Prevention. (1997).

Livestock: Managing Global Genetic Resources: Agricultural Imperatives. Committee on Managing Global Genetic Resources: Agricultural Imperatives. Subcommittee on Animal Genetic Resources. (1993).

Malaria: Obstacles and Opportunities. Committee for the Study of Malaria Prevention and Control: Status Review and Alternative Strategy. (1991).

National Academy of Sciences Colloquium: Genetic Engineering of Viruses and Viral Vectors. Proceedings of the National Academy of Sciences. (1996).

New Vaccine Development: Establishing Priorities; Volume II, Diseases of Importance in Developing Countries. Committee on Issues and Priorities for New Vaccine Development. (1986).

Preventing and Mitigating AIDS in Sub-Saharan Africa: Research and Data Priorities for the Social and Behavioral Sciences. Panel on Data and Research Priorities for Arresting AIDS in Sub-Saharan Africa. Eds. Barney Cohen and James Trussell. (1996).

Preventing HIV Transmission: The Role of Sterile Needles and Bleach. Panel on Needle Exchange and Bleach Distribution Programs. (1995).

Rodents. Institute of Laboratory Animal Resources, Committee on Rodents. (1996).

The Epidemiological Transition: Policy and Planning Implications for Developing Countries: Workshop Proceedings. Committee on Population, Board on International Health. (1993).

The Hidden Epidemic: Confronting Sexually Transmitted Diseases, Summary. Committee on Prevention and Control of Sexually Transmitted Diseases. (1997).

The Social Impact of AIDS in the United States. Committee on AIDS Research and the Behavioral, Social, and Statistical Sciences. (1993).

Vaccines for the 21st Century: A Tool for Setting Priorities. Committee to Develop Priorities for Vaccine Development. Eds. Kathleen R. Stratton, Jane S. Durah, and Michael A. Stoto. (1998).

Valuing Health Risks, Costs, and Benefits for Environmental Decisionmaking: Report of a Conference. Steering Committee on Valuing Health Risks, Costs, and Benefits for Environmental Decisions. Eds. P. Brett Hammond and Rob Coppock. (1990).

[169] WHO (1996a).

[170] Ibid.

[171] Bradley (1994).

[172] WHO (1992).

[173] Dobson et al. (1997).

[174] Lindsay and Birley (1996).

[175] Death from tuberculosis, WHO (1996b): disease and increasing poverty and homelessness in urban areas, Stephens (1996); multidrug resistance, Wilson (1994).

[176] WHO (1996b).

[177] IOM (1992).

[178] See Patz et al. (1996).

 **3** Exploring the Future

T he previous chapter examined past trends and ongoing transitions that will need to be confronted in efforts to navigate a transition toward sustainability. This chapter looks to the future. We recognize that much of the continuing interaction between human development and the environment will be a process of "muddling through." The inevitable trial-and-error of selecting a course, learning, and correction will be carried out less by efforts to think through our futures than by the necessity of acting them out. The decisive factor in determining how effective, fair, and efficient this muddling will be is in our choices not of analytic tools, but rather of the social institutions that help to provide the incentives and feedbacks necessary for social learning. We nonetheless believe that the inevitable trials may be made more productive, and the likelihood of costly and irreversible errors may be reduced through organized efforts to assess the possible future implications of present trends, relying on growing understanding of earth system processes and social goals. The international efforts in recent years to address threats to the stratospheric ozone layer is a case in point. Understanding as much as possible about what the future may hold is important. It can identify things societies should try to avoid. It can give useful insights about what societies should do now to prepare for plausible contingencies. It can even help societies to learn what they ought to want for the future, by helping to illuminate the alternatives before them, and some of the implications of trying to achieve alternative futures.

In some respects, the future is known. Using the laws of physics, the orbital location of the planets 100 years from now can be predicted with considerable precision. While prediction is often possible, however, in many cases it is difficult, impossible, or irrelevant. This may be true because of incomplete causal knowledge, system complexity, insufficient data about current conditions, the engagement of reflective humans in the system, or combinations of all of these factors. Some physical systems are inherently chaotic. At least within broad boundaries, their future performance can not be known. Social systems add another level of complication. People react to their environments. Their preferences and values change, in part because of what they experience, in part because of what their imperfect efforts to look into the future have revealed to them. People and their organizations act strategically, based on what they think others may do in response to different interpretations of the future. Since many of these reactions cannot be predicted, over time they impose progressively more serious limits on our ability to see the shape of possible futures.

Even when the future performance of a system can only be described in the most general terms, however, "what if" analysis can be useful. Such analysis can help societies to explore what contingencies they may face, determine how well they are prepared to deal with those contingencies, and identify indicators for which they should be watchful. If we can find ways to generate a range of plausible alternative futures, we can use them to evaluate different behavioral strategies for their likely efficacy and robustness in the face of a range of alternatives, and for how easily these strategies can be adapted to deal with unanticipated developments.

Efforts to structure and discipline our thinking about future possibilities in the light of present knowledge and intentions may therefore have an important role to play in shaping strategies for a sustainability transition. This chapter explores various approaches that have been used to explore the future toward addressing sustainability concerns. It seeks to evaluate their respective strengths and weaknesses as tools to aid in navigating a sustainability transition, to illustrate the sorts of insights that can emerge from their use, and to identify priorities for improving their performance and practical utility.

STRATEGIES FOR EXPLORING THE FUTURE

Strategies for using science to explore possible futures in policy contexts may be evaluated on at least four criteria: scientific credibility, political legitimacy, practical utility, and effectiveness.[1]

Scientific credibility: Such analytic strategies can make systematic but skeptical use of available scientific knowledge in laying out not only the likely conditions that might be encountered ahead, but also the possible and the impossible ones. Especially important would be these strategies' treatment of uncertainty. Debates over what is known "for sure" are unscientific and not particularly productive. An overemphasis on "consensus" assessments can clearly suppress the discussion of unlikely but not impossible outcomes. Needed as well are tools that can help to structure the inevitable uncertainties—including the possible low-probability, high-consequence events and "surprises"—such that their implications can be critically evaluated and addressed. Also important will be the ways in which known and hypothesized long chains of causal links are concatenated across multiple disciplines and multiple scales of analysis. These issues pose substantial technical challenges. They also raise fundamental questions about who should count as an expert, what should be the meaning and nature of peer review, and how critical evaluations of exploratory tools and the possible futures they illuminate can be most helpfully conducted.

Political legitimacy: Efforts to navigate a transition toward sustainability are inherently social enterprises. Individuals are, of course, free to shape their own private images of the future and may use the results in crafting their own policies. But to the extent that societies seek scientifically based explorations of possible futures to provide a common foundation for collective action, it is crucial that the explorations be viewed as fair and legitimate by those whose futures they might affect. The credibility of future assessments *to users* is therefore also critical. This type of credibility may be related to, but is almost never identical to, scientific credibility. Issues about participation in the design and use of exploratory tools, about transparency and openness in embodied values and assumptions, and about the embedding of assessments in appropriate institutional settings all come to the fore in efforts to satisfy this criterion of political legitimacy.

Practical utility: Tools for exploring the future should also be usable, and used. Above all, this means that they must be relevant to real choices faced by real individuals and institutions. They need to be available to potential users in a timely manner and sufficiently flexible that they encourage exploration of a wide range of possible goals and choices. Often, they will need to enable users to perform "what if" analyses of the possible future consequences of present actions. Since the realm of possible actions is often large, and the range of possible futures so wide, practical utility may also require means for sorting through alternative actions in light of users' values and preferences. Finally, useful assessments must be sparing in their demands for time and other resources that choice makers may find in short supply.

Effectiveness: Finally, tools needed for exploring the sustainability transition should be effective in actually illuminating pitfalls and opportunities in the roads ahead. This is admittedly a post hoc evaluation criterion. But individuals, institutions, and societies have been facing the challenges of grappling with uncertain futures for a long time indeed. It should not be too much to ask of tools for exploring sustainable futures that they be designed, and chosen, at least partially on the basis of their past performances in analogous circumstances.

Various approaches to satisfy these criteria in exploring the future have been adopted in forms that could be applied to sustainability issues. These include (1) qualitative consultation among "knowledgeable" people as in study panels; (2) formal elicitation of expert judgment in forms such as subjective probability distributions; (3) creation of structured and internally consistent narratives or scenarios; (4) various forms of strategic gaming; (5) formal extrapolation of past trends using statistical methods; and (6) a wide variety of different kinds of causal modeling. Often, several of these methods are used together. None of them provide more than partial illuminations of the futures before us. Each is limited in particular ways. Each, however—when used critically, skeptically, and carefully— can make a useful contribution.

Study panels such as those organized under the auspices of the Brundtland Commission, the Intergovernmental Panel on Climate Change (IPCC), the International Council for Science (ICSU) (e.g., the Scientific Committee on Problems of the Environment), the U.S. National Research Council (NRC), and the German Enquette Commissions are common strategies for exploring possible future implications of our current understanding. Such panels often make use of the other strategies outlined below in various combinations. The great strengths of these panels include the ability to draw on a wide range of expertise and stakeholders; to build from data but to tap understanding as well; and to provide environments in which experts can challenge and learn from one another. Common weaknesses include difficulties in quality control; a tendency to exclude disenfranchised stakeholder groups; a vulnerability to groupthink; and the tyranny of consensus-seeking—a special problem in areas as uncertainty-laden as those encountered in efforts to navigate a transition to sustainability.

Of the tools used by study panels and other methods in exploring the future, one extreme consists of causal process models, such as those used to simulate fishery yields and the general circulation of the atmosphere.[2] The strength of approaches to modern modeling lies in their explicit incorporation of scientifically verifiable relationships, and in their ability to make quantitative, if still conditional, forecasts of the implications of those relationships. Among their weaknesses remain their insatiable demands for data, difficulties in incorporating the different types and levels of knowledge and understanding that characterize different disciplines, and a host of computational problems. We turn to recent developments in modeling and integrated assessment that have begun to confront some of these shortcomings in the following section.

At another extreme are strategies built around the use of narratives or scenarios that tell a plausible and coherent story while relying on particular examples to provide context and details.[3] A seminal example is Rachel Carson's account of widespread and enduring ecological damage from some pesticides and other common substances, in her 1962 *Silent Spring*. At their best, these approaches can do a relatively good job at addressing complexity, context, and contingency. A special form of narrative is future history. Future histories have been used effectively to explore surprising futures beyond the normal range of extrapolation or projection.[4] They are also receptive to the explicit incorporation of norms and values. But they tend to be idiosyncratic, only partially constrained by scientific knowledge, and lacking in the precision that many would like to have in a navigational tool. In this chapter, we turn to recent developments that avoid some of these shortcomings under the discussion of scenario-based approaches to exploring sustainability futures.

An intermediate strategy that has proven helpful for exploring the future has been the use of extrapolation, drawing both on past trends and on analogous circumstances elsewhere. Relatively sophisticated examples include work on trends such as decarbonization—the long-term reduction in the amount of carbon produced per unit of energy—and the demographic transition discussed in Chapter 2, the cataloging of environmental degradation syndromes advocated by the German Advisory Council on Global Change, and econometric forecasts of energy use.[5] These approaches work well to the extent that they capture deep underlying forces not readily subject to deflection. Their great weakness is that, in the absence of accompanying causal understanding, the limits to their applicability are unknowable and their visions of the future are thus particularly vulnerable to surprise.

When uncertainty precludes conventional scientific analysis, yet quantitative estimates are needed for use in analysis, it is sometimes possible to obtain the judgments of experts in the form of subjective probability distributions. Such judgments are no substitute for solid understanding of the relevant science. But when decision makers cannot wait for better science, expert judgments can be used on an interim basis to provide some grounds for more informed policy choices. The decision analysis community has developed these methods and employed them in a variety of applications.[6] Formulating interview procedures and obtaining expert judgments relating to large, complex natural and social systems pose significant challenges. However, there are a number of examples of successful applications in such contexts as depletion of stratospheric ozone, long-range transport of sulfur air pollution, the assessment of earthquake structural risks, possible climate change in the face of increased atmospheric carbon dioxide, and energy modeling.[7] Expert elicitation often reveals a richer and more diverse array of expert opinion than is typically captured in the reports of traditional consensus expert panels.[8] But subjective probability distributions can be wrong as often as expert opinion. For example, an elicitation of estimated probabilities of weather modification success from 113 atmospheric scientists in 1968 found universal optimism about the expected success of modifications that 30 years later have either been abandoned or never scientifically validated.[9] Similarly, there is strong evidence that scientists have been overconfident in the past about the accuracy with which they know the value of basic physical constants.[10] Additionally, there is strong evidence of consistent overconfidence in the literature on behavioral decision theory.[11]

A strategy complementary to several of those described above is based on the creation of comprehensive accounts for resource use and pollutant emissions associated with particular futures. Such accounts are important because the multisectoral character of environment-development interactions makes it difficult to avoid analytic blunders such as double-counting the same water in independent agricultural and industrial analyses, or the same land in separate studies of energy and food production. Similarly, in the absence of comprehensive accounting frameworks, emissions of large-scale pollutants such as carbon dioxide can be underestimated when only some sectoral sources are considered. Starting with pioneering work by Resources for the Future in regional environmental management, reflecting integrated studies of the basins of the Potomac, Delaware, and Ruhr rivers, comprehensive accounting frameworks have helped to minimize such errors in careful efforts to explore alternative futures.[12] Such contributions notwithstanding, it is important to realize that accounting strategies provide a tool for exploring the future only when used in conjunction with other approaches.

Finally, a number of assessment methods have begun to emerge that combine elements of representation and deliberation.[13] The most developed of these methods, strategic gaming, is a special form of study panel that developed in military contexts seeking to address major uncertainties in future environments.[14] Military approaches have been adapted for use in civilian contexts, in both corporate planning and a broad range of public policy analyses germane to sustainable development.[15] Strategic gaming has proven an excellent way to integrate scientific models and human ingenuity into evaluations of possible future implications of present decisions. The weakness of this approach is that it is very good at teaching lessons that have little to do with the real world, and that it makes extraordinary demands on the time and resources of the analytic community.

In practice, some of the most interesting and potentially helpful efforts to explore possible futures relevant to a transition toward sustainability have entailed mixed strategies drawing on a combination of those outlined above. The following sections therefore discuss in more detail the present and potential contributions of three mixed strategies that seem particularly promising for exploring such possible futures: integrated assessment models, scenarios building, and institutionally oriented efforts to incorporate such tools into regional systems of policy development and adaptive management.

INTEGRATED ASSESSMENT MODELS

Integrated assessment models seek to link in a consistent fashion formal models of the environment and society.[16] Examples—some discussed in more detail below—include the Club of Rome's *Limits to Growth*, the International Institute for Applied Systems Analysis' RAINS (Regional Air Pollution Information and Simulation) model of acidification in Europe, the Latin American World Model, and the TARGETS (Tools to Assess Regional and Global Environmental and Health Targets for Sustainability) model of regional and global environment and health for sustainability in the Netherlands.[17]

Early Efforts

Early efforts in developing integrated assessment models included systems dynamics studies and, at the global scale, the Club of Rome's *Limits to Growth*.[18] This work helped to draw attention to sustainability issues, but largely failed to satisfy criteria of scientific credibility. A second round of integrated modeling took place in the context of the energy crises of the 1970s.[19] Again, while detailed predictions were not the strong points of these models, they did manage to provide insight into the structure of problems at the interface of society and environment. Lessons learned from these early efforts included the importance of building models to explore a *specific* set of futures rather than general ones, the need to specify realistic model structures and parameter values, the critical role of feedback loops in stabilizing complex systems, and the place of sensitivity analysis in evaluating model results.[20]

More generally, experienced assessors began to question the preeminent focus of the early enterprise on outputs consisting of relatively unconditional predictions. Consistent with trends in the modeling of large-scale economic systems,[21] the most used and useful work began to emphasize instead the role of integrated assessments in providing conditional answers to "what if" policy questions. At the same time, integrated assessment practitioners began to emphasize less the predictions of their models and more the basic insights and understanding that those models could offer about the complex interplay of social and natural processes in shaping possible futures.[22] The reorientation of integrated assessors away from prediction as an end in itself and toward prediction as a means of enhancing and calibrating understanding sometimes seems to be the field's own coming-of-age passage, recapitulated by each generation of modelers on their way to mastery of an important and difficult craft.[23]

Contemporary Efforts

Contemporary integrated assessment modeling has been strongly shaped by the need to address problems of large-scale interactions between economic development and the atmospheric environment. One of the most successful and widely known efforts has been the RAINS model of acidification in Europe developed by the International Institute for Applied Systems Analysis (IIASA) beginning in the mid 1980s.[24]   As developed and applied over a decade and more, RAINS now provides a spatially distributed modeling framework linking emissions and deposition patterns, and estimating local ecological impacts at deposition sites. In "what-if" mode, it allows exploring the ecological consequences of alternative policies for emission reductions. In optimization mode, it allows computation of minimal cost emission reduction schedules for satisfying specified impact constraints. The model, along with the processes of consultation in the science and policy communities in which it is embedded, has been widely credited with influencing policies for the most recent protocols for sulfur dioxide emissions in Europe as negotiated under the Convention on Long-Range Transboundary Air Pollution (LRTAP). [25]

Integrated assessment modeling is now being extensively applied in national and international efforts to address the risk of global climate change. The phenomena of climate change are manifestly complex, involving large-scale socioeconomic forces and the coupled ocean-atmosphere-biosphere system. Seeking to engage with this complicated array of interacting and intersecting phenomena, modelers have created a large variety of integrated assessments linking energy use and other human activities to changes in climate and, more recently, to impacts of climate change on ecosystems and society. In its 1995 report, the IPCC reviewed the 22 such models listed in Table 3.1 and classified them according to the scheme shown in Table 3.2.[26]

Some such classification is necessary to sort through the increasing variety of integrated assessment models being applied in explorations of

TABLE 3.1   Integrated Assessment Models

Model	Modellers
AS/ExM (Adaptive Strategies/Exploratory Model)	R. Lempert, S. Popper (Rand); M. Schlesinger (U. of Illinois)
AIM (Asian-Pacific Integrated Model)	T. Morita, M. Kainuma (National Inst. for Environmental Studies, Japan); Y. Matsuoka (Kyoto U.)
CETA (Carbon Emissions Trajectory Assessment)	S. Peck (Electric Power Research Institute); T. Teisberg (Teisberg Assoc.)
Connecticut (also known as the Yohe model)	G. Yohe (Wesleyan U.)
CRAPS (Climate Research and Policy Synthesis model)	J. Hammitt (Harvard U.); A. Jain, D. Wuebbles (U. of Illinois)
CSERGE (Centre for Social and Economic Research on the Global Environment)	D. Maddison (University College of London)
DICE (Dynamic Integrated Climate and Economy model)	W. Nordhaus (Yale University)
FUND (The Climate Framework for Uncertainty, Negotiation, and Distribution)	R.S.J. Tol (Vrije Universiteit Amsterdam)
DIAM (Dynamics of Inertia and Adaptability Model)	M. Grubb (Royal Institute of International Affairs); M. H. Dong, T. Chapuis (Centre Internationale de recherche sur l'environnement et développement)
ICAM-2 (Integrated Climate Assessment Model)	H. Dowlatabadi, G. Morgan (Carnegie-Mellon U.)
IIASA (International Institute for Applied Systems Analysis)	L. Schrattenholzer, Arnulf Grübler (IIASA)
IMAGE 2.0 (Integrated Model to Assess the Greenhouse Effect)	J. Alcamo, M. Krol (Rijksinstitut voor Volksgezondheid Milieuhygiene, Netherlands)
MARIA (Multiregional Approach for Resource and Industry Allocation)	S. Mori (Sci. U. of Tokyo)

continued

TABLE 3.1 Continued

Model	Modellers
MERGE 2.0 (Model for Evaluating Regional and Global Effects of GHG Reductions Policies)	A. Manne (Stanford U.); R. Mendelsohn (Yale U.); R. Richels (Electric Power Research Institute)
MiniCAM (Mini Global Change Assessment Model)	J. Edmonds (Pacific Northwest Lab), R. Richels (Electric Power Research Institute), T. Wigley (University Consortium for Atmospheric Research [UCAR])
MIT (Massachusetts Institute of Technology)	H. Jacoby, R. Prinn, Z. Yang (MIT)
PAGE (Policy Analysis of the Greenhouse Effect)	C. Hope (Cambridge U.); J. Anderson, P. Wenman (Environmental Resources Management)
PEF (Policy Evaluation Framework)	J. Scheraga, S. Herrod (EPA); R. Stafford, N. Chan (Decision Focus Inc.)
ProCAM (Process Oriented Global Change Assessment Model)	J. Edmonds, H. Pitcher, N. Rosenberg (Pacific Northwest Lab); T. Wigley (UCAR)
RICE (Regional DICE)	W. Nordhaus (Yale U.); Z. Yang (MIT)
SLICE (Stochastic Learning Integrated Climate Economy Model)	C. Kolstad (U. of California, Santa Barbara)
TARGETS (Tools to Assess Regional and Global Environmental and Health Targets for Sustainability)	J. Rotmans, M.B.A. van Asselt, A. Beusen, M.G.J. den Elzen, M. Janssen, H.B.M. Hilderink, A.Y. Hoekstra, H.W. Koster, W.J.M. Martens, L.W. Niessen, B. Strengers, H.J.M. de Vries (Rijksinstitut voor Volksgezondheid en Milieuhygiene, Netherlands)

Source: Weyant et al. (1996). Courtesy of the IPCC (Intergovernmental Panel on Climate Change).

TABLE 3.2 Summary Characterization of Integrated Assessment Models

Model	Forcings 0. CO_2 1. other GHG 2. aerosols 3. land use 4. other	Geographic Specificity 0. global 1. continental 2. countries 3. grids/basins	Socioeconomic Dynamics[1] 0. exogenous 1. economics 2. technology choice 3. land use 4. demographic	Geophysical Simulation[1] 0. Global ΔT 1. 1-D ΔT, ΔP 2. 2-D ΔT, ΔP 3. 2-D Climate	Impact Assessment[2] 0. ΔT 1. Δsea level 2. agriculture 3. ecosystems 4. health 5. water	Treatment of Uncertainty 0. None 1. Uncertainty 2. Variability 3. Stochasticity 4. Cultural Perspectives	Treatment of Decision Making 0. optimization 1. simulation 2. simulation with adaptive decisions
AS/ExM	0	0	0	0	0	1	2
AIM	0,1,2,3	2,3	1,2,3,4	1,2	0,1,2,3,5	0	1
CETA	0,1	0	1,2	0	0	0 or 1	0
Connecticut	0	0	1	0	0	1	0
CRAPS	0	0	1	0	0	1	2
CSERGE	0	0	1	0	0		0
DICE	0	0	1	0	0,1,2,3,4	0 or 1	0
FUND	0,1	1	1,4	0	0	0 or 1	0
DIAM	0	0	1,2	0		0 or 1	0
ICAM-2	0,1,2,3	1,2	1,3,4	1,2	0,1,3	1,2,3	1,2
IIASA	0	0	1	1	2	0	0
IMAGE 2.0	0,1,2,3	3	0,2,3	2	1,2,3	1	1
MARIA	0,1	0,1	1	0	0		0
MERGE 2.0	0,1,2,3	1	1,2	1	0	0 or 1	0
MiniCAM	0,1,2,3	2,3	1,2,3	2	0	0	1
MIT	0,1,2,3	2,3	1	2,3	0,2,3	1	0,1
PAGE	0,1	1,2	1	0	0,1,2,3,4	2	1
PEF	0,1	1,2	1	0	0	2	1
ProCAM	0,1,2,3	2,3	1,2,3,4	2	0,2,3,5	1	1
RICE	0	1	1	0	0	0	0
SLICE	0	1	1	0	0	1	2
TARGETS	0,1,2,3,4	0	1,2,3,4	2	1,2,3,4	4	1,2

Source: Weyant et al. (1996). Courtesy of the IPCC (Intergovernmental Panel on Climate Change).

[1] TARGETS includes ozone depletion, soil erosion, acid rain, and toxic and hazardous pollutant releases.
[2] In AIM, FUND, IMAGE, PAGE, and ProCAM, the impacts are calculated separately for each sector.

the possible futures of climate change. Nonetheless, any classification sufficiently simple to be helpful fails to do justice to the multifaceted character of many of the models classified.[27] For our purposes, it may be sufficient to note that the models fall into two broad classes.[28] Some, such as DICE, RICE, CETA, PAGE, and MERGE, aim at balancing the economic effects of climate change and the policies undertaken to mitigate climate change. These "policy optimizing" models contain relatively simple characterizations of the geophysical systems and the social and physical details of behavior and impacts. Others, such as the Massachusetts Institute of Technology (MIT) Global Systems Model, TARGETS, IMAGE, and ICAM, contain more elaborate or explicit treatments of geophysical, ecological, and socioeconomic systems and have been called "policy evaluation" models.

Methodological development of integrated assessment models is proceeding rapidly, and on a number of fronts. Three are particularly germane to explorations of a future transition towards sustainability.

Uncertainty: While many contemporary integrated assessment models remain deterministic, a number have begun to focus attention on the characterization and treatment of uncertainties, both in the values assumed by specific model coefficients and in the functional form of the models. Those that are most successful tend to have considered uncertainty as a key consideration from the outset. It is often difficult or impossible to do uncertainty analysis in models whose structure has not been chosen with a careful consideration of the needs of uncertainty analysis, although some analytical methods are available.[29] On the other hand, careful uncertainty analysis can sometimes be used to significantly simplify a model, when the second-order consequence of specific details can be shown to be swamped by first-order uncertainties.

When model and coefficient uncertainties are fully explored, the level of uncertainty in model forecasts can easily become too large to provide useful guidance. However, in such models it may still be able to explore the extent to which different behavioral patterns and decision rules are "robust" or "brittle." Robust behaviors may degrade gracefully or lend themselves to easy adaptation across a wide range of possible futures. Brittle ones may tend to lead the decision makers blindly off "cliffs" or into "brick walls." Thus, while the uncertainty may not allow the analyst to say much about what the future will be, such analysis may allow the analyst to conclude that "this behavior is fairly robust" or "this behavior has a high probability of leading to problems."

Human behavior: Many early modeling efforts contained a relatively primitive treatment of human systems and their interactions with natural systems. In the energy field, which was the locus of much modeling work starting in the 1970s, human behavior tended to be described in terms of economic variables such as price or income, or technological variables such as appliance penetration or car usage. More recently, various attempts have been made to model relevant behaviors more directly. A few studies have even begun to combine the two approaches. However, significant challenges remain. Chief among these are the following needs:

• Better representations of the complex dynamics of human behavior, particularly with respect to the twin problems of choice and uncertainty, which interact in complex ways in social systems. Addressing this need will mean making better use of the extensive literature on human behavior in the more qualitative social sciences (sociology, social anthropology, social psychology) on topics related to behavior and attitude change.

• Representations of multiple human causes of global change (driving forces) and human consequences or responses (mitigation, adaptation) in a more integrated way. Of particular importance is the integrated treatment of the relationships among adaptive responses to changes in social, economic, and environmental conditions.

• Involving "users" and stakeholders more directly in the research design and the process of analysis. The resulting knowledge (e.g., traditional environmental knowledge; experience of politics will be more accessible for the policy process as well as for stakeholders), thereby providing an opening for stakeholders' inputs to be fed into the analysis.

• Moving beyond "baseline" or "business as usual" representation of future conditions to a recognition of the wide potential range of future social, economic and environmental conditions; bifurcations and turning points; and different coherent packages of driving forces and responses.

• Addressing the local and regional implications of global change and sustainable development.[30]

Simplification: The deliberate simplification of complex integrated assessment models has been used since the early 1970s to investigate the important interconnections of long-term, large-scale phenomena.[31] The emergence of integrated assessment illustrates how studying these interconnections has become increasingly plausible in the climate change research arena, even though the underlying science is incomplete and variable in its predictive power across disciplines. But analysis intended to assist near-term decision making—including decisions that may well affect the possibility of a transition to sustainability—must accommodate the limits of current knowledge and the scarcity of time and resources. In attempting to evaluate and model all the key interactions, the process could become so overwhelmed in details that it might never manage to produce usable results. Thus, the analysis requires isolating key portions of the social and natural systems of interest, provisionally ignoring some causal links, and—within clearly articulated sets of assumptions—performing parametric or sensitivity analysis.

For example, many local and regional climate impact studies have started with climate outputs from global circulation models, even though at the subgrid level such models are unable to make confident predictions about such variables as precipitation. That is, the complex global models are too crude to be helpful at the local or regional scale. In such cases, it may make more sense in certain contexts to forego temporarily any effort to model causal connections between global and local phenomena and instead to simply ask "what if?": what would happen if rainfall goes up or down by 10 percent, shifts to other seasons, or changes in some other fashion? These alternatives frame a parametric study of the regional implications of climate change, without awaiting global-scale models accurate enough to support a regional analysis. This approach is being used by the National Synthesis Group of the National Climate Impact Assessment, now in progress in the United States.[32]

Lessons Learned

The accumulating experience from these and other integrated assessment models suggests several important lessons for efforts to apply similar approaches in exploring possible futures of a sustainability transition. Above all, the experience suggests that integrated assessment models can make a difference in society's ability to address complex interactions between environment and development. Those contributions can be made in two different dimensions: by providing analytic insight and by directly informing policy making.[33]

On the insight dimension, we know that formal integrated assessment models can stimulate problem redefinition. This is often the most significant influence of integrated assessment. (It is also a path to effectiveness that is independent of whether the models are analytically able to make credible predictions.) Formal modeling demands specificity and clear thinking, and this discipline has often improved our understanding of the nature of complex problems. For example, several integrated assessment models have shown the dilemma that, in the short run, cleaning up local sulfur and particulate air pollution can accelerate climate warming.

On the policy dimension, the RAINS example discussed above illustrates the potential role of integrated assessment models in supporting international environmental negotiations. This type of influence, which has also been seen for problems such as whaling and stratospheric ozone depletion,[34] nonetheless remains rare and hard to obtain. In a recent review of hundreds of modeling studies estimating the costs of mitigating greenhouse gas effects over the next several decades, and sometimes longer, Working Group III of the IPCC concluded that such studies had value primarily under assumptions that historical development patterns and relationships among key underlying variables will hold constant in the projections.[35] The fact that such assumptions rarely hold in practice means that substantial basic research still needs to be done on what makes assessments useful in international environmental policy making.[36]

Validation of integrated assessment models requires scrutiny of both the structure and the assumed parameters, as well as the initial conditions of the component models. This need is a logical result of the fact that integrated assessment puts together models developed for other purposes. As a consequence, each integrated assessment study has vulnerabilities unique to the particular set of models it links together and the particular data sets drawn upon by those models. Obtaining reasonable quantitative agreement across integrated assessments is accordingly an exercise in which model structure and input assumptions—not just model outputs—need to be sorted out.[37]

Sensitivity testing is essential. Sensitivity testing is the name given to studies of models' behavior when input parameters are varied in a systematic fashion. Coupling models together can produce unexpected instabilities and other behaviors that reflect the models' technical structure rather than those aspects of reality that one seeks to study. Sensitivity testing is a way of locating these problems. Integrated assessment models are most often used for parametric studies—asking "what if" questions; these are in essence sensitivity tests of the models.

Integrated assessment models can be useful probes of the nature of uncertainties and their significance in exploring the possible future implications of current decisions. However, although this lesson is generally accepted, systematic explorations of uncertainties and their implications through integrated assessment models present enormous technical challenges, and have rarely been carried out in practice.

Deliberate simplification of complex integrated assessment models can be an important part of strategies for exploring the future. Again, the value of this approach has long been recognized by experienced modelers of complex nature-society interactions.[38] But the temptation remains to let the search for complex "realism" become an end in itself in integrated assessment modeling. The art of providing useful simplifications remains demanding and underdeveloped.

SCENARIOS

If the world is a play, the future is compatible with many alternative scripts. In the theater, a scenario summarizes a play. Long-range development scenarios are summary stories of how the world might unfold in the 21st century. They are useful for organizing scientific insight, gauging emerging risks, and challenging the imagination. Scenarios do not predict the future, but they bring the future to bear on today's choices by providing a narrative framework in which drivers of change, current trends, and options for action are brought together in an orderly and systematic fashion.[39]

Why Scenarios?

Efforts to explore possible futures for a sustainability transition must consider the interplay and dynamic evolution of social, economic, and natural systems, thus requiring an *interdisciplinary and integrated perspective.* They must go beyond specific themes and sectors—population, economy, water, food, energy, climate—to analyze interconnections, common drivers, and systemwide changes. They must understand the process of securing sustainability as tentative, open and iterative, and involving scientific, policy, and public participation.

A recognition of the importance of possible alternative development paths necessarily raises the question of the basis for choosing among these alternatives. In other words, once the focus extends beyond predicting most likely outcomes, and into the evaluation of the feasibility and consequences of quite different futures, then the analysis necessarily has overtly normative dimensions. Not only must the choice of which preferred futures to analyze (out of a potentially infinite set) be confronted, but also different assumptions about the basis for such choices will be part of the analysis itself. In addressing a topic such as the transition to sustainability, it is necessary to incorporate normative social visions into the analysis. Scenario methods do not resolve the ultimately political choices of which normative visions should be pursued and by whom. But they do provide a transparent framework for exploring the implications of such choices, and even for prodding them toward openness and fairness.

In principle, integrated assessment modeling acknowledges these features of analyzing sustainability and can be organized to deal with them. In practice, addressing all concerns in single integrated causal models of large-scale, long-term dynamics has proven immensely difficult. This situation has led to the growing use of approaches for analyzing socioeconomic futures based on the generation of alternative scenarios, which represent different packages of internally consistent assumptions about human behavior and decision making. In common with the best integrated modeling approaches, the point of scenario analysis is not to predict what long-term outcomes are most likely, but to explore the economic and technical feasibility and costs associated with quite different development paths. Scenario approaches, however, place less stringent demands on comprehensive causal understanding and data about the current state of the world than do looks at the future based exclusively on causal models. This feature of scenario approaches limits them in some ways, but also gives them the ability to explore certain important issues of norms and connections presently beyond the reach of integrated causal models.

Contemporary Efforts

Contemporary scenarios used in the context of sustainability concerns are generally stories interpreting and framing the results of models. Although the models need not be formal causal representations of the kind we described in the section above on "Integrated Assessment Models," many of the examples in contemporary use are built on formal computer models that draw on databases containing information and assumptions about the world as it has been and is expected to be.

Perhaps the best-known example of ongoing (since the early 1970s) scenario analysis has been the work at the Shell International Petroleum Company in London. In two seminal articles, the analysis team argued for the need to use scenario analysis to look beyond conventional projections in order to change the "mental models" of company managers.[40] The Shell team continues to engage in far-reaching analysis of global futures, and the work has been a major contribution to scenario efforts of the World Business Council on Sustainable Development.[41]

Another contemporary effort revisits the earlier Limits to Growth systems dynamics model, World 3.[42] The authors present a set of 13 scenarios ranging from collapse to a transition to sustainability, arguing that in the past 20 years some options for sustainability have narrowed, others have opened up, and that achieving a sustainable future is both technically and economically possible.

Finally, another example of scenario analysis presents three global scenarios, with special focus on the United Kingdom, for the future through the year 2020.[43] A retrenchment scenario projects that, eventually, a recession of such severity will occur that, within a few years, there will be a dramatic collapse in the economic systems of both developed and developing countries. An assertive materialism scenario projects that economic crises will be resolved and there will be a prolonged period of rapid economic growth and technological advances. A caring autonomy scenario projects that the global economy will go though a transition to sustainability, including a shift to decentralized governments.

Most of the global scenarios have the same point of departure defined by the current state of the socio-ecological system and the forces propelling the system forward. The initial conditions of identified trends and patterns of change define the near-term trajectory. Most contemporary scenario efforts adopt points of departure consistent with the trends and conditions we outlined in Chapter 2. Scenario variation arises from alternative assumptions about how development trajectories bifurcate and fracture as critical uncertainties and tensions within the unfolding system are resolved.

Further variation is introduced by assumptions about future conditions that define end-point conditions in backcasting exercises. In this sense, visions of future states act as attractors in scenario analysis. Positive future visions are attractors in the world as well, insofar as they galvanize actions for bending the arc of development toward these positive end points; and, of course, dystopian visions are repellors. Finally, surprising events and phenomena can be imposed on the scenario trajectory—an unexpected technological breakthrough, rise of fundamentalism as a globally dominant ethos, wars, major economic destabilizations, catastrophic natural disasters, and so on.

An indefinite variety of scenarios can be generated depending on how each of the trends, conditions, and visions assumed are specified. The scenarios most relevant for exploring possible futures for a sustainability transition share the characteristics of comprehensive thematic coverage, long-range time horizon, global spatial domain, and openness to a full range of socio-ecological visions and pathways. To give some order to the possibilities, a framework of stylized scenarios[44] was prepared for the Global Scenario Group (GSG)[45] that, in slightly altered form, is presented in Figure 3.1. The framework provides a useful point of departure to structure strategic thinking about the alternative futures that may confront efforts to navigate a transition toward sustainability.

To appreciate the implications of the figure, consider first its three archetypal scenario classes, distinguished by different assumptions about how emergent environmental and social stresses are resolved. The *Conventional Worlds* class assumes that current trends play out without major discontinuity or surprise in the evolution of institutions, environmental systems, and human values. In the *Barbarization* class of scenarios, fundamental social change occurs in a manner that many would feel to be an unwelcome sort, bringing great human misery and collapse of civilized norms. Finally, the *Great Transitions* class of scenarios also represents fundamental social transformation. In this case, however, the changes are in directions that many advocates of sustainable development would view as greatly for the better. Our use of the GSG framework reflects a judgment on neither the desirability nor the likelihood of the strategic alternatives it presents. Rather, we have used it as a reminder of how much is carelessly taken for granted, especially about different possible configurations of underlying socioeconomic conditions, in many explorations of futures relevant to a sustainability transition.

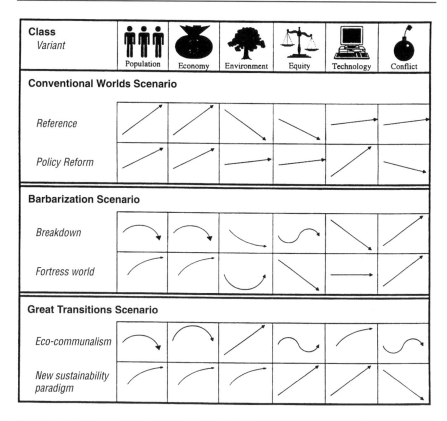

Class *Variant*	Population	Economy	Environment	Equity	Technology	Conflict
Conventional Worlds Scenario						
Reference						
Policy Reform						
Barbarization Scenario						
Breakdown						
Fortress world						
Great Transitions Scenario						
Eco-communalism						
New sustainability paradigm						

FIGURE 3.1   Archetypal scenarios with illustrative patterns of change. The scenario structure shows sketches of behavior over time for six descriptive variables: population growth, economic scale, environmental quality, socio-economic equity, technological change, and degree of social and geopolitical conflict. The curves are intended as rough illustrations of the possible patterns of change only.
Source: Gallopin et al. (1997). Courtesy of the Stockholm Environment Institute.

The utility of the GSG framework can be further appreciated by pursuing it to the next level of detail—one for which six stylized scenarios appear in Figure 3.1. Within the *Conventional Worlds* class, a *Policy Reform* scenario variant complements the business-as-usual of the *Reference* case variant by assuming that strong, comprehensive, and coordinated government action is taken in an effort to foster sustainability. A critical assumption of this scenario is the emergence of the necessary political will for imposing sustainability limits on something not unlike today's growth-driven global economy and consumerist culture. The scenario framework nonetheless lets us identify policy reforms as one (albeit conventional) point of departure for exploring a transition toward sustainability, even as it emphasizes that more basic changes in human institutions and values might ultimately have to play a role in making such reforms possible.

Such changes might draw on elements of the *Great Transitions* scenarios, which in their pure form as described by the GSG are visionary responses to the sustainability challenge—visions that include much strengthened emphasis on the quality of life in matters of human welfare, the valuation of nature, equitable wealth distribution, and social solidarity. The *Eco-communalism* variant embraces the principles of strong decentralization, small technology, and economic autarky. The *New Sustainability Paradigm* variant is a more cosmopolitan vision that would transcend and transform urban and industrial civilization, and maintain global links and solidarity, rather than retreat into localism.

By contrast, if *Conventional World* market and policy adaptations are overwhelmed by increasing environmental and social crises, the GSG framework encourages us to consider whether a transition to *Barbarization* scenarios might take place. In an extreme variant, the GSG *Breakdown* scenarios envision cultural disintegration and economic collapse, a devolution of civilization to a primitive world of all-against-all. The *Fortress World* variant features an authoritarian response to the threat of breakdown. Ensconced in protected enclaves, elites safeguard their privilege by controlling an impoverished majority and managing critical natural resources. Outside the fortress there is repression, environmental destruction, and misery. Again, the question is not whether to "believe" the social vision of this type of scenario, but rather whether treating it in "what if" mode helps to illuminate the challenges and opportunities of the transition toward sustainability. We believe it does.

This framework of scenario classes and variants can be readily made more complex. With a little thought, many variants and subvariants can be devised with differing assumptions, in combinations that vary across global regions and states and include temporal transitions between different scenario trajectories. The proliferation of scenarios—as of model runs—for their own sake is, however, counterproductive. A more compelling goal is the careful explication and analysis of a few archetypal possibilities that can illuminate the contours of alternative futures and aid in preparing for them. To better understand the potential of such approaches, this Board asked a member of our Board and a leader of the GSG[46] to carry out a preliminary scenario analysis of some of the possible futures that would attain the normative goals we set forth in Chapter 1.

The results are presented in further detail in the appendix to this chapter, and described in full in a separate report.[47]

Lessons Learned

The experience summarized above suggests that scenarios to support the study of global futures and the requirements for a transition to sustainability should be rigorous, reflecting the insights of science and modeling. But scenario building must also recognize that the story of the future is not a mere projection of current trends and understanding. Moreover, scenarios are told in the language of words as well as numbers, because some critical dimensions—assumptions about culture, values, lifestyles, and social institutions—require qualitative description.

The spectrum of scenarios to consider should encompass a wide range of possibilities. Contrasting long-range visions should reflect the uncertainty about how the global system might unfold, the possibility of surprise, and a range of worldviews on pathways to a sustainable future. Beyond conventional sensitivity tests (e.g., to assess changes in greenhouse gas emissions associated with a change in population or economic scale), this means exploring fundamentally different assumptions concerning institutions, technology, and values.

To guide the formulation of strategies and policies for sustainability, scenarios need to be sufficiently rich and textured, describing demographic, social, economic, resource, and environmental subsystems in enough detail and disaggregation to evaluate whether a development trajectory is compatible with sustainability goals. These goals can be expressed as criteria by means of various indicators, that gauge the compatibility of a scenario with sustainability (see Chapter 5).

The difference between the indicator values that emerge in the hypothetical world of the scenario and the sustainability goals is a measure of the *unsustainability* of the assumed development trajectory. By describing the timing, character, and degree of the mismatch, scenario analysis becomes "policy relevant," a laboratory for identifying emerging problems and unsustainable patterns of development, and for setting priorities for action. Contributing to both informed action and theoretical insight are the twin goals of the scenario enterprise.

Though our perspective here is global, it should be stressed that a full research program for sustainability would need to be conducted consistently across multiple levels of spatial resolution. For example, global scenarios, generally disaggregated for major regions, clarify planetary level phenomena—climate change, globalization and trade, geopolitics, migration pressure—but are too grainy to pick up sustainability issues at, say, the river basin or ecosystem level. At the other extreme, community-level sustainability studies are able to provide detail on land use patterns and air quality, for example, but reveal little about global change. We turn to a brief survey of the progress made with such regional scale efforts to explore futures relevant to a sustainability transition in the next section of the chapter. Ultimately, a fully developed strategy for exploring sustainability futures would have the capacity to "zoom" across spatial levels, with each nested level providing appropriate insights. Such flexible treatment of scale is a challenge at the forefront of current work in both integrated assessment modeling and scenario analysis.[48]

REGIONAL INFORMATION SYSTEMS

Good integrated assessment models constitute an explicit system of hypothesized causal hypotheses. They can be reproducibly analyzed to illuminate the conditions under which, or the likelihood with which, particular types of global-scale futures would develop if the models represent a reasonable approximation of the real world. Good scenarios also have an explicit structure to assure internal consistency. By relaxing the demand for a complete system of causal links, however, they allow for exploration of a wider range of potential driving forces, intentions, and contingencies, weaving interesting narratives about how those forces might develop and interact over several decades. A third and complementary way that has been used to explore plausible paths toward sustainability is through regional information systems that harness scientific knowledge to support policy and decision making affecting the long-term interactions of development and environment. All such information systems often contain elements of scenario development and integrated modeling, as well as the other forward-looking strategies noted in the introduction to this chapter. The distinguishing feature we wish to pursue here is not the technical aspects of analysis and presentation that lend such efforts scientific credibility, but rather the social processes and institutions that give them political legitimacy and practical utility as strategies for exploring possible transitions toward sustainability in often contentious regional contexts.

Why Regional Information Systems?

Why pursue regional examples of strategies for exploring the future in a report seeking primarily to sketch a global-scale overview of science and the transition to sustainability? One reason is that relative to the global issues on which we have focused in the preceding sections of this review, the quest for sustainability at the regional scale is rich in the variety of institutions, values, and kinds of environmental and social systems it engages. This rich experience seems likely to have a good deal to teach us about providing effective looks into the global futures of the sustainability transition and our attempts to shape them. Moreover, as suggested in previous chapters and argued in detail in Chapter 4, many of the greatest challenges facing a sustainability transition occur at the regional scale. And a substantial number of the historical successes in providing science-based "look ahead" knowledge for managing environment-development interactions have occurred at regional scales. Understanding how scientific information has been used to provide looks at possible regional futures is therefore valuable in its own right as a component of strategies for navigating the path toward sustainability.

By "regional" systems we mean diverse and eclectic sets of circumstances which have in common a spatial template smaller than the world and at that more immediate and easily identified interactions occur between environment and society. In practice, this can mean systems as small as the watersheds on which much of the original work on modeling-based decision support systems was carried out, or as large as the continental-scale airsheds involved in the European acidification models and scenarios discussed above.[49] In the studies we survey below, competing human claims on the environmental and resource components of the region are central. These claims are in turn shaped by institutional arrangements, including jurisdictional borders that do not follow ecosystem boundaries.

Competing claims of stakeholders, expressed through politics, provide one source of information on what is feasible and desirable in a region. A different perspective is provided by scientific analyses, which organize information around natural and social processes and systems. Processes and institutions sometimes can be designed that allow scientific information to be used to complement information derived from politics in ways that facilitate the resolution of competing claims. At least as often, however, political and scientific information clash, with science divorced from or even intensifying conflict. The question is how to design science-based regional information systems for use in exploring contentious futures that are more likely to help than hinder efforts to assess and pursue sustainability. As in the preceding discussions of integrated assessment models and scenarios, the Board's purpose here is to provide a critical appraisal of the utility and limitations of regional information systems for exploring possible futures for a successful transition.

The Range of Experience

Efforts to integrate science-based "what if" analyses in regional resource and environmental management regimes date back to at least the 1950s.[50] By the 1960s, with the impetus of studies at the Harvard Water

Program, Resources for the Future, and elsewhere, such work had become significantly multidisciplinary. Decision analysis, simulation models, and normative scenarios all had significant roles in the emerging "systems analysis" movement.[51] Throughout the 1970s, researchers from the United States' University of Georgia and Canada's University of British Columbia pioneered the development of interactive workshops involving scientists and policy makers in what today would be called the coproduction of simulation models for scenarios exploring the implications of alternative environmental management strategies at the regional scale.[52] Struck by the inevitable incompleteness of the science called upon for such analyses, and by the variety and mutability of the management goals involved, this group also crystallized the importance of viewing the management process *adaptively*.[53] Models came to be viewed less as technologies of prediction and more as sites for a continuing dialog between scientists and policy makers. The "product" of their "what if" views of the future increasingly came to be seen especially as a process of confidence building—an investment in social capacity to continually learn from past management actions to shape future actions better.

Throughout the 1980s, a number of groups experimented with the use of integrated modeling, scenario analysis, and strategic gaming to support the adaptive management of environment-development interactions at the regional scale.[54] A typical but particularly relevant example for our purposes is provided by a striking analysis of Balinese rice culture.[55] Through classic anthropological field methods, a researcher uncovered ways in which local knowledge embedded in religious rituals provided social coordination for complex planting, pest management, and water allocation decisions involved in Balinese rice production. This production system was efficient and had been sustained over periods of hundreds of years. It had also remained invisible to several generations of foreign and domestic resource management experts. When high-yield rice varieties and related cultivation practices were introduced in the 1980s, they interfered with this highly evolved management system, with a resulting severe disruption to both rice production and the local social system.

Experts, local and foreign, almost understood what had gone wrong, but the complex ecology and politics of the situation meant that their diagnosis was difficult to articulate, and almost impossible to communicate persuasively to those who controlled agricultural policy on the island. While others complained about the politics and development advice on the situation, one research group[56] teamed with local experts to build a formal model of the Balinese rice system. The model ended up showing how the traditional system had worked, and how the practices associated with initial high-yield experiments had failed. Because the model had been developed with the input of local experts, and with careful regard for the realities of local politics, it succeeded in providing a "what if" tool that was effectively used in exploring alternative management approaches. Most important, it provided a neutral ground and common language for priests, farmers, and Indonesian agriculture ministry officials to discuss how to integrate the knowledge embodied in high-yielding rice varieties with the knowledge embodied in local temple religious practices to create a higher yield but still maintain a sustainable agricultural system.

A second contemporary example concerning North America's Columbia River Basin stresses how important the integrated design of information systems and management institutions is for the sustainable development of conflicted resource systems.[57] The Columbia River, the fourth largest in North America, was developed by an ambitious federal program of dams, irrigation works, and navigation facilities beginning in 1933. By the time the last dam was completed in 1975, the region—which in several respects included Canada, where the Columbia rises—had achieved an economically successful integration around hydroelectric power. But the building of the dams imposed losses as well as gains: Native American tribes, whose economy was founded on the river's abundant salmon fishery, suffered as the anadromous salmon's migration route to the ocean was progressively blocked and its habitat modified by reservoirs, logging, agriculture, and urbanization.

Rising controversy and the prominent role played by federal hydropower had already prompted Congress to create a new institutional structure in 1980, centered on the Northwest Power Planning Council (NPPC), an interstate agency with a mandate to resolve energy and fisheries conflicts in the Columbia basin. The NPPC's mode of operation was planning: the orderly assembly of information, much of it compiled in an energy-economic model and a separate model of river-basin fish habitat and migration. Together, these models framed an integrated assessment of possible futures for the region and its key interacting components.[58] The NPPC models, developed through a careful consultative process involving scientists and stakeholders, captured the conflicts between the biological needs of the fish and the economics of power with scientific credibility and political legitimacy. The models were used extensively by parties on all sides of the conflict. In contrast to the European acidification models described earlier, however, these models and the deliberations associated with them did not identify solutions that would avoid head-on tradeoffs. The NPPC assessment and policy evaluation models raised the real possibility that under the current state and trends of knowledge and development, coexistence of native salmon and the present day economy of the Columbia Basin may not be sustainable over the scale of the river basin. Whether a transition might be achieved under more radical scenarios that encompass substantial changes in institutions[59] and values is a question that is only now beginning to be explored.

Lessons Learned

Experience in developing information support systems for regional-scale environmental management has led to several significant findings. A regional scale approach grounded in ecosystem knowledge and cooperative and adaptive management constitutes an infrastructure for social learning—a way to lay out scientific knowledge in a form that can be accessible to nonspecialists, a mode of communication and negotiation that can draw opponents together for learning as well as conflict resolution, and a means to continue learning as action proceeds.

Formal models, a common element of the three exploratory approaches discussed in this chapter, play an important role at the regional level in several related ways. First, a formal model is usually necessary for managing the large amounts of information found in coupled natural and social systems. Second, the assembly of that diverse information is a social process that builds links to different communities—resource users, government, citizen groups, and scientists, among others. When this process works well, those stakeholders use model building as a forum in which their views of how knowledge should be integrated can contribute to the model's structure and to the understanding that emerges. Third, the formal modeling provides an impetus for further social and scientific learning; its assumptions and databases are assertions about reality. As experience accumulates, these assertions should be tested and modified to yield an understanding that is not only more accurate but also widely shared within the region.

The regional studies also illuminate hurdles that have not been overcome. Long-term monitoring has been difficult, even in developed nations. Institutional inertia and turbulence has been high, making it difficult to admit failure or surprise—or even to set out to learn in an unbiased fashion. Yet, over times as short as a decade, it is possible to see some institutional changes, such as the formal adoption of a Mediterranean management regime. Similarly, social expectations of the kind that have accompanied the abandonment of nuclear energy in the United States can shift. Such shifts alter the balance of institutions, for example, fostering a widespread acceptance that energy-efficiency is a good business practice.

Work at the regional scale shows that the way human and natural systems interact can be studied and acted upon within an integrated framework. There is real, if often incremental, social learning. Experience over the regional scale and decadal time span—the "large and the long"—can influence choices, although there is as yet little experience in thinking explicitly about how regions are affected by global-scale changes.[60] Despite the hopeful examples, societies are far from having a recipe to achieve sustainable results: to succeed in the context of each region's history and alignments of institutions, power, and economic possibilities requires innovation, resources, staying power, leadership, and no doubt some good luck.

CONCLUSIONS

This chapter has reviewed various approaches that explore possible futures of long-term, large-scale, and also regional interactions between environment and society. These futures are shaped by a variety of factors, including chance, human aspirations, and processes normally studied individually by the natural and social sciences. To be sure, many important factors cannot be summarized in analytical models or computer simulations. Yet, just the knowledge and data that are commonly available challenge individuals' ability to integrate this information on the basis of informed judgment alone.[61] Over the past generation, analysts have sought ways of combining human judgment with the power of information management through processes that are simultaneously scientifically credible and politically legitimate.

The results of our review are promising but mixed. Integrated assessment models have been accepted at the highest levels of international negotiation. But they have not stilled lively controversies about interpreting or responding to emerging evidence that human activity is modifying the global environment. Scenario studies like the one performed by the Global Scenario Group have added considerable breadth and depth to our normative conception of a transition to sustainability. However, they remain controversial, uneasily poised between the domains of facts and values. Regional information systems have combined elements of modeling and scenario analysis to support policy deliberations in relatively circumscribed instances where sustainability issues are highly contested. However, these systems have often merely shifted the domain of controversy from the overtly political realm to an apparently technical context in which political disagreements are merely pushed beneath a surface of numbers and graphs. It is not clear that such shifts help the cause of sustainable resource development.

Often, it must be said, the sorts of methods we have reviewed here have been able to do little more than chart the many ways in which a transition toward sustainability is *not* likely to be achieved over the foreseeable future. At their best, however, these methods have helped determined efforts to probe the future implications of present trends, to identify the likely obstacles to sustainability, and to illuminate alternative options for moving forward toward specific sustainability goals. In doing so, they have helped us to learn a bit about what a transition to sustainability might actually entail. This learning is a process through which notable progress has been made using the methods discussed in this chapter; that is a surprising and optimistic finding in itself.

Our analysis of trends and plausible futures and our commissioned scenarios (in the following appendix to this chapter) further undergird an important conclusion of this study. **Based on our analysis of persistent trends and plausible futures, the Board believes that a successful transition toward sustainability is possible over the next two generations. This transition could be achieved without miraculous technologies or drastic transformations of human societies.** This judgment is illuminated by the analysis in the appendix of a "Hunger and Carbon Reduction Scenario." **What will be required, however, are significant advances in basic knowledge, in the social capacity and technological capabilities to utilize it, and in the political will to turn this knowledge and know-how into action.** There is ample evidence from attitudinal surveys and grassroots activities that the public supports and demands such progress. The remainder of this report seeks to highlight some of the particular capabilities most in need of active development, and some of the institutional and procedural reforms that might help build a more broadly based social commitment to a sustainability transition.

APPENDIX

SCENARIOS FOR A TRANSITION TOWARD SUSTAINABILITY

The detailed articulation of integrated global scenarios is a major undertaking beyond the scope of this inquiry. Nevertheless, we have endeavored to evaluate the use that scenario approaches might have in exploring possible futures for a sustainability transition by adapting and examining a truncated version of the full scenario analysis developed by the Global Scenario Group using the Polestar analytic framework (see Figure 3.1).[62] First, we considered only a subset of the full range of possible social visions, namely, scenarios of the *Conventional Worlds* variety described earlier (and excluding the more extreme scenarios of the *Barbarization* and *Great Transition* worlds). In particular, we developed for reference purposes a *Current Forces and Trends* scenario, in which no major policy initiatives are undertaken to promote sustainability, and compared this scenario to a *Hunger and Carbon Reduction* scenario, in which explicit efforts are made to reach the sustainability goals outlined in Chapter 1. Second, we concentrated on selected issues, rather than a comprehensive appraisal of the many social and environmental dimensions of the sustainability problem. We took the level of global hunger as a proxy for the poverty problem, and greenhouse gas emissions as representative of environmental stress. While these measures are significant indicators of the social and environmental dimensions of a transition to sustainability, there are many others that a full scenario approach would need to include: indicators on food production and land use, toxification, water, social and international equity, geopolitics, and the possibilities of discontinuous institutional adjustments outside the *Conventional Worlds* assumptions. There are many dimensions of the problem.[63]

A Current Forces and Trends Scenario[64]

The *Current Forces and Trends* scenario, based on the *Reference* class scenario of the Global Scenarios Group, is the story of a market-driven world in which the global system gradually unfolds subject to the initial driving forces and trends described in Chapter 2. In this vision, there is institutional continuity, economic globalization, and the slow convergence of developing countries toward the socioeconomic norms of developed regions. In contrast to the *Hunger and Carbon Reduction* scenario discussed below, strong policy actions for a transition toward sustainability are absent. Demographic, economic, and technological assumptions are consistent with those used in other international assessments.

Values for selected projected global variables in the GSG *Current Forces and Trends* scenario for the years 2025 and 2050 are shown in Figure 3.2 relative to 1995 values. (The data for Figure 3.2 are found in attached Sheets 1–8.) By 2050, population increases by more than 50 percent and average income[65] increases by a factor of more than 2.5, as world economic output more than quadruples. Food requirements almost double, driven by population growth and assumed income increases,

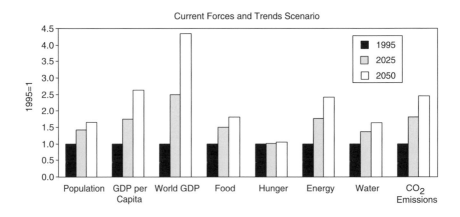

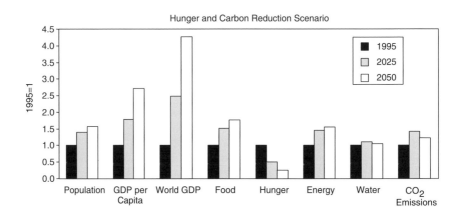

FIGURE 3.2   Overview of *Current Forces and Trends* and *Hunger and Carbon Reduction* scenarios.

Source: Raskin et al. (1998). Courtesy of the Stockholm Environment Institute.

although world hunger remains almost constant, a result of population growth and unequal access to food. Requirements for energy and water increase more slowly than the economy—by factors of 2.4 and 1.6, respectively—due to improving efficiency of use and a shift toward less resource-intensive economic activities such as services versus manufacturing. Global carbon dioxide emissions from energy use increase by a factor of 2.4 over the scenario period.

World population approaches 10 billion by 2050, the UN mid-range projection,[66] with nearly all the additional 3.7 billion people residing in developing regions. Urbanization continues, with almost 7 billion people living in cities in 2050 compared to 2.5 billion in 1995. The OECD regional share of world output decreases from about 78 percent in terms of market exchange rates (MER) or 55 percent in terms of purchasing power parity (PPP) in 1995 to about 60 percent MER or 40 percent PPP in 2050, with population and income growth rates most rapid in developing regions. Absolute national income differences between developing and OECD regions nonetheless increase.

Hunger

The incidence of extreme poverty and hunger are not normally portrayed in integrated global scenarios. Whether, and how, they can be incorporated in scenario efforts are crucial questions in evaluating the suitability of such scenario approaches for exploring possible futures of a sustainability transition.

For the work reported here, the incidence of extreme poverty and hunger was treated as depending on population, economic development, and income distribution. The analysis was carried out at the national level. All else being equal, growth in population adds to the number of people in poverty, while growth in average income decreases it. All else being equal, if income distribution becomes more skewed in the course of development, poverty increases. The degree of income inequality found in the world today varies widely between countries. Future patterns in the scenario assumed are based on trends in developed regions and the assumption of global convergence toward these patterns elsewhere in a context of weak policies for poverty eradication. In particular, the GSG scenario assumes that income inequality continues to increase in the United States, but at half the historical rate. Other countries converge toward the U.S. pattern.

Hunger levels are related to income patterns in the scenario by defining a "hunger line," the income at which dietary requirements for a normally active life are minimally met. National levels of hunger can be computed directly from the income distribution once we know the hunger line. Contemporary data on hunger levels and income distribution define the initial hunger lines used in the scenario. Future hunger lines are assumed to increase as national incomes grow, a pattern that is supported by current data.[67] In the process of urbanization and modernization, it appears that a larger income is required to barely survive, perhaps due to decreased access to informal sources of food (the income-equivalent of informal food gathering is poorly captured in income surveys).

In the scenario, the number of hungry, as defined above, increases gradually over time. Africa shows the sharpest decrease in hunger on a percentage basis, but the largest increase in absolute numbers, while in China and South and Southeast Asia hunger decreases. The hunger reduction goals for the transition toward sustainability set forth in Chapter 1—to reduce by half the number of undernourished people in the world by the year 2015—are not met.

Climate Change

Turning to the implications of the *Current Forces and Trends* scenario for climate change, we focus on carbon dioxide emissions from energy use, the major source of greenhouse gases. The changing regional patterns of energy requirements in the scenario are broadly compatible with the mid-range IPCC IS92a scenario.[68] While global energy needs grow by a factor of 2.4 over the scenario period, developing regions requirements grow by a factor of 3.9. Built into this estimate is an assumed continuing improvement in energy-efficiency. Fossil fuels continue to be the dominant source of energy, though the contributions of modern renewable energy technologies (excluding traditional biomass and hydropower) increase by a factor of 5.2 and nuclear energy increases by a factor of 2.2.

In the GSG *Current Forces and Trends* scenario, carbon dioxide emissions associated with fossil energy use more than double over the 1995-2050 period. The regional composition of emissions changes dramatically as the OECD share of global emissions drops from about 50 to 30 percent over this period. Nevertheless, emissions per capita remain much higher in the developed regions despite the faster growth in poorer regions. For example, emissions per capita in North America are 25 times those in Africa in 1995 but fall to 9 times those in Africa by 2050.

Given the ambiguous goals for managing greenhouse gas concentrations set forth by the international community at Rio and summarized in Chapter 1 (i.e., stabilization "at a level that would prevent dangerous anthropogenic interference with the climate system"), it is impossible to say whether this scenario meets these goals or not. Clearly, however, even the weak interim targets for emission reductions set forth by the Kyoto protocol are not met in this scenario.

A Hunger and Carbon Reduction Scenario

The *Current Forces and Trends* scenario envisions increasing environmental pressures and tenacious poverty, not a vision of a smooth transition to a sustainable world society. Indeed, the surprise-free continuity assumptions of the scenario could well be undermined by the stresses it places on ecological and social systems. By contrast, the *Hunger and Carbon Reduction* scenario assumes that a proactive set of initiatives are instituted to reach sustainability goals. In this case, the international targets for reduction of hunger and greenhouse gas emissions summarized in Chapter 1 are taken as normative goals. The scenario framework is then used to explore what types of initiatives might be effective in moving towards those goals.

Several factors could be altered to move the *Current Forces and Trends* scenario toward patterns that meet the social goals: population levels, the scale of the world economy, the degree of convergence between poor and rich countries (international equity), and the level of income equality within a country (national equity). Our illustrative *Hunger and Carbon Reduction* scenario, which is based on the GSG's *Policy Reform* scenario, assumes slightly lower population growth than the *Current Forces and Trends* scenario due to poverty reduction and more active family planning policies. In the illustrative scenario, non-OECD population in 2050 is assumed to be 95 percent of the UN mid-range forecast value, a reasonable, though modest, assumption given the great uncertainties on the drivers of population growth.

Hunger

In the *Hunger and Carbon Reduction* scenario, hunger goals are met by increasing incomes above minimum threshold levels. In principle, these targets could be met without income shifts, through direct food aid and other targeted welfare programs. Such programs can contribute to a self-sustaining process of raising the incomes of the poor.[69] However, a resilient response to the whole poverty problem will ultimately need to be reflected structurally in income distribution patterns captured by the scenarios.

Not all scenarios of increasing income will meet the target of reducing hunger by one-half by 2025, and half again by 2050. For given levels of total national economic scale, this requires sufficiently high levels of national equity.[70] In the extreme case of no economic growth, very high national equity would be required.[71] Meeting the hunger goals with the equity assumptions of the *Current Forces and Trends* scenario would require, under the assumptions incorporated in the scenario, that average annual growth rates in GDP per capita for non-OECD regions be sustained at levels of more than 5 percent. This "high growth" alternative lies outside what many would consider the realm of plausibility. Moreover, in this variant, the size of the world economy would increase by a factor of 15 by 2025, implying substantially increased environmental pressure.

The *Hunger and Carbon Reduction* scenario developed for this study lies between these extremes. The assumed scale of the world economy in this scenario is very near that of the *Current Forces and Trends* case, with world populations slightly lower and average global income slightly higher comparatively. The distribution of income in the *Hunger and Carbon Reduction* scenario, on the other hand, is very different from that in the *Current Forces and Trends* scenario. The former scenario meets the hunger reduction targets through a more egalitarian distribution of wealth than the latter scenario. In the *Current Forces and Trends* scenario, the ratio of non-OECD to OECD average income (international equity) stays almost constant over the scenario time frame, while in the *Hunger and Carbon Reduction* scenario, the ratio more than doubles, increasing from 0.15 in 1995 to 0.36 in 2050.

National equity decreases from 0.15 to 0.08 in the *Current Forces and Trends* scenario, but remains almost constant in the *Hunger and Carbon Reduction* scenario.[72] While these distribution assumptions imply significantly greater social equity than in the *Current Forces and Trends* scenario, they are not implausible, being near today's values in Europe and those of the 1960s in the United States.

Climate Change

Meeting the climate change goals of Chapter 1 in a *Hunger and Carbon Reduction* scenario also has strong implications for the energy sector and land change. For the purposes of the scenario analysis, we assumed that the Climate Convention goal of "preventing dangerous interference" with the climate system might be met with a cumulative carbon emissions allowance of between 640 and 800 billions of metric tons of carbon (Gt C) between 1990 and 2100.[73] At these levels, an equilibrium carbon dioxide concentration of about 450 ppmv would be reached by the year 2100; this value corresponds to the proposed ecologically based target of limiting human-induced temperature change to no more than 0.1C° per decade.[74] A politically acceptable allocation of these emissions among regions is assumed to involve burden-sharing, with feasible goals for the industrialized countries and some emission increases in developing countries.

In the illustrative *Hunger and Carbon Reduction* scenario, the cumulative carbon budget of 640 to 800 Gt C is met by (1) setting emission abatement targets for OECD countries and regions with transitional economies, (2) allowing developing country regions to increase emissions initially, and (3) gradually converging all regions toward a common per capita emission allowance. This approach balances the various interests while incorporating a long-term equity-based notion of burden-sharing in pursuit of long-term climate stabilization.[75]

Specifically, OECD regions reduce annual energy emissions in the scenario to 10 percent below 1990 levels by 2010 and to 35 percent below 1990 levels by 2025. In the transitional regions, where emissions have dropped precipitously since 1995, scenario emissions increase as their economies recover, and then reduce from 2010 onward. Annual emissions converge everywhere to 0.6 Gt C per capita in 2075, with equal per capita emissions thereafter. In 2100, global emissions are constrained at 3 Gt C per year in order to stabilize carbon dioxide concentrations at 450 ppmv. Finally, developing country emissions increase substantially over the next decades, constrained by the global cap on cumulative emissions of 640 to 800 Gt C and the convergence target. In terms of emissions per capita, the developing regions grow steadily until 2025, but remain substantially below OECD or transitional region levels, before dropping toward the convergence target (Sheet 8). Globally, emissions per capita remain almost constant between 1990 and 2025, and decrease from 2025 to 2100.

To meet these emission constraints, the *Hunger and Carbon Reduction* scenario assumes strong actions for energy-efficiency, renewable energy resource development, and fuel switching.[76] Global energy requirements increase by 56 percent by 2050, which is 36 percent lower than the level foreseen in 2050 in the *Current Forces and Trends* scenario (Sheet 6). Energy requirements in OECD regions decline by over 40 percent by 2050, despite a doubling of GDP (the combined effects of deep energy-efficiency improvements and structural shifts in the economy toward less energy-intensive sectors. On the other hand, energy requirements in developing regions increase by a factor of 3 by 2050, as decreases in energy-intensity per unit of activity are negated by the assumed rapid growth in economic scale (GDP_{PPP} increases by more than a factor of 7 by 2050 for these countries). Analysis of options for implementing these changes suggests that the energy initiatives in the scenario need not require heroic technological assumptions or economic disruption. They will, however, require concerted and sustained efforts at education, capacity building, and the focusing of social attention.[77]

Conclusion

The *Current Forces and Trends* scenario clearly implies that the major elements of a transition toward sustainability cannot be achieved if the forces and trends described in Chapter 2 persist. Human needs will not be met, hunger will not be reduced, and important life support systems will be endangered. There is, however, a suggestion of good news in the *Hunger and Carbon Reduction* scenario.

This brief and limited review of scenarios brings at least an offer of hope. From what we have seen, a transition to sustainability appears to be technically feasible—the hungry can be fed and the human environmental footprint can be kept within reasonable bounds. A much richer, fairer, and environmentally gentler world is conceivable in the 21st century without positing a tumultuous or implausible social transition or revolutionary new technology. Evolutionary adjustments to economic distribution patterns and technological practices would suffice—in principle.

But the scenario is based on another kind of heroic premise—and here is the troubling news. It assumes the emergence of sufficient political will for establishing a comprehensive set of policy reforms for a sustainability transition. It is by no means clear how the required public mobilization and political vision could arise in the context of conventional values, lifestyles, and institutions. Alternative scenarios that transcend conventional visions also require detailed attention in the scientific and social quest for a sustainable future.

Sheet 1: Population

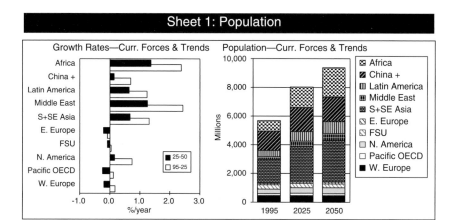

Current Forces and Trends

Region	Population (millions)			Growth Rate (%/year)			Index (95=1)	
	1995	2025	2050	95-25	25-50	95-50	2025	2050
Africa	719	1,454	2,046	2.4	1.4	1.9	2.0	2.8
China +	1,330	1,642	1,704	0.7	0.1	0.5	1.2	1.3
Latin America	477	689	810	1.2	0.6	1.0	1.4	1.7
Middle East	178	365	499	2.4	1.3	1.9	2.1	2.8
S+SE Asia	1,677	2,479	2,925	1.3	0.7	1.0	1.5	1.7
E. Europe	99	97	92	-0.1	-0.2	-0.1	1.0	0.9
FSU	293	297	291	0.0	-0.1	0.0	1.0	1.0
N. America	297	369	384	0.7	0.2	0.5	1.2	1.3
Pacific OECD	149	154	146	0.1	-0.2	0.0	1.0	1.0
W. Europe	467	492	469	0.2	-0.2	0.0	1.1	1.0
Developing	4,382	6,630	7,985	1.4	0.7	1.1	1.5	1.8
Transitional	392	394	383	0.0	-0.1	0.0	1.0	1.0
OECD	913	1,015	998	0.4	-0.1	0.2	1.1	1.1
World	5,687	8,039	9,367	1.2	0.6	0.9	1.4	1.6

Hunger and Carbon Reduction

Region	Population (millions)			Growth Rate (%/year)			Index (95=1)	
	1995	2025	2050	95-25	25-50	95-50	2025	2050
Africa	719	1,425	1,944	2.3	1.3	1.8	2.0	2.7
China +	1,330	1,609	1,619	0.6	0.0	0.4	1.2	1.2
Latin America	477	676	770	1.2	0.5	0.9	1.4	1.6
Middle East	178	358	474	2.4	1.1	1.8	2.0	2.7
S+SE Asia	1,677	2,430	2,779	1.2	0.5	0.9	1.4	1.7
E. Europe	99	95	87	-0.1	-0.3	-0.2	1.0	0.9
FSU	293	291	277	0.0	-0.2	-0.1	1.0	0.9
N. America	297	369	384	0.7	0.2	0.5	1.2	1.3
Pacific OECD	149	154	146	0.1	-0.2	0.0	1.0	1.0
W. Europe	467	492	469	0.2	-0.2	0.0	1.1	1.0
Developing	4,382	6,498	7,586	1.3	0.6	1.0	1.5	1.7
Transitional	392	386	364	-0.1	-0.2	-0.1	1.0	0.9
OECD	913	1,015	998	0.4	-0.1	0.2	1.1	1.1
World	5,687	7,899	8,948	1.1	0.5	0.8	1.4	1.6

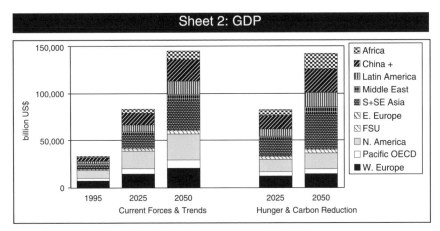

Sheet 2: GDP

Current Forces and Trends

GDP (billion US$)	MER	PPP			Growth Rate (%/year)			Index (95=1)	
Region	1995	1995	2025	2050	95-25	25-50	95-50	2025	2050
Africa	475	1,165	3,958	9,279	4.2	3.5	3.8	3.4	8.0
China +	893	3,839	12,099	22,555	3.9	2.5	3.3	3.2	5.9
Latin America	1,651	2,858	7,449	14,071	3.2	2.6	2.9	2.6	4.9
Middle East	522	938	3,159	6,554	4.1	3.0	3.6	3.4	7.0
S+SE Asia	1,769	4,329	14,160	30,745	4.0	3.1	3.6	3.3	7.1
E. Europe	274	588	1,039	1,396	1.9	1.2	1.6	1.8	2.4
FSU	528	1,206	2,197	3,032	2.0	1.3	1.7	1.8	2.5
N. America	7,464	7,995	18,552	28,016	2.8	1.7	2.3	2.3	3.5
Pacific OECD	5,544	3,146	6,082	8,524	2.2	1.4	1.8	1.9	2.7
W. Europe	9,085	7,352	14,422	20,953	2.3	1.5	1.9	2.0	2.8
Developing	5,310	13,129	40,825	83,204	3.9	2.9	3.4	3.1	6.3
Transitional	802	1,794	3,236	4,427	2.0	1.3	1.7	1.8	2.5
OECD	22,094	18,493	39,056	57,492	2.5	1.6	2.1	2.1	3.1
World	28,205	33,416	83,117	145,124	3.1	2.3	2.7	2.5	4.3

Hunger and Carbon Reduction

GDP (billion US$)	MER	PPP			Growth Rate (%/year)			Index (95=1)	
Region	1995	1995	2025	2050	95-25	25-50	95-50	2025	2050
Africa	475	1,165	6,381	16,427	5.8	3.9	4.9	5.5	14.1
China +	893	3,839	13,762	25,368	4.3	2.5	3.5	3.6	6.6
Latin America	1,651	2,858	8,026	15,177	3.5	2.6	3.1	2.8	5.3
Middle East	522	938	3,501	7,383	4.5	3.0	3.8	3.7	7.9
S+SE Asia	1,769	4,329	17,013	36,417	4.7	3.1	3.9	3.9	8.4
E. Europe	274	588	1,120	1,533	2.2	1.3	1.8	1.9	2.6
FSU	528	1,206	2,501	3,610	2.5	1.5	2.0	2.1	3.0
N. America	7,464	7,995	13,341	16,494	1.7	0.9	1.3	1.7	2.1
Pacific OECD	5,544	3,146	4,742	5,451	1.4	0.6	1.0	1.5	1.7
W. Europe	9,085	7,352	12,202	14,524	1.7	0.7	1.2	1.7	2.0
Developing	5,310	13,129	48,683	100,772	4.5	3.0	3.8	3.7	7.7
Transitional	802	1,794	3,622	5,143	2.4	1.4	1.9	2.0	2.9
OECD	22,094	18,493	30,285	36,468	1.7	0.7	1.2	1.6	2.0
World	28,205	33,416	82,590	142,383	3.1	2.2	2.7	2.5	4.3

Sheet 3: Income (GDP per Capita)

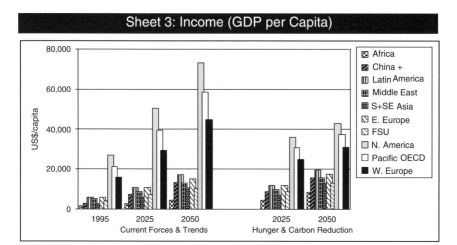

Legend:
- ⊠ Africa
- ▨ China +
- ⬚ Latin America
- ⊞ Middle East
- ▦ S+SE Asia
- ◪ E. Europe
- ◩ FSU
- ☐ N. America
- ☐ Pacific OECD
- ■ W. Europe

Current Forces and Trends

Region	GDP per capita (1995 US$ PPP)			Growth Rate (%/year)			Index (95=1)	
	1995	2025	2050	95-25	25-50	95-50	2025	2050
Africa	1,619	2,722	4,534	1.7	2.1	1.9	1.7	2.8
China +	2,887	7,369	13,234	3.2	2.4	2.8	2.6	4.6
Latin America	5,999	10,804	17,366	2.0	1.9	2.0	1.8	2.9
Middle East	5,261	8,643	13,123	1.7	1.7	1.7	1.6	2.5
S+SE Asia	2,581	5,711	10,512	2.7	2.5	2.6	2.2	4.1
E. Europe	5,946	10,760	15,220	2.0	1.4	1.7	1.8	2.6
FSU	4,111	7,394	10,405	2.0	1.4	1.7	1.8	2.5
N. America	26,946	50,265	72,932	2.1	1.5	1.8	1.9	2.7
Pacific OECD	21,104	39,368	58,544	2.1	1.6	1.9	1.9	2.8
W. Europe	15,727	29,337	44,714	2.1	1.7	1.9	1.9	2.8
Developing	2,996	6,157	10,420	2.4	2.1	2.3	2.1	3.5
Transitional	4,574	8,220	11,558	2.0	1.4	1.7	1.8	2.5
OECD	20,249	38,472	57,589	2.2	1.6	1.9	1.9	2.8
World	5,876	10,339	15,494	1.9	1.6	1.8	1.8	2.6

Hunger and Carbon Reduction

Region	GDP per capita (1995 US$ PPP)			Growth Rate (%/year)			Index (95=1)	
	1995	2025	2050	95-25	25-50	95-50	2025	2050
Africa	1,619	4,479	8,450	3.5	2.6	3.1	2.8	5.2
China +	2,887	8,553	15,668	3.7	2.5	3.1	3.0	5.4
Latin America	5,999	11,879	19,717	2.3	2.0	2.2	2.0	3.3
Middle East	5,261	9,774	15,561	2.1	1.9	2.0	1.9	3.0
S+SE Asia	2,581	7,001	13,106	3.4	2.5	3.0	2.7	5.1
E. Europe	5,946	11,835	17,596	2.3	1.6	2.0	2.0	3.0
FSU	4,111	8,590	13,041	2.5	1.7	2.1	2.1	3.2
N. America	26,946	36,147	42,937	1.0	0.7	0.9	1.3	1.6
Pacific OECD	21,104	30,696	37,437	1.3	0.8	1.0	1.5	1.8
W. Europe	15,727	24,821	30,995	1.5	0.9	1.2	1.6	2.0
Developing	2,996	7,492	13,284	3.1	2.3	2.7	2.5	4.4
Transitional	4,574	9,386	14,131	2.4	1.7	2.1	2.1	3.1
OECD	20,249	29,833	36,530	1.3	0.8	1.1	1.5	1.8
World	5,876	10,456	15,912	1.9	1.7	1.8	1.8	2.7

Sheet 4: Income Distribution

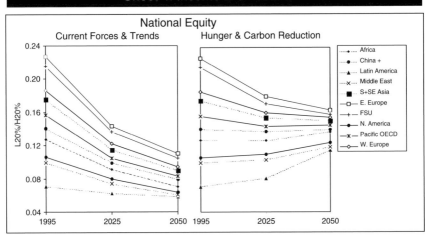

Current Forces and Trends

Region	National Equity (L20%/H20%)			Gini Coefficient		
	1995	2025	2050	1995	2025	2050
Africa	0.13	0.09	0.07	0.42	0.46	0.50
China +	0.14	0.10	0.08	0.38	0.44	0.47
Latin America	0.07	0.06	0.06	0.50	0.51	0.52
Middle East	0.10	0.07	0.06	0.45	0.49	0.51
S+SE Asia	0.18	0.11	0.09	0.34	0.41	0.45
E. Europe	0.23	0.14	0.11	0.29	0.37	0.42
FSU	0.22	0.14	0.10	0.30	0.38	0.43
N. America	0.11	0.08	0.06	0.43	0.47	0.51
Pacific OECD	0.16	0.11	0.08	0.36	0.43	0.47
W. Europe	0.19	0.12	0.09	0.33	0.41	0.45
World (pop. weighted)	0.15	0.10	0.08			

Hunger and Carbon Reduction

Region	National Equity (L20%/H20%)			Gini Coefficient		
	1995	2025	2050	1995	2025	2050
Africa	0.13	0.13	0.14	0.42	0.42	0.39
China +	0.14	0.14	0.14	0.38	0.38	0.38
Latin America	0.07	0.08	0.12	0.50	0.47	0.41
Middle East	0.10	0.10	0.12	0.45	0.44	0.41
S+SE Asia	0.18	0.15	0.15	0.34	0.36	0.37
E. Europe	0.23	0.18	0.16	0.29	0.33	0.35
FSU	0.22	0.17	0.16	0.30	0.34	0.36
N. America	0.11	0.11	0.12	0.43	0.43	0.40
Pacific OECD	0.16	0.14	0.15	0.36	0.37	0.37
W. Europe	0.19	0.16	0.15	0.33	0.36	0.36
World (pop. weighted)	0.15	0.14	0.14			

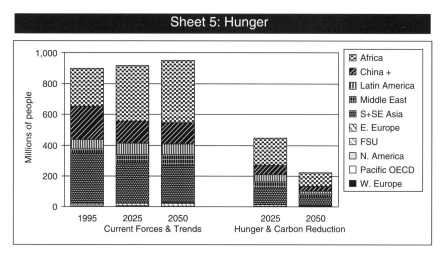

Sheet 5: Hunger

Current Forces and Trends

Region	Incidence (% of population)			Incidence (millions)			Index (95=1)	
	1995	2025	2050	1995	2025	2050	2025	2050
Africa	34	25	20	247	361	404	1.46	1.63
China +	16	9	8	211	142	136	0.67	0.64
Latin America	14	11	9	65	73	72	1.13	1.11
Middle East	16	16	14	29	57	72	1.95	2.45
S+SE Asia	19	10	8	320	259	240	0.81	0.75
E. Europe	1	2	3	1	2	3	2.72	4.24
FSU	4	5	6	11	14	18	1.24	1.55
N. America	2	1	1	7	3	2	0.45	0.34
Pacific OECD	1	1	0	1	1	0	0.53	0.32
W. Europe	1	1	1	4	4	4	1.06	0.94
Developing	20	13	12	873	893	924	1.02	1.06
Transitional	3	4	5	12	16	21	1.33	1.71
OECD	1	1	1	12	8	6	0.64	0.52
World	16	11	10	898	917	951	1.02	1.06

Hunger and Carbon Reduction

Region	Incidence (% of population)			Incidence (millions)			Index (95=1)	
	1995	2025	2050	1995	2025	2050	2025	2050
Africa	34	12	5	247	174	87	0.70	0.35
China +	16	4	2	211	59	29	0.28	0.14
Latin America	14	7	2	65	49	18	0.75	0.28
Middle East	16	11	5	29	40	24	1.39	0.81
S+SE Asia	19	4	2	320	109	54	0.34	0.17
E. Europe	1	1	1	1	1	1	1.01	0.94
FSU	4	2	2	11	7	5	0.57	0.40
N. America	2	1	0	7	4	1	0.50	0.12
Pacific OECD	1	0	0	1	1	0	0.35	0.11
W. Europe	1	1	0	4	3	1	0.69	0.37
Developing	20	7	3	873	431	212	0.49	0.24
Transitional	3	2	1	12	7	5	0.60	0.43
OECD	1	1	0	12	7	2	0.54	0.19
World	16	6	2	898	445	220	0.50	0.25

Sheet 6: Primary Energy Requirements by Region

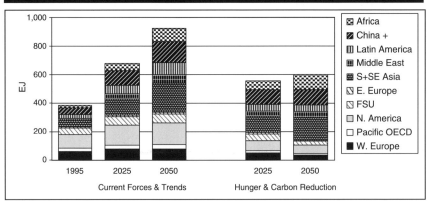

	Africa
	China +
	Latin America
	Middle East
	S+SE Asia
	E. Europe
	FSU
	N. America
	Pacific OECD
	W. Europe

Current Forces & Trends   Hunger & Carbon Reduction

Current Forces and Trends

Region	Primary Energy (EJ)			Growth Rate (%/year)			Index (95=1)		Intensity (MJ/$ PPP)		
	1995	2025	2050	95-25	25-50	95-50	2025	2050	1995	2025	2050
Africa	17	50	98	3.6	2.7	3.2	2.9	5.7	15	13	11
China +	48	105	144	2.7	1.3	2.0	2.2	3.0	12	9	6
Latin America	24	55	84	2.7	1.8	2.3	2.3	3.5	8	7	6
Middle East	18	38	60	2.5	1.9	2.2	2.1	3.3	19	12	9
S+SE Asia	43	114	205	3.3	2.4	2.9	2.7	4.8	10	8	7
E. Europe	10	13	12	0.8	-0.2	0.4	1.3	1.2	17	12	9
FSU	45	60	64	0.9	0.3	0.6	1.3	1.4	38	27	21
N. America	94	138	152	1.3	0.4	0.9	1.5	1.6	12	7	5
Pacific OECD	23	29	31	0.8	0.2	0.5	1.3	1.3	7	5	4
W. Europe	63	76	79	0.6	0.2	0.4	1.2	1.3	9	5	4
Developing	150	361	591	3.0	2.0	2.5	2.4	3.9	11	9	7
Transitional	55	73	76	0.9	0.2	0.6	1.3	1.4	31	22	17
OECD	179	243	262	1.0	0.3	0.7	1.4	1.5	10	6	5
World	384	677	929	1.9	1.3	1.6	1.8	2.4	12	8	6

Hunger and Carbon Reduction

Region	Primary Energy (EJ)			Growth Rate (%/year)			Index (95=1)		Intensity (MJ/$ PPP)		
	1995	2025	2050	95-25	25-50	95-50	2025	2050	1995	2025	2050
Africa	17	63	107	4.4	2.1	3.4	3.7	6.2	15	10	6
China +	48	104	105	2.6	0.0	1.4	2.2	2.2	12	8	4
Latin America	24	45	48	2.1	0.2	1.2	1.9	2.0	8	6	3
Middle East	18	37	41	2.4	0.4	1.5	2.1	2.3	19	11	6
S+SE Asia	43	114	160	3.3	1.4	2.4	2.7	3.8	10	7	4
E. Europe	10	9	6	-0.3	-1.4	-0.8	0.9	0.7	17	8	4
FSU	45	47	28	0.1	-2.0	-0.9	1.0	0.6	38	19	8
N. America	94	73	57	-0.8	-1.0	-0.9	0.8	0.6	12	5	3
Pacific OECD	23	17	12	-1.0	-1.3	-1.2	0.7	0.5	7	4	2
W. Europe	63	49	36	-0.8	-1.3	-1.0	0.8	0.6	9	4	2
Developing	150	363	460	3.0	0.9	2.1	2.4	3.1	11	7	5
Transitional	55	56	35	0.1	-1.9	-0.9	1.0	0.6	31	16	7
OECD	179	138	105	-0.9	-1.1	-1.0	0.8	0.6	10	5	3
World	384	558	599	1.2	0.3	0.8	1.5	1.6	12	7	4

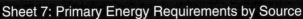

Sheet 7: Primary Energy Requirements by Source

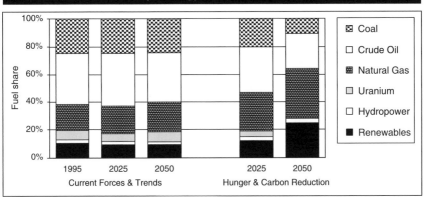

Current Forces and Trends

Fuel	Primary Energy (EJ)			Share of Total (%)			Growth Rate (%/year)			Index (95=1)	
	1995	2025	2050	1995	2025	2050	95-25	25-50	95-50	2025	2050
Coal	95	166	224	25	25	24	1.9	1.2	1.6	1.8	2.4
Crude Oil	141	256	332	37	38	36	2.0	1.0	1.6	1.8	2.3
Natural Gas	73	136	203	19	20	22	2.1	1.6	1.9	1.9	2.8
Uranium	25	39	64	7	6	7	1.5	2.0	1.7	1.5	2.5
Hydropower	9	16	20	2	2	2	1.9	0.9	1.4	1.7	2.2
Renewables	41	64	87	11	9	9	1.5	1.3	1.4	1.6	2.1
Total	384	677	929		100	100	1.9	1.3	1.6	1.8	2.4

Hunger and Carbon Reduction

Fuel	Primary Energy (EJ)			Share of Total (%)			Growth Rate (%/year)			Index (95=1)	
	1995	2025	2050	1995	2025	2050	95-25	25-50	95-50	2025	2050
Coal	95	113	63	25	20	11	0.6	-2.3	-0.7	1.2	0.7
Crude Oil	141	183	153	37	33	26	0.9	-0.7	0.1	1.3	1.1
Natural Gas	73	156	215	19	28	36	2.6	1.3	2.0	2.1	2.9
Uranium	25	22	-	7	4	-	-0.4	-	-	0.9	0.0
Hydropower	9	16	20	2	3	3	1.9	0.9	1.4	1.7	2.2
Renewables	41	68	148	11	12	25	1.7	3.2	2.4	1.7	3.6
Total	384	558	599	100	100	100	1.2	0.3	0.8	1.5	1.6

Sheet 8: Carbon Emissions

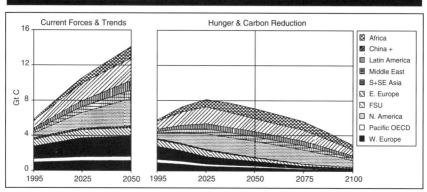

Current Forces and Trends

Region	Total Annual Emissions (Gt C)			Index (95=1)		Annual Per Capita (t C)			Annual Per Dollar GDP PPP (kg C)		
	1995	2025	2050	2025	2050	1995	2025	2050	1995	2025	2050
Africa	0.17	0.65	1.39	3.9	8.3	0.2	0.4	0.7	0.14	0.16	0.15
China +	0.87	2.00	2.60	2.3	3.0	0.7	1.2	1.5	0.23	0.17	0.12
Latin America	0.30	0.75	1.15	2.5	3.8	0.6	1.1	1.4	0.10	0.10	0.08
Middle East	0.25	0.64	0.93	2.5	3.7	1.4	1.8	1.9	0.27	0.20	0.14
S+SE Asia	0.57	1.75	3.22	3.1	5.6	0.3	0.7	1.1	0.13	0.12	0.10
E. Europe	0.19	0.23	0.20	1.2	1.1	1.9	2.3	2.2	0.32	0.22	0.15
FSU	0.75	0.94	0.96	1.3	1.3	2.6	3.2	3.3	0.62	0.43	0.32
N. America	1.49	2.22	2.40	1.5	1.6	5.0	6.0	6.2	0.19	0.12	0.09
Pacific OECD	0.39	0.44	0.44	1.1	1.1	2.6	2.8	3.0	0.12	0.07	0.05
W. Europe	0.95	1.16	1.24	1.2	1.3	2.0	2.4	2.6	0.13	0.08	0.06
Developing	2.16	5.79	9.29	2.7	4.3	0.5	0.9	1.2	0.16	0.14	0.11
Transitional	0.94	1.17	1.16	1.2	1.2	2.4	3.0	3.0	0.52	0.36	0.26
OECD	2.83	3.82	4.08	1.3	1.4	3.1	3.8	4.1	0.15	0.10	0.07
World	5.94	10.78	14.53	1.8	2.4	1.0	1.3	1.6	0.18	0.13	0.10

Hunger and Carbon Reduction

Region	Total Annual Emissions (Gt C)			Index (95=1)		Annual Per Capita (t C)			Annual Per Dollar GDP PPP (kg C)		
	1995	2025	2050	2025	2050	1995	2025	2050	1995	2025	2050
Africa	0.17	0.89	1.19	5.3	7.2	0.2	0.6	0.6	0.14	0.14	0.07
China +	0.87	1.95	1.47	2.2	1.7	0.7	1.2	0.9	0.23	0.14	0.06
Latin America	0.30	0.61	0.61	2.0	2.0	0.6	0.9	0.8	0.10	0.08	0.04
Middle East	0.25	0.61	0.54	2.4	2.2	1.4	1.7	1.1	0.27	0.17	0.07
S+SE Asia	0.57	1.78	1.86	3.1	3.2	0.3	0.7	0.7	0.13	0.10	0.05
E. Europe	0.19	0.15	0.10	0.8	0.5	1.9	1.6	1.1	0.32	0.14	0.06
FSU	0.75	0.68	0.38	0.9	0.5	2.6	2.3	1.4	0.62	0.27	0.11
N. America	1.49	0.90	0.59	0.6	0.4	5.0	2.4	1.5	0.19	0.07	0.04
Pacific OECD	0.39	0.21	0.14	0.6	0.4	2.6	1.4	1.0	0.12	0.05	0.03
W. Europe	0.95	0.59	0.41	0.6	0.4	2.0	1.2	0.9	0.13	0.05	0.03
Developing	2.16	5.83	5.67	2.7	2.6	0.5	0.9	0.7	0.16	0.12	0.06
Transitional	0.94	0.83	0.48	0.9	0.5	2.4	2.2	1.3	0.52	0.23	0.09
OECD	2.83	1.70	1.15	0.6	0.4	3.1	1.7	1.1	0.15	0.06	0.03
World	5.94	8.37	7.30	1.4	1.2	1.0	1.1	0.8	0.18	0.10	0.05

REFERENCES AND BIBLIOGRAPHY

Achebe, Chinua, Goran Hyden, Achola Pala Okeyo, and Christopher Magadza, eds. 1990. *Beyond hunger in Africa: Conventional wisdom and a vision of Africa in 2057.* Nairobi: Henemann Kenya.

Ackerman, B.A., S. Rose-Ackerman, J.W. Sawyer, Jr., and D.W. Henderson. 1974. *The uncertain search for environmental quality.* New York: The Free Press.

Alcamo, J., R. Shaw, and L. Hordijk, eds. 1990. *The RAINS model of acidification: Science and strategies in Europe.* Dordrecht: Kluwer Publishers.

Benedick, Richard Elliott. 1988. *Ozone diplomacy: New directions in safeguarding the planet.* Cambridge, MA: Harvard University Press. Especially Chapter 2.

Blinder, Alan. 1988. Economic policy and economic science: The case of macroeconomics. In *Perspective 2000: Proceedings of a conference sponsored by the Economic Council of Canada, December 1998,* eds. K. Newton, T. Schweitzer, and J-P. Voyer. Ottawa: Canadian Government Publishing Centre.

Bossel, Harmut. 1998. *Earth at a crossroads: Paths to a sustainable future.* Cambridge: Cambridge University Press.

Brewer, G.D. 1986. Methods for synthesis: Policy exercises. Chap. 17 of *Sustainable development of the biosphere,* eds. W. C. Clark and R. E. Munn. Cambridge, UK: Cambridge University Press.

Brewer, G.D., and M. Shubik. 1979. *The War game: A critique of military problem solving.* Cambridge, MA: Harvard University Press.

Budnitz, R.J., P.R. Davis, M.K. Ravindra, and W.H. Tong. 1995. Seismic risk of nuclear power plants under shutdown conditions. In *International conference on structural mechanics in reactor technology* 4. Conference organized by the International Association for Structural Mechanics in Reactor Technology and Universidade Federal do Rio Grande do Sul. Porto Alegre, Brazil: Editora da Universidade Federal do Rio Grande do Sul.

Carson, Rachel. 1962. *Silent spring.* New York: Fawcett Crest.

Cebon, P., U. Dahinden, H.C. Davies, D. Imboden, and C.C. Jaeger. 1998. *Views from the Alps: Regional perspectives on climate change.* Cambridge, MA: MIT Press.

Clark, William C., and Giandomenico Majone. 1985. The critical appraisal of scientific inquiries with policy implications. *Science Technology and Human Values* 10 (Summer 1985): 6-19.

Clark, William C. 1988. Visions of the 21st century: Conventional wisdom and other surprises in the global interactions of population, technology and environment. In *Perspective 2000: Proceedings of a conference sponsored by the Economic Council of Canada, December 1998,* eds. K. Newton, T. Schweitzer, and J-P. Voyer, 7-32. Ottawa: Economic Council of Canada.

Commission on Risk. See Presidential/Congressional Commission on Risk Assessment and Risk Management.

Cronon, William. 1992. A place for stories: Nature, history, and narrative. *Journal of American History* 78: 1347-1376.

Cukier, R.I., H.B. Levine, and K.E. Schuler. 1978. Nonlinear sensitivity analysis of multiparameter model systems. *Journal of Computational Physics* 26: 1-42.

Dowlatabadi, Hadi, and M. Granger Morgan. 1993. Integrated assessment of climate change. *Science* 259, no. 5013: 1813, 1932.

Epple, Dennis, and Lester Lave. 1985. Scenario analysis. In *Climate Impact Analysis,* eds. R. Kates, J. Ausubel, and M. Berberian. London: Wiley.

Fishbone, L.G., and H. Abilock. 1981. MARKAL, a linear-programming model for energy systems analysis: Technical description of the BNL version. *Energy Research* 5: 353-375.

Forrester, J.W. 1968. *Principles of systems.* Cambridge, MA: Wright-Allen Press.

GEA (Global Environment Assessment Project). 1997. A critical evaluation of global environmental assessments: The climate experience. Calverton, MD: Center for the Application of Research on the Environment. [http://environment.harvard.edu/gea].

Gallopin, Gilberto, Al Hammond, Paul Raskin, and Rob Swart. 1997. *Branch points: Global scenarios and human choice.* Stockholm: Stockholm Environment Institute.

Greenburger, M. 1983. *Caught unawares: The energy decade in retrospect.* Cambridge, MA: Ballinger.

Gunderson, Lance H., C.S. Holling, and Stephen S. Light, eds. 1995. *Barriers and bridges to the renewal of ecosystems and institutions.* New York: Columbia University Press.

Guston, D. 1997. Critical appraisal in science and technology policy analysis: The example of "Science, the endless frontier." *Policy Sciences* 30: 233-255.

Haas, Peter M. 1990. *Saving the Mediterranean: The politics of international environmental cooperation.* New York: Columbia University Press.

Haefele, W, project leader. 1981. *Energy in a finite world: A global systems analysis.* Cambridge, MA: Ballinger.

Hammond, A. 1998. *Which world: Scenarios for the 21st century.* Washington: Island Press.

Henrion, Max, and Baruch Fischhoff. 1986. Assessing uncertainty in physical constants. *American Journal of Physics* 54, no. 9: 791-798.

Herrera, A.O., et al. 1976. *Catastrophe or new society?: A Latin American world model.* Fundación Bariloche. Ottawa: International Development Research Centre.

Holling, C.S., ed. 1978. *Adaptive environmental assessment and management.* Chichester, UK: John Wiley.

Hordijk, L. 1988. Linking policy and science: A model approach to acid rain. *Environment* 30, no. 2: 16-20.

Hordijk, L., and C. Kroeze. 1997. Integrated assessment models for acid rain. *European Journal of Operational Research* 102, no. 3: 405-417.

Houghton, J.T., B.A. Callander, and S.K. Varney, eds. 1992. *Climate change 1992: The supplementary report to the IPCC Scientific Assessment.* Cambridge, UK: Cambridge University Press. Published for the Intergovernmental Panel on Climate Change.

Houghton, J.T., L.G. Meira Filho, B.A. Callander, N. Harris, A. Kattenberg, and K. Maskell, eds. 1996. *Climate change 1995: The science of climate change.* Cambridge, UK: Cambridge University Press. Published for the Intergovernmental Panel on Climate Change.

Hourcade, J-C. and B. Lapillonne. 1985. Futurology of energy demand in developing countries: modeling problems. Association d'econometrie appliquee, colloque international 2. Aix-en-Provence, France: Economica Paris.

Hourcade, J-C., R. Richels, and J. Robinson. 1996. Estimating the costs of mitigating greenhouse gases. In *Climate change 1995: Economic and social dimensions of climate change. Contribution of working group III to the second assessment report of the Intergovernmental Panel on Climate Change,* eds. J. Bruce, H. Lee, and E. Haites. Cambridge, UK: Cambridge University Press.

Hourcade, J-C., and J. Robinson. 1996. Mitigating factors: Assessing the costs of reducing GHG emission. *Energy Policy* 24, no. 10/11: 863-873.

IPCC (Intergovernmental Panel on Climate Change). 1992. See Houghton et al. 1992.

_____. 1996. See Houghton et al. 1996.

Jaeger, J., N. Sonntag, D. Bernard, and W. Kurz. 1991. *The challenge of sustainable development in a greenhouse world: Some visions of the future.* Report of a Policy Exercise at Bad Bleiberg, Austria, September 2-7, 1990. Stockholm: Stockholm Environment Institute.

Jorgenson, D.W., and P. Wilcoxen. 1993. Energy, the environment, and economic growth. *Handbook of Natural Resource and Energy Economics* 3: 1267-1390.

Julian, Paul R., Robert W. Kates, and W.R.D. Sewell. 1969. Estimating probabilities of research success in atmospheric sciences: Results of a pilot investigation. *Water Resources Research* 5, no. 1 (February 1969): 215-227.

Kaplan, Robert D. 1994. The coming anarchy: How scarcity, crime, overpopulation, tribalism, and disease are rapidly destroying the social fabric of our planet. *The Atlantic Monthly* 273, no. 2: 44-64.

Keepin, B. and B. Wynne. 1987. The role of models: What can we expect from science? A study of the IIASA world energy model. In *The politics of energy forecasting*, eds. Thomas Baumgartner and Atle Midttun. London: Oxford University Press.

Kennedy, Paul. 1993. *Preparing for the twenty-first century.* New York: Random House.

Kinsman, Francis. 1990. *Millenium: Towards tomorrow's society.* London: W.H. Allen.

Kneese, Allen V., and Blair T. Bower. 1968. *Managing water quality: Economics, technology, institutions.* Baltimore: Johns Hopkins University Press. Published for Resources for the Future.

Lansing, J. Stephen. 1991. *Priests and programmers: Technologies of power in the engineered landscape of Bali.* Princeton: Princeton University Press.

Lee, Kai N. 1993. *Compass and gyroscope. Integrating science and politics for the environment.* Washington, D.C.: Island Press.

Levy, M.A. 1993. European acid rain: The power of tote-board diplomacy. In *Institutions for the earth: sources of effective international environmental protection*, eds. P.M. Haas, R.O. Keohane, and M. Levy. Cambridge, MA: MIT Press.

Maass, A. 1962. *Design of water-resource systems; new techniques for relating economic objectives, engineering analysis, and governmental planning.* Cambridge, MA: Harvard University Press.

Mar, B.W. 1974. Problems encountered in multi-disciplinary resources and environmental simulation models development. *J. Environ. Manage.* 2: 83-100.

McCay, Bonnie J. 1998. *Oyster wars and the public trust: Property, law, and ecology in New Jersey history.* Tucson: University of Arizona Press.

Meadows, D.H., D.L. Meadows, and J. Randers. 1992. *Beyond the limits: Confronting global collapse, envisioning a sustainable future.* Post Mills, VT: Chelsea Green.

Meadows, D.H., D.L. Meadows, J. Randers, and W. W. Behrens. 1972. *The limits to growth.* New York: Universe Books.

Meadows, D.H., J. Richardson, and G. Bruckmann. 1982. *Groping in the dark: The first decade of global modeling.* Chichester, UK: Wiley.

Meadows, Donella H., and J.M. Robinson. 1985. *The electronic oracle computer models and social decisions.* New York: John Wiley & Sons.

Miles, Edward L. 1998. Personal reflections on an unfinished journey through global environmental problems of long timescale. *Policy Sciences* 31, no. 1: 1-33.

Morgan, M. Granger. 1998. Uncertainty analysis in risk assessment. *Human and ecological risk assessment* 4, no. 1: 25-39.

Morgan, M. Granger, and Hadi Dowlatabadi. 1996. Learning from integrated assessment of climate change. *Climatic Change* 34: 337-68.

Morgan, M. Granger, M. Henrion, and M. Small. 1990. *Uncertainty: A guide to dealing with uncertainty in quantitative risk and policy analysis.* New York: Cambridge University Press.

Morgan, M. Granger, and David Keith. 1995. Subjective judgments by climate experts. *Environmental Science and Technology* 29, no. 10: 468-476.

Morgan, M. Granger, S.C. Morris, M. Henrion, D.A.L. Amaral, W.R. Rish, C. De Wispelaere, F.A. Schiermeier, and N.V. Gillani, eds. 1986. *Technical uncertainty in quantitative policy analysis: A sulfur air pollution example.* New York: Plenum Press.

Morris, R.F. 1963. The dynamics of epidemic spruce budworm populations. *Mem. Entomol. Soc. Can.* No. 31.

Nakicenovic, Nebojsa, Arnulf Grübler, and Alan McDonald, eds. 1998. *Global Energy Perspectives.* Cambridge, UK: Cambridge University Press.

National Assessment Synthesis Team. 1998. *A framework for socio-economic and ecological assumptions in climate impact assessment.* Washington, D.C.: US Global Change Research Program.

NPPC (Northwest Power Planning Council). 1994. *Columbia Basin fish and wildlife program.* Portland, OR: Northwest Power Planning Council.

NRC (National Research Council). 1979. *Protection against depletion of stratospheric ozone by chlorofluorocarbons.* Assembly of Mathematical and Physical Sciences (US), Committee on Impacts of Stratospheric Change. Washington, D.C.: National Academy Press.

_____. 1983. *Changing climate.* Carbon Dioxide Assessment Committee. Washington, D.C.: National Academy Press.

_____. 1992. *Policy implications of greenhouse warming: Mitigation, adaptation and the science base.* Washington, D.C.: National Academy Press.

_____. 1994. *Improving the management of US marine fisheries.* Washington, D.C.: National Academy Press.

_____. 1996a. *Understanding risk: Informing decisions in a democratic society.* Committee on Risk Characterization, eds. Paul C. Stern and Harvey V. Fineberg. Washington, D.C.: National Academy Press.

_____. 1996b. *Upstream: Salmon and society in the Pacific Northwest.* Committee on Protection and Management of Pacific Northwest Anadromous Salmonids. Washington, D.C.: National Academy Press.

_____. 1998. *Improving fish stock assessments.* Committee on Fish Stock Assessment Methods. Washington, D.C.: National Academy Press.

Olson, David M. and Eric Dinerstein 1998. The Global 200: A representation approach to conserving the earth's most biologically valuable ecoregions. *Conservation Biology* 12: 502-515.

Parson, Edward R. 1995. Integrated assessment and environmental policy making. *Energy Policy* 23, no. 4/5: 463-475.

Parson, Edward R. 1997. Informing global environmental policy-making: A plea for new methods of assessment and synthesis. *Environmental Modeling and Assessment* 2: 267-279.

Parson, Edward R., and Karen Fisher-Vanden. 1997. Integrated assessment models of global climate change. *Annual Review of Energy and Environment* 22: 589-628.

Pinkerton, Evelyn W. 1992. Translating legal rights into management practice: Overcoming barriers to the exercise of co-management. *Human Organization* 51: 330-341.

Presidential/Congressional Commission on Risk Assessment and Risk Management. 1997. *Framework for environmental health risk management.* Washington, D.C.: U.S. Government Printing Office. Available at www.riskword.com.

Raskin, P., G. Gallopin, P. Gutman, A. Hammond, and R. Swart. 1998. *Bending the curve: Toward global sustainability.* A report of the Global Scenario Group. PoleStar Series Report no. 8. Boston: Stockholm Environment Institute.

Ravallion, Martin. 1992. *Poverty comparisons: A guide to concepts and methods.* Washington, D.C.: The World Bank.

Reisner, Marc P. 1986. *Cadillac desert: The American West and its disappearing water.* New York: Viking.

Ricker, W.E. 1954. Stock and recruitment. *J. Fish. Res. Board. Can.* 11: 559-623.

Rijsberman, F.R., and R.J. Swart. 1990. *Targets and indicators of climate change.* Proceedings of a conference, Rotterdam, Netherlands, April 25-27, 1990. Stockholm: Stockholm Environment Institute.

Robinson, J.B., and D.S. Rothman. 1997. Growing pains: A conceptual framework for considering integrated assessments. *Environmental Monitoring and Assessment* 46, no. 1-2: 23-43.

Rotmans, J. Forthcoming. TARGETS (Tool to Assess Regional and Global Environmental and Health Targets for Sustainability). In *Electronic series in integrated assessment modelling*, eds. J. Rotmans and H. Dowlatabadi. Bussum, The Netherlands: Baltzer Scientific Publishers.

Rotmans, J., and B. de Vries. 1997. *Perspectives on global change: The TARGETS approach.* London: Cambridge University Press.

SCOPE (Scientific Committee on Problems of the Environment, International Council of Scientific Unions). 1978. *Simulation modeling of environmental problems.* SCOPE 9. Chichester, UK: John Wiley.

Spetzler, Carl S., and Staël von Holstein. 1975. Probability encoding in decision analysis. *Management Science* 22, no. 3: 340-358.

Standard and Poors DRI. 1998. *The impact of meeting the Kyoto Protocol on energy markets and the economy.* Lexington, MA: DRI.

Stegner, Wallace. 1954. *Beyond the hundredth meridian: John Wesley Powell and the second opening of the West.* 1982 edition. Lincoln: University of Nebraska Press.

Svedin, U., and B. Aniansson. 1987. *Surprising futures: notes from an international workshop on long-term world development.* Stockholm: Swedish Council for Planning and Coordination of Research.

Tatang, Menner A., Wenwei Pan, Ronald G. Prinn, and Gregory J. McRae. 1997. An efficient method for parameter uncertainty analysis of numerical geophysical models. *Journal of Geophysical Research* 102, no. D18: 21925-21932.

Toth, Ferenc L. 1988a. Policy exercises: Objectives and design elements. *Simulation and Games* 19 (September): 235-255.

Toth, Ferenc L. 1988b. Policy exercises: Procedures and implementation. *Simulation and Games* 19 (September): 256-276.

UN (United Nations). 1998. *World population prospects: The 1996 revision.* New York: United Nations.

UNDP (United Nations Development Programme). 1997. *Human development report 1997.* New York: Oxford University Press.

U.S. Congress, Office of Technology Assessment. 1991. *Changing by degrees: Steps to reduce greenhouse gases.* OTA-O-482. Washington, D.C.: US Government Printing Office.

U.S. Congress, Office of Technology Assessment. 1993. *Preparing for an uncertain climate, Volume II.* OTA-O-568. Washington, D.C.: US Government Printing Office.

WBCSD (World Business Council on Sustainable Development). 1997. *Exploring sustainable development.* WBCSD Global Scenarios 2000-2050 summary brochure. Geneva: WBCSD.

WEC/IIASA (World Energy Council, International Institute for Applied Systems Analysis). 1995. *Global Energy Perspectives to 2050 and Beyond.* London: World Energy Council.

WEFA, Inc. 1998. *Global warming: The high cost of the Kyoto Protocol, nation and state impacts.* Eddystone, PA: WEFA.

WGBU (German Advisory Council on Global Change). 1997. *World in transition: The research challenge.* Annual Report 1996. Berlin: Springer-Verlag. [also available through the Council's home page at http://www.awi-bremmerhaven.de/WBGU].

Wack, P. 1985a. Scenarios: Uncharted waters ahead. *Harvard Business Review* 63, no. 5: 72-89.

Wack, P. 1985b. Scenarios: Shooting the rapids (Part 2). *Harvard Business Review* 63, no. 6: 139-150.

Walsh, S.J., T.P. Evans, W.F. Welsh, B. Entwisle, and R.R. Rindfuss. 1999. Scale-dependent relationships between population and environment in Northeastern Thailand. *Photogrammetric Engineering and Remote Sensing* 65, no. 1: 97-105.

Walters, C.J. 1986. *Adaptive management of renewable resources.* London: MacMillan.

Washington, Warren M., and Claire L. Parkinson. 1986. *An introduction to three-dimensional climate* modeling. Mill Valley, CA: University Science Books.

Watt, K.E.F. 1966. *Systems analysis in ecology.* New York: Academic Press.

Weyant, J., O. Davidson, H. Dowlatabadi, J. Edmonds, M. Grubb, E.A. Parson, R. Richels, J. Rotmans, P.R. Shukla, R.S.J. Tol, W. Cline, S. Fankhauser. 1996. Integrated assessment of climate change: An overview and comparison of approaches and results. Chap. 10 of *Climate change 1995,* ed. James P. Bruce, Hoesung Lee, and Erik F. Haites. Contribution of Working Group III to the Second Assessment Report of the Intergovernmental Panel on Climate Change (IPCC). Cambridge, UK: Cambridge University Press. Published for the IPCC.

World Bank. 1990. *World development report 1990.* New York: Oxford University Press. Published for the World Bank.

Worster, Donald. 1985. *Rivers of empire: Water, aridity, and the growth of the American West.* New York: Pantheon.

ENDNOTES

[1] See, e.g., Guston (1997); Brewer (1986); Clark and Majone (1985).

[2] E.g., Washington and Parkinson 1986; NRC 1994, NRC (1998).

[3] See Cronon (1992).

[4] Svedin and Aniansson (1987); Clark (1988); Achebe et al. (1990); Hammond (1998).

[5] Environmental degradation syndromes, WBGU (1997), see Box 6.2 in Chapter 6; eonometric forecasts of energy use, WEFA (1998), Standard and Poors (1998), Jorgenson and Wilcoxen (1993), Nakicenovic et al. (1998).

[6] Spetzler and von Holstein (1975); Morgan et al. (1990).

[7] Depletion of stratospheric ozone, NRC (1979), Morgan et al. (1990); long-range transport of sulfur air pollution, Morgan et al. (1986); the assessment of earthquake structural risks, Budnitz et al. (1995); possible climate change in the face of increased atmospheric carbon dioxide, Morgan and Dowlatabadi (1996); energy modeling, e.g., NRC (1983).

[8] Morgan and Keith (1995); Morgan (1998).

[9] Julian et al. (1969).

[10] Henrion and Fischhoff (1986).

[11] Morgan et al. (1990).

[12] Integrated studies of river basins, Kneese and Bower (1968); comprehensive accounting frameworks, e.g., Toth (1988a, 1998b).

[13] Parson (1997); NRC (1996a); Commission on Risk (1997).

[14] e.g., Brewer and Shubik, (1979).

[15] Brewer (1986); Jaeger et al. (1991); Toth (1988a,b).

[16] We distinguish here between integrated assessment *models* and integrated assessment *processes* such as some might call the IPCC or the production of an NRC report on policy responses to climate change. As will become clear later in the chapter, our emphasis on models here is not because we underestimate the importance of the process component of successful strategies for exploring the future. Rather, it is because "integrated assessment" as a process has, in the arena of global environmental change policy, come to be used synonymously with virtually any form of science-based assessment or evaluation. This is not necessarily a bad thing. But it does not make for a useful analytic category. Integrated assessment *models*, in contrast, constitute an evolving methodology conducive to critical appraisal, application, and improvement.

[17] Club of Rome, Meadows et al. (1972); RAINS, Alcamo et al. (1990), Hordijk and Kroeze (1997); Latin American World Model, Herrera et al. (1976); TARGETS, Rotmans, and de Vries (1997).

[18] Systems studies, Forrester (1968); Club of Rome, Meadows et al. (1972).

[19] E.g., Haefele (1981), Fishbone and Abilock (1981).

[20] See for example, Meadows et al. (1982); Greenburger (1983); Brewer (1986); Meadows and Robinson (1985); Keepin and Wynne (1987).

[21] See Blinder (1988).

[22] E.g., Holling (1978).

[23] Hourcade and Robinson (1996).

[24] Alcamo et al. (1990); Hordijk and Kroeze (1997).

[25] Levy (1993).

[26] Weyant et al. (1996).

[27] Dowlatabadi and Morgan (1993); Parson and Fisher-Vanden (1997).

[28] Weyant et al. (1996).

[29] Cukier et al. (1978); Tatang et al. (1997).

[30] See Robinson and Rothman (1997); Hourcade and Robinson (1996).

[31] Holling et al. (1978).

[32] See http://www.nacc.usgcrp.gov.

[33] Weyant et al. (1996); Parson (1995); Dowlatabadi and Morgan (1993).

[34] Benedick (1988).

[35] Hourcade et al. (1996).

[36] See GEA (1997).

[37] Hourcade et al. (1996); Hourcade and Robinson (1996).

[38] E.g., Holling (1978).

[39] Epple and Lave (1985).

[40] Wack (1985a,b).

[41] WBCSD (1997).

[42] Meadows et al. (1992).

[43] Kinsman (1990).

[44] Gallopin et al. (1997).

[45] The Global Scenario Group (GSG), part of the Stockholm Environment Institute's Polestar Project, was established to engage a diverse group of development professionals in a long-term commitment to examining the requirements for sustainability. GSG is an independent, international, and interdisciplinary body that represents a variety of geographic and professional experiences and engages in an ongoing process of global and regional scenario development, policy analysis, and public education. Individuals particularly active in the Group's publications have included Gilberto Gallopin, Pablo Gutman, Al Hammond, Paul Raskin, and Rob Swart. Raskin is a member of the Board responsible for this report. Hammond (1998) has published a scenario study of his own, drawing on the GSG work. The GSG is supported by the Nippon Foundation, the Rockefeller Foundation, the UN Environment Program, and the Stockholm Environment Institute. See http://www.gsg.org for more details.

[46] Paul Raskin

[47] Raskin et al. (1998).

[48] National Assessment Synthesis Team (1998); Gallopin et al. (1997); Walsh et al. (1999).

[49] Watersheds, e.g., Maass (1962); airsheds, i.e., Hordijk (1988).

[50] E.g., Ricker (1954); Morris (1963).

[51] E.g., Maass (1962); Watt (1966); Mar (1974); Ackerman et al. (1974); SCOPE (1978).

[52] Holling (1978).

[53] See Walters (1986).

[54] E.g., Gunderson et al. (1995); Cebon et al. (1998).

[55] Lansing (1991).

[56] Stephen Lansing and James Kremer, a systems ecologist.

[57] NRC (1996b); Lee (1993).

[58] NPPC (1994).

[59] In a wide-ranging examination, an NRC panel concluded, "We found no easy answers for institutional change, but many constructive possibilities can be identified." (NRC 1996b), p.325.

[60] Miles (1998).

[61] cf. Kennedy (1993).

[62] As reported in Raskin et al. (1998).

[63] See Raskin et al. (1998) for a discussion.

[64] This scenario assumes that trends such as those toward more efficient technologies continue. The scenario is therefore not simple extrapolations of current data.

[65] Expressed as GDP_{PPP} per capita. In this report, GDP adjusted for purchasing power parity is denoted by GDP_{PPP}, to distinguish it from the more common GDP conversion in market exchange rates (GDP_{MER}).

[66] UN (1998).

[67] Specifically, hunger lines increase to $3,670, the current inferred value for North America, as mean income approaches $21,880 (the value where the linear fit to the national data intersects the constant line at $3,670). This is analogous to the observation that absolute poverty lines tend to rise as average incomes do (Ravallion et al. 1991; World Bank 1990).

[68] IPCC (1992).

[69] UNDP (1997).

[70] Alternative scenarios can be represented as trajectories in a space defined by three coordinates: the size of the world economy, international equity (ratio of non-OECD to OECD average incomes), and national equity average (ratio of incomes of the poorest 20 percent to the richest 20 percent). The sector of the space over which the scenarios can move plausibly is limited. For example, let us require that both the OECD and non-OECD regions exhibit positive economic growth. Let us also assume that, consistent with convergence assumptions of the scenario, incomes grow faster in non-OECD regions than in OECD regions (implying international equity of income should increase throughout the scenario time frame). Finally, based on historical patterns, let us assume a maximum plausible growth rate of GDP_{PPP} per capita of about 4 percent over the large regions and long time periods we are considering. These plausibility constraints define a possible *scenario space*. Both the *Current Forces and Trends scenario* and the *Hunger and Carbon Reduction scenario* lie within this scenario space.

[71] This national equity value would correspond to an average Gini coefficient of only 0.21 in 2025, about two-thirds the current average value in Western Europe. Gini coefficient is a measure of the degree of inequality in a given society. The coefficient is defined with reference to the Lorenz curve, a plot of the fraction of total income held by a given fraction of the population, beginning with the lowest income populations. The coefficent can take values from zero (complete equality) to one (extreme inequality). See Raskin et al. (1998).

[72] This corresponds to an average regional Gini coefficient between 0.35 and 0.41 in 2050.

[73] IPCC (1996).

[74] Rijsberman and Swart (1990).

[75] In addition to these energy-related carbon emissions, about 30 Gt C is emitted in the scenario from land changes over this period, mostly due to deforestation. It is assumed that policies for forest sustainability succeed in decreasing net emissions to zero by the year 2050.

[76] The patterns of energy-efficiency improvement and energy mix change in *Hunger and Carbon Reduction scenario* are comparable to the "ecologically driven" scenario of a recent energy scenario exercise of the World Energy Council and the International Institute for Applied Systems Analysis (WEC/IIASA 1995). However, an important difference is that the WEC/IIASA scenario assumes much lower economic growth rates in developing regions (OECD and transitional region assumptions are comparable) so that developing country GDP_{PPP} in 2050 is only half that of the *Hunger and Carbon Reduction scenario*.

[77] See Raskin et al. (1998) for details.

 **4** | Environmental Threats and Opportunities

The goals for a transition toward sustainability, as we set them out in Chapter 1, are to meet human needs over the next two generations while reducing hunger and poverty and preserving our environmental life support systems. The activities to approach this goal can only move ahead within the constraints set by resources and the environment. Many people have argued that, unless we make dramatic changes in our human enterprises, the development needed to meet future human needs risks damaging the life-support capabilities of the earth—which in turn would of course prevent society from meeting its goals. In this chapter, we therefore ask two related questions:

• What are the greatest threats that humanity will encounter as it attempts to navigate the transition to sustainability?

• What are the most promising opportunities for avoiding or circumventing these threats on the path to sustainability?

Our object is not to predict what environmental damages might be caused by development at particular times and places—a largely futile activity for all but the most specific and immediate development plans. Rather, it is to highlight some of the most serious environmental obstacles that might be met in plausible efforts to reach the goals outlined in Chapter 1 and along development paths such as those explored in Chapters 2 and 3, to take timely steps to avoid or circumvent these obstacles.[1]

This chapter begins with a brief discussion of the approaches and issues we considered in scouting the environmental hazards that societies may confront. We then turn to efforts to assess the relative severity of these hazards for particular times and places. Following the lead of the Brundtland Commission, we next analyze how human activities in a number of crucial developmental sectors might pose important challenges and opportunities for navigating the transition toward sustainability. Finally, we turn to the question of interactions—how multiple developmental activities may interact with complex environmental systems to transform the very nature of the journey before us.

Throughout our discussion, we not only seek to identify potential obstacles to a successful transition, but also to highlight the skills, knowledge, and materials that might be most useful in detecting and understanding the hazards, and in devising solutions or mid-course corrections to address them. We conclude that in any given place there are significant if often place-specific opportunities for societies to pursue goals of meeting human needs while sustaining earth's life support systems. Some of these opportunities are likely to be realized by individual actors—firms, organizations, and states—in the normal course of their self-interested activities. Others, however, will require integrative planning and management approaches.

CONCEPTUAL ISSUES

One of the most difficult challenges of the Board's exercise—and one that has bedeviled other attempts to evaluate the pitfalls to sustainable development—has been to determine which of the many potential problems are truly those that cannot be ignored. Perhaps the easiest approach might be to list as potential concerns for sustainable development every resource limitation or environmental response that can be imagined. Equally clear, however, is that a canoe-steering society that tries to focus public resources on avoiding every possible danger in a river at once will likely be looking the wrong way as it collides with the biggest rock. How can we distinguish those threats that, while not insignificant, are likely to be avoided or adapted to from those with a real potential for sinking the vessel? And how can we devise a system that encourages society to update its priorities among all hazards in light of new information and expertise?

A further difficulty in the analysis arises because hazards have spatial and temporal dimensions and important interactions. However connected the world may be, and however global the transformations humans impose on it, the sustainability transition will be played out differently on a vast number of local stages. Neither population growth, nor climate change, nor water limitations will be the same in Japan as in the Sudan. The environmental hazards that nations and communities find most threatening and the response strategies they look to will continue to be significantly different in different places in the world and at different times. Moreover, some components of the environmental system have impressive resiliency and ability to recover from human-caused or natural stress. Temporal dynamics and variations in the resiliency of systems confound clear illumination of critical hazards. Identification of hazards must also confront the difficulty of identifying, measuring, and predicting cumulative and interactive effects and discontinuous changes. Many of the activities that humans engage in occur at local scales, but as these activities are repeated around the world, their effects accumulate; collectively, local changes can lead to regional and global changes. Many of the worst and of the best-known environmental problems (e.g., stratospheric ozone depletion, anoxia in the Gulf of Mexico) resulted from the slow, day-by-day accumulation of small changes and dispersed activities. Such cumulative effects are only noticed after they have intensified over time, or when nonlinearities in the response of global or regional systems lead to dramatic and unforeseen events. Interactions of multiple changes also lead to surprise. Consequences that are deemed unlikely are often overlooked, yet rare events with extreme or large-scale consequences may influence the sustainability of the global system even more than cumulative effects.

Clearly, uncertainty is rampant and surprise is inevitable. Recent environmental surprises have ranged from the emergence of "new" communicable diseases such as Legionnaires' disease, in a part of the developed world where such things were assumed to be hazards of the past; through the devastation of the developing-world town of Bhopal, India, in a very modern industrial accident; to the belated discovery that the nontoxic, noncorrosive CFCs that had displaced hazardous refrigerants and propellants turned out to have their own serious risks.[2] More such surprises are likely as the earth system comes under increasing pressure from human activities. One difficulty lies in achieving a balance between falsely declaring certainty to engender action and the fatalistic resignation that societies can never know enough to know when or how to act.

In dealing with these difficulties, the Board has attempted to develop a process for setting priorities and for identifying issues that require top concern. While our analysis builds on numerous national and international "stock-taking" efforts, we ultimately focus our attention on those issues that cut across sectors and that interact to simultaneously threaten human and ecosystem health, urban development, industrial advances, and sustained agricultural production. We conclude that integrative solutions—those aimed at interacting challenges across many sectors—will be key to successfully navigating the transition to sustainability.

Perceptions of risk change with circumstances, as pressures increase, information is collected, technology advances, and surprises occur. The environmental challenges that local places face as they navigate the transition to sustainability will also differ, because of inherent variations in resource bases and biophysical, social, and political environments. These variations include differences in geochemical and ecological vulnerability to pollution, social capital formation, and countless other details. Together, they make unsatisfactory any global-scale exercise to rank potential hazards. How do we then focus on challenges and opportunities that are relevant at the global scale yet meaningful locally?

We conclude that the most serious threats are those that (1) affect the ability of multiple sectors of almost any society to move ahead toward our normative goals for sustainability; (2) have cumulative or delayed consequences, with effects felt over a long time; (3) are irreversible or difficult to change; and/or (4) have a notable potential to interact with each other to damage earth's support systems. To identify the problems that fit these criteria, we draw on several approaches. First, we use an environment-oriented analysis,[3] in which hazards are ranked on the basis of the breadth of their consequences (e.g., having human health consequences, ecosystem consequences, and consequences for materials and productivity). Secondly, we use the framework of "common challenges" to development in various sectors proposed by the 1987 Brundtland Commission as the basis for expert group analyses of threats and opportunities for the transition to sustainability. Finally, we identify the threats stemming from the interaction of sectoral activities.

ENVIRONMENTAL PERSPECTIVES

Researchers[4] drew on the UN Environment Program's *The World Environment: 1972-1982*, the U.S. Environmental Protection Agency's *Unfinished Business* and a range of other national and international environmental assessments that had been carried out worldwide, to develop a list of 28 potential environmental hazards that included most issues judged important in one or more of these studies. The hazards fell into five broad categories: land and water pollution, air pollution, contaminants of the human environment (e.g., indoor air pollution), resource losses, and natural disasters. Environmental data and explicit value judgments about the relative importance of present versus future impacts and of human health versus ecological impacts were then combined to generate comparative national rankings of the overall hazards list. From their analysis, it is apparent that the availability of high-quality freshwater is a priority concern in the United States, whether the most weight is given to human health, ecosystem, or materials concerns. Also, the more regional to global problems of stratospheric ozone depletion, climate change, acidification, and tropospheric ozone production and air pollution are common and highly ranked issues of concern across the three areas. Such an approach provides the basis for assigning priorities to environmental threats.

In support of this Board's activities, the list was modified[5] and compared with eight other major efforts to assess environmental hazards, scoring each hazard on the basis of how important the various efforts found them to be (Table 4.1). Looking at Table 4.1 as a whole, some problems such as groundwater contamination and forest degradation stand out as being of nearly universal concern. Others, such as indoor air pollution and contamination, show up less frequently. Over time, there has been a shift from a focus on the depletion of natural resources and contamination of the environment to the loss of particular ecosystems (e.g., forests). In the individual assessments, the environmental threats identified as the most serious are often those most salient to a particular population. For example, the report on India devoted considerable attention to the health hazards of chemicals, both in the workplace and in accidental leakages, largely because at the time of the report the Bhopal disaster was still a major environmental event.

Overall, these analyses suggest that, for most nations of the world, water and air pollution are the top priority issues; for most of the more industrialized nations, ozone depletion and climate change are also ranked highly; while for many of the less-industrialized countries, droughts or floods, disease epidemics, and the availability of local living resources are crucial. The scored hazards approach[6] shows that sufficient data exist to make some relative hazard identifications for both today and the future. It also makes clear that relative hazard rankings—even of global environmental problems— are strongly dependent on the circumstances of the region assessed.

One of the limitations of this approach is its failure to address interactions—for example, the fact that such issues as water quality, acidification, and climate change are intimately linked, and that change in one will have consequences for change in others. In addition, because the approach focuses on the problem rather than the cause, it is not a good pragmatic tool on its own. Solutions are difficult to develop without knowing causes.

DEVELOPMENT PERSPECTIVES

For another type of perspective, we built on the work of the Brundtland Commission's report *Our Common Future*.[7] In the interests of policy relevance, this effort broke with the tradition of analysis focused on environmental issues. Instead, analysis is directed to the "common challenges" to the environment arising from development activities within particular sectors: population and human resource development, cities,

TABLE 4.1   Assessments of the Importance of Environmental Hazards

HAZARDS	Agenda 21	World Development Report	World Resources	The World Environment	A Moment on the Earth	The State of India's Environment	Global 2000	The Challenge of Man's Future
Freshwater—Biological Contamination								
Freshwater—Eutrophication								
Sedimentation								
Ocean Water								
Stratospheric Ozone Depletion								
Climate Change								
Acidification								
Ground Level Ozone Formation								
Metals and Toxics								
Toxic Air Pollution								
Indoor Air Pollutants—Radon								
Indoor Air Pollutants—Non-radon								
Radiation—Non-radon								
Chemicals in the Workplace								
Accidental Chemical Releases								
Food Contaminants								

HAZARDS (continued)	Agenda 21	World Development Report	World Resources	The World Environment	A Moment on the Earth	The State of India's Environment	Global 2000	The Challenge of Man's Future
Salinization, Alkalinization, Waterlogging	Minor		Minor	Major		Minor	Major	
Agricultural Land—Desertification	Major		Minor	Major		Minor	Major	Major
Agricultural Land Soil Erosion	Minor	Minor	Minor	Major	Minor	Major	Major	Major
Agricultural Land—Urbanization	Major		Major		Major	Major	Major	Major
Groundwater	Major		Major	Major		Major	Major	Major
Fish	Major	Minor	Major	Major		Major	Major	Major
Forests	Major		Major	Major	Minor	Major	Major	Major
Biodiversity	Major		Major	Major	Minor		Minor	Major
Nonrenewable Resource Depletion	Major			Minor			Major	Major
Floods	Minor			Minor		Minor	Major	
Droughts	Major			Minor		Minor		
Cyclones				Minor		Minor		
Earthquakes						Minor		
Pest Epidemics						Minor		

Legend: ■ Major environmental concern ▨ Minor environmental concern ☐ Not an environmental concern

Sources: UNCED (1992); World Bank (1992); WRI (1996); UNEP (1982) ; Easterbrook (1995); Centre for Science and Environment (1995); Council on Enviromental Quality and Department of State (1982); Brown (1956).

agricultural production, industry, energy, and living resources. Using the Brundtland "common challenges" concept, we evaluated potential sector-specific resource and environmental impediments to reaching sustainability goals, along with the opportunities each sector offers to reduce, prevent, or mitigate the most serious threats. In addition, we evaluated progress over the last decade in achieving the measures identified by the Brundtland "challenges."

Human Population and Well-Being

In 1987, the Brundtland Commission framed the issue of human population growth in terms of both the balance between population and resources and the need for increased health, well-being, and human rights to self-determination. Today, these issues are strongly linked, and we recognize that the reduction in poverty, poor health, mortality, and the increase in educational and employment opportunities for all are the keys to slowing population growth and to the wise and sustainable use of resources. Thus, one of the most critical challenges for efforts to navigate a transition to sustainability will be to reduce population growth while simultaneously improving the health, education, and opportunities of the world's people.

Population growth is an underlying threat to sustainability due to the increased consumption of energy and materials needed to provide for many more people, to crowding and competition for resources, to environmental degradation, and to the difficulties that added numbers pose in efforts to advance human development. Today, population growth has ended in most industrialized countries and rates of population growth are in decline everywhere except in parts of Africa (see Chapter 2); yet the population of 2050 is nonetheless predicted to reach about 9 billion. In a classic decomposition of future population growth in developing countries, a researcher examined the major sources of this continued growth: unwanted childbearing due to low availability of contraception, a still-large desired family size, and the large number of young people of reproductive age.[8] Currently, 120 million married women (and many more unmarried women) report in surveys that they are not practicing contraception despite a desire for smaller families or for more time between births. Meeting their needs for contraception would reduce future population growth by nearly 2 billion. At the same time, such surveys also show that the desired family size in most developing countries is still above two children. An immediate reduction to the level of replacement (2.1) would reduce future growth by about 1 billion. The remainder of future population growth can be accounted for by so-called population momentum, which is due to the extraordinarily large number of young people. This momentum ensures that population growth will persist for decades even if fertility were to drop to replacement level.

Addressing each of these sources of future growth could reduce fertility and future population numbers further and faster than current trends would project. Opportunities include making contraception more readily available to those who desire it (Table 4.2), accelerating trends that lead to lower desired family size, and slowing the momentum of population growth arising from the large number of prospective parents that are alive today.[9] Linking voluntary family planning with other reproductive and child health services can increase access to contraception for the many who want it. Improving the survival of children, their education, and the status of girls and women has been correlated with and may lead to a desire for smaller families. Increasing the age of child-bearing, primarily by improving the secondary education and income-generating opportunities for adolescent girls, can slow the momentum of population growth. All of these opportunities, if exploited, could contribute directly to our societal goals for a transition to sustainability; at the same time, through these factors' influence on reducing the ultimate size of the population, they would increase the probability of meeting environmental goals.

Threats to human-well being stem from many environmental sources. Environmental factors can affect human health directly—through exposure to air pollution, heavy metals, and synthetic chemicals—and indirectly through loss of natural biological controls over opportunistic agents and vectors of infectious disease. Because of human introductions nearly

TABLE 4.2 Projections of the Population Size of the Developing World With and Without Unwanted Births

Projection	Projected population size (billions) in year	
	2050	2100
Standard* (with unwanted births)	8.6	10.2
Without unwanted births	7.5	8.3
Effect of unwanted fertility	1.1	1.9

*World Bank projection as quoted in Bos et al.

Source: Bongaarts (1994). Courtesy of the American Association for the Advancement of Science.

50 years ago, the global environment now carries a number of synthetic chemicals that can interfere with human physiology, including the endocrine system, the immune system, and neurological function.[10] Additionally, heavy metal deposition in the environment is rising and will continue to increase under development scenarios implicit in meeting our normative goals. Health effects of exposure to heavy metals may be substantial, and include long-term neurological effects on intelligence and behavior. Air pollution is a critical problem of urban systems in many regions of the world, and the increase in air pollution with a rapidly urbanizing world raises serious concerns for human health and the health of crops and natural ecosystems. As described in Chapter 2, over the past several decades, there has been an emergence, resurgence, and redistribution of infectious diseases. The potential eruption of diseases in an increasingly populated world is a serious threat to sustainability goals. These diseases threaten human health, water safety, food security, and ecosystem health.

Fortunately, because of biological and other scientific revolutions and policy reform over the past decades, there are opportunities for addressing the health risks from exposure to environmental threats. Biotechnology holds great promise (for example, in the creation of new medicines and diagnostics, pest-resistant crop species, plants with low-water requirements, and biodegradable pesticides and herbicides). Policies that control the point sources of air pollution, deposition of heavy metals, and disposal of synthetic chemicals help resolve health-related problems for local and regional human populations and can have very significant and long-term payoffs for future generations. Also, the establishment of early warning systems and other predictive capabilities to identify conditions conducive to outbreaks and clusters of infectious disease could be useful for health institutions at all spatial scales.

In addition, a number of opportunities arise via interactions of this human well-being sector with others. For example, reduction in industrial wastes through approaches using industrial ecology would have large advantages for human health, and also for the environment as it is affected by energy and water sectors, through the increased efficiency of these resources' use. Finally, the maintenance of natural ecosystems and the protection of their services can influence human health in many ways, including by providing natural enemies for disease vectors and natural water and air purification and supply systems.

Cities

Over the next half century, urban populations are likely to grow from the present 3 billion to perhaps 7 billion people, with most of the growth occurring in non-OECD (see Chapter 2 and 3).[11] Cities are engines of economic growth and wealth creation, of innovation and creativity, but they are also the sites of extremes of wealth and poverty, unequal access to drinking water and sanitation, pollution, and public health problems. As the Brundtland Commission noted, the growth of urban populations has often preceded development of the housing, infrastructure, and employment needed to sustain that population. In the 10 years from 1985 to 1995, a period during which the Brundtland report was published, the world saw the addition of the equivalent of 81 cities with populations of over a million people.[12] There have been dramatic and successful efforts to improve water, air, and sanitation services in developing world urban centers during this period. But the number of city dwellers without adequate water and exposed to poor sanitation and air pollution has grown as urban population growth has outpaced investments.[13] The health consequences of inadequate drinking water and poor sanitation services are felt most strongly by the poor.

Among the major challenges of urban development is air pollution, produced largely by the interactions of hydrocarbons and nitrogen oxides produced in industrial and transportation processes as well as by heating and cooking.[14] While investments in pollution control in industrialized countries have led to air pollutant reductions in many cities, air pollution is still a major problem in the developed world. In the United States, some 80 million people live in areas that do not meet air quality standards, and in many European cities air pollutant concentrations are also higher than the established standards.[15] At the same time, air quality in the cities of the industrializing world has worsened. Worldwide, the World Health Organization estimates that 1.4 billion urban residents breathe air that fails to meet WHO air quality standards.[16]

Access to water and sanitation services also present enormous challenges to rapidly growing cities. Despite concerted efforts during the 1980s, designated the "International Drinking Water Supply and Sanitation Decade" by the World Health Organization, in 1990 about 200 million urban dwellers were without a safe water supply, and around 400 million were without adequate sanitation.[17] In the largest cities of the industrializing world, the poorest populations in the slums and at the city margins tend to have the least access to safe water. For example, in São Paulo, nearly 20 percent of the city's population lived in slums (called favelas) in 1993; around 85 percent of the favelas had no sewerage service.[18] Innovative technological opportunities—such as condominial sewers,[19] improved ventilated pit latrines, various lower cost sewage treatments, and approaches to reuse of municipal wastewater—are available to provide flexible and cost-effective services and are being used with success in some regions, but have yet to be widely applied. Also, in some areas, such

---

Box 4.1 Mexico City's Water Supply

The population of Mexico City is approximately 20 million and growing, with much migration from rural areas. The continued growth has placed high demand on an unstable water supply network, designed to extract most of the city's water (72 percent) from the Mexico City Aquifer, which underlies the metropolitan area. Increasing land subsidence, groundwater contamination, and inadequate hazardous waste management have made the aquifer and water supply network vulnerable to contamination, posing risks to public health. A 1995 bi-national study of the problem was jointly undertaken by the Mexico Academy of Science, the Mexico Academy of Engineering, and the U.S. National Research Council. The study made recommendations on management of water supply through metering and pricing mechanisms, needed research, treatment of municipal wastewater prior to disposal, demand management approaches, a comprehensive groundwater protection program, a variety of water reclamation schemes, and possible institutional changes related to applying a new cultural perspective to the value of water in Mexico City.[20] It is noteworthy that this comprehensive study recommended several approaches to improved management and conservation of water—and none involving further resource development.

---

as Mexico City (see Box 4.1), high-priority attention can be given to treatment of municipal wastewater as part of a comprehensive plan for improving the balance of water supply, water demand, and water conservation.

In 1900, there were only 16 cities with populations of 1 million or more; by 1994 there were 305 such cities—and of these, 13 had populations of greater than 10 million.[21] Most of this growth has taken place over the last 50 years. As described in Chapter 2, projections of population growth indicate that there will be nearly 7 billion urban dwellers by 2050. The most rapid expansion of high-density cities will be during the next several decades. This trend presents an opportunity to build modern, state-of-the-art facilities and to provide efficient infrastructure systems for the delivery of services. Maintenance and improvement of the quality, adaptability, reliability, cost-effectiveness, and efficiency of these systems are critical to established and aging cities as well. Realizing these opportunities, of course, depends on the foresight, will, capital, and incentives to take advantage of them. Seizing these chances would help to meet the future needs for housing, while reducing the footprint on the land, and, with increases in efficiency, the needs for energy and materials.

Agriculture and Food Security

The task of feeding an additional several billion people in the next 50 years is an unprecedented challenge, one fraught with biophysical, environmental, and institutional hazards and roadblocks. Food demand will rise in response to population growth, growth of per capita income, and attempts to reduce the undernutrition of the very poor. By 2050 food demand could almost double to accommodate the projected population depending on the growth of income and the nature of diet.[22] But the paths to meeting these demands are far from clear. The challenge of feeding this population and reducing hunger requires dramatic advances both in food production, which we focus on here, and in food distribution and access. Production of the globally traded staples (maize, wheat, rice, soybeans, poultry, and swine) will be driven by new technologies already in or rapidly moving toward the private sector.[23] The emergence of genetic biotechnologies, protected by intellectual property rights and patenting, is attracting enormous private investment. Global markets and the movement of private capital into processing and marketing have increased handling efficiencies. Market balance among rich and poor countries, monopoly control, and environmental impacts due to the scale of operations all remain major issues. Industrial technologies are major engines for continued growth. Prospects for growth in production of the numerous "minor" or regional staples, such as cassava, yams, potatoes, grain legumes, millet, white maize, sorghum, and other crops critical to food security for a large segment of the world's poor, are not nearly as optimistic. Such growth is not now in progress nor is it projected for the foreseeable future. The Brundtland Commission recognized that a great strategic effort would be required to meet the challenge of feeding a growing population, yet the past 10 years have seen a reduction in resources for the international agricultural research community along with indicator values that increasingly show world capabilities for increasing food production are stagnating.[24]

During the last half century, the dramatic gains in crop production that have occurred almost worldwide (except, in particular, Sub-Saharan Africa) have come from four interrelated sources: expansion of cultivated land, increased use of fertilizer and pest control chemicals, expansion of irrigated area, and the introduction of high-yielding crop varieties. The continued gains in agricultural production required in the 21st century will be considerably more difficult to accomplish than in the immediate past.[25] There are currently difficulties in raising yield ceilings for the cereal crops, despite a history of rapid yield gains in the past. Incremental response to increases in fertilizer use has declined in many areas. Expansion of irrigated land has become more costly and has slowed dramatically in the past two decades. Because of rising demand for water with growing urbanization, water supplies are increasingly less available to agriculture.[26] The loss of soil fertility and degradation of agricultural lands due to inappropriate management, climate change, and other factors has been reversed in some agricultural areas but at the same time has become an important issue in many other areas.[27] For example, the expansion of irrigated area, combined with the failure to design and implement incentive-compatible irrigation management, has contributed to waterlogging and soil salinity. Reductions in agricultural productivity due to air and water quality changes, some of which emanate from agriculture itself, have also raised concerns.[28] Increasing pest problems because of increasing pesticide resistance stemming from misuse of chemical pesticides, the decimation of natural enemies, and the invasion of new pests are also topics of concern.[29] Any one of these problems alone could impede efforts toward increasing production and yield. Together, these biophysical factors threaten achieving a successful transition toward sustainability.

Perhaps more important still are the threats associated with inadequate investment in the agricultural sector now—for research, education, technological developments, and transfer of knowledge and information to the developing world.[30] Local agricultural research capacity, local public and private capacity to make knowledge, technology, and materials available to producers, and the schooling or informal education of farmers and farm workers are all required for sustained growth in agricultural production. The international agricultural research system and the private sector research community are important sources of new knowledge and new technology,[31] but these systems are effective only in the presence of viable national and regional research systems capable of adapting new technologies to local agroclimatic conditions. Finally, productivity and sustainability depend on the knowledge that farm people bring to the management of their resources and production; education is critical. Institutions must make advances in the technology and management approaches available to farmers, and local financial credit and labor markets must function effectively.

Limitations of institutional capacity may be one of the reasons why Sub-Saharan African countries have failed to realize the gains in productivity that have been achieved by green revolution technology in South and Southeast Asia and Latin America. Institutional limitations, along with political instability, complex land tenure systems, and unique agroclimatic environments may all contribute to the apparent lag in productivity gains there. Understanding the dimensions and factors controlling this failure is critically important because Sub-Saharan Africa is the major region where growth in agricultural production is running behind population growth. One of the major challenges of the sustainability transition will be to develop new and appropriate approaches to improve food production in this region.

If the development of international and national agricultural research systems is maintained, there are many opportunities to enhance our ability to respond to growing world food demand at the same time that we sustain resources and the broader environment. Improved varieties and better management could lead to increases in yield, at least up to fundamental limits set by plant physiology. Scientific and technological breakthroughs, particularly in the area of biotechnology, could over the long term lead to a lifting of the yield ceilings that have been set by the green revolution technologies.[32] Biotechnology is still in its infancy, and its application is controversial. Nevertheless, both the science and the technology are advancing rapidly, and the development and diffusion of biotechnologies may play an important role in increasing and sustaining agricultural production in many areas of the world.

While biotechnology holds substantial hope for improving crop production and efficiency of resource use, many other opportunities exist to increase and sustain food production while decreasing environmental consequences. Protection and careful utilization of soil, water, and biological resources underlie many of these opportunities, and promising management approaches have already been developed and successfully used in some places. For example, integrated nutrient management, like integrated pest management, takes advantage of the ecological processes operating in soils and crop ecosystems and uses them in combination with industrial inputs to optimize productivity and reduce pesticide and nutrient spread.[33] Ecologically based pest management takes advantage of biological diversity to reduce the need for pesticide use. Increased use of efficient irrigation systems will conserve and maintain water supplies and lessen competition with urban and other uses.[34] In breeding programs, increasing attention to flexibility and genetic diversity of crop plants can increase the ability of the agricultural sector to respond to climate and other environmental "surprises."[35] The development of management systems and breeding programs for regional staple crops could also enlarge the food security basket for the poor in many regions. For these opportunities to be useful, new knowledge is needed about both the biophysical crop system and the sociological barriers to implementation. Taking advantage of these opportunities will help to provide the food needs for future human populations, while preserving water in areas of scarcity and reducing pressure on the land.

Industry

Over the next two generations, the global market for goods and services is likely to increase two- to four-fold (Chapter 2 and Chapter 3 appendix). With that increase will come an enormous demand for materials. Avoiding the waste, pollution, and environmental disruption now associated with the extraction, processing, and consumption of materials, and reducing energy and water inputs into industrial production, are the foremost issues during the transition to sustainability. In the 10 years since the Brundtland Commission's challenge to industry to produce more with less, there have been substantial improvements in reducing and re-using materials by both industry and consumers. But the trend toward increasing material use efficiency and dematerialization, discussed in Chapter 2, must be accomplished universally and at much faster rates if it is to offset the rapid increases in production forecasts for the next decades.

The demand for materials to meet expanding markets may in some cases be limited by resource shortages. However, given a supply of energy at competitive prices, the increased demand most likely will result in substantial materials substitutions. Absolute materials shortages are unlikely, at least in the next several decades.[36] The materials challenge, instead, is likely to be associated with pollution due to the "leakage" of materials from the manufacturing, processing, and consumption systems.[37] Such leakages include not only those of nontoxic but valuable materials wasted in the production and consumption streams, and also those of a variety of toxic and hazardous substances used in industrial production. More than 12 billion tons of industrial waste are generated in the United States each year; and municipal solid wastes, which include consumer wastes, are generated at the rate of 0.2 billion tons per year.[38] Clearly, such residual production must be brought under control, or better yet, prevented.

Again, some of these leakages represent not just loss of valuable materials but of substances presenting specific toxicological and ecological threats. More than 100,000 industrial chemicals are in use today, and the number is increasing rapidly in the expanding agriculture, metals, electronics, textiles, and food industries.[39] Some of the effects of these chemicals are well known, but there are insufficient data for health assessment for the majority of these chemicals. Some, like the persistent organic pollutants, are widely distributed beyond their points of origin and concentrate as they move up the food chain. Human exposure to these pollutants can cause immune dysfunction, reproductive and behavioral abnormalities, and cancer. Also, heavy metals such as lead, copper, and zinc can reside in the environment for hundreds of years; human exposure to them can lead to kidney damage, developmental retardation, cancer, and autoimmune responses. Nevertheless, global production, consumption, and circulation of many toxic metals and organics have increased dramatically in the last half century because of their utility in many industrial activities, though production began to level off in the early 1970s and emissions began to decline (Figure 4.1). But numerous opportunities exist to reduce material usage as well as environmentally harmful leakages. Refurbishing or remanufacturing used products or their parts, changing the nature of the product used to a new condition for accomplishing the same purpose (usually provision of a service instead of the product),[40] and recycling and reuse of used subsystems, parts, and materials in products all generally require much less energy, capital, and labor than the original creation of the materials and products. In addition, such processes minimize environmental damage. There is a clear and obvious case for us to examine what we know about the role of industry in the flow of materials, energy, and products, the effects of market forces (e.g., on recycling), and the possibilities for modifying these flows through the system, for more efficient energy use, decreasing environmental damage, and improving the efficiency of providing goods and services.

In recent years, many industries have moved to increase the efficiency of using materials in processing and to control the loss of scrap and other wastes from the production cycle. For example, one corporate plan for introducing customer return programs (copier machines as well as disposable parts like toner cartridges for copiers) led to remanufactured equipment from 30,000 tons of copying machines, thereby reducing both the load on landfills and the consumption of raw materials and energy.[41] Control of leakage is also a means of cost control for industrial production, and there are precedents for the creation of profitable industrial operations based on recapture of consumer materials. Approaches that control the production of garbage and reduce leakage of materials at the consumer end have also been used in some parts of the world. Product recycling has dramatically increased and design of products to facilitate recycling has become a tenet of "industrial ecology."[42] Despite these successes, there is a worldwide loss of valuable materials because of leakage. Thus, one significant set of challenges rests in the development of incentives for higher efficiency and lower leakage from producer and consumer systems. Among such actions would be (1) the provision of incentives to identify heretofore unrecognized economic value of materials; (2) the elimination of historical market distortions (e.g., subsidies) that may interfere with choices that would be more sustainable in the absence of the distortions; and (3) the provision of incentives to move to competitively priced energy whose production does not result in the release of carbon dioxide (i.e., through the use of noncarbon sources or carbon sequestration).

Beyond the challenges related to the reduction and elimination of industrial wastes, the rapidly changing industrial trajectory carries with it the general problem of anticipating problems in new industries and of projecting the dynamics of employment into a future with many more people. The past decade has seen a shift to increasing employment and

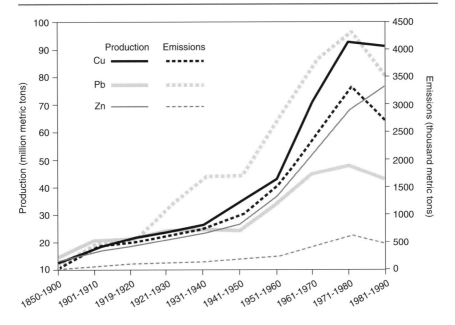

FIGURE 4.1 Global production and consumption of selected toxic metals, 1850-1990. The figure indicates that within the last 20 years, emissions of lead, copper and zinc have begun to decline.
Source: Nriagu (1979). Updated in Nriagu (1996). Courtesy of the Macmillan Magazines, Ltd. and the American Association for the Advancement of Science.

productivity within industry. Nonetheless, the current trends toward production of more by fewer people could lead to persistent unemployment of an expanded population, a spectre not foreseen by the Brundtland Commission.[43]

As the preceding paragraphs make clear, industry is faced with many enormous challenges and much responsibility for reducing and preventing environmental problems related to industrial wastes and leakages. At the same time, however, it also faces a tremendous opportunity for massive market expansion, the development of new technologies (and, therefore new product possibilities, even beyond the products for which the technologies were developed), and the creation of totally new markets based on the requirements of new customers in industrializing countries. There is also great potential for the industrializing world to skip over transitional technologies to new, cleaner technologies without experiencing the same environmental degradation as the industrialized world due to the use of more traditional technologies. The capital, barriers, and incentives to diffusion must be understood and addressed to meet this potential. Meeting the coupled objectives of designing and producing for product competitiveness and for environmental protection and resource conservation is the critical challenge to industry in the next century, and the resulting effects will be felt in all other sectors. Involving industry directly in these challenges and in finding the means to meet them is an opportunity to bring creative actors into the process voluntarily, as well as under incentive and regulatory forces.

Energy

Energy is a critical ingredient in most activities of industrialized and industrializing economies. It is required to extract, process, fabricate and recycle materials, to heat and cool homes and places of business, to produce foods, to move people and goods, and to power communications. For a successful transition to sustainability, energy sources must grow at sufficient rates to maintain other energy-dependent activities, yet at the same time must impose few if any environmental costs in the form of local air pollution, carbon dioxide, toxic residuals, and despoiled land. The world will need to find a way that allows 9 billion people or more to enjoy a lifestyle that requires energy while at the same time protects and sustains human health and the health of the biosphere from local to global scales.

Numerous environmental hazards, including climate change, acidification of water and soil, and air pollution, stem from our dependence on fossil fuel energy. Alone or together, these significant and accumulating hazards can influence a transition toward sustainability. These environmental risks, rather than any limitations of fossil fuel energy resources, are the most significant factors facing the energy sector today. In most industrialized nations, emissions controls are beginning to bring local and regional pollution under control. In contrast, in much of the developing world, local and regional pollution poses serious and growing problems. Regarding global atmospheric changes, in the 10 years since the Brundtland report, much of the world has come to acknowledge the threat from greenhouse gas emissions via international conventions and agreements, but with few exceptions serious constraints on emissions have not been implemented (see Chapters 1 and 2).

For years there have been concerns about limited reserves of fossil fuel. Modern estimates, however, suggest that despite extensive past extraction, the world has very large reserves. In the absence of "externality" taxes (taxes imposed on these fuels to cover their environmental costs) or other policy changes, fossil fuels are likely to remain abundant and cheap for decades to come. A number of direct and indirect subsidies to energy suppliers and technologies have shaped and continue to shape the evolution of the current fossil energy system. Today, most energy is derived from fossil fuels: coal, oil, and natural gas. Oil is primarily used to power transportation. Recent trends in electric power production, especially in the industrialized world, show a move away from coal toward natural gas (see Chapter 2).

Fossil fuel combustion is the source of critical air pollution problems throughout the world.[44] In the leading industrialized countries, emissions of primary particulates and oxides of sulfur and nitrogen are now being aggressively controlled such that local and regional air quality has improved considerably in recent decades, although standards are frequently not met and the adequacy of some standards is still uncertain.[45] At the same time, these problems are increasing in many developing regions. Problems with secondary pollutants formed though photochemical reactions and with long-range transport continue to be significant. For example, while sulfuric acid deposition in the United States has been reduced primarily through the reduction of sulfur emissions from combustion, nitric acid deposition has not declined (Figure 4.2). Globally, CO_2 emissions from fossil fuel combustion continue to grow and threaten to produce notable climate change by modifying the planetary heat balance (see Chapters 2 and 3). While a shift from coal to natural gas may reduce carbon dioxide emissions, emissions of a still more potent greenhouse gas, methane, could result if natural gas energy systems are not leak-free.

Nonfossil energy sources circumvent the serious local, regional, and global air pollution problems of fossil fuels, but each holds its own set of limitations and challenges.[46] Most available sources of hydroelectric power have already been developed in industrialized countries. A number of developing economies such as China, Nepal, and Brazil have large-scale hydroelectric development programs in progress, but concerns about environmental effects on river systems have slowed these programs' growth. The growth of nuclear power has slowed in many parts of the industrialized world due to high costs, public concerns about nuclear wastes, regulatory complications prompted by environmental and safety debates, security issues, and philosophical concerns. However, developing countries such as China and Korea continue to have active programs of nuclear power. Various renewable energy systems have been developed to drawn on such sources as wind, sunlight, and biomass fuels. While these systems show promise, they have had difficulty making headway, even with significant subsidies, in the face of abundant and low-cost fossil fuel.

Opportunities can be seized to increase efficiency and develop or utilize new technologies to reduce the threats associated with meeting the energy needs of the world's population. The efficiency of industrialized

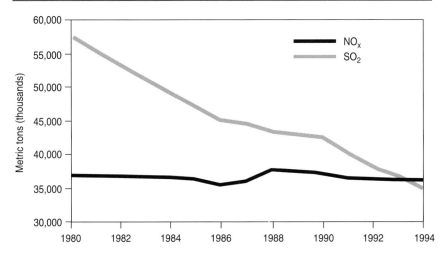

FIGURE 4.2   Trends in SO_2 and NO_x emissions in North America and Europe (OECD countries only), 1980-1994 (excludes Australia, Greece, Japan, Mexico, New Zealand, and Turkey due to incomplete data).
Source: OECD (1997), Swedish Secretariat on Acid Rain (1996). Courtesy of WRI (World Resources Institute).

economies' energy use to produce goods has been gradually improving (Chapter 2), but energy-efficiency opportunities have only partly been exploited. There are also many new technologies (e.g., photovoltaics, electric cars) that may help provide the energy the world needs with far fewer adverse local, regional, and global environmental impacts. As environmental regulations, including emissions fees and emission trading regimes, come into play, market incentives will induce the adoption of cleaner technologies. This is already apparent in the switch of many electric power systems from coal to gas. If this process is to continue and accelerate, ways must be found to reflect directly or indirectly the full environmental costs of fossil fuel in the market place. This can be done directly with fossil fuel taxes or indirectly through mechanisms such as fuel-efficiency standards for motor vehicle fleets and green energy requirements on electric power systems.

While there are many cleaner energy technologies and more efficient end-use technologies now available, the current stock of technology is not sufficient to support the transition to a sustainable energy system. The market is most likely to commercialize technologies that have already been developed to the point where they show short- to medium-term promise for commercialization. If the energy system is to undergo the major transition that will be required to meet the needs of the world without serious environmental consequences, a much larger investment will be needed in energy-related basic technology research.[47] Traditional government R&D will be unlikely to meet all of this need, so new mechanisms must be found to support such research. Some of these mechanisms are discussed in Chapter 6. In designing and evaluating institutions and incentives to encourage sustainable energy technologies, it is important to carefully examine their objectives and implications at the system level, using such strategies as material balance modeling and economic input-output analysis coupled with considerations of environmental loadings. Without such a systematic assessment, polices that appear to promote better solutions may in the long run have serious undesirable consequences, such as problems in recycling and disposing new materials.

Living Resources

The human population rests its requirements for food, shelter, and other essential goods on the shoulders of earth's living and other resources. The grassland, forest, freshwater and marine ecosystems of the world provide such goods as food, timber, forage, fuels pharmaceuticals, and precursors to industrial products. The harvest and management of these resources form the base of enormous economic and social enterprises as well. In addition, ecosystems and the species within them provide vastly underrecognized services such as recycling of water and chemicals, mitigation of floods, pollination of crops, and cleansing of the atmosphere.[48] Humans have enjoyed these goods and services for millennia, and in many regions it has been possible to make use of them without degrading their long-term viability or the life support systems they influence. However, our ever-intensifying use and misuse of ecosystem services is now doing much to imperil them, and, consequently, our own long-term welfare. Moreover, the indirect consequences of the other human endeavors discussed in this chapter also exert enormous pressure on these services. In 1987, the Brundtland Commission described the challenge of managing living natural resources for sustainable development as one of implementing conservation measures in the national interest. Among the most critical challenges of the transition to sustainability over the coming decades will be to develop approaches that sustainably manage both the resources societies use directly and the benefits that we accrue indirectly from the world's living capital.[49]

Human use of land to obtain goods and services is one of the most significant alterations of the global system. Land transformations and use in forestry, grazing, and agriculture have modified nearly 50 percent of the earth's land surface.[50] Agriculture and urban areas cover 10 to 15 percent, pastures cover 6 to 8 percent, and substantially more land is dedicated to forestry and grazing systems. Harvesting of wood for fuel and fiber and the clearing of land for agriculture removed on the order of 13 million hectares of forest per year between 1980 and 1995.[51] Human alterations of freshwater and marine systems (especially coastal zones and fisheries) have also been great in scale and effect. For example, approximately 50 percent of mangrove ecosystems globally have been transformed or destroyed by human activities, and humans use about 8 percent of the primary production of the oceans.[52] Beyond direct use, human activities affect all lands and waters through their effects on the atmosphere and water systems, biogeochemical cycles, and biotic systems.[53] Elevated CO_2 affects all ecosystems; air pollution and acid deposition affect even those we think we are protecting.

The nonsustainable use of living resources carries a number of critical consequences for humans and the other species of earth. Most obviously, overuse and misuse lead to a reduction or loss of resources and thus directly affect human well-being. For example, a number of recent analyses have raised alarms over the nonsustainable management of ocean fisheries (see Chapter 2). Recent assessments[54] suggest that half of the world's fish stocks are now fully exploited, nearly a quarter are overexploited, and many fisheries have collapsed. Fisheries provide direct employment to about 200 million people, and account for 19 percent of the total human consumption of animal protein.[55] Their degradation has grave implications for economic and food security.

Equally important, however, is the fact that the misuse of resources like fisheries, forests, grasslands, and agricultural systems has tremendous unintended effects on the functioning of ecosystems more generally and on the services these ecosystems provide. For example, land transformation is the primary driving force in the loss of biological diversity worldwide. Biotic extinction rates have increased 100 to 1,000 times preindustrial rates and species are being driven to extinction thousands of times faster than new ones can evolve.[56] With loss of biological diversity and alteration or loss of the ecosystems that support them, many social and economic consequences follow. For example, land use changes in watersheds can seriously degrade the water purification processes of soil/plant systems at enormous cost to urban communities.[57] Degradation and loss of wetlands can expose communities to increased flood and storm surge damage. Decimation of pollinating insects has had important negative consequences on yields of particular crops.[58] Introductions and invasions of nonnative species such as killer bees, fire ants, and zebra mussels through human activities cause enormous damage to living resources and threaten human health.

Clearly, at the heart of the sustainability transition is the challenge to manage all of the earth's ecosystems to maintain populations, species, and ecosystems in the face of human domination, and thereby to sustain the goods and services the ecosystems provide to humans. Reducing population growth and levels of consumption and waste are central to meeting this objective because by doing so societies relieve some of the pressures now experienced by ecosystems. Beyond this is the need to develop holistic management approaches that take into consideration the interacting components of ecosystems and landscapes rather than simply focusing on a single species or product. Experiments in ecosystem management are in progress in fisheries and forests around the world, and we can draw knowledge from these experiments for social learning. Finally, the management of living resources must acknowledge and plan for the links among human and natural systems at the landscape and regional scales; and research, management, and development plans must integrate intensive land and water uses (e.g., for agriculture and cities) in the context of areas managed for conservation, water catchments, and purification, air quality services, and recreation purposes.[59]

INTERACTION PERSPECTIVES

Over the past several decades, most decision making and much research has chosen to treat environmental problems and the human activities associated with them in relatively narrow, discrete categories such as "soil erosion," "fisheries depletion," and "acid rain." This narrow framing of environmental problems is evident in our reviews of "Environmental" and "Development" perspectives presented earlier in this chapter, and in the organization of environmental ministries, regulation, and research administration around the world. Both understanding and management have benefited substantially from these narrowly focused traditional approaches. Much has also been missed, however. It has become increasingly clear that much of the workings of the world, and the challenges and opportunities those workings entail for a transition to sustainability, lie in the *interactions* among environmental issues and human activities that have previously been treated as largely separate and distinct. Recognition of the importance of such interactions has been central to emerging international research programs such as those of the International Geosphere-Biosphere Program (IGBP), the International Human Dimensions Program (IHDP), and DIVERSITAS.[60] Such recognition has even begun to emerge in international policy discussions, as exemplified by recent efforts of the UN Environment Program (UNEP), World Bank, and others to draw attention to the connections among global environmental issues and human needs.[61] Despite some progress in implementing these grand designs, however, research support and political action remain largely confined within the narrow categories of traditional thinking.

Today and in future decades, emphasis will have to be given to the interactions among environmental problems. For example, no longer can we ask about the consequences of climate change on agricultural ecosystems; instead, we must ask about the combined effects of climate change, increased climate variability, elevated carbon dioxide, soil quality changes, crop management changes, and tropospheric and stratospheric ozone changes on crop productivity. Also, it makes little sense to ask how climate change affects one system (e.g., coral reefs), when other changes related to human activities (e.g., land use and urban, industrial, and agricultural effluents) act in concert with global changes to alter these systems.[62] Nor does it make sense to ask about the effects of elevated CO_2 on forest uptake and the storage of carbon when these can only be predicted by accounting for such changes as nitrogen deposition, land use change, air pollution, acidification, and climate change.[63] In the next decade we will see research and problem-solving shift in focus from single issues to multiple interacting stresses.[64]

Threats from human activities will result in profound changes in future climate, earth chemistry, and terrestrial biological systems. Environmental transitions expected over the next 50 years and estimations of uncertainty are summarized by the Board in Table 4.3. These estimates reflect the consensus of a large group of international scientific experts based on evidence in the 1995 report by the Intergovernmental Panel on Climate Change (IPCC). The experts conclude with a high degree of confidence that the next 50 years will bring a warmer world, mainly at night; a cooler stratosphere; increased atmospheric water vapor; higher sea level and smaller glaciers. The atmosphere will contain higher concentrations of CO_2, nitrogen compounds, hydrofluorocarbons (HFCs), and smog. Due to human activities, natural habitat will continue to degrade and to be invaded by exotics, while some plants will flourish as a result of increased CO_2 in the atmosphere.

Just as environmental threats and challenges operate interactively, they are caused by the activities of several sectors and have the potential to influence the transition toward sustainability in many sectors. In the following paragraphs, we discuss three integrative, interactive challenges. The changes underlying these challenges are cumulative and are likely to result in surprise.

Water

The earth's water resources are influenced by almost all human activities, and water supports and links the sustainability of industry, en-

TABLE 4.3 Expectations Of Global Environmental Change Over the Next 50 Years

Level of confidence	Changes in Climate System	Changes in Earth Chemistry	Change in Terrestrial Biological Systems [1]

High	global surface warming
	stratospheric cooling
	higher nighttime surface temperatures
	decreased spring snowfall at higher latitudes and elevations
	decreased glaciers in most areas
	increased sea level
	increased water vapor
	global precipitation increase
	ground temperature warming
		Greenhouse Gases
		  increased CO_2
		  increased methane
		  increased nitrous oxide
		  increased nitrogen compounds
		  increased tropospheric ozone
		  decreased HCFCs, decreased CFCs and increased HFCs[2]
		Aerosols
		  decreased sulfate from combustion
		  increased biomass burning
		  increased biogenic sources, including pesticides
		Soil and Water
		  increased nitrogen compounds in soils
		Ocean
		  increased pollution of coastal regions
		  increased sediment loading in some regions
		  interactions with land use
			loss and degradation of habitat
			increase of drought stress on crops
			increase of airborne pollution (e.g., ozone) on plants
			increased CO_2 induced crop productivity (assuming other factors are constant)
			latitudinal and altitudinal expansion of plant species
			increased soil salinity in some regions
			longer growing season in some regions
			loss of biodiversity

Medium	enhanced arctic winter surface warming winter hemisphere precipitation increase subtropics precipitation decrease tropics precipitation increase arctic precipitation increase changes in precipitation magnitude reduced polar sea ice increased drought probability in mid-continental regions regional surface warming in most regions	Greenhouse Gases decreased stratospheric ozone Soil and Water increased heavy metals increased endocrine disrupters	spread of exotic species spread of pests decreased global forests
Low	increased climate variability changes in precipitation frequency regional surface cooling in some regions changes in extreme weather events (e.g., severe storms) increased intensity and frequency of tropical storms (e.g., hurricanes) increased high, mid-level, convective clouds slowing ocean circulation	Ocean increased ocean pollution	
Uncertain	changes in freshwater runoff change in ENSO[3] magnitude and frequency	Aerosols increased volcanic activity	

1 Changes in terrestrial biological systems will be regional and highly variable.
2 (HCFC) hydrochlorofluorocarbon, (CFC) chlorofluorocarbon, (HFC) hydrofluorocarbon.
3 (ENSO) El Niño-Southern Oscillation.

ergy, human health, urban development, agriculture, and the diversity and functioning of biological systems. Like energy, the availability of water is a critical resource for nearly all human activities. At the global level, the supply of fresh water has been dramatically altered by these activities. Water was not identified by the Brundtland Commission among its "Common Challenges," but, clearly, significant challenges related to water confront future populations. As noted in Chapter 2, although there have been slowing water withdrawals, water quality continues to be a concern, particularly in developing countries, and water supply can be regionally or locally scarce.

Global numbers suggest adequate per capita water worldwide. But global numbers are deceiving—variable distributions of fresh water lead to great disparities in access to water, with scarcities in some areas and excess supply in others. Thus, in a number of regions, water is in short supply relative to needs, in some cases because of insufficient amounts and in others because of poor water quality. As regional populations grow and urban systems develop, these stresses are accelerating with conflicting and increasing demands for water supply. Some estimates suggest that a dozen or more nations in semi-arid climates cannot currently provide minimum per capita water requirements for their citizens and that many more will fail to do so in the future as a result of climate change[65] (see Table 4.4). It should be noted that comparing water availability by nations is suggestive but neglects options for management and sharing among nations as explained below. In many parts of the world, conflicts over water rights are sources of continuing social and economic stress. Also, as noted in the "Cities" section, many people in urban and rural areas do not have access to clean drinking water or sanitation services, and some 250 million new cases of waterborne disease are reported each year, resulting in 5 to 10 million deaths.[66] Thus, water scarcity and water degradation are growing threats to a transition to sustainability, and a major challenge is the need to supply both more water and cleaner water to the growing population.

The demands for and status of water resources reflect interactions across all sectors. For example, the price of energy influences water options; increases in the cost of energy increase the cost of groundwater extraction, pumping, and irrigation operation. In turn, demands on water influence energy options. Increasing agricultural production, either by increasing yield or land under production, will carry with it increased demand for irrigation; and, at the same time, rapidly urbanizing populations will demand greater water for consumptive purposes, increasing the potential for conflicts about the balance between consumptive and nonconsumptive water uses. As more marginal water supplies are used

TABLE 4.4   Per Capita Water Availability Today and in 2025, Selected
Countries

Country	Water availability per capita in 1990 cubic metres/person/year	Projected water availability per capita in 2025 cubic metres/person/year
AFRICA		
Algeria	750	380
Burundi	660	280
Cape Verde	500	220
Comoros	2040	790
Djibouti	750	270
Egypt	1070	620
Ethiopia	2360	980
Kenya	590	190
Lesotho	2220	930
Libya	160	60
Morocco	1200	680
Nigeria	2660	1000
Rwanda	880	350
Somalia	1510	610
South Africa	1420	790
Tanzania	2780	900
Tunisia	530	330
NORTH AND CENTRAL AMERICA		
Barbados	170	170
Haiti	1690	960
SOUTH AMERICA		
Peru	1790	980
ASIA/MIDDLE EAST		
Cyprus	1290	1000
Iran	2080	960
Israel	470	310
Jordan	260	80
Kuwait	< 10	<10
Lebanon	1600	960
Oman	1330	470
Qatar	50	20
Saudi Arabia	160	50
Singapore	220	190
United Arab Emirates	190	110
Yemen (both)	240	80
EUROPE		
Malta	80	80

Note: Water use of 500 m^3 per person per year might suffice in a semi-arid society with
extremely sophisticated water management.
Source: Reprinted from Gleick (1992). Computed from UN population data and estimates;
water availability data from WRI (1990). Courtesy of Cambridge University Press.

for irrigation, the need to manage for salinity and drainage will intensify to avoid negative impacts on agricultural productivity.

Increased removal of water from surface water systems, whether for agriculture, urban use, or industry, will potentially damage the functioning of the aquatic ecosystems and the marine systems from which they are taken and into which they empty. Damages to aquatic systems may, in turn, affect the quality and quantity of water available for human use, ultimately influencing the spread of disease and toxic water. Competing human demands will lead to a decrease in the amounts of water available for natural ecosystems, including highly valued lakes, riparian zones, and watersheds. Deforestation and urban developments alter runoff and groundwater recharge patterns. Moreover, pollutants including nitrates from agricultural fertilization and acidic deposition; metals such as copper, cadmium, zinc, and lead from mining; industrial and agricultural activities; and organic pollutants from industrial and agricultural activities have increased in many of the freshwater and coastal marine ecosystems of the developed world.[67] Although reduction of a number of these pollutants has been observed in a number of lakes and rivers,[68] the negative consequences of these changes for aquatic ecosystems and the diversity of biota they hold are enormous. The feedback effects to human welfare argue for the necessity of management approaches that explicitly protect aquatic ecosystems for the services they provide to humans (Table 4.5).

The likely effects of climate change on regional water balances are uncertain. Water supply could be decreased through increased evapotranspiration (caused by warmer air temperatures), especially in areas that already experience arid and semi-arid climates. In other regions, precipitation is likely to increase; depending on the timing and amount of change, water storage and control systems may come under considerable strain. Elsewhere, water resources could prove more plentiful. Rising sea level can produce saltwater intrusion into freshwater reservoirs. In some regions, current reservoir and water-retaining systems may be unable to maintain water supply during drought periods. Finally, dramatic shifts in ocean circulation patterns, should they occur through global climate change, could have major impacts on regional rainfall patterns and climate.

Integrated Strategies for Water Management

Many current technologies can be employed to increase the efficiency and effectiveness of water use, but for those technologies to be applied and new ones to be developed, a new vision of water management will be required. For example, one new paradigm accounting for trends in water

TABLE 4.5 Threats to Aquatic Ecosystem Services from Human Activities

Human Activity	Impact on Aquatic Ecosystems	Values/Services at Risk
Dam construction	Alters timing and quantity of river flows, water temperature, nutrient and sediment transport, delta replenishment; blocks fish migrations.	Habitat, sports, and commercial fisheries; maintenance of deltas and their economies
Dike and levee construction	Destroys hydrologic connection between river and floodplain habitat	Habitat, sports, and commercial fisheries; natural floodplain fertility; natural flood control
Excessive river diversions	Depletes streamflows to ecologically damaging levels	Habitat, sports, and commercial fisheries; recreation; pollution dilution; hydropower; transportation
Draining of wetlands	Eliminates key component of aquatic environment	Natural flood control, habitat for fisheries and waterfowl, recreation, natural water filtration
Deforestation/ poor land use	Alters runoff patterns, inhibits natural recharge, fills water bodies with silt	Water supply quantity and quality, fish and wildlife habitat, transportation, flood control
Uncontrolled pollution	Diminishes water quality	Water supply, habitat, commercial fisheries, recreation
Overharvesting	Depletes living resources	Sport and commercial fisheries, waterfowl, other living resources
Introduction of exotic species	Eliminates native species, alters production and nutrient cycling	Sport and commercial fisheries, waterfowl, water quality, fish and wildlife habitat, transportation
Release of metals and acid-forming pollutants to air and water	Alters chemistry of rivers and lakes	Habitat, fisheries, recreation
Emission of climate-altering air pollutants	Has potential to make dramatic changes in runoff patterns from increases in temperature and changes in rainfall	Water supply, hydropower, transportation, fish and wildlife habitat, pollution dilution, recreation, fisheries, flood control
Population and consumption growth	Increases pressures to dam and divert more water, drain more wetlands, etc.; increases water pollution, acid rain, and potential for climate change	Virtually all aquatic ecosystem services

Source: Daily (1997). Courtesy of Island Press.

withdrawals has the objective of increasing the productive use of water by increasing the efficiency of meeting needs and allocating water wisely among different uses.[69]   Several other strategies that hold promise for better integrated water use and planning recognize the interconnected nature of sectors and activities of humans and life support systems. Strategies for watershed management go beyond the typical framework of hydrology and engineering to consider water resources in the context of interacting physical, biological, and chemical systems that control water cycling and use at a landscape scale. These strategies take into account land use, water quality, and ecosystem processes and protection, as well as urban and economic requirements. Local examples of watershed management abound. On larger scales, work on the Chesapeake Bay and the Columbia Basin[70] provides particularly insightful treatments of the challenges and opportunities for sustainability and adaptive management.

Regional water planning also takes a watershed perspective and seeks an explicit allocation of watershed resources to a mix of water applications, including withdrawals for agriculture, industry, and urban use, and in-stream activities such as waste assimilation, ecosystem and species maintenance and preservation, and recreation. For regional water planning to work, major changes in the way water is valued, allocated, and managed will be required. Regional planning must look seriously at such issues as restructuring agriculture for more efficient use of water, dramatically reducing outdoor urban water use, particularly in arid and semi-arid areas, increasing recycling, and determining and providing environmental water requirements (e.g., for protection of wetlands, fisheries, and endangered species). A number of studies have shown that water is chronically overused because it is underpriced.[71]   Pricing policies that reflect the cost of water for particular uses at particular times and that encourage more efficient use and adaptation of conservation, reuse, and recycling approaches will be crucial. Meeting some of these objectives may be exceedingly difficult in poor regions. Changes in approaches to water-related regulation, education, laws, markets, and information dissemination also will be necessary. In addition, heightened efforts to diffuse available technology to all regions without access to appropriate technology are necessary, as are training and institutional arrangements that make their use possible.

Atmosphere and Climate

Changes in atmospheric chemical composition and chemistry also reflect the activities of multiple human endeavors, as well as natural processes. The cumulative and interactive consequences of gas emissions associated with industry, fossil fuel consumption, and agriculture are linked via atmospheric circulation and chemistry, and the influence of those chemical and physical interactions is felt from regional to global scales. Lessons from the past tell us that we cannot solve urban air pollution problems without evaluating the multiple gases from multiple sources that together regulate air chemistry and pollution. In the case of urban smog in the United States, for example, a decade or more of regulation of hydrocarbons emissions from industrial processes failed to improve air quality; recognition and regulation of the nitrogen oxides emitted from automobiles is now seen as an additional critical factor in controlling pollution.[72] Moreover, while we once thought of smog and tropospheric ozone production as an urban-scale phenomenon, it is now clear that it can be regional in scale. For example, studies in the southeastern United States have indicated that urban emissions of hydrocarbons (volatile organic compounds, VOCs) and nitrogen oxides (NO_x), in conjunction with nitrogen oxide emissions from the agricultural sector and hydrocarbon emissions from natural forests, combine to affect regional-scale pollution events (Figure 4.3).[73] Such broad-scale pollutant levels may feed back to reduce agricultural productivity[74] as well as combine to impair human health and the health of natural ecosystems.

Atmospheric changes that were once characterized as local to regional in scale have now been recognized for their role in global atmospheric and climatic change. Sulfur aerosols emitted from a variety of combustion processes are a source of acid deposition and have been under regulation for the last 30 years. Only recently has it been shown that those aerosols that form regionally may have resulted in an increase in earth's reflectance sufficient to offset some of the effects of greenhouse gas increases.[75] Similarly, burning associated with land use changes such as deforestation or agriculture, alone or in combination with industrial air pollution, can have tremendous impacts on the health of people and ecosystems. Fires associated with tropical deforestation and burning for agricultural purposes emit carbon, nitrogen, and sulfur gases into the atmosphere, where they undergo chemical reactions and lead to the production of tropospheric ozone and acidic precipitation. Consequently, high-ozone episodes and acid rain are experienced by people and ecosystems in areas far removed from urban activity.[76]

The interaction of multiple atmospheric changes also holds surprises for the regional and global system. For example, the deposition of compounds of nitrogen, a regional change produced by intensive agricultural and combustion processes,[77] may interact with elevated atmospheric CO_2 concentrations, a global-scale change, to affect the ecological and biological responses of terrestrial and marine ecosystems. Models suggest that increased nitrogen deposition in North America and Europe may increase the ability of forests to absorb carbon dioxide,[78] although a measurement

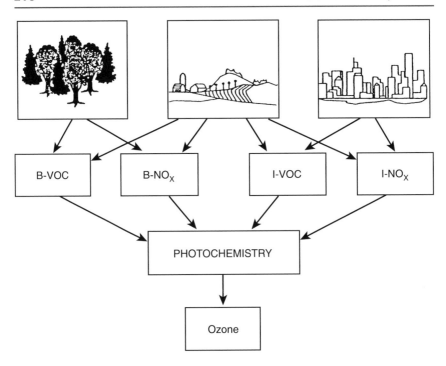

FIGURE 4.3   The evaluation of the effectiveness of VOC-based and NO_x-based strategies for ozone pollution abatement is confounded by the potential significant contribution of VOC and NO_x emissions from biogenic and other natural sources.   In the figure, I-VOC and I-NO_x is used to denote industrial VOC and NO_x, respectively, and B-VOC and B-NO_x is used to denote biogenic VOC and NO_x, respectively.

Source: Chamedies and Cowling (1995). Courtesy of North Carolina State University.

has not confirmed this.   There is reason to doubt that this effect, if it occurs, would continue indefinitely.   Long-term nitrogen deposition resulting from human activities is likely to damage vegetation, thereby decreasing its carbon uptake. Moreover, nitrogen deposition may also increase the emissions of other greenhouse gases.[79]

Integrated Strategies for the Atmospheric Environment

As for water resources, managing for air quality and for the atmospheric environment requires a different strategy than societies have seen in the past decades.   An approach is needed that accounts for the multiple sources of materials released to the atmosphere, the natural and human-influenced processing of those materials, and the multiple and interacting effects on exposed systems. In the case of the atmosphere, the scale at which this integrated management must take place ranges from the urban airshed to the globe. New strategies must be developed to evaluate the understanding of factors driving air pollution and integrated solutions to air pollution, such as tropospheric ozone, at regional to continental scales. Consortia of local, state, and national and international agencies, industries, and scientists will have to come together to develop research and management programs with longer time horizons and greater spatial domains.

Efforts to improve regional air quality are now under way in the United States and Europe. Scientifically based implementation strategies that control emissions across large regions are being developed for areas of the United States.[80] Similarly, the European Community, in its Convention on Long-Range Transboundary Air Pollution, has developed integrated approaches to controlling sulfur and nitrogen emissions on the basis of both the location of sources and the sensitivity of deposition sites.[81]

Global-scale atmospheric changes also require integrated solutions. Many activities (e.g., energy use, agriculture) cause concomitant changes in the atmosphere at local, regional, and global scales, and the tradeoffs and conflicts among alternative strategies must be evaluated across all scales. For example, the burning of natural gas (about 90 percent of which is methane), as opposed to other fossil fuels, has been encouraged because of its higher energy yield per molecule of CO_2 released in combustion and its lesser impact on regional air quality. On the other hand, methane is a very effective greenhouse gas (about 20 times as potent as CO_2 per molecule), so inadvertent emissions of methane used in energy production could offset benefits from reducing CO_2 emissions. Thus, as gas usage increases worldwide, loss rates from gas field drilling and from wellheads must be decreased along with losses from gas distribution lines. Another global methane source, rice paddies, are strongest emitters when fresh organic matter such as post-harvest stubble is plowed into the paddy soil.[82] Burning the rice stubble is an historical alternative to placing the rice stubble in the soil. Yet some areas such as Sacramento, California, in efforts to prevent regional air pollution, are requiring the stubble to be plowed back into the soil, thereby potentially increasing methane emissions in the following growing season. Thus, a balance is needed between decreasing pollution sources and increasing other environmental effects through responsive technological fixes—for example, balancing the risks of local air pollution against greenhouse forcing of global climate change.

Species and Ecosystems

A third area in which interactions and cumulative effects are exceedingly important is the biological component of the earth system. The welfare of species and ecosystems in a rapidly developing world is of critical importance in meeting the normative goals of a sustainability transition. These resources provide many of the goods and services needed to sustain human life—goods such as timber, forage, fuels, pharmaceuticals, precursors to industrial products, and services such as recycling of water and chemicals, mitigation of floods, pollination of crops, and cleansing of the atmosphere. Beyond the importance of these goods and services, the diversity of genes, species, and ecosystems is valued intrinsically, and loss of biological diversity is of major concern because it is irreversible.[83]

The major forces or stresses on biological diversity and ecosystem functioning under our scenarios for the transition are likely to be simply an intensification of trends already seen today (see Chapters 2 and 3), with significant and mostly negative effects on the functioning of ecosystems.[84] Some appraisals of possible increases in agricultural productivity suggest that significant land areas could be returned to natural or more varied ecosystems.[85] Nevertheless, as the human population grows, land conversion for agriculture, extractive uses, and urban settlements exert tremendous influence on biological diversity and on the ability of ecosystems to act as biogeochemical buffers and water suppliers (as noted in Chapter 2). Increased use of biofuels could place even more pressure on land use. Atmospheric and water pollution due to industrial and agricultural activities can have effects on species and ecosystems as significant as they have on human health, and the resulting alterations in the functioning of ecosystems can also feed back to affect human well-being. For example, industrial, agricultural, and urban pollution that leads to eutrophication of estuaries can lead to the production of toxic algal blooms and fish kills, thus affecting industry and human health. Climate and atmospheric changes that result from industrial and agricultural activities will affect ecosystems in multiple and interacting ways. Some changes may have seemingly positive effects on ecosystems; for example, plant "fertilization" due to elevated carbon dioxide concentrations in the atmosphere may lead to enhanced growth and carbon storage in some ecosystems and thus serve as a negative feedback to atmospheric and climate change, at least in the short term. Ultimately, however, climate and atmospheric changes will alter the structure and composition of ecosystems and the services they provide in unpredictable ways.[86]

To the degree that our actual development paths involve ever-increasing pressures on natural ecosystems, the goals of a transition to sustainability cannot be met. One of the major threats to ecosystem goods and services is the lack of understanding about how specific eco-system functions and services may change with ecosystem transformations and about the options for reducing those functional changes. A second threat is a lack of knowledge about, or incorrect valuation of, ecosystems' worth to society. Effective strategies for sustaining species and ecosystems will have to address both of these issues.

Integrated Strategies for Sustaining Species and Ecosystems

Many of the opportunities discussed above in the areas of energy, water, agriculture, industry, urban systems, and human health are ultimately opportunities for sustaining biological resources and the services they provide. For example, numerous opportunities exist for combining management for sustainable forestry and sustainable agriculture with management for biodiversity and ecosystem integrity.[87] Management of agricultural landscapes to optimize for natural pollinators and natural predators of agricultural pests will at the same time conserve species and ecosystems, because in doing so patches of diverse natural vegetation adjacent to agricultural systems are maintained.[88] Management of regions to maximize water supply and water quality for urban systems can at the same time conserve and sustain the natural systems that provide watershed services. Improvements in efficiency of water and chemical use in agricultural systems (thereby reducing the demands on and losses from these systems) will sustain the quality of down-wind and down-stream ecosystems at the same time they protect human health.[89] Opportunities to restore degraded lands have direct relevance to sustainable agriculture and forestry as well as to natural ecosystems.

The focus of preservation efforts is shifting from management of single species to that of multiple species and their interactions with each other and their physical environments. This expansion of the scope of preservation also greatly increases the complexity of the choices to be made both scientifically and in the way that human activities are considered and reshaped. Integrated conservation plans that can simultaneously preserve ecosystems and their species while fostering carefully planned regional economic development illustrate integrated management in which human societies and "nature" are both winners. To take advantage of these and other opportunities, institutions and policies that allow designating regional or landscape-level prescriptions for land use and that enable evaluating and maintaining them over long time scales are likely to be necessary. Development decisions that protect and take advantage of the services natural ecosystems provide will help strengthen prospects for achieving a sustainability transition and therefore should be encouraged.

INTEGRATED APPROACHES IN A PLACE-BASED CONTEXT

This chapter has illustrated the strong linkages and interactions that exist between resources and human activities across many different issues, sectors, and scales. Efforts to reach the goals we have sketched for a transition to sustainability cannot be expected to succeed if they are pursued within narrow disciplinary or sectoral frameworks that ignore these interactions. Rather, many of the greatest opportunities identified here for navigating that transition are integrative in defining the problems and seeking the solutions.

As a result of this review of the environmental challenges and opportunities facing a sustainability transition, the Board believes that the most significant threats to it are likely to be the cumulative, interactive consequences of activities across a number of sectors. Society and its decision makers must recognize that agricultural, urban, industrial, and ecosystem processes interact with each other and must be evaluated as an integrated system. This conclusion is shared by other groups that have addressed analogous questions over a period extending back several years, but has been achieving renewed emphasis in recent years.[90]

Recognizing the importance of interactions among environmental problems, and of the need for integrated approaches to understand and manage these interactions, still leaves open some questions of appropriate spatial scale. In one sense, the answer is simple: because interactions occur at all scales, integrative research and management are needed at all scales. This is certainly correct as far as it goes. But it is not a particularly helpful observation in improving existing research and management systems. As a step toward developing such guidance, the Board drew on the history of efforts to develop and sustain improvements in agricultural productivity around the world. A major lesson of that experience has been the "location specific" character of useful knowledge and know-how that involves biological and social systems. In the agricultural realm, efforts simply to transfer understanding or technologies created in one part of the world across scales or places have generally not succeeded. Instead, as summarized by a major restrospective sponsored by the Rockefeller Foundation—

> The location-specific nature of biological technology meant that the prototype technologies developed at the international centers could become available to producers in the wide range of agroclimate regions and social and economic environments in which the commodities were being produced only if the capacity to modify, adapt, and reinvent the technology was available. It became clear that the challenge of constructing a global agricultural research system capable of sustaining growth in agricultural production required the development of research

capacity for each commodity of economic significance in each agroclimatic region.[91]

This Board's work suggests that the insights from experience with agricultural production systems have general applicability to the challenges of navigating a transition to sustainability. As the examples covered in the preceding section of this chapter suggest, many of the most successful integrated analyses of challenges to sustainability have focused on specific places. Like the earlier agricultural efforts, they have prospered to the extent that they have been able to integrate general principles and knowledge of global relationships with specific understanding of local environmental circumstances and social institutions. There is no magic scale for such effective integrations—they have ranged from the planetary work on ozone depletion, through continental assessments of acid rain and regional efforts to restore the Columbia Basin, to highly localized efforts to design sustainability strategies for particular communities. What effective integrative analyses do seem to have in common is the ability to take seriously questions of scale and linkages, and to shape research, development, and management strategies to discover the conceptualizations of "place" most relevant to the problem at hand. To emphasize our beliefs that attention to scale matters in efforts to promote a sustainability transition, but that no particular scale has a "natural" rightness for all the challenges likely to be faced, we have chosen to highlight here the need for "place-based" integrative analysis. As suggested in the Chapter 1 review of the progress towards sustainability reported at the 1997 Special Session of the UN General Assembly, selected leaders in government, industry, and advocacy groups have begun to recognize the need for such integrated, place-based assessments of the challenges and opportunities for a transition to sustainability. In Chapters 5 and 6, we turn to a consideration of the indicators, research, and institutions needed to realize the potential of these analyses.

CONCLUSION

This analysis shows that progress has been made toward identifying environmental hazards and toward a greater understanding of the challenges in each of the sectors identified 10 years ago by the Brundtland Commission. It has also identified some of the difficulties in overcoming these hazards, and the opportunities to address them. What has become evident in the past decade is the overwhelming degree to which there is increasing interaction among the sectors, and the degree to which the consequences of these interactions are cumulative, sometimes nonlinear, and subject to critical thresholds. Therefore, **we conclude that most of** the individual environmental problems that have occupied most of the world's attention to date are unlikely in themselves to prevent substantial progress in a transition toward sustainability over the next two generations. Over longer time periods, unmitigated expansion of even these individual problems could certainly pose serious threats to people and the planet's life support systems. Even more troubling in the medium term, however, are the environmental threats arising from multiple, cumulative, and interactive stresses, driven by a variety of human activities. These stresses or syndromes, which result in severe environmental degradation, can be difficult to untangle from one another, and complex to manage. Though often aggravated by global changes, they are shaped by the physical, ecological, and social interactions at particular places, that is locales or regions. Developing an integrated and place-based understanding of such threats and the options for dealing with them is a central challenge for promoting a transition toward sustainability.

REFERENCES AND BIBLIOGRAPHY

Aber, J.D., A. Magill, S.G. McNulty, R.D. Boone, K.J. Nadelhoffer, M. Downs, and R. Hallett. 1995. Forest biogeochemistry and primary production altered by nitrogen saturation. *Water, Air and Soil Pollution* 85, no. 3: 1665-1670.

Aber, J.D., K.J. Nadelhoffer, P. Steudler, and J.M. Melillo. 1989. Nitrogen saturation in northern forest ecosystems. *BioScience* 39: 378-386.

Allen, D.T., and N. Behmanesh. 1994. Wastes as raw materials. In *The Greening of Industrial Ecosystems*. National Academy of Engineering, B.R. Allenby, D.J. Richards, eds. Washington, D.C.: National Academy Press.

Allen, D.T., and R. Jain. 1992. Special issue on industrial waste generation and management. *Hazardous Waste and Hazardous Materials* 9, no. 1: 1-111.

Andreae, M.O. 1993. The influence of tropical biomass burning on climate and the atmospheric environment. In *Biogeochemistry of global change: Radiatively active trace gases*, ed. R.S. Oremland, 113-150. New York: Chapman and Hall.

Ausubel, J.H. 1996. Can technology spare the earth? *American Scientist* 84: 166-178.

Bell, David E., William C. Clark, and Vernon W. Ruttan. 1994. Global research systems for sustainable development: agriculture, health and environment. In *Agriculture, environment and health: Sustainable development in the 21st Century*, ed. Vernon W. Ruttan, 358-379. Minneapolis: University of Minnesota Press.

Bender, William H. 1997. How much food will we need in the 21st Century? *Environment* 39, no. 2: 6-14.

Berry, Brian J.L. 1990. Urbanization. In *The earth as transformed by human action*, ed. B.L. Turner II. W.C. Clark, R.W. Kates, J.F. Richards, J.T. Matthews, and W.B. Meyer. New York: Cambridge University Press.

Bongaarts, J. 1994. Population policy options in the developing world. *Science* 263: 771-776.

Bos, E., M.T. Vu, A. Levin, and R. Bulatao. *World population projections 1992-93 Edition.* Baltimore: Johns Hopkins University Press. Published for the World Bank.

Botsford, L.W., J.C. Castilla, and C.H. Peterson. 1997. The management of fisheries and marine ecosystems. *Science* 277: 509-515.

Brundtland Commission. See WCED, 1987.

Cassman, K.G., D.C. Olk, and A. Dobermann. 1997. Scientific evidence of yield and productivity declines in irrigated rice systems of tropical Asia. *International Rice Commission Newsletter* 46: 7-18.

Chameides, W.L., and E.B. Cowling. 1995. *The state of southern oxidants study: Policy-relevant findings in ozone pollution research 1988-1994.* Raleigh: North Carolina State University.

Chameides, W.L., P.S. Kasighatla, J. Yienger, and H. Levy II. 1994. Growth of continental scale metro-agro-plexes, regional ozone pollution, and world food production. *Science* 264, no. 5155: 74-77.

Chapin, F.S., B.H. Walker, R.J. Hobbs, et al. 1997. Biotic controls over the functioning of ecosystems. *Science* 277, no. 5325: 500-504.

Chichilnisky, G., and J. Heal. 1998. Economic returns from the biosphere. *Nature* 391, no. 6668: 629.

Clark, William C. 1985. Scales of climate impacts. *Climate Change* 7: 5-27.

Clark and Patt. 1997. Working paper for the NRC Board on Sustainable Development

Conway, Gordon. 1997. *The doubly green revolution: Food for all in the twenty-first century.* London: Penguin Books.

Costanza, R., and J. Greer. 1998. The Chesapeake Bay and its watershed: A model for sustainable ecosystem management? Chap. 18 in *Ecosystem Health,* eds. D. Rapport et al., 261-302. Oxford: Blackwell Science, Ltd.

Covich, A.P. 1993. Water and ecosystems. In *Water in crisis: A guide to the world's fresh water resources,* ed. P.H. Gleick. New York: Oxford University Press.

Crosson, P. 1995. Soil-erosion estimates and costs. *Science* 269, no. 5223: 461-464.

DIVERSITAS. 1998. About DIVERSITAS. http://www.lmcp.jussieu.fr/icsu/DIVERSITAS/index.html.

Daily, G.C., ed. 1997. *Nature's services: Societal dependence on natural ecosystems.* Washington, D.C.: Island Press.

Daily, G.C., P. Dasgupta, B. Bolin, P. Crosson, J. du Guerny, P. Ehrlich, C. Folke, A.M. Jansson, B.O. Jansson, N. Kautsky, A. Kinzig, S. Levin, K.G. Mäler, P. Pinstrup-Andersen, D. Siniscalco, and B. Walker. 1998. Food production, population growth, and the environment. *Science* 281: 1291-1292.

EPA (U.S. Environmental Protection Agency). 1987. *Unfinished business: A comparative assessment of environmental problems.* Washington, D.C.: EPA.

_____. 1990. *Characterization of municipal solid waste in the United States, 1970-2000.* EPA/530-SW-89-015A. Washington, D.C.: EPA.

Earth System Sciences Committee, NASA Advisory Council. 1988. *Earth system science: A closer view.* Washington, D.C.: NASA.

Edwards, C.A., R. Lal, P. Madden, R.H. Miller, G. House. 1990. *Sustainable agricultural systems.* Delray Beach, Florida: St. Lucie Press.

FAO (Food and Agriculture Organization of the United Nations). 1994. *Review of the state of world marine fishery resources.* FAO Technical Paper 335. Rome: United Nations.

_____. 1997. *Review of the state of world's forests.* Rome: United Nations.

Fredricksen, H. D. 1996. Water crisis in developing world: Misconceptions about solutions. *Journal of Water Resources Planning and Management* 122, no. 2: 79-87.

Galloway, J.N., W.H. Schlesinger, H. Levy, A. Michaels, and J.L. Schnoor. 1995. Nitrogen fixation: Anthropogenic enhancement-environmental response. *Global Biogeochemical Cycles* 9, no. 2: 235-252.

Gleick, P.H. 1992. Effects of climate change on shared fresh water resources. In *Confronting climate change: Risks, implications and responses,* ed. Irving M. Mintzer. Cambridge, UK: Cambridge University Press.

_____. 1993. Water in the 21st Century. In *Water in crisis: A guide to the world's fresh water resources,* ed. P.H. Gleick. New York: Oxford University Press.

_____. 1998. *The world's water 1998-1999: Biennial report on freshwater resources.* Washington, D.C.: Island Press.

Goulder, Lawrence H., and Donald Kennedy. 1997. Valuing ecosystem services: Philosophical bases and empirical methods. In *Nature's Services: Societal dependence on natural ecosystems,* ed. Gretchen C. Daily. Washington, D.C.: Island Press.

Graedel, T.E. and P.J. Crutzen. 1993. *Atmospheric change: An earth system perspective.* New York: W.H. Freeman and Co.

Heal, G.M. 1998. *Valuing the future: Economic theory and sustainability.* New York: Columbia University Press.

Holdgate, Martin W., Mohammed Kassas, and Gilbert F. White, eds. 1982. *The world environment 1972-1982: A report by the United Nations Environment Programme.* Dublin: Tycooly International Publishers.

Holling, C.S., ed. 1978. *Adaptive environmental assessment and management.* Chichester, UK: John Wiley.

Hornung, M., and R.A. Skeffington, eds. 1993. *Critical loads: Concept and applications: Proceedings of a conference held on 12-14 February 1992 in Grange-over-Sands under the auspices of the British Ecological Society Industrial Ecology Group and the Natural Environment Research Council, and partly sponsored by the National Power/PowerGen Joint Environmental Programme.* Institute of Terrestrial Ecology Symposium no. 28. London : HMSO Publications Centre.

Houghton, J.T., L.G. Meira Filho, J. Bruce, H. Lee, B.A. Callander, E. Haites, N. Harris, and K. Maskell. 1994. *Climate change 1994: Radiative forcing of climate change.* Cambridge, UK: Cambridge University Press. Published for the Intergovernmental Panel on Climate Change (IPCC).

Houghton, J.T., L.G. Meira Filho, B.A. Callander, N. Harris, A. Kattenberg, and K. Maskell. 1996. *Climate change 1995: The science of climate change.* Cambridge, UK: Cambridge University Press. Published for the Intergovernmental Panel on Climate Change (IPCC).

IGBP (International Geosphere-Biosphere Programme). 1994. *The IGBP in action: The work plan 1994-1998.* Stockholm: IGBP.

IHDP (International Human Dimensions Program). 1998. *About IHDP.* http://ibm.rhrz.uni-bonn.de/IHDP/about.html.

_____. 1995. *Climate change 1994: Radiative forcing of climate change and an evaluation of the IPCC IS92 emission scenarios.* Cambridge, UK: Cambridge University Press.

IPCC (Intergovernmental Panel on Climate Change). 1996. See Houghton et al. 1996.

Kates, R.W., and W.C. Clark. 1996. Environmental surprise: Expecting the unexpected? *Environment* 58, no. 2: 6-11, 28-34.

Kates, R.W., B.L. Turner II, and W.C. Clark. 1990. The great transformation. In *The earth as transformed by human action,* eds. B.L. Turner, W.C. Clark, R.W. Kates, J.F. Richards, J.T. Matthews, and W.B. Meyer. Cambridge, UK: Cambridge University Press.

Kendall, H.W., R. Beachy, T. Eisner, F. Gould, R. Herdt, P.H. Raven, J.S. Schell, and M.S. Swaminathan. 1997. Bioengineering of crops: Report of the World Bank Panel on Transgenic Crops. Washington, D.C.: The World Bank.

Lawton, J.H., and R.M. May. 1995. *Extinction rates.* Oxford: Oxford University Press.

Lee, K.N. 1993. *Compass and gyroscope: Integrating science and politics for the environment.* Washington, D.C.: Island Press.

Matson, P.A., W.H. McDowell, A.R. Townsend, and P.M. Vitousek. 1999. The globalization of nitrogen deposition: ecosystem consequences in tropical environments. *Biogeochemistry* 46: 67-83.

Matson, P.A., W.J. Parton, A.G. Power, and M.J. Swift. 1997. Agricultural intensification and ecosystem properties. *Science* 277: 504-509.

Mitchell, David L., and W. Michael Hanemann. 1994. *Setting urban water rates for efficiency and conservation: A discussion of issues: A report for the California Urban Water Conservation Council.* Sacramento, CA: The Council.

NAE (National Academy of Engineering). 1990. *Energy production, consumption, and consequences.* J.L. Helm, ed. Washington, D.C.: National Academy Press.

_____. 1994a. *The greening of industrial ecosystems.* B.R. Allenby and D.J. Richards, eds. Washington, D.C.: National Academy Press.

_____. 1994b. *Technological trajectories and the human environment.* J.H. Ausubel and H.D. Langford, eds. Washington, D.C.: National Academy Press.

_____. 1997. *Environmentally significant consumption: Research directions.* Committee on the Human Dimensions of Global Change. Eds. Paul Stern, Thomas Dietz, Venon Ruttan, Robert Socolow, and James Sweeney. Washington, D.C.: National Academy Press.

NRC (National Research Council). 1988. *Air quality, environment, and energy.* Transportation Research Board. Washington, D.C.: National Academy Press.

_____. 1990. *Fuels to drive our future.* Committee on Production Technologies for Liquid Transportation Fuels. Washington, D.C.: National Academy Press.

_____. 1991a. *Rethinking the ozone problem in urban and regional air pollution.* Committee on Tropospheric Ozone Formation and Measurement. Washington, D.C.: National Academy Press.

_____. 1991b. *Toward sustainability: A plan for collaborative research on agriculture and natural resources management.* Panel for Collaborative Research Support for AID's Sustainable Agriculture and Natural Resource Management. Washington, D.C.: National Academy Press.

_____. 1992a. *Plant biology research and training in the 21st century.* Committee on Examination of Plant Science Research Programs in the United States. Washington, D.C.: National Academy Press.

_____. 1992b. *Toward sustainability: An addendum on integrated pest management as a component of sustainability research.* Subpanel on Integrated Pest Management for the Sustainable Agriculture and Natural Resource Management Program of the US Agency for International Development. Washington, D.C.: National Academy Press.

_____. 1994. *The role of terrestrial ecosystems in global change: A plan for action.* Board on Global Change. Washington, D.C.: National Academy Press.

_____. 1995. *Mexico City's water supply: Improving the outlook for sustainability.* The Joint Academies Committee on the Mexico City Water Supply. Washington, D.C.: National Academy Press.

_____. 1996. *Upstream: Salmon and society in the Pacific Northwest.* Committee on Protection and Management of Pacific Northwest Anadromous Salmonids. Washington, D.C.: National Academy Press.

_____. 1997a. *Environmentally significant consumption: Research directions.* Committee on the Human Dimensions of Global Change. P.C. Stern, T. Dietz, V.W. Ruttan, R.H. Socolow, and J.L. Sweeney, eds. Washington, D.C.: National Academy Press.

_____. 1997b. *Toward a sustainable future: Addressing the long-term effects of motor vehicle transportation on climate and ecology.* Committee for a Study of Transportation and a Sustainable Environment. Washington, D.C.: National Academy Press.

_____. 1998a. *Global environmental change: Research pathways for the next decade.* Committee on Global Change Research. Washington, D.C.: National Academy Press.

_____. 1998b. *Research priorities for airborne particulate matter: I. Immediate priorities and a long range research portfolio.* Committee on Research Priorities for Airborne Particulate Matter. Washington, D.C.: National Academy Press.

_____. 1999a. *Sustaining marine fisheries.* Committee on Ecosystem Management for Sustainable Marine Fisheries. Washington, D.C.: National Academy Press.

_____. 1999b. *Hormonally Active Agents in the Environment*. Committee on Hormonally Active Agents in the Environment. Washington, D.C.: National Academy Press.

Nabhan, G., and S. L. Buchmann. 1997. Services provided by pollinators. Chap. 8 in *Nature's services: Societal dependence on natural ecosystems*, ed. G.C. Daily. Washington, D.C.: Island Press.

Nash, L. 1993. Water quality and health. In *Water in crisis: A guide to the world's fresh water resources*, ed. P.H. Gleick. New York: Oxford University Press.

Naylor, R.L., and P.R. Ehrlich. 1997. Natural pest control services and agriculture. In *Nature's services: Societal dependence on natural ecosystems*, ed. G.C. Daily. Washington, D.C.: Island Press.

Noble, I.R., and R. Dirzo. 1997. Forests as human-dominated ecosystems. *Science* 277: 522-525.

Norberg-Bohm, V., W.C. Clark, B. Bakshi, J. Berkenkamp, S.A. Bishko, M.D. Koehler, J.A. Marrs, C.P. Nielsen, and A. Sagar. 1992. *International comparisons of environmental hazards: development and evaluation of a method for linking environmental data with the strategic debate management priorities for risk management*. Cambridge, MA: Center for Science and International Affairs, John F. Kennedy School of Government, Harvard University.

Nriagu, J.O. 1979. Global inventory of natural and anthropogenic emissions of trade metals into the atmosphere. *Nature* 279: 409-411.

Nriagu, J.O. 1996. History of global metal pollution. *Science* 272, no. 5259: 223-224.

OECD (Organisation for Economic Co-Operation and Development). 1997. *OECD environmental data compedium 1997*. Paris: OECD.

Odum, Howard T. 1994. *Ecological and general systems: An introduction to systems ecology*. Niwot, CO: University Press of Colorado.

PCAST (President's Committee of Advisers on Science and Technology). 1999. *Powerful partnerships: The federal role in international cooperation on energy innovation*. Washington, D.C.: PCAST.

_____. 1997. *Federal energy research and development for the challenges of the twenty-first century*. Washington, D.C.: PCAST.

_____. 1998. *Teaming with life: Investing in science to understand and use America's living capital*. Washington, D.C.: PCAST.

Pauly, D., and V. Christensen. 1995. Primary production required to sustain global fisheries. *Nature* 374, no. 6519: 255-257.

Pimentel, D., and C.A. Edwards. 1982. Pesticides and Ecosystems. *Bioscience* 32, no. 7: 595.

Pinstrup-Andersen, P., and R. Pandya-Lorch. 1996. Food for all in 2020; Can the world be fed without damaging the environment? *Environmental Conservation* 23, no. 3: 226-234.

Pinstrup-Anderson, P., R. Pandya-Lorch, and M.W. Rosegrant. 1997. *The world food situation: Recent developments, emerging issues, and long-term prospects*. Washington: International Food Policy Research Institute.

Postel, S. 1992. *Last oasis: Facing water scarcity*. New York: W.W. Norton and Co.

_____. 1993. Water and agriculture. In *Water in crisis: A guide to the world's fresh water resources*, ed. P.H. Gleick. New York: Oxford University Press.

Postel, S.L., G.C. Daily, and P. Ehrlich. 1996. Human appropriation of renewable freshwater. *Science* 271: 785-788.

Postel, S.L., and S. Carpenter. 1997. Freshwater ecosystem services. In *Nature's services*, ed. G.C. Daily. Washington, D.C.: Island Press.

Raskin, P., M. Chadwick, T. Jackson, and G. Leach. 1996. *The transition toward sustainability: Beyond conventional development*. Stockholm: Stockholm Environmental Institute.

Richards, D.J., B.R. Allenby, and R.A. Frosch. 1994. The greening of industrial ecosystems: Overview and perspective. In *The greening of industrial ecosystems*, NAE, eds. B.R. Allenby and D.J. Richards. Washington, D.C.: National Academy Press.

Risch, S.J., D. Pimentel, and H. Grover. 1986. Corn monoculture versus old field: Effects of low levels of insecticides. *Ecology* 67, no. 2: 505.

Rodhe, H., and R. Herrera. 1988. *Acidification in tropical countries*. Scientific Committee on Problems of the Environment (SCOPE) Series, 36. New York: John Wiley and Sons.

Ruttan, Vernon W. 1994. Challenges to agricultural research in the 21st century. In *Agriculture, environment, and health: sustainable development in the 21st century*, ed. Vernon W. Ruttan. Minneapolis: University of Minnesota Press.

_____. 1996. Population growth, environmental change and technical innovation: Implications for sustainable growth in agricultural production. In *The impact of population growth on well-being in developing countries*, eds. Dennis A. Ahlburg, Allen C. Kelly, and Karen Oppenheim Mason. Berlin: Springer.

Schimel, D.S. 1994. Terrestrial ecosystems and the carbon cycle. *Global Change Biology* 1:77-91.

Schultz, Theodore W. 1964. *Transforming traditional agriculture*. New Haven, CT: Yale University Press.

Socolow, R., C. Andrews, F. Berkhout, and V. Thomas, eds. 1994. *Industrial ecology and global change*. Cambridge, UK: Cambridge University Press.

Smith, R.A., R.B. Alexander, and K.J. Lanfear. 1992. *National water summary 1990-91. Stream water quality in the conterminous United States—Status and trends of selected indicators during the 1980s*. USGS Water Supply Paper 2400. Reston, VA: U.S. Geological Survey.

Strong, Maurice, Chair, System Review Panel. 1998. *The third system review of the Consultative Group on International Agricultural Research (CGIAR)*. Washington, D.C.: The World Bank.

Swedish Secretariat on Acid Rain. 1996. *Acid News 5*. Göteborg, Sweden: Int. Försurningssekretariatet.

Thies and T. Tscharntke. 1999. Landscape structure and biological control in agroecosystems. *Science* 285:893-895.

Townsend, A.R., B.H. Braswell, E.A. Holland, and J.E. Penner. 1996. Spatial and temporal patterns in terrestrial carbon storage due to deposition of fossil fuel nitrogen. *Ecological Applications* 6, no. 3: 806-814.

Turner, B.L., W.C. Clark, R.W. Kates, J.F. Richards, J.T. Matthews, and W.B. Meyer, eds. 1990. *The Earth as transformed by human action: Global and regional changes in the biosphere over the past 300 years*. New York: Cambridge University Press.

UN (United Nations). 1995. *World urbanization prospects: The 1994 revision*. New York: United Nations.

UNEP (UN Environment Programme), NASA (US National Aeronautics and Space Administration), and The World Bank. 1998. *Protecting our planet, securing our future*. Nairobi: UNEP.

Vitousek, P.M. 1994. Beyond global warming: Ecology and global change. *Ecology* 75:1861-1876.

Vitousek, P.M., H.A. Mooney, J. Lubchenco, and J.M. Melillo. 1997. Human domination of earth's ecosystems. *Science* 277: 494-499.

WBGU (German Advisory Council on Global Change). 1993-1997. *World in transition: The research challenge*. Annual report. Berlin: Springer-Verlag. (Also available through the Council's home page at http://www.awi-bremmerhaven.de/WBGU.)

WCED (World Commission on Environment and Development). 1987. *Our common future*. New York: Oxford University Press.

WHO (World Health Organization). 1997. *Health and environment in sustainable development: Five years after the Earth Summit.* Geneva: WHO.

WHO (World Health Organization) and UNEP (United Nations Environment Program). 1992. *Urban air pollution in megacities of the world.* Oxford, UK: Blackwell Publications.

WRI (World Resources Institute). 1996. *World resources 1996-1997: A guide to the global environment: The urban environment.* A joint publication by the World Resources Institute, the United Nations Environment Programme, the United Nations Development Programme, and the World Bank. New York: Oxford University Press.

_____. 1998. *World resources 1998-1999: A guide to the global environment: Environmental change and human health.* A joint publication by the World Resources Institute, the United Nations Environment Programme, the United Nations Development Programme, and the World Bank. New York: Oxford University Press.

Waggoner, P.E. 1994. *How much land can ten billion people spare for nature?* Ames, Iowa: Council for Agricultural Science and Technology.

Watt, K.E.F. 1966. *Systems analysis in ecology.* New York: Academic Press.

Weyant, J., O. Davidson, H. Dowlatabadi, J. Edmonds, M. Grubb, E.A. Parson, R. Richels, J. Rotmans, P.R. Shukla, R.S.J. Tol, W. Cline, and S. Fankhauser. 1996. Integrated assessment of climate change: An overview and comparison of approaches and results. Chap. 10 of *Climate change 1995,* ed. James P. Bruce, Hoesung Lee, and Erik F. Haites. Contribution of Working Group III to the Second Assessment Report of the Intergovernmental Panel on Climate Change (IPCC). Cambridge, U.K.: Cambridge University Press. Published for the IPCC.

Woomer, P.L., and M.J. Swift. 1994. *The biological management of tropical soil fertility.* Chichester, UK: Wiley.

World Bank. 1992. *World development report 1992: Development and the environment.* New York: Oxford University Press. World Bank. 1998. *Environmental Matters.* Annual review, Fall 1998. The World Bank Group.

XEROX Corporation. 1997. Environment, Health and Safety Program Report. Xerox corporation company document. Stamford, CT: Xerox Corporation.

Yagi, K., and K. Minami. 1990. Effect of organic matter application on methane emissions from paddy fields. *Soil Science and Plant Nutrition* 36: 599-610.

ENDNOTES

[1] Possible large social, economic, or political threats such as war, terrorism, crime, financial collapse, or substance abuse are not part of this analysis. In part, this is because of the configuration and expertise of the board, but more so because of the absence of the kind of thinking and studies of such social threats that makes possible the comparative ranking and analysis of environmental threats that we undertake in this chapter.

[2] Kates and Clark (1996).

[3] Norberg-Bohm et al. (1992).

[4] Researchers developing the list, Norberg-Bohm et al. (1992); UNEP program on *The World's Environment,* Holdgate et al. (1982); EPA program on *Unfinished Business,* EPA (1987).

[5] Norberg-Bohm et al. (1992) list modified by Clark and Patt (1997).

[6] Scored hazards approach by Clark and Patt (1997).

[7] WCED (1987).

[8] Bongaarts (1984).

[9] Ibid.

[10] NRC (1999b).

[11] WRI (1996).

[12] Personal communication with Thomas Buettner, United Nations.

[13] World Bank (1992); WRI (1996).

[14] NRC (1991a, 1997b).

[15] WRI (1998).

[16] WHO and UNEP (1992).

[17] World Bank (1992).

[18] Ibid.

[19] The condominial sewerage system, which is used in northeast Brazil, has a shorter grid and shallower feeder sewers running through backyards, resulting in shallower connections to the main pipes, lower construction costs (20 to 30 percent lower than for conventional systems), and less pipe.

[20] NRC (1995).

[21] Berry (1990); UN (1996).

[22] Bender (1997); Ruttan (1996); Daily et al. (1998); see Chapter 3.

[23] Pinstrup-Anderson et al. (1997).

[24] NRC (1991b); Pinstrup-Anderson and Pandya-Lorch (1996); Ruttan (1996); Strong (1998).

[25] NRC (1991b); Ruttan (1996); Cassman et al. (1997).

[26] Postal et al. (1996).

[27] Matson et al. (1997); NRC (1991b).

[28] Chameides et al. (1994).

[29] Naylor and Ehrlich (1997); NRC (1991b).

[30] NRC (1991b), (1992b); Ruttan (1996).

[31] See Strong (1998).

[32] Kendall et al. (1997); Conway (1997).

[33] Matson et al. (1997); NRC (1991b, 1992b); Woomer and Swift (1994).

[34] Postel (1992, 1993).

[35] NRC (1992a).

[36] NAE (1997).

[37] NAE (1994a); NRC (1997a).

[38] Industrial waste, Allen and Jain (1992); municipal solid wastes, EPA (1990).

[39] Raskin et al. (1996).

[40] E.g., selling the cleaning of the factory or office ("selling the factory") as opposed to selling cleaning products and tools.

[41] Xerox (1997).

[42] Product recycling, NAE (1994b); industrial ecology, NAE (1994a,b), and Socolow et al. (1994).

[43] NAE (1994b).

[44] NRC (1990, 1991a).

[45] NRC (1990, 1998b).

[46] PCAST (1997).

[47] PCAST (1997, 1999).

[48] Daily (1997).

[49] PCAST (1998).

[50] Vitousek et al. (1997).

[51] FAO (1997); Noble and Dirzo (1997).

[52] Mangrove ecosystems, WRI (1996); oceans, Pauly and Christensen (1995).

[53] Vitousek et al. (1997).

[54] FAO (1994); NRC (1999a).

[55] Botsford et al. (1997).

[56] Lawton and May (1995); PCAST (1998).

[57] E.g., Chichilnisky and Heal (1998).

58 Nabhan and Buchmann (1997).

59 Noble and Dirzo (1997); Vitousek et al. (1997); Matson et al. (1997).

60 See, e.g., IGBP (1994); IHDP (1998); DIVERSITAS (1998); and the NRC's "Pathways" report [NRC (1998a)].

61 UNEP et al. (1998); World Bank (1998).

62 Vitousek et al. (1997).

63 Schimel (1994); IPCC (1996); NRC (1994).

64 NRC (1998a).

65 Gleick (1992).

66 Gleick (1998).

67 Nash (1993).

68 Smith et al. (1992).

69 Gleick (1998).

70 Chesapeake Bay, e.g., Costanza and Greer (1998); Columbia Basin, e.g., Lee (1993), and NRC (1996).

71 E.g., Mitchell and Hanemann (1994).

72 NRC (1991a).

73 Chameides and Cowling (1995).

74 Chameides et al. (1994).

75 IPCC (1995).

76 Graedel and Crutzen (1993); Andreae (1993); Rodhe and Herrera (1988).

77 Galloway et al. (1995); Vitousek et al. (1997).

78 Schimel (1994); Townsend et al. (1996).

79 Aber et al. (1989); Aber et al. (1995); Matson et al. (1999).

80 Chameides and Cowling (1995).

81 Hornung and Skeffington (1993).

82 Yagi and Minami (1990).

83 NRC (1992a).

84 Vitousek et al. (1997); Chapin et al. (1997).

85 Ausubel (1996); Waggoner (1994).

86 See chapter 2 NRC (1998a).

87 Daily (1997).

88 Risch et al. (1986); Pimental and Edwards (1982); Matson et al. (1997); Thies and Tscharntke (1999).

89 Matson et al. (1997); Crosson (1995).

90 Several decades, e.g., Odum (1994), Watt (1966), and Holling (1978); recent years, e.g., the *World in Transition* reports of the German Advisory Council on Global Change (WBGU 1993-1997); see also Chapter 6, Box 6.1.

91 Bell et al. (1994), p. 362; see also Schultz (1964).

 **Reporting on the Transition**

I f a transition toward sustainability does emerge over the next two generations, it will likely be guided by the mosaic of information outlined in previous chapters. Its accomplishment will be determined by societies' ability to shape the trends toward the transitions described in Chapter 2, foresight of the future using tools presented in Chapter 3, and skill in navigating successfully the threats and challenges identified in Chapter 4, in order to meet the normative goals laid out in Chapter 1. In this chapter we explore the contributions that appropriate monitoring and indicator systems might make to our navigational abilities toward the goals of sustainability in a turbulent world of surprise and inevitable policy failure. These indicators assess the trends that signal a transition. More important, these indicators can stimulate social learning—going beyond research, and beyond science and policy debate—to attain the actual policy and behavioral changes needed for a successful course. Learning of this kind, though difficult to achieve, can be influenced by a set of indicators that shape the awareness and actions of individuals, organizations, and societies in much the way that weather forecasts and economic indicators already influence short-term behavior.

INDICATORS

Indicators are repeated observations of natural and social phenomena that represent systematic feedback. They generally provide quantitative measures of the economy, human well-being, and impacts of human activities on the natural world. The signals they produce sound alarms, define challenges, and measure progress. For example, measurements of carbon dioxide levels in the atmosphere warn of possible climate change, population statistics show trends in the rate of growth of the human species, and Gross Domestic Product statistics attest to a nation's prosperity. Generally, indicators are most useful when obtained over many intervals of observation so that they illustrate trends and changes. Their calculation requires concerted efforts and financial investments by governments, firms, nongovernmental organizations, and the scientific community.

Indicators are essential to inform society over the coming decades how, and to what extent, progress is being made in navigating a transition toward sustainability. Numerous efforts are under way to collect, analyze, and aggregate the information needed to form sets of indicators of environmental, societal, and technological change. These efforts range on an ecological scale from watersheds to the whole planet, and on a political scale from municipal to international institutions and activities. **For reporting on a sustainability transition, however, it is clear that multiple indicators are needed to chart progress toward the goals for meeting human needs and preserving life support systems, and to evaluate the efficacy of actions taken to attain these goals.** Indicators will be needed to monitor and report on human welfare and planetary life support at global, regional, and local scales to catch the appropriate signals. These signals will tell us if societies are on track or if they are headed toward unsustainability. If such indicators focus on different levels of human-environment interactions, it should be possible to measure the directions in which humanity is headed. Another set of indicators will be needed to aid navigation, and thus, help humanity steer a course toward sustainability.

We begin with an overview of the current use of indicators, and then outline an approach formulated on the basis of the Board's normative objectives; finally, we address the role of indicators in navigating the uncharted waters of a transition toward sustainability.

THE USE OF INDICATORS

Humans have made repeated, precise measurements of some phenomena since ancient times. As archeologists have deciphered the use of astronomical observations in agrarian societies, it has become clear that environmental indicators have long been used to guide human behavior. The use of indicators has expanded with efforts of industrial societies to measure and manage a widening variety of environmental and societal parameters.

In an information age, the abundance of quantitative data along with digital imagery (from satellites and ground-based observation systems) and broadband communications helps us to perceive multiple parameters in our complex and dynamic world. Yet much of the data available was understandably shaped by the conventions and precedents of scientific research, and was not specifically collected to assess progress toward selected goals for humanity and to manage future developments. Indicators are evolving to fill this gap by condensing complex trends into convenient index numbers, giving researchers, policy makers and the public concise assessments of trends and guidance for how to shape future policies and actions. Whether indicators signal the ability to understand, predict, or control important environmental or social parameters depends on the relevance and accuracy of the selected goals and measurements. How the understanding that such indicators provide is used to guide human behavior is a matter for society and its governance.

Efforts to Formulate Indicators

In day-to-day life societies use prices, news and weather reports, and other routine methods of monitoring to guide behavior and expectations. Indicators perform parallel functions for long-term changes and large-scale actions. As the members of the European Community prepared to institute a common currency, they agreed to meet numerical guidelines for their budget deficits as a fraction of gross domestic product, and this indicator was closely watched. This is a striking instance of the influence of indicators that are widely accepted in defining valued social conditions. For complex conditions such as sustainable development (or a transition toward sustainability), no single indicator can adequately track their state or changes; sets of indicators are commonly used to gauge various parameters that together indicate multi-dimensional trends in social and environmental change.

The development of sets of indicators for sustainability has aimed at combining assessments of three aspects of nature and society: economy, environmental quality, and human well-being. One major effort to achieve such a combination is the Pressure-State-Response (PSR) framework presented, for generic environmental variables, in Figure 5.1.[1] This framework is a guideline to formulate sets of indicators that assess aspects of environmental and societal trends influencing sustainability.

Illuminating the interactive nature of sustainability, the Pressure-State-Response framework posits links between human actions and environmental consequences. Human activities exert *pressures*, such as burning gasoline in cars, that alter the *state* of environmental variables, such as the quality of city air. Those impaired states, in turn, elicit *responses*, such

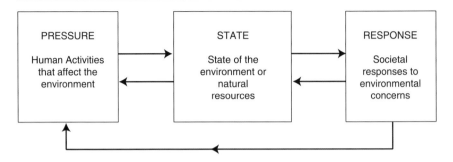

FIGURE 5.1   Pressure-State-Response framework for indicators of sustainable development.
Source: U.S. Interagency Working Group on Sustainable Development Indicators (1999).

as regulations governing pollution control technology in new vehicles. These three classes of variables identified by PSR can be measured using data that often are already collected for administrative purposes.   Combining these data with a simple but flexible scenario captures a fundamental idea of sustainable development: that humans can impair the life support systems of the natural world, calling forth responses intended to protect environmental quality. Feedbacks are also possible.   As the arrows in Figure 5.1 indicate, some responses can directly change the state of environmental variables, which in turn can affect the pressures exerted on people in some instances.   For instance, the creation of a national park alters expectations of future uses of that land, affecting a spectrum of pressures of human origin.   Some indicators, such as the value of adjacent private property, may rise, while others, such as mining permits, may decline.   Also, it is straightforward to expand PSR to include the impact of economic development on equity, hunger, and other aspects of human welfare; the scenarios analyzed in Chapter 3 provide examples.

Using the PSR framework, governments and nongovernmental organizations have compiled numerous sets of indicators for sustainable development using various measurement regimes.   Table 5.1 shows one set of indicators advanced recently by a working group in the U.S. government.[2] Figure 5.2 elaborates one of these indicators, high poverty census tracts, and describes how it is measured.   The simplicity of this indicator set highlights the need for each of these major indicators to be backed by sound scientific understanding to evaluate their limitations for detailed interpretations.

TABLE 5.1 An Illustrative Set of Indicators for Sustainable
Development in the U.S.

Issue	Selected Indicators
Economic Prosperity	Capital assets
	Labor productivity
	Domestic product
Fiscal Responsibility	Inflation
	Federal debt-to-GDP ratio
Scientific and Technological Advancement	Investment in R&D as a percentage of GDP
Employment	Unemployment
Equity	Income distribution
	People in census tracts with 40% or greater poverty
Housing	Homeownership rates
	Percentage of households in problem housing
Consumption	Energy consumption per capita and per dollar of GDP
	Materials consumption per capita and per dollar of GDP
	Consumption expenditures per capita
Status of Natural Resources	Conversion of cropland to other uses
	Soil erosion rates
	Ratio of renewable water supply to withdrawals
	Fisheries utilization
	Timber growth to removals balance
Air and Water Quality	Surface water quality
	Metropolitan air quality nonattainment
Contamination and Hazardous Materials	Contaminants in biota
	Identification and management of Superfund sites
	Quantity of spent nuclear fuel
Ecosystem Integrity	Acres of major terrestrial ecosystems
	Invasive alien species
Global Climate Change	Greenhouse gas emissions
	Greenhouse climate response index
Stratospheric Ozone Depletion	Status of stratospheric ozone
Population	U.S. population
Family Structure	Children living in families with one parent present
	Births to single mothers
Arts and Recreation	Outdoor recreation activities
	Participation in the arts and recreation
Community Involvement	Contributing time and money to charities
Education	Teacher training level and application of qualifications
	Educational attainment by level
	Educational achievement rates
Public Safety	Crime rate
Human Health	Life expectancy at birth

Source: Based on U.S. Interagency Working Group on Sustainable Development Indicators
(1998).

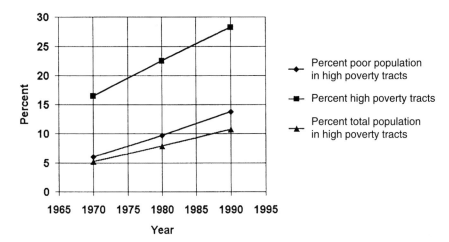

FIGURE 5.2 An illustrative indicator: high poverty census tracts. Census tracts have been defined for metropolitan areas, covering 75 percent of the total population. The poverty line is defined as the income level at which the estimated cost of a low-cost food plan for a family of three or more would consume 33 percent of the family's total income. A high poverty census tract is defined as one in which 40 percent or more of the population is below the poverty line. The percentage of poor people living in high poverty census tracts is a measure of the concentration of poverty in cities. It is widely believed that poor people are worse off living in areas of concentrated poverty than they would be in other areas, and that society as a whole suffers when these areas of concentrated poverty exist. The graph shows three measures of the concentration of poverty in urban areas: (1) the percentage of the population below the poverty line living in high poverty census tracts (from 16.5 percent in 1970 to 28.2 percent in 1990); (2) the percentage of census tracts defined as high poverty tracts, with 40 percent or more of the population below the poverty line (from 6 percent in 1970 to 13.7 percent in 1990); and (3) the percentage of total population living in high poverty census tracts (from 5.2 percent in 1970 to 10.7 percent in 1990).

Source: U.S. Department of Housing and Urban Development as published in U.S. Interagency Working Group on Sustainable Development Indicators (1999).

Indicators of Sustainable Development

Despite widespread agreement on the relevance of the Pressure-State-Response framework in formulating sets of indicators for sustainable development, diverse interests in the progress and definition of sustainable development have led to controversy over an acceptable set of indicators for its measurement.[3] Quantitative indicators are often scrutinized more for their moral, economic, and political implications than for their scientific substance. This is in part because there is no widely accepted operational definition of the term "sustainable development"[4] from which to guide the selection of the indicators (see Chapter 1). A result is that no single set of available indicators satisfies criteria for evaluation acceptable to all sides of the debate. This controversy often hinders the further collection of data, even when new studies are needed to appraise the reliability and accuracy of the measurements being taken.

Despite these difficulties, there are numerous efforts underway to assemble indicators of sustainable development. These efforts range on a political scale from municipal to international and on an ecological scale from watersheds to the planet as a whole.[5] Hundreds of indicators and numerous schemes to collect, analyze, and aggregate the information needed to form indicator sets have been proposed and various attempts have been made to rationalize them. For example, a recent effort vigorously attempts a "whole system" framework from existing schemes to provide a base for both information systems and dynamic modeling.[6] Five separate projects are discussed here with the intent of outlining what is being done rather than providing an exhaustive survey. These include two global (United Nations, World Bank), two national (Netherlands, United States), and one local (Seattle, Washington) projects.[7] A schematic overview of these studies is contained in Table 5.2, where they are sorted by the concepts of sustaining and developing set out in Chapter 1.

As Table 5.2 illustrates, sets of indicators for sustainability tend to focus on maintaining the life support systems important to humans and on monitoring development and economic activity. Many indicators, particularly in the environmental sector, do not have long time series, so their ability to discern environmental trends is weak compared to the determinations possible with economic and social data series. In addition, coverage is uneven; although environmental indicators outnumber the rest, there is greater depth of coverage in economic and some social indicators (e.g., education and health), especially in the large UN indicator set. Numerous indicators are available at the level of the nation-state, but apart from information collected on urban settlements and land cover, few indicators are available at smaller spatial scales.

The two American efforts included in Table 5.2, one by a federal interagency task force (see Table 5.1) and the other by an ad hoc citizen

Table 5.2 Indicators of Sustainable Development Proposed in Various Projects

	Sustain		
	Nature	Life Support	Community
Indicator group	**UN Commission on Sustainable Development (1997)**		
environmental	7	50	2
social	1	7	
economic		13	
institutional			6
totals	8*	70*	8*
	World Bank, *Expanding the Measure of Wealth* (1997)		
		1	
Indicator group	**Netherlands Environmental Policy Performance Indicators Adriaanse (1993)**		
environmental themes		7	
economic			
totals	0	7	0
Indicator group	**U.S. Interagency Working Group (1998)**		
environmental	8	12	1
social			7
economic		2	6
totals	8*	14*	14*
Indicator group	**Sustainable Seattle (1995)**		
environment, population	2	8	3
economy			2
health, community, education			8
totals	2	8	13

* Column totals are greater than total number of indicators because some are counted in more than one category.

† Numbers marked with a dagger indicate the number of indicators that are potentially available in spatial (geo-referenced) form, at a level of resolution finer than national boundaries.

Source: Based on US Interagency Working Group for Sustainable Development Indicators (1998).

| Develop | | | Availability of Indicators | | | |
People	Econ-omy	Society	yes	no	unknown	number of indicators
	5	5	8	27	20	55
17	7	13	37	3	1	41
	16	1	12	2	9	23
	4	9	6	3	6	15
17	32*	28*	63	35	36	134
1	1		1	2		3
			7			7
	6	1	7			7
0	6	1	14			14
	4		16/13†			16
7	4	5	11/11†			11
3	14	4	13/8†			13
10*	22*	9*	40			40
	2		15			15
4	2	1	9			9
4		4	16			16
8	4	5	40			40

panel in the city of Seattle, each chose about 40 variables, sifting from a larger number but converging on sets of indicators considerably more numerous than those typically used, for example, to assess sports leagues, financial markets, or local weather. Both the national and Seattle indicator sets include variables probing the sustaining of community, the aspect of sustainable development that has been least studied. The national set includes participation in arts and recreation, while the Seattle set includes a measure of gardening activity. The federal task force made a deliberate attempt to emphasize large-scale, long-range phenomena, similar to the Board's interest in a long-term transition toward sustainability.

The efforts by the UN Commission on Sustainable Development (CSD) and the World Bank complement one another. The CSD indicators were assembled using a Driving Force–State–Response framework similar to that seen in Figure 5.1. Selected through a consensus process without an agreed-upon operational definition of sustainable development, the CSD indicators are numerous, diverse in the methods used to measure development or sustainability, and include a large number of indicators for which reliable measurements do not exist.

The World Bank, in contrast, has estimated three capital accounts. Each attempts to capture the value to national economies of a vital aspect of the world. The most familiar account, of "produced" capital, is what is normally called national wealth—physical capital and financial claims—and is marked in the "economy" column in Table 5.2. A second account measures natural capital—the resources and capitalized value of services provided by the natural world—and is marked in the "life support" column in Table 5.2. In principle, this would include standing timber, soil fertility, fish stocks, potable water, and the value of flood control by wetlands. Natural capital estimates are as yet primitive in comparison to those for produced capital. The most recent World Bank study takes into account only the use values of natural resources,[8] an approach that ignores unpriced damage to ecosystems, as well as ecosystem services like the flood control capabilities of wetlands and aesthetic or moral dimensions of resource value. The third component of wealth, quantitatively the largest, is human resources—the economic value of labor, knowledge, and social institutions—and is marked in the "people" column in Table 5.2. The Bank estimates this dimension of wealth as a residual, by inferring the value of human resources needed to explain the generation of the actual flows observed in national income accounts. All three accounts, including the one measuring "produced" capital, are subject to errors of estimation. Already, the World Bank study has launched debates, but has succeeded in broadening the key issue about how to capture different measures of value in a transition toward sustainability.

Although the Bank's indicators are highly aggregated and estimated using drastic assumptions, they are conceptually clear. The wealth of nations should be considered in three parts. At least at the margins wealth can be transferred from one account to another in ways advantageous to people. By contrast, the United Nations CSD indicators do not warn unambiguously of imminent hazards in any ecosystem or society, nor do they provide guidance on how to pursue sustainable development.

Only the United Nations CSD indicator set includes variables that are not now being measured. This is a notable strength of the CSD process, the realization that much of what needs to be assessed about sustainable development remains unclear. Another strength of the CSD process is its recognition of the need to transfer reliable measurement methods to developing countries. The UN also has sponsored a wide-ranging, if still diffuse, research effort under the aegis of the Scientific Committee on Problems of the Environment (SCOPE) of the International Council for Science.[9] In evaluating measurements being taken in various categories, the SCOPE effort outlines a broad research agenda for indicators (based on filling methodological gaps, resolving inadequate existing efforts, making better use of existing designs), but does not provide a framework for monitoring indictors.

In sum, the Board finds that there is no consensus on the appropriateness of the current sets of indicators or the scientific basis for choosing among them. Their effectiveness is limited by the lack of agreement on what to develop, what to sustain, and for how long—that is, there is a lack of agreement on the meaning of sustainable development (see Chapter 1), on the specificity or aggregation of indicators, or on the use of existing as opposed to desired data sets. The projects carried out over the decade since the Brundltand Commission popularized the idea of sustainable development have drawn on the large bodies of work done in past decades on the measurement of human welfare and the condition of the environment. These efforts bring together many sources of illumination, but have yet to produce a set of goals for social and natural conditions that can plausibly lead to prosperity for all while conserving the life support systems on which human economies rest. Consequently, they have not provided indicators set on goals for sustainability.

The fact that societies do not have a clear path to a sustainable future is hardly surprising in light of the long time scales, large spatial reach, and unexpected turns of the future described in Chapters 1, 2, and 3. Yet controversy over the definition of sustainable development and the set of indicators to monitor its evolution has hindered scientific and political progress. In an effort to overcome these barriers, the Board now turns to the task of defining a framework for indicators to measure essential environmental and human parameters, and whose monitoring might guide societies toward our normatively defined transition toward sustainability.

INDICATORS FOR A SUSTAINABILITY TRANSITION

Although a compact set of indicators cannot comprehensively measure the complex and qualitative dimensions of a transition to sustainability, indicators provide a clear and concise reading on progress which can have a powerful impact on both the public and policy makers, leading to essential changes in policies and behaviors. In addition, sets of indicators testify to varying claims on what matters in a transition. The Board's claims are implicit in our normative perspective: to meet human needs while maintaining life support systems and reducing hunger and poverty.

While indicators are not by themselves an answer to the question of what constitutes a transition toward sustainability, they are indispensable in helping to successfully answer that question. Multiple indicators will be needed to chart progress toward the goals for human welfare and planetary life support, and to evaluate the effectiveness of actions taken to attain these goals.

Charting Progress Toward the Goals

First, we describe five kinds of information that is monitored or needs to be monitored at different spatial scales that shed important light on whether human needs are being met and whether human activities are compatible with sustaining life support systems (see Tables 5.3 and 5.4):

• Human welfare is now being monitored by quantitative indicators that are appropriate in concept but implemented with inadequate coverage and frequency.

• Quantitative indicators to measure global phenomena are now monitoring planetary circulatory systems affected by human activity.

• Critical zones of human-environment vulnerability at regional scales are being identified, but there is not a single set of indicators that can monitor the combination of social and natural factors that lead to irreversible damage.

• Indicators are needed to describe the management requirements of ecosystems that support rapidly growing cities. Productive landscapes at local scales will help reconcile accelerated urbanization and the overall needs of human settlements.

• Inventories of ecosystems will assist conservation at local scales. Protected areas, managed to enable their biota to persist indefinitely, are being identified on a place-by-place basis, rather than through a consistent set of appraisals of their long-term sustainability.

For each of these settings, indicators form an indispensable but in-

TABLE 5.3   Global and Regional Indicators for Meeting Human Needs

NEEDS	INDICATOR	Agency	Frequency of estimate	IN NEED [year of estimate]
Providing Food and Nutrition Under-nourished	Number and percentage chronically underfed for work, health, and growth	FAO	5-year intervals [1970-]	828 million [1996]
Nurturing Children Under 5 Mortality	Number and rate of deaths 0-5 yrs.	UNICEF	Annual	12 million [1997]
Underweight	Number and percentage of 0-5 yrs. <2SD median weight for age.	UNICEF	Annual	183 million [1997]
Micronutrient deficiencies	*Iodine*: Number and percentage age 6-11 with palpable or visible goiter	WHO	Irregular; current status reviewed in de Onis and Blössner (1997)	18% [1991]
	Iron: Number and percentage of mothers and children anemic	WHO	See above	51% < 4 yrs. [1991]
	Vitamin A: Number and percentage of pre-school children at risk (living in areas where defieciency and its consequences occur)	WHO	See above	190 million [1991]
Finding Shelter Water	Number and percentage with access to safe water	WHO	Irregular; current status reviewed in WRI (1998, Table 8.7)	1,115 million [1994]
Sanitation	Number and percentage with access to adequate sanitation	WHO	See above	2,873 million [1994]
Housing	Number and percentage living in housing where lives and health are at risk	UNCHS	10 years	600 million

Sources: WHO (1996), UNCHS (1996), FAO (1998), UNICEF (1998).

complete part of the intelligence needed to discern a transition toward sustainability in the decades to come.

Meeting Human Needs, Reducing Hunger and Poverty

As discussed in Chapter 2, human societies have reduced hunger and poverty in relative terms as population has grown. Yet even these impressive improvements leave large absolute numbers of the destitute, together with a widening inequality between rich and poor across nations and within national economies. Human population growth is slowing, with the rate of absolute increase falling over the past decade. Urbanization of the human race is still accelerating, with roughly half of the world's population currently living in cities, a fraction that is projected to continue to increase over the next two generations. These changes seem likely to alter much of social life, including some of the ways we define human needs.

Meeting human needs is a near-term imperative, one that the world community has pursued with some success for at least two generations. Some quantitative data series are available in this area, often over times longer than a generation, together with proven analytical structures in demography, public health, and other applied social sciences.

Yet, as shown in Table 5.3, there is only a rudimentary system of indicators in place to assess human needs, hunger, and poverty. For example, a precise estimate of the number of poor and hungry people in the world remains elusive: hunger and poverty are difficult to define, the statistical data are weak and scattered, and efforts to improve data collection and analysis have been limited. In addition, resources devoted to the measurement and reporting of hunger and poverty are meager in comparison to the effort put into reporting population or economic growth. The reason is simple: national governments are rarely motivated to inquire into the fate of those for whom they have not provided. The existing indicators also reflect the implicit hierarchy of needs discussed in Chapter 1, favoring children and people in disasters—feeding and nurturing first, followed by education. Housing adequacy is rarely estimated globally and comprehensive employment not at all.

Nonetheless, with the exception of employment, a baseline of regional and global estimates exists against which progress in meeting human needs and reducing hunger and poverty could be measured. Examples are shown in Table 5.3. In all cases, such indicators are based on either national aggregates or on special populations within nations. Most of these data are actually nonrandom samples, but as much data is missing even when a condition is reported on; this can be seen, for example, in the data for 193 nations in the latest UNICEF report.[10] The number undernourished is inferred from the annual estimates of agricultural production and the resulting estimate of dietary energy supply for every country in the world made by the UN Food and Agricultural Organization. Many of the estimates in Table 5.3 are based on measured surveys, but even more rely on informed judgment or guesses for some countries.[11] Recognizing the difficulty of assembling comprehensive coverage, the UN estimate of 600 million inadequately housed relies heavily on a housing indicators program begun in 1990 that uses consultants in 52 cities containing 10 percent of the world's urban population to estimate 25 key indicators such as floor area per person.[12]

Broadly speaking, indicators of human need are of two types: those based on direct measurement of a condition that is symptomatic of the condition to be assessed, and indicators one step removed, measuring the number "at risk." The following examples are drawn from studies of hunger.[13] Measurements for *underweight* are mostly direct, based on measurements of children's weight carried in national demographic and health surveys in 120 countries.[14] Those data are supplemented by more recent UNICEF-sponsored multiple-cluster indicator surveys carried out in 60 countries in 1995 and 1996,[15] as well as reports from key clinical programs in developing countries. But even when weight is adequately sampled, measured, and reported, age estimates remain a problem. There is also a lively debate about the adequacy of the reference standard (based on weight for age in industrialized countries) from which underweight is calculated. Other direct measurements of human need may include observing goiters for iodine deficiency, anemia for lack of iron, and xerophthalmia incidence for vitamin A deficiency. In contrast, *undernourished* is an "at risk" estimate, an effort to calculate the numbers resident in households whose income or food production is insufficient to provide a minimal diet sufficient for work, health, and child growth. Key assumptions in such calculations, in addition to dietary energy supply, are the minimal dietary requirements and the distribution of income and food production within a national account. Other at-risk estimates have been made of numbers resident in areas with extensive iodine or Vitamin A deficiencies.

It is clear that a responsibility of the world community should be to report quantitatively on human well-being, with particular attention to hunger and poverty, on an annual or biennial basis sufficient to mark movement toward or away from the agreed-upon goals for basic human needs. Achieving regular reporting with usable accuracy could build on the efforts now put into the annual report of the UN Development Program, extending the already widespread use of targeted surveys (e.g., health, population, living standard), and incorporating reporting mechanisms with the creation of international targets and goals.

Monitoring Planetary Circulatory Systems

Indicators also play a role in monitoring global threats to a sustainable future. Earth has biophysical circulatory systems—rapid circulation in atmosphere and oceans, driven by solar energy, and slower changes in the lithosphere, as tectonic plates move, and the biosphere, as migration patterns shift and species radiate—that act as an analog to human vital signs. To these circulatory patterns, humans have added travel, technology, and trade—moving people and their companion life forms with increasing speed and momentum across spatial and biogeochemical domains (see Table 5.4).

An objective of worldwide scientific studies of planetary circulatory systems is to search for phenomena and potential surprises that may affect the stability of natural systems and the sustainability of human endeavors and well-being. Trouble in the circulatory systems is important because the scale of circulation can involve the entire planet more rapidly or persistently than governments can address through regulation. The transportation of infectious diseases by human travelers has been cited recently.[16] Less noticeable but sometimes more important surprises lurk, as global phenomena increasingly interact with other forces to cause unanticipated consequences. The interactions of nitrogen deposition and elevated CO_2, and of sulfur aerosols and climate, both discussed in Chapter 4, are such examples. Such interactions are difficult to predict and, once discovered, can be hard to manage when they involve processes important to human economic activities, as almost by definition they do. More generally, changes in planetary circulatory systems are subtle and largely invisible in the short run without scientific measurements and their theoretical interpretation.[17] Thus, long-term monitoring programs must include supportive fundamental scientific research. While indicators sometimes provide signals that are valuable and comprehensible, numerous examples, such as the failure to recognize seasonal depletion in polar stratospheric ozone,[18] underscore the value of scientific research as a social resource for recognizing surprising threats and opportunities that indicators on their own do not delineate.

Indicators of important chemical changes in the atmosphere have become well utilized in recent years. There is agreement that changes in atmospheric composition indicate changes in the radiative balance of the planet, with consequences that are likely to include long-term and large-scale modifications of climate.[19] The search for reliable indicators of human-caused climate change is well under way. Similarly, some monitoring of ozone and of the gases that deplete the stratospheric ozone layer is in place as part of an international legal regime aimed at eliminating ozone-depleting chemicals. At the regional level, long-range transport of air pollutants including ozone, sulfates, and oxides of nitrogen is being monitored in many places in an attempt to implement regulations that cross political boundaries.

Planetary circulatory systems of increasing significance are the networks of communications and trade, and migration and travel, now expanding rapidly. These evolving networks carry direct threats already identified (see Chapters 2 and 4), such as the transfer of diseases and exotic species, together with a large spectrum of opportunities (such as the expanding telecommunications and computing networks) both to develop and to sustain human welfare. To date, study of this network from a scientific perspective has been done within the framework of the social sciences. Those studies have illuminated the conflicts between the transformations driven by global trade and the goals of environmental protection and economic equity.[20] But few analyses have been done of the effect of communications and computer technology (especially the increasing use of the Internet) on work or consumptive patterns, or on productivity and efficiency, to determine how these networks might mitigate the threats associated with meeting the needs of a more crowded, more consuming human population. Indicators of trade are now reported at high levels of aggregation[21] with data organized by dollar volume and nation. Datasets with much finer resolution on the production of specific commodities are now becoming available.[22] But these more detailed data do not become useful indicators without an agreed-on framework of specific questions. The Board has not studied trade indicators at the global level, although we believe the long-term growth of trade will play a significant role in a transition to sustainability; we have listed trade as an indicator in Table 5.4 as a placeholder for this belief.

Identifying Critical Regions

While indicators of circulatory systems monitor the directions of human and environmental systems on a planetary basis, indicators are needed to catch the signals of critical change at the regional level, thereby identifying stresses on ecosystem services resulting from human mismanagement and overexploitation.[23] Although humans were modifying the natural world on local and regional scales even before the invention of agriculture, the scale and scope of human-induced change has accelerated over the past century as both population and consumption have increased. Accordingly, it is useful to consider a definition proposed recently by an international team of geographers: a critical environment is one in which the extent or rate of environmental degradation precludes the maintenance of current resource-use systems or levels of human well-being, given feasible adaptations and the community's capacity to mount a re-

TABLE 5.4 Global and Regional Indicators for Life Support Systems

System	Indicator
Circulatory Systems Atmospheric composition	Concentration of carbon dioxide, other greenhouse gases, and patterns of global temperature, precipitation, snow, ice, sea level, and ocean circulation
	Cross-border transport of air pollutants (Europe, N. America)*
Infectious diseases	Alerts of emergent diseases
Invasive exotic species	No regular monitoring Studies of particular sites, e.g., San Francisco Bay
Trade across ecosystems	Economic transactions across governmental boundaries (not ecosystems)
Critical Regions Natural setting	Region-specific; not identified
Social capacity to respond	Region-specific; not identified
Feasible steps to mitigate or restore	Region-specific; not identified
Productive Metropolitan Landscapes	None defined in terms of ecosystem damage or cost to rehabilitate
Protected places	Total area protected
	Effectiveness of preservation

Note: EMEP, Geneva Protocol on Long-term Financing of the Cooperative Programme for Monitoring and Evaluation of the Long-range Transmission of Air Pollutants in Europe; EPA, U.S. Environmental Protection Agency; WHO, World Health Organization; IMF, International Monetary Fund; NRC, National Research Council.

*A North American monitoring program for transboundary air pollutant flows is being developed under the 1991 U.S.–Canada Air Quality Agreement (United States–Canada Air Quality Committee (1999)). Additional datasets may be found in Center for Air Pollution Impacts and Trends Analysis (1999). In addition, the RAINS Asia project at the International Institute for Applied Systems Analysis (IIASA 1999) has estimated emissions for East Asia.

Agency	Frequency of Estimate	Condition
Carbon Dioxide Information Analysis Center (1999)	Annual	Climate change in progress
EMEP (1984) (Europe); US EPA (1998a,b)	Annual (Europe only)	Controls on emissions being negotiated and implemented
WHO	As found	Increasing frequency (see NRC (1992a))
None	—	High frequency in some places (see NRC (1995e,f))
IMF (1998)	Annual	Threat to life-support systems unclear
—	—	Locally severe damage
—	—	Unknown
—	—	Unknown
—	—	Unknown
World Conservation and Monitoring Centre (1999)	Every 3 years	Unknown (see Green and Paine (1997))
—	—	Unknown

sponse.[24]   A comparative study of nine regions, each of which had at-
tracted scientific notice as a potentially critical region, concluded that one
of the nine, the Aral Sea in the former Soviet Union, was in a critical state.
Two others were firmly in the region marked "endangered" in Figure 5.3,
eastern Sundaland—Borneo and peninsular Malaysia—which has experienced severe deforestation and consequent forest fire damage, and the
basin of Mexico, the scene of rapid industrialization and population increase during the 20th century.[25] Thus, regional environments move
through trajectories from sustainable to critical as their ability to recover
from damage diminishes and the ability of society to sustain the costs of
mitigation or substitution of environmental services increases.

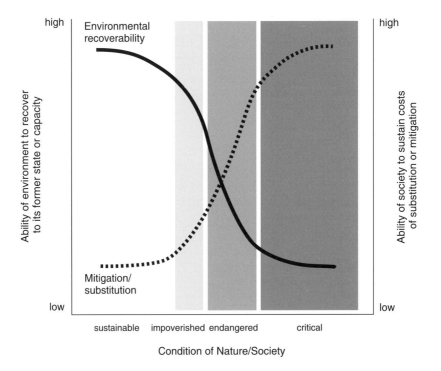

FIGURE 5.3   Regional trajectories and emerging criticality. The criticality of
a region is a joint function of the ability of the environment to recover to its
former state or capacity and the ability of society to sustain the costs of
mitigation of damage or substitutes of environmental services.

Source: Redrawn from Kasperson et al. (1995). Courtesy of United Nations
University Press.

Whether a region is on a path to criticality depends on three factors: the state and vulnerability of the natural setting, the social capacity to recognize, and choose to cure, the problems brought about by human activity, and the feasible steps available to avoid irreversible damage. Note that these factors are explicitly grounded in human interest. (Preservation of ecosystems and species is discussed separately below.)

The risks facing potentially critical regions are a function of their social systems as well as their natural settings. All three key elements of critical damage—pressure on natural systems, capacity to respond, and adaptations that would constitute an effective response—are conditioned by history. The risks to a region, accordingly, are "contingent upon unique socioeconomic structures."[26] Those structures may include international markets or other forces involving societies and actors from afar. Although the critical risk has a local impact, its cause may be distant.

The highlighting of the social variables here does not mean that natural variables are unimportant, but rather that both social and natural variables matter (see Figure 5.3). Pressure on natural systems is typically measured using variables from the natural sciences, but the pressures are exerted by human activities. Feasible adaptations are often described in engineering terms, but whether they are feasible is a social question and whether the adaptations are put in place is an institutional matter. Risks to sustainability are specific to the social and natural history of the region. In part for that reason, researchers have no satisfactory means as yet of comparing risks to sustainability across different regions.

These facts imply that useful indicators of regional unsustainability will reflect the specific conditions of each region. Researchers suggested a generic set of trajectories (Figure 5.3): as intensity of exploitation increases, the modifications made to ecosystems decrease the potential for complete recovery; correspondingly, the costs to mitigate ecosystem damage or to provide substitutes for the goods and services provided by the regional ecosystem rise.[27] In the critical zone, costs rise so much that irreversible damage to both natural and social systems is done. Of global relevance are the criteria for critical damage—irreversible losses and threats to human well-being or economic sustainability. The dynamics of criticality are local, but criticality in any region is an indicator of global significance.

Criticality is not a quantitative indicator, however, but a judgment informed by a combination of social and natural system considerations. It is a judgment likely to be contested. In the current state of understanding, the assessment of whether a region is headed for unsustainable damage and of whether its resident social system is capable of avoiding that damage cannot be reduced to a computational algorithm.

Given this constraint, researchers should search for quantitative and qualitative information that can inform different kinds of judgments:

• Identify regions at risk of critical damage. Develop region-specific indicators to assess critical risks.

• Provide information to the world community on the scope and scale of potential critical risks and on the costs of avoiding irreversible damage.

• Advance basic understanding of the social processes and natural vulnerabilities that expands knowledge of the potential risks associated with damage.

• Advance basic understanding of the social processes—including politics, markets, and culture—that both form and undermine the capacity to sense and to avoid critical damage.[28]

• Working with regional communities, develop ways to recognize critical decline before irreversible damage is done, and develop means of learning from experience so that capacity to respond will strengthen over time. As necessary, work in support of external intervention to forestall critical decline.

Although these activities make use of quantitative indicators, these analytical tasks cannot all be routinized into the standard protocols that define an indicator. Nonetheless, the social functions served by indicators would be realized if the tasks were reasonably well carried out.

Conserving Productive Landscapes

As human settlements—particularly cities—grow in the coming century, it will be important that patterns of growth take into account the dependencies of populations on local ecosystems.[29] For some resources such as food supply, it is possible to meet the needs of urban dwellers economically by importing goods over longer and longer distances. For others, such as water or air, it is costly or infeasible to build technological systems to substitute for the natural systems already in place. The conservation of productive landscapes is implicit in the Pressure-State-Response framework (Figure 5.1). One task of society is to anticipate the pressures of future populations, designing infrastructures that respond to those pressures in ways that can be sustained by an affordable fraction of the economic surplus generated by the population of a settlement or urban region. Sensing the pressures upon environmental services and resources with enough lead time and analytical vision to respond is a challenge that is being met, imperfectly, by the indicators gathered by governing authorities.[30] For example, the Sustainable Seattle project (Table 5.2) includes measures of soil erosion, air quality, and solid waste generation and recycling. Yet none of these measures is explicitly stated in a way that provides insight into the relationships among increasing pressure, declining ecosystem recoverability, and increasing costs of mitigating or providing substitute services shown in Figure 5.3.[31] Such insight is important for sensing irreversible damage, but it is difficult to provide (Table 5.4).

The spatial and temporal structure of ecosystem services is often not apparent to humans and the institutions and markets through which they organize their activities. As a result, the development of human activities and settlements frequently does not take into account the patterns and vulnerabilities of ecosystem services. Unsustainable development then results, a pattern of settlement far more costly to maintain than expected;[32] in severe cases, the region may also face a larger risk of critical environmental damage. Metropolitan sprawl has been criticized as a form of unsustainable development, although there is lively controversy about whether sprawl is wasteful in an economic sense.[33] Unsustainable development is further accelerated and reinforced by pressures to accommodate urgent human needs rapidly when investment capital is scarce.

For centuries, physical infrastructure—sewers, aqueducts, roads— have been used to overcome the imperfect match between human needs and the supply of ecosystem services. In the great urbanization underway, however, it makes sense in many places to anticipate greatly increased human demands and to design infrastructure so that those demands may be met efficiently by resources nearby. Ecosystems are valuable to people, frequently in ways that are literally irreplaceable in practical terms.[34] The design of urban infrastructure should reflect the value of ecosystems, especially freshwater ecosystems in their value for future water resource needs, wetlands, flood plain habitat, commercial fisheries and other services.

Such an approach requires, however, understanding and nurturing the ecosystems surrounding urbanizing sites—an understanding that comes in part from long-term studies of those ecosystems. Improved understanding would also illuminate the nonmarket value of species and ecosystems, permitting better-informed choices when utilitarian values and conservation biology come into unavoidable conflict.[35] The required long-term ecosystem monitoring and supporting field science is just beginning with the creation of the first two long-term ecological research stations in Baltimore and Phoenix.[36]

Preserving Ecosystems

We described in Chapter 4 how the preservation of species, habitats, and ecosystems has become a significant part of the effort to conserve and maintain biodiversity and to effect a sustainable biosphere.* In spite of its importance, preservation remains controversial for social and scientific reasons. Improved understanding of which conservation methods are biologically effective would assist in implementing preservation strategies. As noted in Chapter 2, there is no question that many ecosystems are at critical risk and that irreversible losses of species are under way at a pace and scale seen only five times before in the history of life.[37] But translating that grim reality into indicators at the scale of ecosystems managed by humans for purposes of preservation remains one of the significant challenges of a transition toward sustainability.

The realization that human activities are causing a wave of species extinctions that have only been met or exceeded a few times in the entire geological record is itself a recent discovery.[38] The massive endangerment of species and ecosystems has stimulated two responses over the past several decades—worldwide effort to preserve species and areas, and the field of conservation biology. Land or waters that contain species harvested by humans are not protected easily. Various approaches have emerged for overcoming resistance to preservation. International environmental activism has played a significant role in influencing national governments to preserve habitats. Transnational arrangements for bioprospecting and debt-for-nature swaps have provided financial support for changes in the use of terrestrial and aquatic ecosystems.[39] But conflict persists, as illustrated by the legal and political struggle over private property rights brought about by passage of the Endangered Species Act in the United States.[40]

As described in Chapter 4, preservation efforts are moving away from an emphasis on single species to an emphasis on management of multiple species and their interactions with one other and their physical environments.[41] This expansion of the scope of preservation also greatly increases the complexity of the choices to be made, both scientifically (especially in selecting indicators for monitoring change) and in the way that human activities are considered and reshaped to ensure the maintenance of critical interactions.

The flowering of conservation biology has made clear that the pressure on the world's biological wealth cannot be gauged simply by counting land area being converted or fishing grounds being overharvested. Biodiversity is a complex geographic phenomenon, requiring new tools to assay its richness. An initial attempt to identify a set of large ecosys-

---

*In this discussion the word "preservation" means setting aside land (or water) for the maintenance or recovery of species, habitats, or ecosystems that are judged to be vulnerable to extinction, failing an explicit decision to preserve them.

tems that would in aggregate provide complete representation of all types of ecosystems and habitats is the Global 200 nominated by the World Wildlife Fund,[42] shown in Figure 5.4. Large-scale conservation is slow work that must contend with the urgent demands of poor people and the powerful forces of governments, trade, and greed.

Innovative methods are now being developed—including rapid assessment methods to assess habitats quickly; population and genetic models that combine information from museum collections and field studies to inform judgments about how species and ecosystems may respond to anthropogenic changes; and fundamental studies of the relationships between the diversity of ecological communities and their stability when subjected to disturbance.[43]

In parallel with conservation science, there has emerged a social capacity to elicit and focus the concern of citizens, governments, and philanthropists. The ideas of conservation biology are now being applied in a wide variety of situations. In addition to the seed banks and zoos that have long provided living collections of biota, captive breeding of animals has enabled a small number of species to be preserved outside the wild.[44] Biotechnology has also been applied to extract desirable traits from the

FIGURE 5.4 Global 200 ecoregions proposed by the World Wildlife Fund. The shaded areas would, if successfully conserved, provide representation for all ecosystem and habitat types. Because of the large size of the ecoregions, nearly all will be permanently inhabited by humans. The human economies in these ecoregions would need to join in a sustainability transition accordingly.

Source: Olson and Dinerstein (1998). Courtesy of the World Wildlife Fund.

genomes of some wild species, such as the capacity to make medicinal compounds like taxol, originally discovered in the Pacific yew.[45]

The most visible and controversial efforts in preservation may be protected areas, terrestrial and aquatic habitats in which human use is excluded or altered so as to be compatible with the continued survival of these habitats' biotic communities and wild species.[46] Protected areas have now been declared in many nations around the world, with a quarter of the land base of Costa Rica now in national parks and biological reserves.[47] Often, the social choice to preserve a habitat is organized around a biological indicator—an appealing "flagship" species, such as the salmon of the Pacific Northwest, which may or may not be an effective indicator of the conservation of the habitat as an ecosystem.[48] Without the protected area, there would usually be little chance to sustain or restore valued species and habitats, but without monitoring and assessment there will be no chance of learning what works and, just as important, what does not work, to preserve ecosystems.

A focus of worldwide research should be on sharing and improving methodologies for monitoring and assessment, to evaluate strategies for meeting management objectives (e.g., spatial boundaries, legal status, funding, and personnel), for protecting targeted species (e.g., population parameters such as size, fecundity, and some dimensions of genetic variability), for furthering understanding of how species interact with their environments, and for taking into account the human populations that inhabit regions of high biological diversity (e.g., measuring use, restricting access, maximizing opportunities for traditional land use practices).[49] The indicators collected in each area should be selected to maximize the effectiveness of the protected area in meeting the identified goals of preservation.

Evaluating the Efficacy of Actions

Indicators of human welfare and life support systems identify urgent needs. Indicators selected to evaluate different levels of human-environment interactions can help to steer a course toward sustainability, because in each of these levels of interactions there are hazards that we must strive to avoid. Success in responding to the hazards has been uneven and is likely to continue to be so. There is also the question of navigation, of the long-term directions in which humanity should aim, in light of the possibilities hinted at by the scenarios of Chapter 3 and the goals we laid out in Chapter 1. In this task, quantitative information complements the narratives provided by scenarios. We comment briefly on four different approaches for evaluating the efficacy of actions taken to achieve the goals for sustainablity (see Table 5.5) below, with the aim of provoking debate on navigational aids for a sustainability transition.

National Capital Accounts

Most of the planet will continue to lie outside critical regions and protected areas for the immediately foreseeable future. How should we monitor the evolution of this part of the world for signs of trouble or improvement in a transition toward sustainability? Large fractions of freshwater and solar energy are already appropriated by humans, in the sense that we make use of them directly and indirectly in our economies.[50] Yet what is occurring is hard to see, in part because its human driving forces are decentralized.

It is in this context that the World Bank's studies of the wealth of nations provide a usefully provocative approach: to estimate the state of the world through three national accounts, described earlier in this chapter—accounts of natural, human, and produced capital.[51] In this economic formulation, each of these categories of capital might be transformed by human activity, but so long as a nation's total capital increases over time, its trajectory is in roughly the right direction to contribute to a transition toward sustainability.

The word "roughly" is important. An economic accounting is inadequate to assess sustainability, even without the many major assumptions made in the Bank's current estimates. These studies also demonstrate anew the difficulty of valuing human resources, social institutions, and environmental stewardship using only a utilitarian metric. But the capital accounts make two important contributions. First, the framework draws attention to transformations among forms of wealth—transformations that will continue through, and beyond, any long-term search for sustainability. Monitoring those transformations is useful to highlight them and to acknowledge the importance of undervalued natural capital. Second, the accounting framework is one that can be disseminated via the United Nations' System of National Accounts, an intellectual infrastructure that encourages the finance ministries and governments of the world to use common accounting standards. This is one means for transferring technical assistance, particularly to developing countries, so that the rudimentary reporting of today can be improved over time and made comparable and reliable.[52]

There is a larger question here, though, of whether some sort of "weak" sustainability[53] might be appropriate in the long run—an approach in which many natural assets might not be preserved in perpetuity, but in which the stock of natural assets would vary in response to the needs of humans. The Board believes that we are too early in the pursuit

TABLE 5.5 Navigational Aids for a Sustainability Transition

Navigational Aid	Indicator	Agency	Frequency of estimate	Comments
Economic	National capital accounts: — Natural assets — Human resources — Produced assets	World Bank	Under development; needed at 5-year intervals	Utilitarian framework incomplete in principle; approximations in practice add further errors; simplicity valuable
Policy	PSR indicators used in adaptive management	Needed at local to regional scales	—	Difficult to implement but yields reliable knowledge when successful
Ongoing Transitions				
	Energy intensity (joules/GDP)* carbon intensity (tonnes C/GDP)	WRI, UN, World Bank	Climate convention assessments	"De-carbonization" of energy supply[†]
	Material flows and recycling	Not implemented	Tied to economic reporting	"De-materialization," closing of material flow cycles
	Population	UN	Annually	Demographic transition
Surprises	None, by definition	—	—	Warning of factors not taken into account; opportunity to improve management—and run larger risks.

Note: PSR, Pressure-State-Response model; GDP, Gross Domestic Product.

*This data series is not regularly reported but is readily calculated from standard sources. Estimates for 1993 are in WRI (1996, Table 12.2, pp. 286-287).
[†]Nakicenovic (1997).

of sustainable development even to frame this question tractably. What we emphasize here instead is that the World Bank accounts constitute a useful starting point for discussion and learning.

Assessing Policies

The Pressure-State-Response framework envisions indicators as policy assessment tools. It is important that indicators become the basis for learning, an approach called adaptive management. Adaptive management treats policies as experiments, designing them so that lessons may be learned reliably from the implementation of policies, even those that fail. In the PSR framework, this means assembling pressure and state indicators to test the effectiveness of responses. Then, as the responses are carried out, the indicators provide two kinds of learning. First, they should inform those who manage the responses of how to do their work better. Second, the indicators should permit better appraisals of whether the responses are effective at all, so that better responses may be designed as necessary. These simple goals have turned out to be remarkably difficult to achieve.[54] Yet, over the generational time scale of a transition toward sustainability, there is reason to think that a deliberately adaptive approach to policies will yield benefits.[55]

Adaptive management borrows the idea of experiments from laboratory science, where three concepts could be said to underpin the process of learning. First, if an experiment is to produce reliable understanding, the effect must be repeatable. Cold fusion was discarded as a promising energy source because other laboratories could not reproduce the results claimed by the original discoverers. In policy assessment, this means that an effectively designed policy should work in different contexts to some reasonable degree of generalization.

Second, to pin down what makes the experiment work, there must be controls—ways to turn off the causal agent to see if the result also declines or ceases. If a medicine works to moderate pain, then the pain will remain intense if the medicine is withheld and the patient receives a placebo. In policy, in theory this means that there should be circumstances in which *only* the policy is omitted, while all else is the same, to be sure that it is the policy that is making the difference, though obviously this is extremely difficult to do.

Third, it is hard to detect weak effects, so in many cases it is important to provide a large enough experimental manipulation to see the effect. Efforts to restore the ecosystems of Western rivers need large releases of water, so that a rough approximation of the spring flood can recreate the ecological effects that have been eliminated by upstream dams.[56] The technical name for this idea is assuring adequate power of test. In a policy context, it means designing responses that are large enough to have observable impacts on the state or the pressure indicators under study.

None of these three conditions is readily achieved. Policies adopted by governments are usually implemented with little attention to gathering data on the policies' effectiveness. Moreover, neither those who originally advocated a policy (often against stiff opposition) nor those implementing it welcome news that the policy is failing. Finally, many policies are assessed by their cost or other inputs, rather than by their results. It is accordingly easy when resources are scarce to cut back spending so that no observable result can be obtained.

Because the conditions for adaptive management are often difficult to achieve, policies that fall within the framework of a set of indicators can provide important opportunities for learning. The indicators will usually be in place already, in support of a commitment to sustainable development or for other reasons, so that it may be easier to tackle the issues of repeatability, controls, and power of test without securing the cooperation of the agencies and people implementing the policy. A by-product of a well-functioning set of indicators should thus be social learning through adaptive management.

Monitoring Ongoing Transitions

A transition to sustainability is a dynamic process. It will be essential to monitor the trends identified in Chapter 2 to determine whether the specific transitions involved (for example, the globalization of the economy and changes in demographics, consumption patterns, health, energy-intensity, pollution per unit value produced by the economy, and the role of the state in global governance) actually occur on a global basis. In particular, if economies are to continue to grow as populations level off, it will be essential to improve technology and energy efficiency so that humans can accomplish more, economically, with less impact on the natural world.

There is no assurance, however, that the trends described in Chapter 2 will unfold in the direction of greater material efficiency. So it is important to update and to argue over the questions raised by those and other data. In particular, it is important to see if the long-term trend of "decarbonization"* (Figure 5.5) can be accelerated, so that energy for growing economies can be supplied in ways that cause less disturbance to the climate. Ideas on this and other fronts are described more fully in

---

*The term "decarbonization" is used to refer to the decrease in tons of carbon emitted per unit of energy consumed.

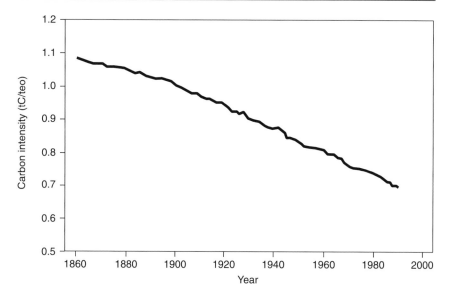

FIGURE 5.5   Carbon intensity of global energy consumption (tC/toe—tons of carbon per tons of oil equivalent).

Source: Nakicenovic (1997).

Chapter 6. The point here is that quantitative indicators are necessary to monitor ongoing transitions and trends.

As transitions do and do not take shape in these areas, people are likely also to develop a clearer idea of how a sustainable economic order is beneficial or easily obtained, and of the ways in which sustainability is costly or infeasible. Navigation is more than avoiding hazards, it is also a way of identifying desirable destinations.

Surprise Diagnosis

A transition to sustainability is an improbable development after a half-millennium of especially restless and sometimes heedless expansion of the human footprint on the planet. Many of the continuities and discontinuities of the past century were not anticipated by leading thinkers of the time. Neither the continuation of economic growth at the end of the Second World War nor the end of the Cold War in 1989-1991 was expected; both were positive surprises for the United States. There is no reason to think that the coming century will have fewer surprises.

Reflecting on environmental surprises over the past three decades, researchers concluded that events like the deadly industrial accident at Bhopal, India, or the discovery of the effect of chlorofluorocarbons on the stratospheric ozone layer shared several characteristics.[57] First, the events were surprises, confounding social expectations. Second, however, they were not incomprehensible in retrospect, but arose from causes that were known in principle, often driven, in part, by variables that were being monitored, even though the surprise itself was not anticipated. Third, these surprises have the potential to harm large numbers of people and have actually done so in instances like Bhopal.

Fourth, after the surprises occurred, the understanding of their causes provided opportunities to increase the social capacity to manage problems in the future. This is a promising finding: it says that societies can learn from surprises, so that they can better anticipate, avoid, or mitigate their consequences. But knowing how to improve management is also a temptation to operate closer to the edge.[58] Surprises could therefore become *more* frequent as humans gain better knowledge of the world. This possibility qualifies the conventional notion that science is valuable because it improves our ability to control or at least predict danger. Even when we do gain knowledge, the fact that social systems may use that understanding to venture further into the unknown may lead to more frequent surprises.

From this perspective, surprises are valuable indicators in themselves, both identifying particularly fragile or brittle endeavors and pointing to phenomena and processes that humans need to take into account. It is well accepted that surprises should produce humility. Surprises should also produce curiosity. On the time scale of the transition toward sustainability, curiosity and the learning it prompts are likely to be important, whether or not control can be extended in the short term.

INDICATORS AND SOCIAL LEARNING

The lack of an operational definition of sustainable development leads to disagreement about which indicators societies should use to measure progress toward or away from sustainability. Without that agreement, one should expect spirited debates over the value, biases, and meanings of indicators. In the related sphere of economic policy, one can observe over the past half-century sharp disputes in the United States over economic growth, the incidence of poverty, unemployment, and inflation. All these characteristics have been indicators that American politicians think will influence voter behavior.[59] Remarkably, the independence of the data gathering and analytical organizations has survived, despite their location within government agencies.[60]

This is one lesson for science: the independence of science is central to the social value of scientific information in a transition to sustainability. Preserving that independence requires prudent judgments about the use of science as a political resource.[61]

Another lesson emerges from the incomplete understanding of the nature of a transition to sustainability. Indicators are useful in the scientific quest for that understanding, but the collection and appraisal of those indicators must be part of a *research* enterprise that goes beyond what is conventionally called monitoring. Looking over the 50 year horizon for a transition toward sustainability, such an enterprise involves creative inclusion of both knowledge and know-how; it will have to go beyond the typically exclusionary lines drawn between science and technology. In Chapter 6, we call this sustainability science; indicators are an important element of study in that science.

A third lesson is that surprise is itself a valuable indicator. Governments and societies should anticipate unexpected things to happen. In a policy context, the inevitability of surprise calls for a kind of precautionary principle: because surprise is likely, action should be undertaken with thought, humility, and caution. These qualities are not quantifiable, but that does not diminish their significance.

Indicators used to report on a transition toward sustainability are likely to be biased, incorrect, inadequate, and indispensable. Getting the indicators right is likely to be impossible in the short term. But not trying to get the indicators right will surely compound the difficulty of enabling people to navigate through a transition to sustainability.

REFERENCES AND BIBLIOGRAPHY

Aber, J.D. 1992. Nitrogen cycling and nitrogen saturation in temperate forest ecosystems. *Trends in Ecology and Evolution* 7: 220-223.

Aber, J.D., A. Magill, S.G. McNulty, R.D. Boone, K.J. Nadelhoffer, M. Downs, and R. Hallett. 1995. Forest biogeochemistry and primary production altered by nitrogen saturation. *Water, Air and Soil Pollution* 85: 1665-1670.

Adriaanse, Albert. 1993. *Environmental policy performance indicators: A study on the development of indicators for environmental policy in the Netherlands.* Netherlands: Sdu Uitgeverij Konintginnegracht. ISBN 90 12 08099 1.

Baltimore Ecosystem Study. 1998. *Baltimore ecosystem study.* Available, http://www.baltimore.umbc.edu/lter/. Visited 5/13/99

Barinaga, Marcia. 1996. A recipe for river recovery? *Science* 273: 1648-50.

Benedick, Richard Elliot. 1991. *Ozone diplomacy: New directions in safeguarding the planet.* Cambridge: Harvard University Press.

Carbon Dioxide Information Analysis Center. 1999. *Current greenhouse gas concentrations.* Oak Ridge, TN: Oak Ridge National Laboratory. For this and related data series, including temperature, see http://cdiac.esd.ornl.gov/trends/trends.htm. Visited 4/27/99.

Center for Air Pollution Impacts and Trends Analysis (CAPITA). 1999. Washington University, St. Louis. Available, http://capita.wustl.edu/, visited 4/29/1999.

Central Arizona-Phoenix Long-Term Ecological Research Project. 1998. Available, http://www.asu.edu/ces/CAPLTER.htm. Visited 5/13/99.

Chadwick, D. 1998. Rebirth on the great plains. *National Wildlife* 36: 20-28.

Daily, Gretchen C., ed. 1997. *Nature's services: Societal dependence on natural ecosystems.* Washington, D.C.: Island Press.

di Castri, F., and T. Younes, eds. 1996. *Biodiversity, science and development: Towards a new partnership.* London: CAB International.

Duncan, Joseph W., and William C. Shelton. 1978. *Revolution in United States Government statistics, 1926-1976.* A report of the U.S. Department of Commerce, Office of Federal Statistical Policy and Standards. Washington: US Government Printing Office.

EMEP. 1984. See Meteorological Synthesizing Centre-West.

Eaton, J. 1998. An absence of condors. *Terrain* 29: 24-31.

Egan, Timothy. 1996. Urban sprawl strains western states. *New York Times*, December 29, 1, 20.

_____. 1996. Drawing the hard line on urban sprawl. *New York Times*, December 30, A1, A12.

Eisner, T. 1994. Bioprospecting. *Issues in Science and Technology* 10, no. 3: 18.

Ewing, Reid. 1997. Is Los Angeles-style sprawl desirable? *Journal of the American Planning Association* 63, no. 1: 107-126.

FAO (Food and Agricultural Organization of the United Nations). 1998. *The state of food and agriculture 1998.* Rome: FAO.

FAOSTAT (Food and Agriculture Organization of the United Nations Statistical Database). 1999. Rome: FAO. Available http://faostat.fao.org/.

Farrell, A., and M. Hart. 1998. What does sustainability really mean?: The search for useful indicators. *Environment* 40, no. 9: 4. See also http://www.subjectmatters.com/indicators/.

Fiedler, P.L. and P.M. Kareiva. 1997. Preface and Prologue. In *Conservation biology.* 2nd edition, eds. P.L. Fiedler and P.M. Kareiva, xvi-xx. New York: Chapman and Hall.

Franklin, J.F. 1993. Preserving biodiversity: Species, ecosystems, or landscapes? *Ecological Applications* 3: 202-205.

Gamez, R. 1996. Inventories: Preparing biodiversity for non-damaging use. In *Biodiversity, science and development: Towards a new partnership,* eds. F. di Castri and T. Younes, London: CAB International.

Garrett, Laurie. 1994. *The coming plague: newly emerging diseases in a world out of balance.* New York : Farrar, Straus and Giroux.

Gordon, Peter, and Harry W. Richardson. 1997. Are compact cities a desirable planning goal? *Journal of the American Planning Association* 63, no. 1: 95-106.

Goulder, L.H., and D. Kennedy. 1997. Valuing ecosystem services. In *Nature's services: Societal dependence on natural ecosystems,* ed. G.C. Daily, 23-48. Washington, D.C.: Island Press.

Green, Michael J.B., and James Paine. 1997. *State of the world's protected areas at the end of the twentieth century.* Paper presented at IUCN World Commission on Protected Areas Symposium on "Protected Areas in the 21st Century: From Islands to Networks," Albany, Australia, 24-29 November 1997. Cambridge, UK: World Conservation Monitoring Centre. Available, http://www.wcmc.org.uk/protected_areas/albany.htm.

Groom, M.J., and M.A. Pascual. 1997. The analysis of population persistence: an outlook on the practice of viability analysis. In *Conservation biology* 2nd ed., eds. P.L. Fiedler and P.M. Kareiva, 4-27. New York: Chapman and Hall.

Gunderson, Lance H., C.S. Holling, and Stephen S. Light, eds. 1995. *Barriers and bridges to the renewal of ecosystems and institutions.* New York: Columbia University Press.

Heal, Geoffrey. 1998. *Valuing the future: Economic theory and sustainability.* New York: Columbia University Press.

Holmes, Steven A. 1998. Political interests arouse raging debate on census. *New York Times,* April 12, sec. 1, 1, 20.

Hopkins, J.W. 1995. *Policymaking for conservation in Latin America.* Westport, CT: Praeger.

Houghton, J.T., L.G. Meira Filho, B.A. Callander, N. Harris, A. Kattenberg, and K. Maskell. 1996. *Climate change 1995: The science of climate change.* Cambridge, UK: Cambridge University Press. Published for the Intergovernmental Panel on Climate Change (IPCC).

IIASA (International Institute for Applied Systems Analysis). 1999. RAINS-ASIA web site. Available, http://www.iiasa.ac.at/~heyes/docs/rains.asia.html. Visited 4/27/99.

IISD (International Institute for Sustainable Development). 1998. *Compendium of sustainable development indicator initiatives and publications.* Available: iisd1.iisd.ca/measure/compinfo.htm. Visited 4/6/98.

IMF (International Monetary Fund). 1998. *Annual report of the executive directors for the fiscal year.* Washington: International Monetary Fund.

_____. Monthly periodical. *International Financial Statistics.* Washington: IMF.

Kaiser, J. 1997. When a habitat is not a home. *Science* 276: 1636-1638.

Kasperson, Jeanne X., Roger E. Kasperson, and B.L. Turner II, eds. 1995. *Regions at risk: Comparisons of threatened environments.* Tokyo: United Nations University Press.

Kates, Robert W., and William C. Clark. 1996. Expecting the unexpected. *Environment* 38, no. 2: 6-11, 28-34.

Korten, David C. 1995. *When corporations rule the world.* West Hartford, CT: Kumarian Press; San Francisco, CA: Berrett-Koehler Publishers.

Lee, Kai N. 1993. Compass and Gyroscope. Washington, D.C.: Island Press.

Lowe, P.D., and J.M. Goyer. 1993. Environmental Groups in Politics. London: Allen and Unwin.

Lubchenco, J., A. Olson, L.B. Brubaker, S.R. Carpenter, M.M. Holland, S.P. Hubbell, S.A. Levin, J.A. MacMahon, P.A. Matson, J.M. Melillo, H.A. Mooney, C.H. Peterson, H.R. Pulliam, L.A. Real, P.J. Regal, and P.G. Risser. 1991. The sustainable biosphere initiative: An ecological research agenda. A report from the Ecological Society of America. *Ecology* 72, no. 2: 371-412.

Ludwig, Donald, Ray Hilborn, and Carl Walters. 1993. Uncertainty, resource exploitation, and conservation: Lessons from history. *Science* 260: 17, 36.

Magnuson, John J. 1990. Long-term ecological research and the invisible present. *BioScience* 40: 495-501.

Matson, P.A., W. McDowell, A. Townsend, and P. Vitousek. Forthcoming. The globalization of N deposition: Ecosystem consequences. *Biogeochemistry,* in review.

Meadows, Donella. 1998. *Indicators and information systems for sustainable development.* A report to the Balaton Group. Hartland Four Corners, VT: The Sustainability Institute.

Meteorological Synthesizing Centre-West (EMEP 1984). *Tables of anthropogenic emissions in the ECE region.* Oslo: Norwegian Meteorological Institute. Available, http://www.unece.org/env/emep_tbl/tab1.htm. Visited 4/27/99. The synthesizing center implements provisions of the Protocol to the Convention on Long-range Transboundary Air Pollution on the Financing of the Co-operative Programme for Monitoring and Evaluation of the Long-range Transmission of Air Pollutants in Europe.

Mickelwright, S. 1993. The voluntary movement. In *Conservation in progress,* eds. F.B. Goldsmith and A. Warren, 321-334. New York and Chichester, UK: John Wiley and Sons.

Moldan, Bedrich, and Suzanne Billharz. 1997. Introduction, in *Sustainability indicators. A report on the project on indicators of sustainable development*, eds. Bedrich Moldan, Suzanne Billharz, and Robyn Matravers. Chichester and New York: John Wiley & Sons. Published on behalf of the Scientific Committee on Problems of the Environment.

Moldan, Bedrich, Suzanne Billharz, and Robyn Matravers, eds. 1997. *Sustainability indicators. A report on the project on indicators of sustainable development*. Chichester and New York: John Wiley & Sons. Published on behalf of the Scientific Committee on Problems of the Environment.

NAE (National Academy of Engineering). 1999. *Measures of environmental performance and ecosystem conditions*. Ed. Peter Schulze. Washington, D.C.: National Academy Press.

NRC (National Research Council). 1989. *Measuring and understanding coastal processes*. Committee on Coastal Engineering Measurement Systems. Washington, D.C.: National Academy Press.

_____. 1990. *Managing troubled waters: The role of marine environmental monitoring*. Committee on a Systems Assessment of Marine Environmental Monitoring. Washington, D.C.: National Academy Press.

_____. 1991. *Four-dimensional model assimilation of data: A strategy for the earth system sciences*. Panel on Model-Assimilated Data Sets for Atmospheric and Oceanic Research. Washington, D.C.: National Academy Press.

_____. 1992a. *Emerging infections: Microbial threats to health in the United States*. Committee on Emerging Microbial Threats to Health, Institute of Medicine. Washington, D.C.: National Academy Press.

_____. 1992b. *The national energy modeling system*. Committee on the National Energy Monitoring System. Washington, D.C.: National Academy Press.

_____. 1993a. *A biological survey for the nation*. Committee on the Formation of the National Biological Survey. Washington, D.C.: National Academy Press.

_____. 1993b. *Setting priorities for land conservation*. Committee on Scientific and Technical Criteria for Federal Acquisition of Lands for Conservation. Washington, D.C.: National Academy Press.

_____. 1993c. *Toward a coordinated spatial data infrastructure for the nation*. Mapping Science Committee. Washington, D.C.: National Academy Press.

_____. 1994a. *GOALS (Global Ocean-Atmosphere-Land System) for predicting seasonal-to-interannual climate: A program of observation, modeling, and analysis*. Climate Research Committee. Washington, D.C.: National Academy Press.

_____. 1994b. *Promoting the national spatial data infrastructure through partnerships*. Mapping Science Committee. Washington, D.C.: National Academy Press.

_____. 1995a. *Earth observations from space: History, promise, and reality*. Committee on Earth Studies. Washington, D.C.: National Academy Press.

_____. 1995b. *Finding the forest in the trees: The challenge of combining diverse environmental data*. Committee for a Pilot Study on Database Interfaces. Washington, D.C.: National Academy Press.

_____. 1995c. *Infectious diseases in an age of change: The impact of human ecology and behavior on disease transmission*. Ed. Bernard Roizman. Washington, D.C.: National Academy Press.

_____. 1995d. *Measuring poverty: A new approach*. Eds. Constance F. Citro and Robert T. Michael. Panel on Poverty and Family Assistance: Concepts, Information Needs, and Measurement Methods. Washington, D.C.: National Academy Press.

_____. 1995e. *A Review of the biomonitoring of environmental status and trends program: The draft detailed plan*. Committee to Review the Department of the Interior's Biomonitoring of Environmental Status and Trends Program. Washington, D.C.: National Academy Press.

_____. 1995f. *Review of EPA's environmental monitoring and assessment program: Overall evaluation.* Committee to Review the EPA's Environmental Monitoring and Assessment Programs. Washington, D.C.: National Academy Press.

_____. 1995g. *Science and the endangered species act.* Committe on Scientific Issues in the Endangered Species Act. Washington, D.C.: National Academy Press.

_____. 1995h. *Understanding marine biodiversity.* Committee on Biological Diversity in Marine Systems. Washington, D.C.: National Academy Press.

_____. 1996a. *Linking science and technology to society's environmental goals.* Committee on the National Forum on Science and Technology Goals: Environment. Washington, D.C.: National Academy Press.

_____. 1996b. *Upstream: Salmon and society in the Pacific Northwest.* Committee on the Protection and Management of Pacific Northwest Anadromous Salmonids. Washington, D.C.: National Academy Press.

_____. 1998. *Sustaining marine fisheries.* Committee on Ecosystem Management for Sustainable Marine Fisheries. Washington, D.C.: National Academy Press.

_____. 1999a. *Indicators for monitoring aquatic and terrestrial environments.* Water Science and Technology Board. Washington, D.C.: National Academy Press.

_____. 1999b. *Integrated environmental and economic accounting.* Committee on National Statistics. Washington, D.C.: National Academy Press.

_____. In progress. *Review of environmental monitoring and research in the Grand Canyon.* Grand Canyon Monitoring and Research Committee. Washington, D.C.: National Academy Press.

NSF (National Science Foundation). 1997. NSF funds first long-term studies of urban ecology. Press Release, 10/20/97. Available http://www.lternet.edu.

Nakicenovic, Nebojsa.1997. Freeing energy from carbon. In *Technological trajectories and the human environment*, NAE 1997, eds. Jesse H. Ausubel and H. Dale Langford. Washington, D.C.: National Academy Press.

The Nature Conservancy. 1982. Private, academic and local government activities. Vol. 3 of Preserving our natural heritage. Washington, D.C.: US National Park Service, Office of the Chief Scientist.

_____. 1996. *Conservation by design: A framework for mission success.* Arlington, VA: The Nature Conservancy.

_____. 1997. *Designing a geography of hope: Guidelines for ecoregion-based conservation.* Arlington, VA: The Nature Conservancy.

O'Connor, John C. 1995. Toward environmentally sustainable development: Measuring progress. In *A Sustainable World: Defining and measuring sustainable development,* ed. Thaddeus C. Trzyna. Sacramento, CA: International Center for the Environment and Public Policy, for the International Union for the Conservation of Nature (IUCN).

Olney, P., G.M. Mace, and A.C.T. Feistner, eds. 1994. *Creative conservation: Interactive management of wild and captive animals.* London: Chapman and Hall.

Olson, David M., and Eric Dinerstein. 1998. *The Global 200: A representation approach to conserving the earth's distinctive ecoregions.* Draft paper. Washington, D.C.: World Wildlife Fund US, March.

Ostrom, Elinor. 1990. *Governing the commons: The evolution of institutions for collective action.* Cambridge, UK: Cambridge University Press.

Pearce, David W., and Giles D. Atkinson. 1993. Capital theory and the measurement of sustainable development: An indicator of 'weak' sustainability. *Ecological Economics* 8: 103-08.

Pearce, David W., and J.J. Warford. 1993. *World without end: Economics, environment and sustainable development.* Oxford, UK: Oxford University Press.

Postel, Sandra L., Gretchen C. Daily, and Paul R. Ehrlich. 1996. Human appropriation of renewable fresh water. *Science* 271: 785-88.

Reid, W.V., S.A. Laird, R.G. Elmex, A. Sittenfeld, D.H. Janzen, M.A. Gollin, and C. Juma, eds. 1993. *Biodiversity prospecting.* Washington: World Resources Institute.

Rogers, P.P., K.F. Jalal, B.N. Lohani, G.M. Owens, C-C. Yu, C.M. Dufournaud, J. Bi. 1997. *Measuring environmental quality in Asia.* The Division of Engineering and Applied Sciences, Harvard University and the Asian Development Bank. Cambridge, MA: Harvard University Press.

Rothman, Dale S., John B. Robinson, and Dave Biggs. In press. *Signs of life: Linking indicators and models in the context of QUEST.* Paper presented to second workshop of the SCOPE/UNEP project of Integrated, Adaptive Ecological Economic Modeling and Assessment, 31 July - 4 August, 1996. Boston: SCOPE/UNEP.

Sasson, A. 1996. Biotechnologies and the use of plant genetic resources for industrial purposes: Benefits and constraints for developing countries. In *Biodiversity, science and development: Towards a new partnership,* eds. F. di Castri and T. Younes. London: CAB International.

Schimel, D.S. 1995. Terrestrial ecosystems and the carbon cycle. *Global Change Biology* 1: 77-91.

Slocombe, D.S. 1993. Implementing ecosystem-based management: Development of theory, practice, and research for planning and managing a region. *Bioscience* 43(9): 612-622.

Spirn, Anne Whiston. 1984. *The granite garden: Urban nature and human design.* New York: Basic Books.

Stork, N.E., and M.J. Samways. 1995. Inventorying and monitoring of biodiversity. In *Global biodiversity assessment,* ed. V.H. Heywood, United Nations Environment Program. Cambridge, UK: Cambridge University Press.

Stork, N.E., T.U.B. Boyle, V. Dale, H. Eeley, B. Finegan, M. Lawes, N. Manokaran, R. Prabhu, and J. Soberon. 1997. Criteria and indicators for assessing sustainability of forest management: Conservation of biodiversity. Working Paper No. 17. Bogor, Indonesia: Center for International Forestry Research.

Sustainable Seattle. 1995. *1995 Indicators Report.* Sustainable Seattle, Metrocenter YMCA, Seattle, WA. Available at: http://www.scn.org/sustainable/indicators.html. Visited 3/16/98.

Tangley, L. 1992. *Mapping biodiversity: Lessons from the field I.* Washington, D.C.: Conservation International.

Tenner, Edward. 1996. *Why things bite back: technology and the revenge of unintended consequences.* New York: Knopf.

Tilman, David. 1997. Biodiversity and ecosystem functioning. Chap. 6 of *Nature's services: Societal dependence on natural ecosystems,* ed. Gretchen C. Daily. Washington, D.C.: Island Press.

Tobin, Richard J. 1990. *The expendable future: U.S. politics and the protection of biological diversity.* Durham, NC: Duke University Press.

Townsend, A.R., B.H. Brasswell, E.A. Holland, and J.E. Penner. 1996. Spatial and temporal patterns in terrestrial carbon storage due to deposition of fossil fuel nitrogen. *Ecological Applications* 6: 806-814.

Tufte, Edward R. 1978. *Political control of the economy.* Princeton, NJ: Princeton University Press.

UN (United Nations). Department of International Economic and Social Affairs. 1989. *World population at the turn of the century.* Population Studies, no. 111. New York: United Nations.

_____. 1998. System-wide web site on national implementation of the Rio Commitments. Available: www.un.org/esa/agenda21/natlinfo, visited 4/6/98.

UNCHS (UN Centre for Human Settlements). 1996. *An urbanizing world: Global report on human settlements, 1996.* Oxford, UK: Oxford University Press.

UNCSD (UN Commission for Sustainable Development). 1996. *Indicators of sustainable development: Framework and methodologies.* UN publication E.96.II.A.16, August. New York: United Nations, Division for Sustainable Development.

UNFAO (UN Food and Agriculture Organization). 1998. *The state of food and agriculture 1998.* New York: United Nations.

_____. 1999. *FAOSTAT statistical database 1997.* CD-ROM, available in part on-line, http:// apps.fao.org/. Visited 4/27/99.

UNICEF (UN Fund for Children). 1998. *The state of the world's children 1999.* New York: United Nations.

US EPA (Environmental Protection Agency). 1998a. *National Air Quality and Emissions Trends Report, 1997.* (EPA 454/R-98-016) Research Triangle Park, NC: Office of Air Quality Planning & Standards, US EPA. December 1998. [http://www.epa.gov/oar/ aqtrnd97/]

_____. 1998b. *National Air Pollutant Emission Trends Update: 1970-1997.* (EPA 454/E-98-007). Research Triangle Park, NC: Office of Air Quality Planning & Standards, US EPA. December, 1998. [http://www.epa.gov/ttn/chief/trends97/emtrnd.html]

US Interagency Working Group on Sustainable Development Indicators. 1998. *Sustainable development in the United States: An experimental set of indicators.* December. Washington: U.S. Interagency Working Group on Sustainable Development Indicators. Available: http://www.sdi.gov/. Visited 8/25/99.

United States-Canada Air Quality Committee. 1999. *Ground level ozone: Occurrence and transport in Eastern North America.* Washington, D.C.: US EPA. Available, http:// www.epa.gov/oar/oaqps/publicat.html#uscanaq, visited 4/29/99.

Uvin, Peter. 1994. The state of world hunger. In *The hunger report, 1993,* ed. Peter Ivin. Yverdon, Switzerland: Gordon and Breach.

Vitousek, Peter M., Paul R. Ehrlich, Anne H. Ehrlich, and Pamela A. Matson. 1986. Human appropriation of the products of photosynthesis. *Bioscience* 36: 368-73.

Volkman, John M., and Willis E. McConnaha. 1993. Through a glass, darkly: Columbia River salmon, the Endangered Species Act, and adaptive management. *Environmental Law* 23: 1249-72.

WHO (World Health Organization). 1996. *Water supply and sanitation sector monitoring report 1996 (Sector status as of 1994).* New York: Water Supply and Sanitation Collaborative Council and UNICEF.

WRI (World Resources Institute). 1996. *World resources 1996-97: The urban environment.* A joint publication by the World Resources Institute, the United Nations Environment Programme, the United Nations Development Programme, and the World Bank. New York: Oxford University Press.

Weiss, C., and T. Eisner. 1998. Partnerships for value-added through bioprospecting. *Technology in Society* 20, no. 4: 481-498.

Wernick, Iddo K., Robert Herman, Shekhar Govind, and Jesse H. Ausubel. 1996. Materialization and dematerialization: Measures and trends. *Daedalus* 125, no. 3: 171-198.

Wilson, E.O., and Frances M. Peter, eds. 1988. *Biodiversity.* National Forum on Biodiversity. Washington, D.C.: National Academy Press.

Wilson, E.O. 1993. *The diversity of life.* Cambridge: Harvard University Press.

World Bank. 1997. *Expanding the measure of wealth: Indicators of environmentally sustainable development.* Environmentally Sustainable Development studies and monographs series no. 17. Washington, D.C.: The World Bank.

World Conservation and Monitoring Centre. 1999. Protected Areas and Landscapes Programme (current). Available, http://www.wcmc.org.uk/protected_areas/. Visited 4/27/99.

ENDNOTES

1 See Adriaanse (1993).

2 Note that this set is relatively long, and yet still too simple for many purposes, such as sensing trends in health or work.

3 Farrell and Hart (1998); http://www.subjectmatters.com/indicators/.

4 Moldan and Billharz (1997), pp. 1-5.

5 For a compilation, see IISD (1998).

6 The Balaton Group, see Meadows (1998).

7 UN Commission on Sustainable Development (1997); World Bank (1997); Netherlands Environmental Policy Performance Indicators, see Adriaanse (1993); US Interagency Working Group (1998); Sustainable Seattle (1995).

8 World Bank (1997), p. 21.

9 Moldan et al. (1997).

10 UNICEF (1998).

11 Uvin (1994).

12 UNCHS (1996).

13 See Uvin (1994) for a discussion.

14 Uvin (1994).

15 UNICEF (1998).

16 E.g., Garrett (1994); NRC (1995c).

17 Magnuson (1990).

18 Benedick (1991).

19 Houghton et al. (1996).

20 E.g., Korten (1995).

21 E.g., IMF (1998).

22 E.g., FAOSTAT (1999).

23 Franklin (1993); Slocombe (1993); Stork et al. (1997).

24 Kasperson et al. (1995).

25 Ibid.

26 Kasperson et al. (1995), p. 14.

27 Kasperson et al. (1995).

28 Regions that appear to be at risk of critical damage have one or more important common-pool resources—natural assets that cannot be readily managed by individual owners. Common-pool resources themselves are not a defining characteristic, however, because there are numerous examples of communities that depend on such resources and that have managed them well over long periods. A useful perspective on the governance structures that have enabled management to succeed has been advanced by Ostrom (1990). Ostrom's findings underscore the importance of monitoring and enforcement, so that individuals who engage in irresponsible behavior can be detected and brought back in line with community norms. Practical application of that analysis, to strengthen the capacity of communities to manage common-pool resources, has been slow because the social dynamics of communities are both complex and resistant to intervention by outsiders. The logic of monitoring as a precursor to corrective action is implicit in the discussion of indicators generally in this report.

29 WRI (1996), Ch. 1.

30 UN (1998), WRI (1996).

31 For an example of work that seeks to build such a context, see Rothman et al. in press.

32 E.g., Egan (1996).

33 Metropolitan sprawl, Ewing (1997); economics of sprawl, e.g., Gordon and Richardson (1997).

34 Daily (1997).
35 Goulder and Kennedy (1997).
36 NSF (1997); Baltimore Ecosystem Study (1998); Central Arizona–Phoenix Long-Term Ecological Research Project (1998).
37 Wilson (1993).
38 Wilson and Peter (1988).
39 Bioprospecting, Weiss and Eisner (1998); Eisner (1994); Reid et al. (1993); debt for water swaps, Pearce and Warford (1993); Hopkins (1995).
40 Endangered Species Act and private property rights, NRC (1993a, 1995h); Tobin (1990); environmental activism and habitat preservation, Lowe and Goyer (1993); Nature Conservancy (1982); Mickelwright (1993); Hopkins (1995).
41 Lubchenco et al. (1991).
42 Olson and Dinerstein (1998); The Nature Conservancy (1996, 1997).
43 Rapid assessment, e.g., Tangley (1992); response and anthropogenic changes, Groom and Pascual (1997), Fiedler and Kareiva (1997), diversity and stability, Tilman (1997).
44 Olney et al. (1994).
45 Sasson (1996).
46 Fiedler and Kareiva (1997); NRC (1998).
47 Gamez (1996).
48 NRC (1996b).
49 See, e.g., Stork and Samways (1998) for a treatment of monitoring and assessment of biodiversity.
50 Vitousek et al. (1986); Postel et al. (1996).
51 World Bank (1997).
52 UN (1998).
53 Pearce and Atkinson (1993).
54 Lee (1993); Gunderson et al. (1995).
55 E.g., Volkman and McConnaha (1993).
56 Barinaga (1996).
57 Kates and Clark (1996).
58 Tenner (1996).
59 Tufte (1978).
60 See Duncan and Shelton (1978).
61 Lee (1993), Ch. 7; cf. Holmes (1998).

6 Integrating Knowledge and Action

We must consider our planet to be on loan from our children, rather than being a gift from our ancestors ... As caretakers of our common future, we have the responsibility to seek scientifically sound policies, nationally as well as internationally. If the long-term viability of humanity is to be ensured, we have no other choice.

Gro Harlem Brundtland[1]

NAVIGATING A TRANSITION TOWARD SUSTAINABILITY

The idea of sustainable development has become a significant and dynamic force in political dialogue around the world. It emerged in the early 1980s from scientific perspectives on the relationships between society and the environment, and has evolved since in tandem with significant advances in our understanding of these relationships. Nonetheless, for the last decade and more the evolving idea of sustainable development has been shaped more by political than by scientific perspectives. Reciprocally, strategic priorities for science and technology have been little influenced by the development of sustainability thinking. The present study has been an effort to reinvigorate the needed strategic connections between science and sustainable development.

In conducting its work, the Board has focused its efforts on the next two generations, when many of the stresses between environment and development will be most acute and when a transition toward sustainability will need to take place if the earth's human population and life support systems are not to significantly damage both. This next half-century, like any future, is not knowable and will provide at least its share of surprises. But certain trends and transitions of population and habitation, wealth and consumption, technology and work, connectedness and diversity, and environmental change are likely to persist well into the coming century (Chapter 2). They provide the context for scientific analysis of some of the threats to, and opportunities for, sustainable development that the future may hold (Chapter 4). In such analysis lies the prospect for informed investment in research, capacity building, action, and policy that can make more attractive the prospects for our common journey.

In the Board's judgment, a transition to sustainability over the next two generations should aim to meet the needs of a much larger but stabilizing human population, to sustain the life support systems of the planet, and to substantially reduce hunger and poverty. For each of these dimensions of a successful transition, there is wide international agreement about minimal goals and targets.

The current trends mentioned above are likely to persist well into the coming century and could significantly undermine the prospects for sustainability. If they do, we conclude that many human needs will not be met, life support systems will be dangerously degraded, and the numbers of hungry and poor will increase. Even the most alarming current trends, however, may experience transitions that enhance the prospects for sustainability. Based on our analysis of persistent trends and plausible futures, we believe that a successful transition toward sustainability is possible over the next two generations. This transition could be achieved without miraculous technologies or drastic transformations of human societies. What will be required, however, are significant advances in basic knowledge, in the social capacity and technological capabilities to utilize it, and in the political will to turn this knowledge and know-how into action.

The individual environmental problems that have occupied most of the world's attention to date are unlikely in themselves to prevent substantial progress in a transition toward sustainability over the next two generations. Over longer time periods, unmitigated expansion of even these individual problems could certainly pose serious threats to people and the planet's life support systems. Even more troubling in the medium term, however, are the environmental threats arising from multiple, cumulative, and interactive stresses and driven by a variety of human activities. These stresses or syndromes, which result in severe environmental degradation, can be difficult to untangle from one another and complex to manage. Though often aggravated by global changes, they are shaped by the physical, ecological, and social interactions at particular places, that is, locales or regions. Developing an integrated and place-based understanding of such threats and the options for dealing with them is a central challenge for the development of a useful "sustainability science" for promoting a transition toward sustainability.

There are no maps for navigating a transition toward sustainability. Our common journey is nonetheless already under way. This Board's study has suggested the need for navigational strategies that can better integrate avowedly incomplete knowledge with necessarily experimental action into programs of adaptive management and social learning. Our goal in this chapter is to sketch such a strategy.

Why a strategic approach? "Muddling through" the changing challenges and opportunities presented by the trends discussed in Chapter 2 can take us part of the way toward sustainability goals in the future as it has in the past—especially where political systems and markets are so structured that they provide appropriate incentives and timely feedbacks. But as examples and analysis presented in earlier chapters of this report suggest, *mere* muddling through would leave untapped substantial opportunities for promoting a sustainability transition. It would also leave society unnecessarily vulnerable to a variety of foreseeable threats, as well as to the sorts of surprises that cannot be foreseen but can be prepared for.

Needed to complement the strengths and compensate for the weaknesses of "muddling through" are, therefore, strategic efforts dedicated to improving the prospects for sustainable development. Many such efforts are possible. As discussed in Chapter 1, some are well under way. Our intention here is to sketch elements of one such strategy: a strategy for mobilizing scientific knowledge in programs of purposive social learning and adaptive management committed to the promotion of a sustainability transition. We see such a strategy as a vehicle through which the science and technology community can significantly increase its contribution to the goal of "providing the energy, materials, and information to feed, house, nurture, educate, and employ many more people than are alive today—while preserving the basic life support systems of the planet, and reducing hunger and poverty."

What kind of strategy? Along with others that have studied the problem, we believe that knowledge is a crucial resource for navigating the transition toward sustainability—a resource that arms us, however imperfectly, to cope with the threats and opportunities that may be encountered along the way.[2] A capacity for long-term, intelligent investment in the production of relevant knowledge, know-how, and the capacity to use them both must therefore be a component of any strategy for the transition to sustainability. Some of that knowledge will be produced in libraries, on web sites, and in laboratories around the world. Such are the concerns before us, however, that much of what societies need to know will only emerge in the course of applying knowledge to actions. A strategy for navigating the transition toward sustainability must therefore be a strategy not just of thinking but also of doing. Our explorations suggest that such a strategy should include a spectrum of initiatives ranging from curiosity-driven research addressing fundamental processes of environmental and social change, to focused policy experiments designed to promote specific sustainability goals. We suggest a number of such initiatives below under the general headings of "Priorities for Research" and "Priorities for Action," while recognizing that in practice these realms will often blend together. We also provide an appraisal of the institutional matters that will have to be surmounted if this—or some similar—strategy for integrating knowledge and action is to realize its potential for contributing to the successful navigation of a transition toward sustainability. To be implemented, all of these initiatives would require more detailed elaboration and planning involving a wider array of groups and national perspectives than could be involved in this Board's present study. Our goal has not been to preempt that broader endeavor, but to encourage it and to suggest some initial directions.

PRIORITIES FOR RESEARCH

At least three dilemmas bedevil any effort to set priorities for scientific research in support of a sustainability transition. While these dilemmas are not unique to sustainability issues, they do pose special considerations for the strategy we seek to outline here.

First is the tension between broadly based and highly focused research strategies. This tension has been addressed in the recent NRC "Pathways" report on research priorities for understanding global environmental change.[3] Broadly based programs are desirable in light of the frequency with which important insights in one area emerge from research trying to investigate something else.[4] Moreover, they are needed to allow for the likelihood of surprising and unexpected developments in the interactions between the environment and development.[5] On the other hand, in fields as complex and multifaceted as those bearing on global change, much less the still broader field of sustainable development, there is a widespread consensus among the scientific community that much of the progress that has been achieved has come through research programs focused on "critical scientific issues and the unresolved questions that are most relevant to pressing national policy issues."[6]

A second tension exists between integrative, problem-driven research and research firmly grounded in particular disciplines. It has been recognized for more than a decade that many of the central challenges to sustainability involve multiple, interactive environmental stresses arising from multiple, overlapping human development activities.[7] Unfortunately, our collective ability to create reliable scientific knowledge about such integrated problems remains limited due to the inadequacies of observational data, the immaturity of relevant theory, and the underdevelopment of an appropriate professional community to provide meaningful criticism and peer review. In contrast, it is precisely the strengths of the established disciplines in the areas related to sustainable development that continue to make these fields our most effective engines for the generation of reliable—if more narrowly focused—scientific knowledge.

Finally, a tension exists between the quest for generalizable scientific understanding of sustainability issues and the place-specific aspects of the environment-society interactions that give rise to those very issues and generate the options for dealing with them. Again, this is not a dilemma unique to sustainability issues—it has been a central concern for scientific research in fields as diverse as agricultural production and public health for at least a generation.[8] Moreover, the tension between generalizable and place-specific understanding is increasingly confronting those seeking to provide useful research on the regional impacts of climate change and other global environmental issues.[9]

None of these tensions should be interpreted as either-or choices. Indeed, some of the most exciting and important research seems to arise precisely in circumstances where the tensions are high but successfully managed. From the Board's efforts to understand these tensions and their implications have emerged three priority tasks for advancing the research agenda of what might be called "sustainability science":

1. Develop a research framework for the science of sustainable development that integrates global and local perspectives to shape a place-based understanding of the interactions between environment and society.

2. Initiate focused research programs on a small set of understudied questions that are central to a deeper understanding of those interactions.

3. Promote better utilization of existing tools and processes for linking knowledge to action in pursuit of a sustainability transition.

We expand on these priorities in the sections that follow.

A Research Framework for Sustainability Science

Meeting the demands of a sustainability transition will require a substantial expansion in the capacity of the world's system for discovering new things. As suggested in earlier chapters of this report, the needs run broad and deep. They include the needs for both generalizable knowledge about the workings and interactions of the world's environmental, economic, and social systems, and specific understanding of particular places, problems, and solutions. Much of what societies need to know is sufficiently clear, and how to learn it is sufficiently understood, that specifically targeted research and development is surely justified. We turn to a discussion of some of these targeted areas in the following section.

But history suggests that it would be an enormous mistake to rely only or even primarily on such targeted research and development in our strategies to navigate a transition toward sustainability. Research and development are good investments. But they pay off in ways frequently unimagined by those who funded and even those who performed the seminal work. In fact, technologies have frequently transformed societies—in the nature of work, medicine, and communications. For example, a health sciences revolution is taking place as a result of our new understanding of molecular biology and genetic engineering. In addition, a transformation in communications and modeling has been brought about by the development of high-speed computers and modern communication devices.

Thus, basic research is essential for assuring that, as societies enter future stages of the transition to sustainability, markets, governments, and other players have the intellectual capital available to address the problems they face and to create the products and processes they need. If science and technology are to live up to their potential in meeting the needs of the sustainability transition, a fundamental requirement is a healthy, globally distributed system for conducting basic research across a wide range of topics and disciplines.

Precisely because of the breadth of the needed endeavor, however, a framework is also necessary to identify what the NRC "Pathways" report has called "the coherent domains of research that are likely to provide efficient and productive progress for science…" while still encompassing the range of issues that concern us.[10] What sort of research framework might be appropriate for "sustainability science"?

Intellectual Foundations

The fundamental knowledge needed to support our common journey is rooted in the core sciences of nature and society and has been nurtured in the interdisciplinary soil of scholarship and engineering practice concerned with the interactions between environment and development. Over the last generation, four related, sometimes overlapping, but nonetheless distinct, research-based components of sustainability have grown from this soil (Figure 6.1).

The first is essentially biological, emphasizing the intertwined fates of humanity and the natural resource base on which it depends for sustenance. This branch of research originated in the conservationist thinking of the 19th and early 20th centuries.[11] Internationally, it began to take shape in 1973 with the pathbreaking *Ecological Principles for Economic Development*, blossomed in 1980 as the *World Conservation Strategy* (which first popularized the term "sustainable development"), matured to em-

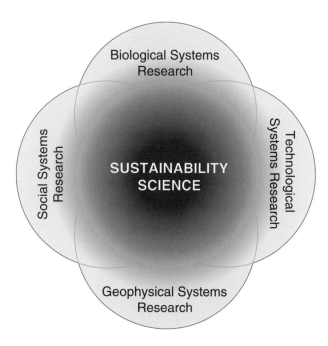

FIGURE 6.1   Four interlinked, research-based components of sustainability science.

brace the social dimensions of resource use with the report *Caring for the Earth*, and now supports the international DIVERSITAS program on biodiversity and sustainable use of the earth's biotic resources.[12]   Within the United States, recent offshoots of this branch of research include the *Sustainable Biosphere Initiative* of the Ecological Society of America and the *Teeming with Life* initiative of the President's Council of Advisors on Science and Technology.[13]

A second branch of research relevant to sustainability has been essentially geophysical, emphasizing the interconnections among the earth's climate and biogeochemical cycles, including their response to perturbation by human activities. This branch originated and has remained grounded in efforts to understand the earth as a system. Early impetus was provided by projects undertaken during the International Geophysical Year of 1957 and by concerns about human-induced changes to the global climate and stratosphere, concerns that took shape in the late 1960s. An international, interdisciplinary approach to research on earth systems science was nurtured through the 1970s by early studies of the International Council for Science's Scientific Committee on Problems of the Environment (SCOPE), and given form and strength with the emergence of the World Meteorological Organization's World Climate Research Program in 1979 and the International Council for Science's International Geosphere-Biosphere Program in 1986. U.S. contributions to and pursuit of this earth systems science agenda, which began with NASA's global habitability program in the early 1980s, have recently been reviewed in the "Pathways" report of the National Research Council.[14]

A third branch of relevant research has been primarily social, focusing on how human institutions, economic systems, and beliefs shape the interactions between societies and the environment. This branch is rooted in geographers' efforts to sort out long-term, large-scale relationships among resources, landscapes, and development. At an early stage, this branch of research produced divergent shoots, addressing topics as different as the economics of natural resource use, institutions for governing environmental "commons," the determinants of human vulnerability to environmental hazards or risks, and methods for environmental impact assessment and policy design. Interdisciplinary studies seeking to integrate these disparate strands became widespread in the 1970s, especially in the area of natural resource management, and were drawn into early efforts to understand global issues such as climate change.[15] By the mid-1980s, a wide variety of social science programs had begun to address issues of global environmental change.[16] A comprehensive international effort was launched in 1990, and today is moving forward as the International Human Dimensions Program.[17] Recent reviews of the content and concerns of this line of research are available.[18]

Finally, a fourth branch of relevant research has been the development of basic technological knowledge and the design of products and processes for producing more social goods with less environmental harm. This effort has occurred in several overlapping areas, such as energy technology, emissions control and treatment technologies, and green process and product design. It has involved many efforts, including both market- and regulatory-driven development in industry, technology spillovers among industrial sectors (e.g., the use of aero-derivitive gas turbines for electric power generation), and collaborative research among private institutes, government laboratories, universities, and nonprofit organizations. [19] As engineering practice, this branch reaches back into the earliest work on sanitation, air pollution control, and agricultural practices for soil conservation. By the early 1980s, such practices had been codified as basic engineering principles for pollution prevention, addressing both end-of-pipe treatment and disposal technologies.[20] In addition, basic technology research in the areas of energy, materials, biology, and information have led to efficiency improvements and materials substitutions that continue to reduce the environmental pressures associated with the production of social goods and services.[21] Finally, a broader systems perspective on technology, environment, and development began to emerge in the mid-1980s, focused not on individual technologies or processes but rather on minimizing waste produced by whole sectors of human activity.[22] Under the rubrics of "industrial ecology" and "industrial transformation," this systems approach to environmental engineering has become a centerpiece of both international and U.S. research programs on global change.[23]

Integrative Science

A research framework for sustainability science will need to build on these established branches of scholarship and their respective research programs, practices, and observation systems. Assuring the health of these foundational programs and their priority endeavors is therefore a fundamental prerequisite for sustainability science. But sustainability science will need to be broader yet, spanning the individual branches to ask how, over the large scale and the long term, the earth, its ecosystems, and its people can interact for mutual sustenance.

In keeping with our exploratory theme, we neither know how such science will evolve or if its ambitious rubric—sustainability science—will ever take hold. We do know, however, from the material reviewed in Chapter 4 and elsewhere[24] that many of the most problematic threats to people and their life support systems arise from multiple, cumulative, and interactive stresses resulting from a variety of human activities. Sustainability science will therefore have to be above all else *integrative* science—science committed to bridging barriers that separate traditional modes of inquiry. In particular, it will need to integrate across the discipline-based branches of relevant research described above—geophysical, biological, social, and technological. The same can be said for sectoral approaches that continue to treat such interconnected human activities as energy, agriculture, habitation, and transportation separately. In addition, sustainability science will need to integrate across geographic scales to eliminate the sometimes convenient but ultimately artificial distinctions between global and local perspectives. Finally, it will need to integrate across styles of knowledge creation, bridging the gulf that separates the detached practice of scholarship from the engaged practice of engineering and management.

Fortunately, integrative research approaches to address environment and development issues at the ecosystem scale are not wholly new.[25] Today, for example, forest management strives to encompass social systems and natural resources in an inclusive and interacting systems framework.[26]   In addition, integrated water management approaches are forming a new paradigm in water management, and research has been undertaken to understand the interactions of urban, agricultural, industrial, and natural ecosystem requirements for water resources, and the policy implications for water management.[27]   In agriculture, especially in systems designed for high-yield, successful production is more likely when crop selection, pest management, irrigation systems, and local culture are considered (see Chapter 3).[28]   At a broader scale, the international global change research program has made tremendous progress in the task of integrating previously separate disciplines.   For example, 15 years ago atmospheric chemists and biologists had not combined their knowledge to study atmospheric change, despite the fact that biological processes exert major regulation on atmospheric composition.   Furthermore, neither had been well integrated into atmospheric physics, oceanography, or climate research.   Today, these disciplines are much more closely linked, and integrated research, analysis, and assessment are at the heart of our understanding of global change.[29]

But if the first steps toward an integrative science of sustainability have been taken, the great leaps forward lie ahead. While the international global change research community has made great headway in linking the relevant natural science disciplines, it has made far less progress—despite significant national and international effort—in understanding the interactions of natural and social systems. The same can be said about the incorporation of biodiversity considerations in contemporary global climate change studies. As a result, the scientific community now knows much about what emissions cause various global environmental changes, but too little about what drives those emissions, what impacts they will have on people and other species, and what to do about them. Likewise, although integrated forest ecosystem management programs have progressed to the point of including people in the ecosystem at a local scale, there is much less progress in planning and assessment at broader regional scales, where issues such as air and water pollution and determinants of human population migration and density distribution begin to exert tremendous control. In short, if there is no longer much doubt about *whether* integrative approaches to research are needed in support of a sustainability transition, *how* to achieve such integration in rigorous and useful research programs remains problematical. For if in many cases systems are strongly coupled, then how is one to avoid the practical impossibility of having to study everything in order to know anything? We describe below one approach to this dilemma that our studies have suggested is especially worth pursuing: integrating research for sustainability not around particular disciplines or sectors, but rather around the study of interactions between development and environment in particular places.

Place-Based Science

In Chapter 4, we argued that the major threats and opportunities of the sustainability transition are not only multiple, cumulative, and interactive, but also place-based. In other words, it is in specific regions with distinctive social and ecological attributes that the critical threats to sustainability emerge, and where a successful transition will need to be based. Fortunately, "place" also provides a conceptual and operational framework within which progress in integrative understanding and management are possible (Figure 6.2). Not surprisingly, for the examples of threats and opportunities emerging from the interactions of multiple sectoral activities and environmental components as characterized in Chapter 4, we found the best examples of analytic and policy progress in work on particular places.

To argue that sustainability science will be integrative and place-based is to beg the question for the time being of what constitutes an appropriate classification of "place." In part, the distinction is surely one of scale. In Chapter 5, for example, we suggested that indicators of planetary circulation made sense at a global scale, and those of critical unsustainability at a regional scale, while productive landscapes and ecosystems require more localized indicators. A grand query of sustainability science will be these scale relationships. Understanding the links between macroscale and microscale phenomena is one of the great querries of our age in a wide array of sciences.[30] The pursuit of such understanding will also be a central task of sustainability science.

Whatever spatial scales turn out to be most appropriate for examining particular sustainability issues, however, there remains the task of classifying the "kinds" of pressures and stresses that occur at those scales. While any such classification is necessarily somewhat arbitrary, and will lump together places exhibiting differences, without some classification scientists are left with the dismal prospect of approaching each "place" as though it were altogether unique. One approach to this dilemma certainly worth pursuing in a "place-based" framework for sustainability science has been put forward in the concept of recurrent "degradation syndromes" (See Box 6.1).

However defined, sustainability science as a place-based science will benefit from the many ongoing efforts to regionalize environment-development relationships. The START (SysTem for Analysis, Research and Training) initiative of the International Geosphere-Biosphere Program, the World Climate Research Program, and the International Human

(A)

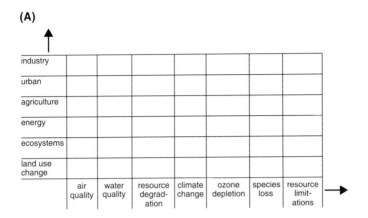

(B)

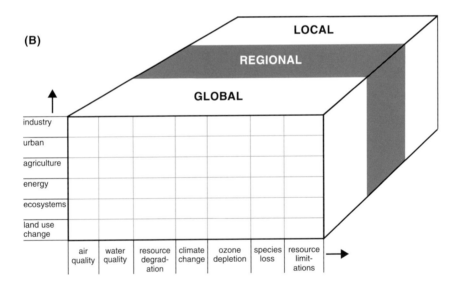

FIGURE 6.2 (A) Traditional approach to sustainability research, in which the effects of multiple human activities on environmental changes are assessed separately. (B) Place-based, integrative approach to sustainability science. Most challenges and opportunities exist at midrange scales.

BOX 6.1   Degradation Syndromes

The "degradation syndromes" concept was originally developed by Canadian scientists to classify regional ecosystems under stress (Rapport et al. 1981; Regier and Baskerville 1986) and later applied to the analysis of global change in the NRC's 1986 assessment of initial priorities for U.S. contributions to the International Geosphere-Biosphere Program (NRC 1988, pp. 161ff). More recently, the degradation syndrome concept was substantially elaborated by the German Advisory Council on Global Change (WBGU): "... interactions in certain regions between human societies and the environment frequently operate along typical lines. These functional patterns (*syndromes*) are unfavorable and characteristic constellations of natural and civilizational trends and their respective interactions, and can be identified in many regions of the world." (WBGU 1997, pp. 112)

The Council's report goes on to postulate the 16 global change syndromes listed below, and to develop an elaborate set of criteria for ranking their relative importance for various societies (WBGU, Box 18). It also employs the syndromes as a framework for defining priorities for future research.

"Utilization" Syndromes
1. Overcultivation of marginal land: *Sahel Syndrome*
2. Overexploitation of natural ecosystems: *Overexploitation Syndrome*
3. Environmental degradation through abandonment of traditional agricultural practices: *Rural Exodus Syndrome*
4. Nonsustainable agroindustrial use of soils and bodies of water: *Dust Bowl Syndrome*
5. Environmental degradation through depletion of nonrenewable resources: *Katanga Syndrome*
6. Development and destruction of nature for recreational ends: *Mass Tourism Syndrome*
7. Environmental destruction through war and military action: *Scorched Earth Syndrome*

"Develoment" Syndromes
8. Environmental damage of natural landscapes as a result of large-scale projects: *Aral Sea Syndrome*
9. Environmental degradation through the introduction of inappropriate farming methods: *Green Revolution Syndrome*
10. Disregard for environmental standards in the course of rapid economic growth: *Asian Tigers Syndrome*
11. Environmental degradation through uncontrolled urban growth: *Favela Syndrome*
12. Destruction of landscapes through planned expansion of urban infrastructures: *Urban Sprawl Syndrome*
13. Singular anthropogenic environmental disasters with long-term impacts: *Major Accident Syndrome*

"Sink" Syndromes
14. Environmental degradation through large-scale diffusion of long-lived substances: *Smokestack Syndrome*
15. Environmental degradation through controlled and uncontrolled disposal of waste: *Waste Dumping Syndrome*
16. Local contamination of environmental assets at industrial locations: *Contaminated Land Syndrome*

Dimensions Program on global environmental change has focused on the regional dimensions of global change since its inception.[31] It is now addressing issues ranging from determinants of land use change to industrial transformation to implications of environmental change for national security. The flagship international scientific assessment of climate change by the Intergovernmental Panel on Climate Change produced an addendum of 10 regions to its second assessment [32] and will base its third assessment on such regional analyses. The recommendations of the German Advisory Council on Global Change have already been noted (see Box 6.1). In the United States, the first assessment of climate change and impacts is being done for 19 regions.[33] Analogous efforts are under way in the European Union, as well as Canada and a number of other countries.[34] Implicit in many of these efforts is the search for parsimony—the identification of the smallest number of regions that can capture the diversity of nature-society relationships and still be manageable without constraining scientific understanding, organizational capacity, and budget. Common to all these approaches is a need for basic advances in our ability to understand interactive, cumulative effects of global change in particular regional contexts. Promoting such advances across a broad front is perhaps the central challenge of a place-based, integrative sustainability science.

Focused Research Programs

It would be premature here to suggest a comprehensive research agenda for a still-nascent sustainability science. The potentially vast scope of such an agenda was explored in ICSU's conference on "An Agenda of Science for Environment and Development into the 21st Century," conducted in 1991 as part of the preparations for the UN Conference on Environment and Development in Rio de Janiero.[35] The chapter on "Science for Sustainable Development" in "Agenda 21" carried forward this broad conception of research needs, and has served as a template for subsequent progress reports by the UN Commission on Sustainable Development. Those reports, and others reviewed above, show that several research programs relevant to sustainability have grown notably over the last decade, especially within the four central branches of scholarship described in the preceding section. Much research in what might well be seen as the sustainability science agenda is clearly moving along now. It remains true, however, that the very breadth of the science that could contribute to understanding long-term, large-scale interactions between environment and society brought with it the risk that the overall research program actually carried out would remain relatively diffuse, underfunded, and unproductive. Evidence presented at the 1997 UN General Assembly's Rio+5 review[36] for the most part bore out this expectation. Several opportunities for international efforts to address these issues and reinvigorate a science agenda for environment and development were scheduled for the turn of the century. These include the 1999 World Conference on Science arranged by UNESCO and ICSU in Budapest and the Conference on the Transition to Sustainability planned by the InterAcademy Panel on International Issues for the year 2000 in Japan.[37]

In hopes of contributing to such efforts, this Board followed the thrust of recent NRC reviews of global change research that have "consistently emphasized the need ... to focus on critical scientific issues and unresolved questions that are most relevant to pressing national policy issues."[38] In particular, we list below seven critical areas of inquiry that are central to the pursuit of a sustainability transition and are amenable to research. Most are understudied in existing research programs. The causes for this relative lack of attention are varied: only now are some of the relevant sciences matured to the point of being able to address some of the critical questions; some critical questions fall between disciplines; and some of these questions acquire new urgency in the context of a transition to sustainability. Independent of the reasons for current neglect, we set these seven issues forward as candidates for focused research programs in sustainability science.

Critical Loads and Carrying Capacities

To pursue the goal of "preserving the basic life support systems of the planet" is, among other things, to look for limits beyond which those systems should not be pushed. Both process understanding and practical experience suggest that relatively sharp boundaries do sometimes exist separating relatively normal and radically transformed states of life support systems.[39] Moreover, scientists know that the abrupt changes associated with the crossing of such boundaries provide special "windows of opportunity" for mobilizing political action and institutional reform.[40] Finally, the indicator systems discussed in Chapter 5 lose much of their attraction if they provide no signal of the approach of a "dangerous threshold" or nonlinear relationship between the indicator variable and adverse environmental or social consequences.

For all of these reasons, it should not be surprising that efforts to establish "safety" limits for the earth's life-support and ecological systems are long-standing and widespread. Under various circumstances, these efforts have sought to specify critical indicator values in each of the "pressure," "state," and "response" categories described in Chapter 5. Debates about the "carrying capacities" of the earth and its component ecosystems for domestic animals or the people that herd them have been active since at least the 17th century.[41] Efforts to determine the shape of dose-response relationships for human health effects at low levels of ex-posure to radiation and chemical pollutants suggest that there may be practical limits to how far the conventional predictive risk assessment paradigm can be pushed. This ambition to identify safe levels for "state" indicators has led European states to specify "critical loads" for the depo-sition of acidifying compounds on ecosystems.[42] It shows up again in the Framework Convention on Climate Change, which calls for "stabilization of greenhouse gas concentrations ... at a level that would prevent danger-ous anthropogenic interference with the climate system."[43] Finally, some scholars have sought to identify critical thresholds of damage beyond which whole regional ecosystems lose their ability for self-renewal and slide inexorably into deeper and deeper degradation.[44]

While many of these efforts to specify safety limits for human pres-sures on the biosphere have been helpful, the Board's inquiries found that the underlying concepts have proven to be contentious, ambiguous, and frustrating. Carrying capacities turn out to depend on available technolo-gies and consumption practices. Efforts to specify actual critical loads or safety levels are undermined by the heterogeneity of the environment and populations at risk. In addition, thresholds turn out to be less often absolute than relative. Finally, a good case can be made that the viability of ecosystems depends less on critical levels that may be exceeded during particular episodes of stress than on the longer term regime of stresses that includes, but cannot be reduced to, such single-valued characteris-tics.[45]

We encountered all these difficulties in the present study, as we failed in our effort to develop criteria that could provide a "bright line" test for significant degradation of regional ecosystems and their life-support func-tions (see Chapter 4). Though we had no trouble identifying cases in which life support systems had been degraded or even destroyed, we were unable to turn the concepts of "critical loads," "carrying capacities," and their cousins into useful tools for navigating the transition toward sustainability. This is clearly an area that needs further work. Either a robust scientific foundation needs to be built under the idea of "safe lim-its," or the scientific community needs to come up with alternative con-cepts for guiding action toward sustainability. The historical experience of efforts to determine whether threshold or linear responses best charac-terize dose-hazard relationships for human health and exposure to radia-tion suggest that this will not be an easy task.[46]

Understanding and Monitoring the Transitions

The persistent trends in environment and development that we have discussed in this report (Chapters 2 and 3) can, if properly understood, serve as important guides to a sustainability transition. They are the great currents of our uncharted sea—large-scale, persistent forces that will shape, though not fully determine, our paths to the future. Over the last two decades, many of the global trends most important for the sustainability transition have become much better documented and understood. These advances have occurred in both the social and environmental realms, and in studies of their interactions.[47]

The search for fundamental *transitions*—or breaks in trends—in the relationships between society and environment has been harder. In this report we have identified one powerful transition that is both credible and interesting: the change in population regimes from those of high birth and death rates to those of low birth and death rates. This transition is *credible* because it meets scientific criteria: it is partly supported by theory, matches the data well, and has predictive power. It is *interesting* because it appears to be not simply a continuous trend, but rather a transition from one relatively stable state of affairs to another. Several other candidate "transitions" seem almost as compelling: in settlement regimes, the transition from predominantly rural to predominantly urban regimes; in agricultural productivity, the transition from increases in production deriving from additions in the amount of land farmed to increases deriving from additions to local yields based on knowledge and its use (e.g., physical inputs such as fertilizers and pesticides). Other possible transitions were noted—for example, the globalization of the economy and changes in consumption patterns, energy intensity, pollution per unit value produced by the economy, and the role of the state in global governance—that are surely interesting, but are not as well understood or as globally documented as the others. Improving that documentation and understanding, especially for those transitions that transcend the normal disciplinary boundaries of scholarship, should be a priority objective for sustainability science (see Chapter 5 on indicators).

Consumption Patterns: Determinants and Alternatives

One of the biggest obstacles for a successful transition to sustainability is the desire of so many people for lifestyles requiring much larger flows of energy and materials. Yet relatively little work has been done in addressing consumption in this fundamental sense, as energy and materials, rather than in terms of "final" consumer goods and services. For example, although much work has been done on documenting trends of dematerialization and decarbonization,[48] an explanatory theory to account for variations in rates of decreasing mass per unit of service has not yet been developed. There is also the need for methodology to separate out resource-depleting or environmentally damaging consumption from general consumption, and to substitute modes of consumption that are less damaging and depleting of energy and materials for the more damaging ones. Little-studied of late, but particularly important in activities as diverse as agriculture and air conditioning, is the systemic potential for substituting information for energy and material use.

Turning to the demand side of consumption, advertising and culture appear remarkably effective in encouraging emulation of high-consumption lifestyles. Nonetheless, the human behavior driving consumption is still poorly understood, especially the potential for alternative consumption patterns, and the value systems that would support them.[49] A small but growing effort has explored people's satisfaction with their current levels of consumption and their willingness to substitute other values for material things.[50] Such values include reducing work time for more leisure, social, or family time, diminishing household burdens on environment, and enjoying simplified life styles.[51] A rigorous, comparative research program is needed into how the values underlying alternative consumption patterns are formed, stabilized, and undermined in contemporary societies.[52]

Finally, it is clear that any number of economic interventions—tax policies, removal or introduction of subsidies, tariffs, and trade restrictions, more effective use of markets, market intervention through regulatory initiatives, among others—may have an impact on consumption. Unfortunately, societies have an inadequate understanding of the responses of complex and interconnected economies (and the vested interests therein) to such interventions, so that there will be tremendous concerns and some danger in implementing such mechanisms, and in learning from their actual performance.

Incentives for Technical Innovation

Innovative technologies that produce more human value with less environmental damage will surely be a central element of any transition to sustainability. When the economic benefits of such technologies can be captured by private parties, markets offer the most efficient way to move the basic knowledge created by research into practical new products and processes. Many new products and capabilities that will contribute to a successful sustainability transition—from efficient heat pump technology to systems for recycling aluminum cans—are already being widely adopted as a result of success in the marketplace. Markets, however, do not always produce the desirable products and processes, or the desirable solutions to social allocation problems. The conditions associated with such market failure include unpriced externalities, public goods, and insecure or uncertain property rights.* Standard remedies are equally well known, generally involving government regulation of externalities, provision of public goods, or enforcement of property rights.

More systematic application of existing remedies for market failure would surely help to align incentives for technical innovation with the needs of a transition toward sustainability—for example, through the realistic pricing of water used for agriculture and industry. But as necessary as such measures may be, they are almost certainly insufficient. The spatial and temporal extent of sustainability issues means that incentives must function across national boundaries and across generations—exactly the domain in which the national governments responsible for most past remedies to market failure are least likely to be helpful. The information-intensive character of much of the innovation needed to navigate a transition poses extraordinary hurdles for handling intellectual property rights, as can be seen in recent debates over biotechnology. In addition, a global trend to commercialize data is manifest in emerging national legislation (proposed in the United States; ratified in Europe as the European Database Directive) and international organization discussions (e.g., World Meteorological Organization, World Intellectual Property Organization) on intellectual property rights. These bills and agreements are of great concern to the international scientific and technical communities because they could give database producers perpetual and exclusive rights to the contents of their databases, without regard to fair use exceptions such as research and education.[53] A concerted research program on the kinds of incentives, market and otherwise, needed to promote technological innovations for a sustainability transition, on the options for providing such incentives in a highly uncertain, multi-actor, globalizing world, and on their actual performance in that world is surely worth pursuing.

Institutions for Navigating a Transition Toward Sustainability

If institutions are the norms, expectations, and rules through which societies figure out what to do and organize themselves to get things

---

*"Externalities" are relationships among actors that are not taken into account in the market transactions between them. An example is the pollution from one actor's energy production falling on another. "Public goods" are those whose benefits can be taken advantage of, not only by those who invested in the goods' provision, but also by others who did not. An example is the construction of sewage treatment plants. "Property rights" issues arise when a potential investor in a technology or sustainable use practice cannot retain the benefits of that investment. Open access commons such as ocean fisheries are a well-known example, where a current "investment" in restricted, but sustainable, fishing levels are not recouped in later harvests because the investor cannot assure that others will exercise the same restraint.

done, then the institutions with which society will navigate the transition toward sustainability may be quite different from those with which it has the most experience to date.   As noted elsewhere in this report, those institutions will likely be less government-centered than in the past, involving as well substantial roles for a variety of private sector and nonprofit actors. [54] Moreover, they could well be less centered at the level of nation-states, spanning instead scales from the local to the global. Finally, they will almost certainly be substantially more information-intensive than the institutions of the past, with increasing tasks of monitoring, assessment, and reporting.[55]   Within these emerging multi-actor, multi-scalar, information-rich institutions, initiatives are less likely to be pushed by the familiar individual actor groups—a UN agency, a national government, or a single firm or sector—than by ad hoc networks of advocates temporarily united around a shared purpose.[56]

Today, we have very limited understanding of what these emergent institutions are or might be. We know even less about the factors determining their effectiveness in promoting a sustainability transition, though issues of participation, credibility, capacity, and linkage immediately come to the fore. Nonetheless, recent work has begun to sketch the outlines of what a long-term research program on institutions for a sustainability transition might include.[57] Central to this emerging agenda is the need for a better understanding of when enlightened self interest provides sufficient grounds for state and nonstate actors to engage in behaviors promoting a sustainability transition, when various forms of collective action are also necessary, and how such collective action can be promoted.[58] A focused effort to develop and pursue this emerging institutional agenda is needed.

Indicator Systems

We have argued in this report that an informed dialogue on goals for the transition toward sustainability is necessary if societies are to take some measure of responsibility for where they ought to be headed, rather than merely acquiescing to where the currents of demographic, economic, and environmental transformation take them. But even in the best of circumstances, goals alone are only distant intentions. To become operationally useful, they need to be translated into specific indicators that can be monitored, reported on, and evaluated throughout the journey. Seen in this manner, indicators become part of an information feedback system through which societies can assess progress, adjust directions, and obtain warnings of unsustainability.

Chapter 5 reviewed the vast range of efforts that have been carried out around the world to develop indicator systems relevant to the sustainability transition. These range from global accounts of people and carbon, through regionally integrated "sustainability" metrics, through corporate environmental audits. Although further conceptual development of such indicators systems will be important, the most pressing need is to facilitate the wider application of existing knowledge about indicators to specific management situations. The experience reviewed in this report suggests that to be used, such applications need to be developed in ways that involve stakeholders and ultimate users as well as the technical community. The same experience also suggests, however, that user-driven indicator systems can often overlook some of the more strategic functions of indicators we outlined in Chapter 5. We believe that a research effort focused on bridging this gap between practice-driven and theory-driven indicator systems for sustainability could reap significant benefits.

Assessment Tools

In Chapter 3, we described the need for methods and processes to perform "what if" explorations of possible trends, transitions, and policy options. We presented examples of how the tools of integrated assessment models, scenarios, and regional information systems had helped to integrate knowledge and action in a variety of efforts to promote sustainability. Despite their potential contributions to the navigation of a transition toward sustainability, however, the best assessment methods are not nearly as widely used as they might be. Several steps could help to remedy this.

First, the international development of a set of reference scenarios could play a significant role in developing a common understanding of a sustainability transition, just as has been done in the narrower case of stratospheric ozone depletion. The focus of such scenario efforts should be on the interactions among the needs of future generations, and the impacts on life support systems of satisfying these needs through technologies and institutions of the future. Examples of what such explorations might entail are provided in a number of recent publications.[59] Further development of scenarios should be encouraged by establishing a global scenarios forum, learning from the experience of groups such as the IPCC Special Report on Emissions Scenarios, the Energy Modeling Forum, the Global Scenario Group of the Stockholm Environment Institute[60] and other similar efforts. Whatever the specific character of the forum, the goal should be to bring into the discussion broad expertise in environment and development, as well as representatives from multiple regions and nations.

A second assessment initiative stems from the growing realization that the credibility of international science-based assessments (e.g., the IPCC assessment of climate change) and their use by individual countries is strongly conditioned by the extent of a country's meaningful participation in the assessment.[61] This same lesson has been repeatedly learned at national and local levels, and is a central issue for ongoing U.S. national efforts to conduct regions-based assessments of global change.[62] Critical experimentation with a variety of methods for achieving legitimacy-enhancing participation without undue cost to scientific credibility is badly needed.[63] New information technology may have much to offer such experiments. But empirical data on the conditions under which, and the degree to which, remote engagement can replace face-to-face interaction in legitimacy-building participation efforts remains almost non-existent.[64]

Integrative methods that bring a variety of disciplinary perspectives into the formulation of assessment questions and strategies must also be developed. Fortunately, there is substantial activity on this front, with truly integrative approaches replacing earlier models that simply used the social sciences to supplement assessments framed primarily by the natural sciences.[65]

Finally, much of the knowledge and decision making necessary for navigating a transition toward sustainability is, as we have noted, tied to particular places and circumstances. Scenarios and assessment models used in support of sustainability efforts therefore require both global perspective and local context. Bridging multiple scales of analysis has long been a particularly vexing problem in both the natural and social sciences. Despite these difficulties, however, recent progress has been seen in pragmatic efforts to bring global sustainability perspectives to bear on practical problems of ecosystem, watershed, and community management.[66] Some of these, such as recent efforts dealing with sustainable futures for the Columbia Basin and Alpine regions of Europe, have become quite sophisticated in their integration of global modeling with local stakeholder perspectives, knowledge bases, and decision-making needs.[67] Such experience needs to be codified so that it can be assessed, adapted, and learned from in capacity-building efforts throughout the world.

Toward More Usable Knowledge

A great deal of knowledge, know-how, and capacity for learning relevant to sustainable development has already been assembled in various observation systems, laboratories, and management regimes around the world. Unfortunately, relatively little of this rich resource is currently utilized in even a fraction of the situations where it could contribute to navigating the transition to sustainability successfully. Even as the science and technology community pursues new research and development endeavors of the sort described elsewhere in this chapter, it therefore faces the additional task of promoting better use of what is already known.

In general, the need is for two-way, dynamic processes for transforming what one person, group, firm, or nation knows into something useful for the particular challenges and opportunities faced by another. Increasingly, such processes are taking the form of collaborations or partnerships rather than the one-directional "pipeline" model that characterized earlier efforts in information diffusion and technology transfer. Newly emerging information technologies almost certainly have a role to play in making such collaborations both effective and global in reach. Much remains to be understood, however, about the potential opportunities and risks posed by these new technologies, and about the social and technological infrastructures needed to assure their effective and equitable use.[68] Effective two-way collaborations have emerged in engineering, agricultural development, and renewable resource management as well as research-intensive private sector activities. There is a continuing need for advancing our understanding of what underlies these effective collaborations in moving knowledge into action, for making that understanding part of the normal training for professionals engaged in research, and for applying it systematically in promoting better and more widespread use of what is already known to the pursuits of a sustainability transition.

One implication of the emerging "collaborative" view of knowledge and technology dissemination is already clear, however. Making knowledge more usable means enhancing the capacity of groups around the world not only to obtain and interpret it, but also to critique it and adapt it to their own place-specific contexts. This is as true for the current undertakings of shaping useful assessments of climate change as it has been for the classical concerns of agricultural extension. And it is as important—if not more so—for the nongovernmental organizations, private enterprises, and regional authorities destined for central roles in the sustainability transition as it is for the national governmental bodies that have been the conventional focus of capacity-building efforts. Aggressive and inclusive fostering of local capacity in science and technology must therefore be a centerpiece of any strategy for the sustainability transition. This has been generally recognized in international discussions on measures for promoting sustainable development. Programs to do something with this realization nonetheless remain largely inadequate.[69]

As we discuss below, the successful production and application of the knowledge needed for a sustainability transition will require significant strengthening of institutional capacity in at least four areas: linking long-term research programs to societal goals; coupling global, national, and local institutions into effective research systems; linking academia, government, and the private sector in collaborative research partnerships; and integrating disciplinary knowledge in place-based, problem-driven research efforts. None of these needs are unique to sustainability science; strengthening our institutional capacity to address them will benefit society more broadly as well. The specific institutional forms and processes needed will be a function of the particular problems and places involved. Nonetheless, several general needs for the development of institutional capacity seem clear.

Linking Long-Term Research Programs to Societal Goals

As we have repeatedly emphasized in this report, some of the knowledge and know-how needed for navigating the transition to sustainability will be produced without need of strategic design or priority setting by governments or international bodies. Given adequate support for curiosity-driven research, incentives for private sector research, and spillovers from short-term research on immediate problems, much of value will be discovered and disseminated. Nonetheless, there remains a great deal of knowledge that would be useful—and may be necessary—to meet the goals of the transition, yet which is unlikely to be produced through such channels. These types of knowledge include most monitoring data with large geographical coverage, much "public good" understanding about the interactions of social and environmental systems (i.e., understanding useful to everyone once it is discovered by someone), and certain know-how lacking near-term prospects of generating competitive returns on investment. To create and disseminate such knowledge, society needs the institutional capacity to design and sustain the full array of long-term monitoring, research, and development programs that are required to attain sustainability goals.

In the United States, as in most other countries, the lack of such capacity is generally acknowledged.[70] Creating it will require, first of all, institutional structures that can promote the articulation of a broadly shared, politically viable consensus on sustainability goals. Second, it will need mechanisms for designing, setting priorities, and providing stable funding for the research programs that could help to achieve those goals. Successful efforts to link long-term research programs to social goals are not without precedent, having been carried out internationally in the effort to eliminate smallpox, and domestically in the U.S. in certain areas of the space program (e.g., Apollo), defense (e.g., the Atlas rocket development), and health (e.g., polio). Submissions to the 1977 UN General Assembly Special Session showed that a number of countries have made substantial progress toward articulating goals relevant to sustainability.[71] And the

European Union's Fifth Framework Program for research and development (1998-2002) makes the link between sustainability goals and priority research programs explicit.[72]

Forging similar long-term linkages in the U.S. political context will be particularly difficult given the government's fractionation of domestic and international policy making.[73] The Carnegie Commission advanced a number of general recommendations for enhancing the nation's capacity to link science and technology to societal goals in 1992; a number of followup efforts are now in play.[74] Most of these entail some form of coordinated effort involving a number of congressional committees and federal agencies under leadership of the White House offices of Science and Technology Policy and Management and Budget. Focused efforts are now needed to adapt the general recommendations emerging from these various efforts to the challenges of designing and implementing particular long-term research programs in support of sustainability goals.

Integrating Global, National, and Local Institutions into Effective Research Systems

The knowledge base to support a transition to sustainability will have to be attuned to the unique characteristics of particular places and issues. At the same time, it must be able draw on research that addresses phenomena of regional or even global scale. Societies need arrangements that connect the local end-users—including corporations, farmers, households, land use planning commissions, and regional research centers—and the international science and technology community into a global research system. This system needs to link local use and the best that international science has to offer in a way that provides relevant scientific guidance for a sustainability transition. In this sense, sustainability science is like the agricultural science that supported the Green Revolution, or the health science that has brought about the reduction of many infectious diseases. The analogy is an important one, for it highlights both the potential and the pitfalls of problem-driven research systems that span multiple geographic scales.[75] The design of an integrated research system of sustainability science will have to evolve on its own course. Nonetheless, the following elements seem almost certain to play a role and merit serious attention.

At the international level, sustainability science would benefit from a set of international research institutes somewhat analogous to the CGIAR (Consultative Group on International Agricultural Research) of The World Bank, Food and Agricultural Organization of the United Nations (FAO), UN Development Program (UNDP), and UN Environment Program

(UNEP) with centers located in regions reflecting major sustainability challenges. One such CGIAR-derived approach has in fact been recommended.[76] The new efforts could well be based in or affiliated with the regionally oriented START centers of the IGBP, WCRP, and IHDP, or related institutions such as the Inter-American Institute for Global Change Research. Mandates for each institute should almost certainly include research responsibility for one or more sustainability science issues of particular relevance to the region in which it is located, and responsibility for global leadership on an issue particularly relevant to its region, but with clear relevance to a larger community.

If the international institutes are to be effective, they must be able to work with strong national research systems. Such systems must have the capacity to set priorities, mobilize resources, carry out the necessary R&D, and assess progress in areas such as energy, agriculture, environment, and other priority areas outlined here. National capacity is also important in producing the knowledge and analysis needed by national governments and national constituencies to make decisions about research priorities and technology development and investment, and to establish policies and programs that will advance the sustainability transition. In the United States, a national mechanism should be developed to promote research and development on critical issues that do not fall within the charter of established mechanisms. The Science and Technology Centers of the National Science Foundation, and the military's earlier ARPA (Advanced Research Projects Agency) materials and computer labs might provide informative models for consideration in the design of such collaborations.[77]

In addition to national capacity, all countries, except for the very smallest, will need decentralized research (and education and training) capacity at the regional, local, and firm level. With appropriate incentives, decentralized systems can make important contributions to the generation, transfer, and communication of locally relevant knowledge. The network should be organized and funded in a manner that provides incentives for it to contribute to local-level sustainability concerns (e.g., the eutrophication of lakes or contamination of groundwater) by performing what has been termed "routine science" (e.g., monitoring or operational research) and technology development.

Linking Academia, Government, and the Private Sector in Collaborative Partnerships

Linkages are also needed that facilitate collaboration among academics, governmental and private sectors, and nongovernmental actors in research partnerships to promote the sustainability transition. It is by now generally accepted that one of the greatest shortcomings in the efforts to enhance worldwide agricultural production through the CGIAR system was the failure to provide incentives and institutional arrangements that would link private sector actors into that system.[78] Similar difficulties have plagued efforts to enhance family planning and basic public health around the world. Even efforts to transfer relatively discrete technologies across national borders have been shown to require collaborative, two-way partnerships among public and private interests if they are to have much hope of success.[79] Societies need to enhance these collaborative efforts if substantial opportunities to harness science and technology to the sustainability transition are not to be lost.

Multisector research and development partnerships need not be formally codified. Many of the most successful collaborations consist almost entirely of the flow of people among sectors, with young university-trained scientists and engineers heading into the commercial world, business people serving terms in government, and so on.[80] While these exchanges often work reasonably well within nations, there is a case to be made for substantial strengthening of mechanisms to promote two-way exchanges of scientists and engineers across national as well as sectoral boundaries.

However successful informal partnerships of these sorts may be, the need will remain to foster more structured cross-sectoral partnerships to promote sustainability science. Although national governments have a role to play in such endeavors, it seems likely that an important locus for integration may be at the subnational level, where organizational arrangements can be more readily tailored to specific needs and opportunities.[81] This emphasis on cross-scale issues in institutional design reemphasizes the point made earlier about the importance of tending to linkages among local, national, and global actors in the science and technology system. Especially as such linkages extend across national boundaries, creative institutional designs will be needed to assure that incentives for participation in research partnerships remain high and stable. This seems to be one area in which the contributions of dedicated private foundations could be particularly effective.

Integrating Disciplinary Knowledge in Place-Based, Problem-Driven Research Efforts

Finally, sustainability science will require progress in institutional designs that foster integration of research planning and support across disciplines and sectoral missions to address system interactions in particular regions and locales.

This need runs counter to deeply held organizational biases that emphasize individual intellectual disciplines within academia, and individual sectoral missions within governments. Thus, it is vastly easier to mount a study of the people or plants or hydrology or soils of a watershed than of their interactions. Studies of the implications of energy use on one region and land use change on another are more likely than an integrated study of how all human activities on a particular landscape affect it jointly. A variety of arrangements involving Presidential initiatives, lead agencies, multi-agency coordinating committees and task forces, and other mechanisms have been tried in the U.S. science policy structure to address these issues, none with uniform success.

That said, substantial progress has been made over the last decade in bridging disciplinary and even occasionally sectoral perspectives in addressing problems of global environmental change.[82] Even this limited progress, however, has proven tenuous and enormously difficult to sustain.[83] And it has not fared at all well in providing long-term support for the integrative, place-based science that this Board has identified as central to the successful navigation of the transition toward sustainability. A priority for enhancing institutional capacity to foster sustainability science is therefore the design of an S&T policy system that puts control of more research funds in the hands of place-based institutions with a mission of promoting integrative, policy-driven knowledge and know-how. Some precedent for such an approach exists in the old land-grant agricultural colleges and in a variety of novel regional partnerships of academia, government, and industry that have emerged in areas of high technology R&D. Internationally, institutions such as the START system could—if properly supported—provide the testing ground for such integrative, place-based efforts.

PRIORITIES FOR ACTION

This section applies the strategy sketched above to the core sectoral challenges for sustainable development identified more than a decade ago by the Brundtland Commission. For each sector—population, settlements, agriculture, energy and materials, and living resources—we begin by recapitulating the Brundtland Commission's call for action. We then draw from our own studies of developments since the Brundtland report to suggest plausible, high-priority sectoral goals for a sustainability transition, assess the knowledge most needed for the journey, and propose specific steps that could help society to move along a suitable pathway. In some sectors, such as population, enough is known to suggest specific policy measures. In others, such as urban systems, where the needed knowledge is less fully developed, enough is known to suggest where to look for guidance. In all cases, what is needed is the iterative, adaptive approach outlined in our strategy for navigation where science both informs action and learns as much as possible from the encounter. Activities related to many of our action priorities are under way with varying but generally inadequate levels of support around the world. Our intent is not to ignore, much less compete with such initiatives, but rather to help focus attention on a few areas where significantly increased concentration or activity seems warranted. Implementation of our recommendations will therefore be a task not only for the National Research Council and its national and international partners in science, but also for the many "knowledge-action collaboratives" involving the international science community, governments, non-governmental organizations, and the private sector around the world.

Human population: Accelerate current trends in fertility reduction

> "Giving people the means to choose the size of their families is not just a method of keeping population in balance with resources; it is a way of assuring—especially for women—the basic human right of self-determination. The extent to which facilities for exercising such choices are made available is itself a measure of a nation's development." WCED, 1987

By the middle of the next century, in just 50 years, global population is currently projected to be about 9 billion in the UN mid-range forecast, with much higher and somewhat lower populations within the current range of projections. These projections are based on the assumed trajectory of the demographic transition, with fertility reduced to a level just adequate for replacement over the next generation. Could, and should, the pace of this fertility reduction be increased? In many ways, smaller generations could ease a transition to sustainability. By reducing the number of people to feed, nurture, house, educate, and employ, the tasks become less daunting. Consumption of energy and materials would be reduced while available investment for both human development and economic growth would be potentially increased. On the other hand, too much fertility reduction, accomplished too quickly, can clearly bring on transition problems of its own. Especially troublesome are those associated with the creation of populations characterized by high ratios of elderly people relative to productive workers. On balance, however, for most parts of the world still exhibiting high fertility, accelerating the rates of reduction will almost certainly ease the transition toward sustainability.

Goals

An achievable goal for population is to accelerate current trends in fertility reduction. After reviewing the continuing reduction in fertility and the potential for accelerated reductions (notably, in addressing the unwanted childbearing due to lack of available contraception), we believe that achieving a 10 percent reduction in the population now projected for 2050 is a desirable and attainable goal.[84] Nearly a billion less people would ease the transition toward sustainability.

Knowledge

As noted in Chapter 4, the three major sources of high fertility and continued rapid population growth are the unmet need for contraception, the still high desired family size, and the large number of young people entering reproductive age. Improving access to contraceptive services, and linking these to reproductive and child health services can over the next decade reduce the unmet needs for contraception. On the whole, enough is now known about providing access to such services to meet these needs in the course of a decade. The potential of private markets to deliver contraceptives, however, has not been fully explored by national programs. In other areas, more knowledge is called for. Thus, more needs to be learned about the factors that determine desired family size and the nature and effectiveness of incentives to postpone marriage and delay reproduction. Fundamental research on the factors influencing the timing and speed of the demographic transition is also still required. For example, while diminished fertility seems to correlate with increasing income over the long term, it also seems to respond to shorter term diminution in income. Further, fertility has dropped below replacement in most industrial countries (contrary to the constant replacement assumption of most projections) and future trends are uncertain. And, a better understanding is needed of the implications that enhanced fertility reduction rates and age-specific mortality factors such as AIDS will have for social issues related to the future age distributions of the populations they create.

Actions

Despite these knowledge needs, societies know enough to seek a reduction of the 2056 projected levels of population by 10 percent. Research and decomposition analyses have shown that such reductions should be possible. Desired family size diminishes with increased incomes, child survival, educational and employment opportunities for women, and access to birth control. As discussed in Chapter 4, all of these measures tend to be correlated and each—separately and together—has been hypothesized as a key lever in fertility reduction. In practice, attaining the reductions will require behavioral as well as cultural changes, with much energetic and coordinated action by national governments, international organizations, and other institutions, as well as by individuals.

Over the short-term, the most obvious strategy is to meet the unsatisfied demand for contraception by increasing the knowledge about and availability of existing technologies to those who might want to use them. Over the medium term, strategies are needed to aim for reduced family size through efforts to enhance the status of women, particularly developing incentive structures for educating girls and women. Education is a reasonably well-known and tested intervention, with additional critical benefits for individuals and societies; but accelerating education for women will require new and sustained efforts. Finally, looking over the longer term, the most promising effect would be achieved by delaying the onset and increasing the spacing of childbearing. Postponing having children through education and job opportunities (thereby, in most societies encouraging marriage at a later age) and addressing such difficult issues as adolescent sexuality have the potential to slow population momentum. But more specific programs—such as the novel program in Hyderabad, India, that provides dowries to empower young women to stay in school and to postpone marriage—are needed. All these actions require a level of collaboration not usually found—bringing together initiatives in family planning, reproductive health, education, women's rights, adolescent pregnancy, and employment to accelerate fertility reduction.

Cities: Accommodate an expected doubling to tripling of the urban system in a habitable, efficient, and environmentally friendly manner

"In many developing countries, cities have thus grown far beyond anything imagined only a few decades ago—and at speeds without historic precedent... These projections put the urban challenge firmly in the developing countries. In the space of 15 years ...the developing world will have to increase by 65 percent its capacity to produce and manage its urban infrastructure, services, and shelter—merely to maintain present conditions." WCED, 1987

Over the next two generations, the human population is expected to become predominantly urban, with the great majority of new human settlement expected in urbanized areas in developing countries. Using current projections for population and rates of urbanization, the transition will be from a world with 3 billion people in cities to one with 7 billion in cities—a doubling to tripling of urban systems. Almost all of this growth will take place in and around existing cities; truly new cities such as Abuja and Brasilia have been and are likely to continue to be rare.

The challenges posed by this projected urban population growth are daunting.[85] Nonetheless, a number of opportunities present themselves and stem in part from the same trends that present challenges. The growth of high-density cities provides an opportunity for economic and energy-efficient provision of services and infrastructure (e.g., the marginal cost of providing each additional unit of public service is lower in urban areas than in rural areas). The fact that growth will be rapid means that most of the infrastructure will be built in the next several decades, providing an opportunity to build modern and efficient facilities. Key to these opportunities, of course, is the foresight, will, and capital required to take advantage of them.

Goals

An achievable goal is to accommodate a doubling to tripling of the urban system in a habitable, efficient, and environmentally friendly manner. The cities emerging from such growth should meet the needs for housing, nurturing, educating, and employing the 4 billion additional persons expected to be urban dwellers by the middle of the 21st century. By utilizing the potential efficiencies provided by both increased density and the opportunity to build anew, these cities should meet human needs while reducing their "ecological footprint" and providing more environmentally friendly engines of development.

Knowledge

Cities are very complex places. The knowledge and know-how required to expand and manage them are diffused across a broad range of disciplines, practitioners, and institutions. The urban social sciences study the forces, needs, and impacts of growth; architects, engineers, and planners address the built environment's form and function. These professions, as well as politicians, developers, financiers, and the construction industry create the built environment. Environmental scientists seek to maintain the needed ecosystem services and lessen the impacts of cities on their own environs.   Habitability, efficiency, and environmental health are all goals of clusters of disciplines and professions. An extensive literature related to each is available.[86] Lacking, however, is the knowledge and know-how for sustainable cities that brings these goals together to drive research and development programs to better meet urban residents' needs, reduce hunger and poverty, and lessen stresses on life support systems. For example, not enough is known about the tradeoffs among sustainability goals as cities grow to different sizes, in different configurations, or at different rates. Lacking even more is the understanding of how to manage such tradeoffs within the realities of the urban politics and economics that characterize different regions of the world. For example, better understanding is needed of the relation between the growth of cities and the development of capital markets in developing countries that can mobilize funds for housing.

Actions

Humanity is in the midst of a transition from a world with 3 billion people in cities to one with 7 billion in cities, mostly in developing countries. Over the next two generations, the equivalent of nearly 1,000 great cities will be built, in and about existing cities—an average of almost 20 of these cities every year. The challenge that faces urban areas and all high-density population areas is to achieve settlement patterns that make efficient use of land and infrastructure and impose reduced burdens on material and energy use, while providing satisfactory levels of living. This challenge poses both an enormous necessity and a grand opportunity to seek new behaviors, institutions, policies (public and private), technologies, urban forms, environmental management (water, wastes, air quality), and infrastructure configurations to move urban areas toward sustainability. Now is the time to bring together the science and technology of habitability, efficiency, and environment with the practice of planning, building, and financing the cities of tomorrow. Such a collaborative partnership of disciplines, professions, and major institutions of finance and development can seek the needed knowledge to urgently address this still dimly recognized enormous challenge and opportunity, which is only dimly recognized today.

Agricultural production: Reverse the declining trends in agricultural production in Africa; sustain historic trends elsewhere

> "Global food security depends not only on raising global food production, but on reducing distortions in the structure of the world food market and on shifting the focus of food production to food-deficit countries, regions and households." WCED, 1987

The last 50 years have seen an increase in agricultural production that has outpaced population growth, reduced hunger, and improved diets almost everywhere around the world. The great failure has been Africa, where per capita production has generally been declining over the last several decades. Food demand in the next 50 years will continue to rise in response to population growth, per capita income growth, and attempts to reduce the undernutrition of the very poor. Meeting the challenge of feeding the population and reducing hunger while sustaining life support systems will require dramatic advances both in food production, on which we focus here, and in food distribution and access. The Brundtland Commission recognized the multiplicity of strategies that would be required to meet the challenge. Yet the past 15 years have seen stagnation in real spending on international agricultural research and increasing indications that societies' capabilities for rising food production are inadequate worldwide, with a special problem in Africa.[87]

Goals

An achievable goal is to reverse declining trends in agricultural production in Africa while sustaining historic trends elsewhere. The most critical near-term aspect of this goal is to reverse the decline in agricultural production capability in Sub-Saharan Africa, the only region where population growth has outpaced growth in agricultural production.

Knowledge

The gains in agricultural production during this century were made possible by the ability of public and private sector research institutions to incorporate new knowledge and technology into new production materials and new production practices that could be transmitted to producers. Advances in education, both in schooling and in nonformal education (such as agricultural extension), have been important factors in enabling farm families to utilize the new knowledge and technology more productively. In recent decades, the production increases associated with the Green Revolution technologies of improved seed, nutrients, and pest control have slowed, while numerous social and environmental concerns about those technologies have been raised. Thus, the next 50 years are seen as requiring a "green-green" revolution, in which new biology-based technologies are used to renew yield increases and diminish negative environmental and social effects.[88] Whether such knowledge—and the institutions necessary to produce and apply it—can be created quickly enough to enable a transition toward sustainability remains a subject of much debate.

Actions

Societies know enough to take many of the needed actions now. The challenge that faces agriculture is to intensify production on robust soil areas, to reduce the intensity of agricultural use on fragile land areas, and to restore productivity on degraded lands. Sustainable increases in output per hectare of about two (perhaps three) times present levels will be required by 2050. Substantial progress has been made by developing countries in Asia and Latin America in establishing the institutional capacity to achieve these objectives. In addition, food production and food quality improvements have been introduced in many regions through biotechnology, agricultural runoff prevention from minimum tillage practices, efficient water use by targeted application, and reduction of farm inputs from precision applications based on computer analysis.

Africa, however, remains the only major region where growth in production lags behind growth in demand. Why this should be so remains a puzzle to African governments and aid agencies, as well as to students of African economic development. It is possible to point to the difficult problems of managing agricultural soil resources, the constraints resulting from traditional land tenure institutions, limited agricultural capacity, urban bias in agricultural and food policy, and to a lack of stability in economic governance and political institutions. But the weights that should be given to these several factors and the actions that must be taken to "get agriculture moving" is a source of substantial disagreement. A collaborative effort involving African governments, the African scientific community, African farmers, and nongovernmental organizations will be needed to address the underlying causes and the actions that are needed for the countries of Sub-Saharan Africa to implement the technical and institutional changes required to get agriculture moving, and to build the agriculturally based development required for an African transition toward sustainability.

Industry and energy: Accelerate improvements in the use of energy and materials

"If industrial development is to be sustainable over the long term, it will have to change radically in terms of the quality of that development... In general, industries and industrial operations should be encouraged that are more efficient in terms of resource use, that generate less pollution and waste, that are based on the use of renewable rather than non-renewable resources, and that minimize irreversible adverse impacts on human health and the environment.... The period ahead must be regarded as transitional from an era in which energy has been used in an unsustainable manner. A generally acceptable pathway to a safe and sustainable energy future has not yet been found." WCED, 1987

The extraction of raw materials and their conversion into material products of all kinds requires large amounts of energy and poses great environmental burdens and damages. In a more crowded and more consuming world, one required transition is toward the production of the goods and services to meet the far greater needs and wants of human society with a much smaller environmental impact. This achievement will require a smaller loss to the environment of the basic ingredients of energy and materials that sustain life, and a system of production and delivery that is less disruptive of environmental systems. In the 10 years since the Brundtland challenge to industry to produce more with less, there have been substantial improvements in this direction both by industry and by consumers. But this trend toward greater efficiency and dematerialization must be accomplished universally and at much faster rates than the historical ones described in Chapter 2 if it is to offset the rapid increases in production forecast for the next decades. The energy system has been moving toward improved end-use efficiency and declining emissions of carbon dioxide per unit of energy production, but rapid rates of population and economic growth have outstripped these trends of increasing efficiency and decarbonization.

Goals

An achievable goal is to accelerate efficiency improvements in the use of energy and materials. Some analysts have set improvement goals on the basis of an increase in the eco-efficiency ratio of a process, firm, or economy: useful (saleable) outputs divided by resource inputs (materials and energy).[89] Long-term rates of improvement in energy efficiency has averaged about 1 to 2 percent per year since the beginning of the Industrial Revolution. A reasonable energy goal for the transition toward sustainability discussed in this report may be to double this historical rate of energy efficiency improvement. Others have suggested as much as a 10-fold increase in eco-efficiency for materials use in the developed world over the same 50 years.[90] Aggregate goals do not distinguish among resources with high and low environmental impacts. Instead, they point generally in the right direction, leaving freedom for experimentation with diverse methods, while conveying a simple but essential message.

Knowledge

Research and development should focus on improving processes and generating technologies that can reduce the energy and materials required per unit of economic output, as in the many efforts under way to improve household energy efficiency; build low-polluting, energy-efficient automobiles; and reduce waste. The emergent field of study and action known as industrial ecology seeks to use the mechanisms of markets, competition, and efficiency to minimize the throughput of energy and materials and the output of wastes from industrial processes. The means include improved eco-efficiency, reuse, recycling, and the substitution of services for products. Many new energy technologies are being developed—for example, fuel cells, photoelectric conversion systems, carbon separation and sequestration technologies, advanced storage technologies, high-temperature superconductors, and advanced power electronics. Much, if not enough, is known about the kinds of research partnerships and incentives that will most effectively and efficiently move such promising developments into the "pre-competitive" stage of product demonstration. Still more is understood about the factors influencing the rate and pattern of adoption of new technologies once they become competitive in open markets. Great challenges remain, however, in the middle ground in understanding the institutional and incentive requirements for bringing promising technologies from the pre-competitive into competitive stages of their development.

In designing and evaluating institutions and incentives to encourage sustainable technologies, it is important to consider their implications carefully at a system level over the technologies' full life cycles, using such strategies as material balance modeling and economic input-output analysis coupled to evaluation of environmental loadings. Without such a systematic assessment, policies that appear to promote better solutions may in the long run have serious undesirable consequences, such as creating difficult problems for the recycling and disposal of materials.

Over the long term, there is a great opportunity to increase human sustenance without increasing environmental burdens through new basic and applied knowledge in the science and engineering of biological processes, new energy sources and transmission technologies, new materials, and more generally in the substitution of information for energy and materials.

Actions

Businesses are likely to pursue reductions in the intensity of energy and materials use if provided with the needed incentives such as the potential to reduce costs or regulatory provisions. Approaches to accelerate efficiency trends through industry leaders (some already committed to "green" practices) and through trade and industry associations (e.g., the Conference Board, the International Organization for Standardization [ISO]) seem likely to have major effects on large and medium size firms. Attracting the interest of the large numbers of small firms in long-established industries, most of which have little capacity for investment in change, will be more difficult and require special efforts.

Even when consumer and public attitudes are neutral, or in favor of change, however, the barriers to efficiency improvements that are embodied in subsidies, statutes and regulations are likely to be difficult to reverse. This will be especially true of those involving long-standing differential incentives, or those that will penalize some industries in favor of others. However, given current trends toward "green" attitudes to recycling and green advertising by product and service suppliers, the pressure by environmental organizations and by government, especially if coordinated, might be effective in encouraging change.

To achieve the increased efficiency objective with respect to energy provisions, ways must be found to reflect the full environmental costs of various fuels through the marketplace. This can be done through means that include fuel use taxes, fuel-efficiency standards for appliances and motor vehicle fleets, and green energy requirements on electric power systems. Direct "externality" taxes on fuels are believed by most economists to be much more efficient, and to produce fewer perverse incentives, than indirect methods, though they tend to be politically unpopular in some countries.

In the short term, societies need to promote more rapid adoption of existing in-use efficiency technologies and practices worldwide. Many efficient technologies are already available to be used in places around the world where they are needed. But societies also need to move beyond simply using what is available to promoting some technologies in a demonstration phase that encourages further development of these technologies. Renewables seem to show enough promise to rate some special nurturing in this category. For the longer term, societies need to commit to fostering and supporting a broadly based, collaborative program of basic energy research and development, involving both public and private sectors in all the varied ways made possible by trends toward deregulation and multiple scale developments. Finally, experience has suggested that a transition toward sustainability will be hastened by research on materials. This should be a broad program, driven by our knowledge that materials innovations will be important for increased production and product efficiency, not simply by a quest for the particular materials that societies now need. These individual research initiatives can usefully be viewed as a portfolio within which technology choices for the future can be based on an integrated view of sustainable production.

Living resources: Restore degraded ecosystems while conserving diversity elsewhere

"The challenge facing nations today is no longer deciding whether conservation (of living natural resources) is a good idea, but rather how it can be implemented in the national interest and within the means available in each country.... the economic values inherent in the genetic materials of species are alone enough to justify species preservation." WCED, 1987

Species, ecosystems, and their services are critical elements of the life support systems of the planet and represent important natural capital for the human economic and social enterprise. Humans have become integral parts of most of the earth's ecosystems.[91] As described in Chapter 4, human activities that modify ecosystems, primarily land use change and overharvesting of renewable resources, constitute the major threats to sustaining these systems. As described in Chapter 2, unprecedentedly high rates of species extinctions are being driven primarily by continuing loss of habitat. Changes in species and ecosystems also imply losses in natural capital stocks. One estimated value of U.S. species (agricultural crops and livestock, hunted animals, forest products) to the worldwide economy is $434 billion.[92] The value of marine fisheries for human consumption worldwide is estimated to be between $50 and $100 billion.[93] One estimate of ecosystem services on a global basis has generated a value of $33 trillion/year.[94] Unfortunately, species valuation is rudimentary. Also, numbers alone often do not lead to preservation (see Box 6.2). Nonetheless, expansion of the human population and human activities threatens many living resources and ecosystems. Humanity must not await the arrival of future generations before taking action to preserve the present stock of biodiversity.

Goals

An achievable goal is to restore degraded systems while conserving diversity elsewhere. For the human-dominated ecosystems undergoing degradation from multiple demands and stresses, the goal should be to work toward restoring and maintaining their function and integrity so that their services and use for humans may be sustained over long time frames. Other ecosystems have been less influenced by human activities.

Box 6.2 Valuation of Rain Forests

There has been much speculation about natural product chemistry and the potential value of rainforests for pharmaceuticals. If rain forests were an extremely rich and valuable source of pharmaceutical precursor opportunities, their preservation should be assured by market forces, which would not allow their destruction. Unfortunately, they have been oniy occasionally found to be such a resource. Indeed, one study valuing biodiversity for use in pharmaceutical research cites the "maximum possible value of a marginal species is slightly less than $10,000,"[95] which is not enough to mobilize corporate attention for preservation. Thus, the preservation of species must be assured through other interventions, both scientific and political.

Some of them represent the last reserves of earth's biological diversity, providing a treasure for future generations as a storehouse of biodiversity and because of their aesthetic and spiritual qualities. For these systems, the goal is to protect and conserve biological diversity, both by dramatically reducing current rates of land conversion and by planning for conservation.

Knowledge

Much is known about ecosystem function and how ecosystems and species respond to anthropogenic changes. Some of that information has already been integrated into management approaches. A growing number of recent efforts have integrated knowledge of ecosystem processes and the services they provide into both conservation and development planning. Most of these management approaches are in fact experiments, and adaptive learning is a requisite characteristic of them. The field of restoration ecology, for example, is yielding information about successes and failures as well as providing critical knowledge to help reverse the trend of habitat modification and to establish new habitats for biodiversity. In addition, knowledge from conservation biology is used in managing protected areas, as well as in identifying appropriate species-rich habitats for conservation purposes. To apply these approaches more widely will require additional research, learning, and information dissemination at the interface between the social sciences, natural sciences, and technology.

Beyond these applications, new knowledge is needed in three general areas—fundamental understanding, ecosystem management, and monitoring. In the realm of fundamental understanding of how biological systems work, better knowledge is needed of both the dynamics of population processes and the seasonal and interannual variations in ecosystem processes. We also need an increased understanding of the roles of genes, species, and functional groups in ecosystem processes; the response of ecosystems, species, and population dynamics to multiple and interacting anthropogenic changes; and an assessment of what kinds of species and ecosystems are distributed worldwide and how they can be best used and valued by people.[96]

A second general area of needed information addresses how ecosystems can best be managed at the landscape or regional scale, while accommodating human needs and activities (sometimes termed "ecosystem management"). New knowledge is required to understand the components of decision making for land and resource use across scales and political boundaries; identify the socioeconomic determinants of over-exploitation; develop the ability to predict and correctly value the services provided by ecosystems; and develop more sustainable management and harvesting techniques. Moreover, new institutions may be required to integrate the diverse range of knowledge.

Finally, in the area of monitoring, research that allows evaluating the usefulness of the indicator species concept and the concept of fragile or sentinel ecosystems is needed. Monitoring programs must make better use of ecological knowledge gleaned from basic research programs. In addition, evaluations of comparable methods for data gathering and analysis, the strengths and weaknesses of current and future remote-sensing systems, and the criteria for species and habitat protection and use will be necessary before reliable monitoring systems can be developed.

Actions

Enough is already known to better manage human-dominated eco-systems and to preserve biodiversity. Restoration ecology and conservation biology have grown both in theory and in experience through applications to problems of protecting and managing species and ecosystems. Land conservation is made possible through easements, joint partnerships, "debt-for-nature swaps," grants from the Global Environment Facility, and other transactions. Nevertheless, there are lingering tensions or debates about preservation versus conservation* (e.g., wildlife parks in Kenya), best practices, incentives, and the valuation of natural resources. Resolution of these and related issues will require a better integration of the biological and social sciences, including better understanding of the beliefs, attitudes, and needs of local communities, the private sector, and governments.

The restoration of degraded systems will require focusing on better management of human-dominated systems, including using ecological knowledge in decision making and removing incentives that encourage exploitation of systems and replacing them with incentives that sustain the systems. Examples of successful land restoration abound, and with application of new biotechnologies such as phytoremediation, even the most seriously damaged terrestrial ecosystems have a chance for restoration and recovery of values and services. More attention should also be focused on restoring "marginal" lands of low agricultural value and use, because such areas with lower quality soils may support higher biodiversity than more heavily exploited agricultural lands with higher quality soils.[97] These and other "manipulation" experiments are underway to evaluate the applications of ecology in restoring degraded systems; the management of forests, agriculture, and oceans, while retaining

---

*To preserve is to protect from any change, whereas to conserve is to use with regard to dangers of overuse.

ecosystem services; the effects of species reintroductions (e.g., recovering marine mammal populations) and species invasions (e.g., exotics) on ecosystem structure and functioning; and multiple-use management in forests, protected areas, and coastal and marine ecosystems.

A comprehensive, comparative analysis is needed to determine what these experiments reveal for adaptive management and what useful information is transferable from one species, one ecosystem, or one scale to another. This knowledge—together with removal of the incentives for forestry, irrigation, and fisheries that encourage land degradation or over-exploitation of living resources—would help restore degraded systems, encourage the sustainable use of renewable resources, and build natural capital for future generations.

Biodiversity can be managed in part by setting aside protected areas. Unfortunately, many existing protected sites were established because of convenience, threat of overuse, or aesthetic reasons, not because of biodiversity. Fortunately, many programs are under way to evaluate important areas for protecting species diversity (e.g., identification of "hot spots," or areas of high biodiversity at greatest risks of disturbance; and establishment of wilderness areas, or ecosystems protected from human interference); engage local communities in conservation efforts (e.g., UNESCO's Biosphere Reserves); and establish buffer zones around protected areas as transition zones. These efforts provide opportunities for identifying appropriate sites for long-term protection of biodiversity and for balancing the ecological needs of species with the economic needs of society.

Integrative Interactions:
Water, Atmosphere and Climate, Species and Ecosystems

Our elaboration of navigational needs in each of the Brundtland "sectors" demonstrates that it is possible to identify appropriate next steps in each sector through the integration of what societies know—both the lessons learned over the last decade and the projected needs for knowledge and know-how over the coming decades—with what societies can do, namely, the policy actions that move us in the right directions and the indicators that can monitor their progress. Achievements in each of the sectors toward the specified goals will improve our chances of attaining the overall goals of a sustainability transition. But it is clear that achievements in one sector do not imply improvements in others, and that the interactions among the sectors also must be taken into account in terms of the resources they require and the environmental effects to which they contribute. To meet our normative goals, an integrated approach is necessary.

For example, as we discussed in Chapter 4, progress in reducing a pollution-causing gas emission from one sector may not reduce urban or regional smog, because gaseous emissions from many sectors, including stationary and mobile combustion sources, industry, agriculture, and natural ecosystems together contribute to the atmospheric chemistry that produces regional air pollution. Also, improvements in the efficiency of water use and reuse and the water quality at its outflow in urban systems may be meaningless to downstream users if similar efficiency improvements are not made in adjacent agricultural areas. Likewise, efforts to preserve natural ecosystems for ethical or aesthetic reasons, or for the goods and services they provide us, may ultimately fail if these efforts do not account for the longer term changes likely to be introduced by atmospheric pollution, climate change, or human population encroachment.

These examples and others in Chapter 4 argue strongly for the need to develop both a thorough understanding of the most critical interactions, often at a regional scale, and an integrated strategy for planning and management that is focused on sustaining critical life support systems. Such strategies require research and policies that go beyond the typical framework of sectoral or scientific disciplines. For example, any integrated approach to sustaining the world's water supplies must extend from hydrology and engineering to consider water resources in the context of the interacting physical, biological, chemical, and human systems that control water cycling and use at a landscape scale. An integrated perspective, therefore, takes into account land use, water quality, ecosystem processes and protection, as well as urban and economic requirements. Similarly, any approach to the sustainability of atmosphere and climate requires the integration of industrial, energy, urban, and agricultural planning and management.

Knowledge

An integrative strategy for the sustainability transition is one that views, studies, and manages the world as a dynamic, interacting system. Such a strategy is already under development and application, albeit in its very early steps. It must be built on the knowledge and know-how of the individual disciplines and sectors addressed above. Indeed, it is the advanced state of knowledge in those areas that allow integrative approaches to proceed. However, the strategy now required demands a new way of working and thinking, including new concepts and theories that link the areas of knowledge and that account for feedbacks and interactions among both biophysical and social systems.

Researchers and managers have begun developing and testing such approaches under the various names of ecosystem management, adaptive management, integrated conservation and development planning, integrated water resource planning, and so on. For example, the U.S. Forest Service is carrying out a series of regional integrated forest planning and management efforts, including work in the Appalachians, Columbia River, and Sierra Nevada.[98] Also, several U.S. funding agencies have in the past few years initiated research opportunities that aim to integrate across disciplines and sectors.[99] To date, the results and application of these activities toward sustainability science are unclear. Perhaps the most important outcome of these early efforts will be the emergence of a new body of theory about how to ask integrative questions, acquire and integrate knowledge, and apply that knowledge using adaptive approaches.

Actions

For issues in energy, agriculture, human population, and living resources, discussed earlier in this section and in the report, the immediate actions to be taken build on a long record of advancement in knowledge and know-how and in concepts and theories. In the area of integrative science, the scientific community has much less experience, and in many ways our immediate action must be to learn by doing and redoing. There are several dimensions to this action. First, we must ask in rigorous and careful ways about the determinants of success or failure in our ongoing experiments in integrative research (see, e.g., the earlier discussion in this chapter of research on degraded ecosystems), a point that we have also made more generally in this report about social learning and adaptive management. Second, much more effort must be focused on truly integrative research at all spatial scales. While funding institutions around the world are increasingly willing to provide resources for patching together different kinds of disciplinary information, fewer funding agencies have been willing to invest in studies that are interdisciplinary and integrative from their inception, and it is these studies that have the best chance of developing the conceptual underpinnings of integrative science. Third, new frameworks for interactions among industry, academia, foundations, and other nongovernmental organizations must be developed in which all partners contribute to the analysis of sustainability at local to regional scales.

TOWARD A SUSTAINABILITY TRANSITION

The challenge of mobilizing science and technology for a transition toward sustainability is daunting. Relevant knowledge needs to be integrated from the natural and social sciences, engineering, and management practice. Approaches to learning how to navigate the transition need to extend from the most basic research, to the active design and interpretation of large-scale policy experiments, to the informed diffusion of technologies around the world. Collaboration needs to occur across scales, extending from the local to the global, and across industrial sectors, nonstate actors, and governments. Judgments about priorities need to balance a respect for individual initiative and the inevitability of surprise with a responsiveness to urgent national and international needs.

The United States does not have in its national history a precedent for conducting such an enterprise. However, the role of science and technology in the agricultural, defense, and health complexes may provide partial and instructive analogies. Each of these broad areas has involved collaboration among an extended community of universities, businesses, and government agencies to address a specific set of social problems. Each also has involved the development of mission-oriented laboratories and experiment "stations" (e.g., agricultural experiment stations in the United States). These latter institutions were essential in promoting the development of hospitable settings in which a critical mass of scientists and engineers could come together, conduct world-class research on unconventional, problem-driven topics, and receive recognition from their peers in the larger R&D community—settings now in short supply for the kind of sustainability science that we believe is increasingly needed.[100]

An assessment of the extent and implications of similarities between the agriculture, defense, and health complexes and the needs of sustainability science was beyond the charge of this study and has yet to be undertaken. What this study has suggested is that the magnitude of the challenges to science posed by sustainability concerns in the 21st century may well be as great as the challenges posed by food, health, and security concerns in the 20th century. It is therefore past time to begin thinking about the institutional capacity for funding and promoting sustainability science in terms that are commensurate with the magnitude of the task ahead.

In establishing the Board on Sustainable Development and this project, the National Academies undertook their own experiment in social learning. There was great risk of failure. The legacy of the Academies' experiment—a commitment to sustainable development, to the pursuit of a sustainability science, and to the implications for future work—probably poses a more formidable challenge than the initial task of laying out the strategic framework contained in these pages. In the national history of the scientific enterprise, the National Academies have no precedent for conducting nor following up this type of study. Instead, they will need to continue the process of social learning by exercising their convening role to pursue priorities for research; help establish collaborative partnerships to advance the priorities for action; and work internationally with the scientific and technical community and the private sector. The United States has a special obligation to join and help guide the journey. In addition to having a robust scientific and technological capacity, the US public is a major consumer of global resources. Moreover, sustainable communities have not been realized across the US landscape.

Today, we have an opportunity to shape a sustainable world, if not necessarily for our children or grandchildren alive today, quite possibly for our great-grandchildren. All societies must seize the opportunity by applying what they know toward what they should do. Our common journey toward—or away from—sustainability has already begun.

REFERENCES AND BIBLIOGRAPHY

Adams, William Mark. 1990. *Green development: environment and sustainability in the Third World*. London; New York: Routledge.

Alston, J.M., B.J. Craig, and J. Rosenboom. 1998a. Financing agricultural research: International investment patterns and policy perspectives. *World Development* 26: 1057-1071.

Alston, J.M., P.G. Pardy, and V.H. Smith. 1998b. Financing agricultural R&D in rich countries: What is happening and why. *The Australian Journal of Agricultural and Resource Economics* 42, no. 1: 51-82.

Arrow, K. 1962. The economics of learning by doing. *Review of Economic Studies* 29: 155-173.

Baumgartner, Frank R., and Bryan D. Jones. 1993. *Agendas and instability in American politics*. Chicago: University of Chicago Press.

Bell, David E., William C. Clark, and Vernon W. Ruttan. 1994. Global research systems for sustainable development: agriculture, health and environment. In *Agriculture, environment and health: Sustainable development in the 21st Century*, ed. Vernon W. Ruttan, 358-379. Minneapolis: University of Minnesota Press.

Bossel, Hartmut. 1998. *Earth at a crossroads: Paths to a sustainable future*. Cambridge, UK: Cambridge University Press.

Branscomb, Lewis. 1998. *Defining successful partnerships and collaborations in scientific research*. Testimony hearing on March 11, 1998. Washington, D.C.: The US House of Representatives Committee on Science.

Brundtland, Gro Harlem. 1997. The scientific underpinning of policy. *Science* 277, no. 5325: 457.

Bull, K.R. 1991. The critical loads/levels approach to gaseous pollutant emission control. *Environmental Pollution* 69: 105-123.

Burton, Ian, Robert W. Kates, and Gilbert White. 1993. *The environment as hazard*. 2d ed. Oxford: Oxford University Press.

CENR (Committee on Environment and Natural Resources). 1997. *Integrating the nation's environmental monitoring and research networks and programs: A proposed framework*. Washington: National Science and Technology Council.

Carnegie Commission on Science, Technology and Government. 1992. *Environmental research and development: Strengthening the federal infrastructure*. New York: Carnegie Corporation.

Cash, David W., and Susanne C. Moser. 1998. *Information and decision making systems for the effective management of cross-scale environmental problems: A theoretical concept paper.* Global Environmental Assessment Project Working Paper. Cambridge, MA: Center for Science and International Affairs, Kennedy School of Government, Harvard University. Available through the Project's home page at http://www.environment.harvard.edu/ gea.

Cebon, Peter, Urs Dahinden, Huw Davies, Dieter M. Imboden, and Carlo C. Jaeger. 1998. *Views from the Alps: Regional perspectives on climate change.* Cambridge, MA: MIT Press.

Center for a New American Dream. 1997-1999 (quarterly). *Enough! A Quarterly Report on Consumption, Quality of Life, and the Environment.* Burlington, VT: Center for a New American Dream.

Clark, William C. 1985. Scales of climate impacts. *Climate Change* 7: 5-27.

Clark, William C. 1988. Visions of the 21st century: Conventional wisdom and other surprises in the global interactions of population, technology and environment. In *Perspective 2000: Proceedings of a conference sponsored by the Economic Council of Canada, December,* eds. K. Newton, T. Schweitzer, and J.-P. Voyer, 7-32. Ottawa: Economic Council of Canada.

Clark, William C., and R. E. Munn, eds. 1986. *Sustainable development of the biosphere.* Cambridge, UK: Cambridge University Press.

Climate Analysis Center. 1998. *Climate assessment* (annual report). Washington: US Department of Commerce, National Oceanic and Atmospheric Administration, National Weather Service, National Meteorological Center.

Cohen, Joel. 1995. *How many people can the earth support?* New York: Norton.

Conway, Gordon. 1997. *The doubly green revolution: Food for all in the 21st century.* London: Penguin.

Costanza, Robert, and Carl Folke. 1997. Valuing ecosystem services with efficiency, fairness, and sustainability as goals. In *Nature's services: Societal dependence on natural ecosystems,* ed. Gretchen C. Daily. Washington, D.C.: Island Press.

Crutzen, P.J., and T.E. Graedel. 1986. The role of atmospheric chemistry in environment-development interactions. Pp. 213-251 in *Sustainable development of the biosphere,* W. C. Clark and R. E. Munn, eds. Cambridge, UK: Cambridge University Press.

DIVERSITAS. 1998. About DIVERSITAS. http://www.lmcp.jussieu.fr/icsu/DIVERSITAS/ index.html.

Daily, G.C., and P.R. Ehrlich. 1996. Socioeconomic equity, sustainability, and Earth's carrying capacity. *Ecological Applications* 6, no. 4: 991-1001.

Dobson, A.P., A.D. Bradshaw, and A.J.M. Baker. 1997. Hopes for the future: Restoration ecology and conservation biology. *Science* 277, no. 5325: 515-522.

Dooge, J.C.I., G.T. Goodman, J.W.M. la Rivière, J. Marton-Lefèvre, T. O'Riordan, F. Praderie, eds. 1992. *An agenda of science for environment and development into the 21st century.* Cambridge, UK: Cambridge University Press.

Dowlatabadi, H., and M.G. Morgan. 1993. A model framework for integrated assessment of the climate problem. *Energy Policy* 21 (March): 209-221.

Durning, Alan. 1992. *How much is enough? The consumer society and the future of the earth.* New York: Norton.

ESA (Ecological Society of America). 1998. *The sustainable biosphere initiative.* http://esa.sdsc.edu/ sbi.htm

ESRC (Economic and Social Research Council) Global Environmental Change Programme (UK) and the Social Sciences and Humanities Research Council (Canada). 1998. *Interactive research: Exploring the practice: Case studies in environmental research.* Report of a Workshop, University of Sussex, Brighton, UK, 2-4 March, 1998. Brighton, UK: University of Sussex.

EU (European Union). 1998. The fifth framework programme of the European community for research, technological development and demonstration activities, 1998 to 2002. PE-CONS 3626/98. Brussels: European Union. Further information and text of the program available through the web site http://www.cordis.lu/fifth/home.html.

Eicher, C.K. 1994. Building productive national and international agricultural research systems. In *Agriculture, environment and health: Sustainable development in the 21st century*, ed. Vernon W. Ruttan, 77-103. Minneapolis: University of Minnesota Press.

FCCC (Framework Convention on Climate Change). 1992. New York: United Nations.

Francis, George, and Sally Lerner. 1996. Making sustainable development happen: Institutional transformation. In *Achieving sustainable development*, eds. Ann Dale and John B. Robinson. Vancouver: University of British Columbia.

Frink, C.R., P.E. Waggoner, and J.H. Ausubel. 1999. Nitrogen fertilizer: Retrospect and prospect. *Proceedings of the National Academy of Sciences* 96, no. 4: 1175-1180.

Fritz, Jan-Stephan. 1998. *Report on international scientific advisory processes on the environment and sustainable development*. Background Paper No. 21, Commission on Sustainable Development, 6th Session. UN Department of Economic and Social Affairs DESA/DSD/1998/21. New York: United Nations. Also available via gopher://gopher.un.org/oo/esc/cn17/ 1998/background/ 21scienc.wpd.

Frosch, R.A. 1996. Toward the end of waste: Reflections on a new ecology of industry, *Daedalus* 125, no. 3: 199-212.

GEA (Global Environmental Assessment Project). 1997. *A critical evaluation of global environmental assessments: The climate experience*. Calverton, MD: Center for the Application of Research on the Environment. Available at the project's web site: http://environment.harvard.edu/gea.

Gibson, Clark, Elinor Ostrom, and Toh-Kyeong Ahn. 1998. *Scaling issues in the social sciences*. IHDP Working Paper No. 1. Bonn: International Human Dimensions Programme on Global Environmental Change. Available through the Programme's home page at http://ibm.rhz.uni-bonn.de/IHDP.

Goody, Richard. 1982. *Global change: Impacts on habitability*. Report by the Executive Committee of a Workshop held at Woods Hole, MA, June 16-21, 1982. JPL D-95. Pasadena, CA: National Aeronautics and Space Administration, Jet Propulsion Laboratory, California Institute of Technology.

Graedel, T.E., and P.J. Crutzen. 1989. The changing atmosphere. *Scientific American* 261, no. 3: 58.

Grübler, A. 1998. *Technology and social change*. Cambridge: Cambridge University Press.

Gunderson, Lance H., C.S. Holling, and Stephen S. Light, eds. 1995. *Barriers and bridges to the renewal of ecosystems and institutions*. New York: Columbia University Press. Especially chapters 1 and 12.

Guston, D. 1997. Critical appraisal in science and technology policy analysis: The example of "Science, the endless frontier." *Policy Sciences* 30: 233-255.

Haas, Peter M., R.O. Keohane, and Mark A. Levy, eds. 1993. *Institutions for the earth: Sources of effective international environmental protection*. Cambridge, MA: MIT Press.

Hardin, Garrett. 1968. The tragedy of the commons. *Science* 162: 1243-1248.

Hammond, Allen. 1998. *Which world? Scenarios for the 21st century*. Washington: Island Press.

Herman R., S.A. Ardekani, and J.A. Ausubel. 1989. Dematerialization. In *Technology and Environment*, NAE (National Academy of Engineering), Advisory Committee on Technology and Society, eds. J.H. Ausubel and H.E. Sladovich, 50-69. Washington, DC: National Academy Press.

Holling, C.S., ed. 1978. *Adaptive environmental assessment and management*. Chichester, UK: Wiley.

_____. 1986. The resilience of terrestrial ecosystems: local surprise and global change. In *Sustainable development of the biosphere*, eds. Clark, William C., and R.E. Munn. Cambridge, UK: Cambridge University Press.

Houghton, J.T., L.G. Meira Filho, B.A. Callander, N. Harris, A. Kattenberg, and K. Maskell. 1996. *Climate change 1995: The science of climate change*. Cambridge, UK: Cambridge University Press. Published for the Intergovernmental Panel on Climate Change (IPCC).

Hughes, Thomas P. 1998. *Rescuing Prometheus*. New York: Pantheon Books.

IGBP (International Geosphere-Biosphere Programme). 1991. *Global Change System for Analysis, Research and Training (START)*. Eds. J.A. Eddy, T.F. Malone, J.J. McCarthy, and T. Rosswall. Stockholm: IGBP.

_____. 1994. *The IGBP in action: The work plan 1994-1998*. Stockholm: IGBP.

IHDP (International Human Dimensions Program). 1998. *About IHDP*. http://ibm.rhrz.uni-bonn.de/IHDP/about.html.

IUCN (International Union for Conservation of Nature and Natural Resources), UNEP (United Nations Environment Programme), WWF (World Wide Fund for Nature). 1980. *World conservation strategy: Living resource conservation for sustainable development*. Gland, Switzerland: IUCN.

_____. 1991. *Caring for the earth: A strategy for sustainable living*. Gland, Switzerland: IUCN.

Issacs, Stephen L., and James R. Knickman, eds. 1998. *To improve health and health care: The Robert Wood Johnson Foundation anthology*. San Francisco: Josey-Bass Publishers.

Johnson, K. Norman, Richard Holthausen, Margaret A. Shannon, and James Sedell. 1998. Forest management ecosystem management assessment team assessment. In *Bioregional Assessments*, eds. K. Norman Johnson, Frederick Swanson, Margaret Herring, and Sarah Greene. Washington, D.C.: Island Press.

Kasperson, Jeanne X., Roger E. Kasperson, and B.L. Turner II, eds. 1995. *Regions at risk: comparisons of threatened environments*. UN University studies on critical environmental regions. Tokyo: United Nations University Press.

Kates, R.W., and W.C. Clark. 1996. Environmental surprise: Expecting the unexpected? *Environment* 58, no. 2: 6-11, 28-34.

Kates, Robert W. 1997. Climate change 1995: Impacts, adaptations, and mitigation. (A review of the IPCC report). *Environment* 39, no. 9: 29-33.

Kates, Robert W. 1999. Population and consumption: From more to enough. In *Sustainable development: The challenge of transition*, eds. Jurgen Schmandt and C.H. Ward. New York: Cambridge University Press.

Kaufman, Les, and Paul Dayton. 1997. Impacts of marine resource extraction on ecosystem services and sustainability. In *Nature's services: Societal dependence on natural ecosystems*, ed. Gretchen C. Daily. Washington, D.C.: Island Press.

Keck, M.E., and K. Sikkink. 1998. *Activists beyond borders: Advocacy networks in international politics*. Ithaca, NY: Cornell University Press.

Kempton, Willett, James S. Boster, and Jennifer A. Hartley. 1995. *Environmental values in American culture*. Cambridge, MA: MIT Press.

Kendall, Henry W., Roger Beachy, Thomas Eisner, Fred Gould, Robert Herdt, Peter H. Raven, Jozef S. Schell, and M.S. Swaminathan. 1997. *Bioengineering of Crops: Report of the World Bank Panel on Transgenic Crops*. The International Bank for Reconstruction and Development/The World Bank. Washington, D.C.: The World Bank.

Kingdon, John W. 1984. *Agendas, alternatives and public policies*. Boston: Little Brown.

Landes, David S. 1998. *The wealth and poverty of nations: Why some are so poor and some so rich*. New York: W.W. Norton and Company.

Lansing, J. Stephen. 1991. *Priests and programmers. Technologies of power in the engineered landscape of Bali*. Princeton, NJ: Princeton University Press.

Mathews, Jessica T. 1997. Power shift: The changing role of central government. *Foreign Affairs* 76, no. 1: 50-67.

Merck Family Fund. 1995. *Yearning for balance: Views of America on consumption, materialism, and the environment.* Takoma Park, MD: Merck Family Fund.

Miles, Edward L. 1995. Integrated assessment of climate variability, impacts, and policy response in the Pacific Northwest. *US Globec News* 9 (November): 4-5, 14-15.

Moldan, B., S. Billharz, and R. Matravers, eds. 1997. *Sustainability indicators: A report on the Project on Indicators of Sustainable Development.* SCOPE (Scientific Committee on Problems of the Environment). New York: John Wiley and Sons.

NAE (National Academy of Engineering). 1988. *Cities and their vital systems: Infrastructure past, present and future.* J.H. Ausubel and R. Herman, eds. Washington, D.C.: National Academy Press.

_____. 1989. *Technology and environment.* J.H. Ausubel and H.E. Sladovich, eds. Washington, D.C.: National Academy Press.

_____. 1990. *Energy: Production, consumption and consequences.* John L. Helm, ed. Washington, D.C.: National Academy Press.

_____. 1993. *Keeping pace with science and engineering: Case studies in environmental regulation.* Myron F. Uman, ed. Washington, D.C.: National Academy Press.

_____. 1994. *The greening of industrial ecosystems.* Braden R. Allenby and Deanna J. Richards, eds. Washington, D.C.: National Academy Press.

_____. 1996. *Engineering within ecological constraints.* Peter Schulze, ed. Washington, D.C.: National Academy Press.

_____. 1997a. *The industrial green game: Implications for environmental design and management.* Deanna J. Richards, ed. Washington, D.C.: National Academy Press.

_____. 1997b. *Technological trajectories and the human environment.* Jesse H. Ausubel and H. Dale Langford, eds. Washington, D.C.: National Academy Press.

_____. 1998. *The ecology of industry: Sectors and linkages.* Deanna J. Richards and Greg Pearson, eds. Washington, D.C.: National Academy Press.

_____. 1999a. *Measures of environmental performance and ecosystem conditions.* Ed. Peter Schulze. Washington, D.C.: National Academy Press.

_____. 1999b. *Industrial environmental performance metrics: Challenges and opportunities.* Committee on Industrial Environmental Performance Metrics. Washington, D.C.: National Academy Press.

NCEDR (National Center for Environmental Decision Making and Research). 1998. Stakeholder participation in the US national assessment of possible consequences of climate variability and change. (Tech. Report NCEDR/98-19). Oak Ridge, TN: NCEDR.

NRC (National Research Council). 1981. *Federal research on the biological and health effects of ionizing radiation.* Committee on Federal Research on the Biological and Health Effects of Ionizing Radiation. Washington, D.C.: National Academy Press.

_____. 1985. *Reducing hazardous waste generation: An evaluation and call to action.* Board on Environmental Studies and Toxicology. Washington, D.C.: National Academy Press.

_____. 1986. *Global change in the geosphere-biosphere: Initial priorities for an IGBP.* U.S. Committee for an International Geosphere-Biosphere Program. Washington, D.C.: National Academy Press.

_____. 1988. *The behavioral and social sciences: Achievements and opportunities.* Commission on Behavioral and Social Sciences and Education. Washington, D.C.: National Academy Press.

_____. 1989. *Towards an understanding of global change: Initial priorities for US contributions to the International Geosphere-Biosphere Program.* Board on Global Change. Washington, D.C.: National Academy Press.

_____. 1991. *Toward sustainability: A plan for collaborative research on agriculture and natural resource management.* Washington, D.C.: National Academy Press.

_____. 1995. *A review of the US Global Change Research Program and NASA's Mission to Planet Earth/Earth Observing System* (La Jolla Report). Committee on Global Change Research and Board on Sustainable Development. Washington, D.C.: National Academy Press.

_____. 1996a. *Upstream: Salmon and society in the Pacific Northwest.* Committee on the Protection and Management of Pacific Northwest Anadromous Salmonids. Washington, D.C.: National Academy Press.

_____. 1996b. *Water and sanitation services for megacities in the developing world.* A working paper. Panel on Sustainable Water and Sanitation Services for Megacities, Water Science and Technology Board. Washington, D.C.: National Academy Press.

_____. 1996c. *Meeting the challenges of megacities in the developing world: A collection of working papers.* Washington, D.C.: National Academy Press.

_____. 1996d. *Linking science and technology to society's environmental goals: Report of a National Forum on Science and Technology Goals.* Washington, D.C.: National Academy Press.

_____. 1997a. *Bits of power: Issues in global access to scientific data.* Committee on Issues in the Transborder Flow of Scientific Data. Washington, D.C.: National Academy Press.

_____. 1997b. *Environmentally significant consumption: Research directions.* Paul C. Stern, Thomas Dietz, Vernon W. Ruttan, Robert H. Socolow, and James L. Sweeney, eds. Washington, D.C.: National Academy Press.

_____. 1998a. *Overview: Global environmental change: Research pathways for the next decade.* Committee on Global Change Research. Washington, D.C.: National Academy Press.

_____. 1998b. *Health effects of exposure to low levels of ionizing radiation: Time for reassessment?* Committee on Health Effects of Exposure to Low Levels of Ionizing Radiation (BEIR VII). Washington, D.C.: National Academy Press.

_____. 1998c. *Meeting megacity challenges: A role for innovation and technology.* Committee on Meeting Megacity Challenges. Washington, D.C.: National Academy Press.

_____. 1998d. *New strategies for America's watersheds.* Committee on Watershed Management. Washington, D.C.: National Academy Press.

_____. 1999a (forthcoming). *Human dimensions of global change: Research pathways for the next decade.* Committee on Human Dimensions of Global Change. Washington, D.C.: National Academy Press.

_____. 1999b. *Observing climate variability and change: Adequacy of existing observing systems: A decision maker's perspective.* Panel on Climate Observing Systems' Status, Climate Research Committee. Washington, D.C.: National Academy Press.

NSF (National Science Foundation). 1997. NSF funds first long-term studies of urban ecology. Press release, 10/20/97. Available http://www.lternet.edu.

Nakicenovic, N. 1996. Freeing energy from carbon. *Daedalus* 125, no. 3: 95-112.

National Assessment Synthesis Team. Forthcoming. *First national assessment on climate change impacts.* Washington: National Science and Technology Council. See http://www.nacc.usgcrp.gov/.

NSB/NSF (National Science Board, National Science Foundation). 1999. *Environmental science and engineering for the 21st century: The role of the National Science Foundation.* Interim Report. NSB 99-133. Washington, D.C.: National Science Foundation.

National Science and Technology Council. 1995. *Preparing for the future through science and technology: An agenda for environmental and natural resource research.* Washington, D.C.: Committee on Environment and Natural Resources. National Science and Technology Council.

New York Academy of Sciences. 1997. *Systems for Global Public Health Collaboration: Organizing for a time of renewal.* New York: New York Academy of Sciences.

Nilsson, J., and P. Grennfelt, eds. 1988. *Critical loads for sulphur and nitrogen.* Miljorapport 15. Copenhagen: Nordic Council of Ministers.

Norberg-Bohm, V., W.C. Clark, B. Bakshi, J. Berkenkamp, S.A. Bishko, M D. Koehler, J.A. Marrs, C.P. Nielsen, and A. Sagar. 1992. *International comparisons of environmental hazards: Development and evaluation of a method for linking environmental data with the strategic debate management priorities for risk management.* Cambridge, MA: Center for Science and International Affairs, John F. Kennedy School of Government, Harvard University.

Norberg-Bohm, V., W.C. Clark, M. Koehler, and J. Marrs. 1990. Comparing environmental hazards: The development and evaluation of a method based on a causal taxonomy of environmental hazards. In *Usable knowledge for managing global climatic change,* ed. W.C. Clark, 18-67. Stockholm: Stockholm Environment Institute.

Nye, Joseph, and Robert O. Keohane. 1998. Power and interdependence in the information age. *Foreign Affairs 77,* no. 5: 81-94.

O'Riordan, Timothy. 1997. Climate change 1995: Economic and social dimensions. (A review of the IPCC report). *Environment 39,* no. 9: 34-39.

Ostrom, Elinor. 1990. *Governing the commons: the evolution of institutions for collective action.* Cambridge, UK: Cambridge University Press.

PCAST (President's Committee of Advisors on Science and Technology). 1997. *Federal energy research and development for the challenges of the 21st century.* Report of the Panel on Energy Research. Washington, D.C.: OSTP (Office of Science and Technology Policy).

_____. 1998. *Teeming with life: Investing in science to understand and use America's living capital.* Washington, D.C.: OSTP (Office of Science and Technology Policy).

_____. 1999. *Powerful partnerships: The federal role in international cooperation in energy innovation.* Washington, D.C.: OSTP (Office of Science and Technology Policy).

PCSD (President's Council on Sustainable Development). 1997. *Building on consensus: A progress report on sustainable America.* Washington, D.C.: PCSD.

_____. 1998. *Sustainable communities: Task force report.* Washington, D.C.: PCSD.

Pinstrup-Anderson, P., R. Pandya-Lorch, and M.W. Rosegrant. 1997. *The world food situation: Recent developments, emerging issues, and long-term prospects.* Washington, D.C.: International Food Policy Research Institute.

Policy Research Project on Sustainable Development. 1998. *The road to sustainable development: A guide for nongovernmental organizations.* Lyndon B. Johnson School of Public Affairs, Policy Research Project Report, Number 120. Austin: The Board of Regents of the University of Texas.

Porter, Roger B., and Raymond Vernon. 1989. *Foreign economic policymaking in the United States.* Cambridge, MA: Center for Business and Government, John F. Kennedy School of Government, Harvard University.

Posch, M., and W. de Vries. 1999. Derivation of critical loads by steady-state and dynamic soil models. In *The impact of nitrogen deposition on natural and semi-natural ecosystems,* ed. S.J. Langan, 213-234. Norwell, MA: Kluwer Academic Publishers.

Rapport, D.J., H.A. Regier, and C. Thorpe. 1981. Diagnosis, prognosis and treatment of ecosystems under stress. In *Stress effects on natural ecosystems,* eds. G.W. Barrett and R. Rosenberg. New York: Wiley.

Raskin, Paul, Gilberto Gallopin, Pablo Gutman, Al Hammond, and Rob Swart. 1998. *Bending the curve: Toward global sustainability.* Boston: Stockholm Environment Institute.

Rasmussen, P.E., K.W.T. Goulding, J.R. Brown, P.R. Grace, H.H. Janzen, and M. Körschens. Long-term agroecosystem experiments: Assessing agricultural sustainability and global change. *Science* 282: 893-896.

Rayner, Steve, and Elizabeth L. Malone. 1998. *Human choice and climate change.* 4 vols. Columbus, OH: Battelle Press.

Regier, H.A., and G.L. Baskerville. 1986. Sustainable redevelopment of regional ecosystems degraded by exploitive development. In *Sustainable development of the biosphere*, eds. William C. Clark and R.E. Munn. Cambridge, UK: Cambridge University Press.

Root, T.L., and S.H. Schneider. 1995. Ecology and climate: Research strategies and implications. *Science* 269: 334-341.

Rosenberg, N. 1982. Learning by using. In *Inside the black box: Technology and economics*, ed. N. Rosenberg, 120-140. Cambridge, UK: Cambridge University Press.

Rosswall, Thomas, Robert G. Woodmansee, and Paul G. Risser, eds. 1988. *Scales and global change: spatial and temporal variability in biospheric and geospheric processes*. SCOPE (Scientific Committee on Problems of the Environment) 35. New York: J. Wiley.

Rotmans, J., and H. Dowlatabadi. 1998. Evaluation of methods and strategies. In *Human choice and climate change: An international social science assessment*, eds. S. Rayner and E. Malone. Washington, D.C.: Battelle Press.

Runge, C.F. 1995, Trade, pollution, and environmental protection. In *The handbook of environmental economics*, ed. D.W. Bromley, 353-375. Oxford, UK: Blackwell.

Runge, C.F., F. Ortalo-Magné, and P. Vande Kamp. 1994. *Free trade, protected environment: Balancing trade liberalization and environmental interests*. New York: Council on Foreign Relations.

Ruttan, Vernon W., ed. 1994. *Agriculture, environment and health: Sustainable development in the 21st Century.* Minneapolis: University of Minnesota Press.

_____. 1996. *United States development assistance policy: the domestic politics of foreign economic aid.* Baltimore: Johns Hopkins University Press.

_____. 1997. Induced innovation, evolutionary theory, and path dependence: Sources of technical change. *Economic Journal* 107, no. 444: 1520-1529.

START (Global Change System for Analysis, Research and Training). See http://www.start.org.

Sandler, Todd. 1997. *Global challenges: An approach to environmental, political and economic problems.* Cambridge, UK: Cambridge University Press.

Schelling, Thomas C. 1996. Research by accident. *Technological Forecasting and Social Change* 53, no. 1: 15-20.

Settle, William H., Hartjahyo Ariawan, Astuti Endah Tri, Cahyana Widyastama, Hakim Arief Lukman, Hindayana Dadan, Lestari Alifah Sri, Pajarningsih Sartanto. 1996. Managing tropical rice pests through conservation of generalist natural enemies and alternative prey. *Ecology* 77: 1975-1988.

Simpson, R. David, R.A. Sedjo, and J.W. Reid. 1996. Valuing biodiversity for use in pharmaceutical research. *Journal of Political Economy* 104: 163-185.

Skeffington, R.A., and E.J. Wilson. 1988. Excess nitrogen deposition: Issues for consideration. *Environmental Pollution* 54: 159-184.

Socolow, R., C. Andrews, F. Berkout, and V. Thomas, eds. *Industrial ecology and global change.* Cambridge, UK: Cambridge University Press.

Stokes, Donald E. 1997. *Pasteur's quadrant: Basic science and technological innovation.* Washington, D.C.: Brookings Institution Press.

Strong, Maurice, Chair, System Review Panel. 1998. *The third system review of the Consultative Group on International Agricultural Research (CGIAR).* Washington, D.C.: The World Bank.

Turner, B.L., W.C. Clark, R.W. Kates, J.F. Richards, J.T. Mathews, and W.B. Meyer, eds. 1990. *The Earth as transformed by human action: global and regional changes in the biosphere over the past 300 years.* Cambridge; New York: Cambridge University Press (especially Chapter I).

UN (United Nations). 1997. *Report of the UN Conference on Human Settlements* (Habitat II), Istanbul, 3-14 June, 1996. New York: United Nations. Available http://www.undp.org/un/habitat/agenda/.

_____. 1998. *Knowledge societies: Information technology for sustainable development.* UN Commission for Science and Technology for Development. R. Mansell and U. When, eds. Oxford: Oxford University Press.

_____. 1999. UN sustainable development web site: Success stories. http://www.un.org/esa/sustdev/.

UNCSD (United Nations Commission on Sustainable Development). 1997. *Overall progress achieved since the UN Conference on Environment and Development.* Addendum on International institutional arrangements. UN E/CN.17/1997/2/Add.28. New York: United Nations.

UNDP (United Nations Development Programme). 1998. *Human development report 1998: Consumption for human development.* New York: United Nations.

UNEP (UN Environment Programme), NASA (US National Aeronautics and Space Administration), and The World Bank. 1998. *Protecting our planet, securing our future.* Nairobi: UNEP.

USGCRP (United States Global Change Research Program). 1998. *Our changing planet: The FY 1999 US Global Change Research Program: A report by the Subcommittee on Global Change Research.* Washington, D.C.: National Science and Technology Council.

_____. Forthcoming. US National Assessment: The Potential Consequences of Climate Variability and Change: Synthesis Report. Washington, D.C.: National Science and Technology Council. See http://www.nacc.usgcrp.gov/.

US House of Representatives. 1998. *Unlocking our future: Toward a new national science policy: A report to Congress by the House Committee on Science.* Washington, D.C.: The US House of Representatives Committee on Science.

Vitousek, P.M., H.A. Mooney, J. Lubchenco, and J.M. Melillo. 1997. Human domination of earth's ecosystems. *Science* 277: 494-499.

WBGU (German Advisory Council on Global Change). 1997. *World in transition: The research challenge.* Annual Report 1996. Berlin: Springer-Verlag. Also available through the Council's home page at http://www.awi-bremmerhaven.de/WBGU.

WCED (World Commission on Environment and Development). 1987. *Our common future.* Oxford, UK: Oxford University Press.

WRI (World Resources Institute). 1998. *World resources 1998-99: A guide to the global environment.* A joint publication by the World Resources Institute, the United Nations Environment Programme, the United Nations Development Programme, and the World Bank. New York: Oxford University Press.

Watson, Robert T., Marufu C. Zinyowera, and Richard H. Moss, eds. 1998. *The regional impacts of climate change: An assessment of vulnerability: A special report of IPCC Working Group II.* New York: Cambridge University Press. Published for the Intergovernmental Panel on Climate Change (IPCC).

Wernick, I.K. 1996. Consuming materials the American way. In *Technological Forecasting and Social Change* 53: 111-122.

Wernick, I.K., R. Herman, S. Govind, and J.H. Ausubel. 1996. Materialization and dematerialization: Measures and trends. *Daedalus* 125, no. 3: 171-198.

Wilbanks, T., and R.W. Kates. Forthcoming. Global change in local places: How scale matters. *Climate Change.*

Williams, Jill, ed. 1978. *Carbon dioxide, climate and society.* Oxford, UK: Pergammon Press.

World Bank. 1992. *World development report: Development and the environment.* New York: Oxford University Press.

_____. 1997. *World development report 1998: Knowledge for development.* Washington, D.C.: The World Bank.

ENDNOTES

1   Editorial in *Science*, Vol. 277, July (1997).
2   see, e.g., World Bank (1997); UN (1998).
3   NRC (1998a).
4   Schelling (1996).
5   Kates and Clark (1996).
6   NRC (1998a), p. 18; see also NRC (1995).
7   Clark and Munn (1986); UNEP et al. (1998).
8   E.g., Ruttan (1994).
9   NRC (1998a); Watson et al. (1998).
10 NRC (1998a), p. 9.
11 Adams (1990).
12 *Ecological Principles*, IUCN et al. (1980, 1991); *World Conservation Strategy*, IUCN et al. (1991); *Caring for the Earth* (1991); DIVERSITAS (1998).
13 *Sustainable Biosphere Initiative*, ESA (1998); *Teeming with Life*, PCAST (1998).
14 Global habitability program, Goody (1982); "Pathways" report, NRC (1998a).
15 Natural resource management, e.g., Holling (1978); global issues, e.g., Williams (1978).
16 See, e.g., the review in NRC (1988), pp. 196ff.
17 IHDP (1998).
18 See Rayner and Malone (1998) and NRC (1999a).
19 For a history of these efforts, see, e.g., Helm (1990); NAE (1993, 1994, 1996, 1997a,b, 1998, 1999); NRC (1996d).
20 E.g., NRC (1985).
21 E.g., NRC (1997b); PCAST (1997, 1999).
22 E.g., NAE (1994).
23 NRC (1998a); EU (1998); IHDP (1998).
24 E.g., NRC (1998a), UNEP et al. (1998).
25 E.g., Gunderson et al. (1995); NRC (1996a).
26 E.g. Johnson et al. (1998).
27 NRC (1998d).
28 Studies of rice paddies as ecosystems discovered that pest species can be controlled with a multispecies community ecology regime that uses far less pesticide while allowing higher yields. Insights from the study of culture and ecology have led to a new vision of how humans can feed themselves with lower impacts on life support systems vital to the well-being of a rural society (see Lansing 1991).
29 Houghton et al. (1996; NRC 1998a).
30 Gibson et al. (1998); Root and Schneider (1995); Wilbanks and Kates, forthcoming; Cash and Moser (1998); Gunderson et al. (1995); Rosswall et al. (1988); Clark (1985); NRC (1998c); Turner et al. (1990).
31 IGBP (1991, 1994); IHDP (1998); START, http://www.igbp.kva.se/start.html.
32 Watson et al. (1998).
33 USGCRP (forthcoming); See http://www.nacc.usgcrp.gov/.
34 These include the European Union's Fifth Framework Program for research, EU (1998), http:www.cordis.lu/fp5/home.html; the Canadian Tri-Council Eco-Research Program, http:www.sdri.ubc.ca/gbfp/tricerp.html; and the Inter-American Institute for Global Change Research, HtmlResAnchor http://www.iai.int/. For a broad overview of other initiatives see UNCSD (1997).
35 Dooge et al. (1992).
36 UNCSD (1997).

[37] Information on the "World Conference on Science: Science for the 21st Century, A New Commitment" is provided on UNESCO's web page http://www.unesco.org; information on the "Conference on the Transition to Sustainability" is provided on http://www4.nationalacademies.org/oia/iap/IAPHome.nsf/all/2000+Conference. Visited 8/27/99.

[38] NRC (1998a), p. 18.

[39] Holling (1986); Clark (1988).

[40] Kingdon (1984); Baumgartner and Jones (1993); Burton et al. (1993); Gunderson et al. (1995).

[41] Hardin (1968); Cohen (1995); Daily and Ehrlich (1996).

[42] Nilsson and Grennfelt (1988); Skeffington and Wilson (1988); Bull (1991); Posch and de Vries (1999).

[43] FCCC (1992), Article 2.

[44] E.g., Kasperson et al. (1995).

[45] See also Cohen (1995); Posch and de Vries (1999).

[46] NRC (1981, 1998b).

[47] Landes (1998); NRC (1998a); Grübler (1998); Turner et al. (1990).

[48] E.g., Herman et al. (1989); Nakicenovic (1996); Wernick et al. (1996); NRC (1997b); Grübler (1998).

[49] NRC (1997b); Kates (1999); Policy Research Project on Sustainable Development (1998).

[50] Kempton et al. (1995); Merck Family Fund (1995).

[51] Durning (1992); Center for a New American Dream (1997-1999).

[52] UNDP (1998).

[53] NRC (1997a).

[54] Mathews (1997).

[55] Nye and Keohane (1998).

[56] E.g., Keck and Sikkink (1998).

[57] Ostrum (1990); Haas et al. (1993); NRC (1997b); Rayner and Malone (1998); Francis and Lerner (1996).

[58] Sandler (1997).

[59] E.g., Raskin et al. (1998); Hammond (1998); Bossel (1998).

[60] The Global Scenario Group (GSG), part of the Stockholm Environment Institute's Polestar Project, was established to engage a diverse group of development professionals in a long-term commitment to examining the requirements for sustainability. It is an independent, international, and interdisciplinary body that represents a variety of geographic and professional experiences and engages in an ongoing process of global and regional scenario development, policy analysis, and public education.

[61] Fritz (1998); GEA (1997).

[62] USGCRP (forthcoming); See http://www.nacc.usgcrp.gov.

[63] As an example of such work, see *Interactive Social Science: Environmental Research*, the report of a workshop sponsored by the Economic and Social Research Council's Global Environmental Change Programme (UK) and the Social Sciences and Humanities Research Council (Canada), University of Sussex, Brighton, UK, 2-4 March 1998.

[64] NCEDR (1998).

[65] Dowlatabadi and Morgan (1993); Rotmans and Dowlatabadi (1998); NRC (1998a).

[66] E.g.,. Gunderson et al. (1995); PCSD (1997); UN (1999).

[67] Cebon et al. (1998); NRC (1996a); Miles (1995).

[68] UN (1998).

[69] UNCSD (1997).

[70] E.g., Carnegie Commission on Science, Technology and Government (1992).

71 UN (1999).

72 EU (1998).

73 Porter and Vernon (1989).

74 E.g. NSTC (1995); NRC (1996); NSB (1999).

75 Ruttan (1994); Strong (1998).

76 In 1992, the Carnegie Commission on Science, Technology, and Government suggested establishing a Consultative Group for Research on the Environment (CGREEN), patterned after the Consultative Group on International Agricultural Research to Integrate Environmental Science. Carnegie Commission (1992, pp. 22ff).

77 The Advanced Research Projects Agency (ARPA), later named the Defense Advanced Research Projects Agency, was established by the U.S. Department of Defense in 1958 to foster and fund cutting-edge research related to defense needs. The ARPA-supported work in universities led to development of the Internet and optical communications, among other accomplishments. For an account of ARPA's support of the development of what became the Internet, see Hughes (1998).

78 Bell et al. (1994); Strong (1998).

79 Norberg-Bohm et al. (1990); Norberg-Bohm et al. (1992).

80 Branscomb (1998).

81 U.S. House of Representatives (1998); Guston (1997).

82 USGCRP (1998); NRC (1998d).

83 NRC (1998a).

84 This conclusion is based also on discussions at the board's 1997 Workshop on the Decomposition of Complex Issues in Sustainable Development, held at The H. John Heinz III Center for Science, Economics and the Environment, Washington DC, February 27-28, 1997.

85 In the years since the Brundtland report, there have been dramatic successes in efforts to improve water, air, and sanitation services in urban systems. But the number of city dwellers without decent housing or adequate water and exposed to poor sanitation and air pollution has grown (World Bank 1992, Ch. 4) to 600 million, while another 100 million have no home at all (UN 1997, Chs. 1-16). Meeting the housing and employment needs for these urban dwellers and the billions yet to come will inevitably lead to massive conversion of the productive agricultural and forest resources adjacent to the city and along the connecting highways and rail lines. More distant water resources will be diverted or polluted, and airborne pollutants will cross continents and national boundaries.

86 E.g., NAE (1988); UN (1997); NRC (1996b, 1998c).

87 Declining research spending, Alston et al. (1998b), p. 61; food production capabilities, Alston et al. (1998a,b).

88 Green Revolution, Conway (1997); bioengineering of crops, Kendall et al. (1997).

89 See, e.g., NAE (1999a,b); UNEP (1998); WRI (1998).

90 Raskin et al. (1998).

91 Recently, the U.S. National Science Foundation began support of studies focused on human-dominated ecosystems. The long-term ecology of urban environments is being studied in Phoenix, Arizona, and Baltimore, Maryland, as part of the NSF's Long Term Ecological Research (LTER) program. (See NSF 1997 and Chapter 5 of this report.)

92 PCAST (1998).

93 Kaufman and Dayton (1997).

94 Costanza and Folke (1997).

95 Simpson et al. (1996), p. 177.

96 PCAST (1998); NSB/NSF (1999).

97 Dobson et al. (1997).

[98] U.S. Department of Agriculture, National Forest Service, http://www.usfs.gov.

[99] E.g., NSF's Water and Watersheds Program, NASA's Land Use/Land Cover Change Program.

[100] The Board is indebted to Harvey Brooks of Harvard University for helping to clarify its thinking on the potential analogies discussed here.

 Appendixes

APPENDIX A

Biographical Information on Board Members and Staff

CHAIR

Edward A. Frieman is director emeritus of the Scripps Institution of Oceanography. He also has served as vice chancellor for Marine Sciences at the University of California, San Diego, deputy director of the Princeton Plasma Physics Laboratory, and director of energy research for the US Department of Energy. A fellow of the American Physical Society and a member of the National Academy of Sciences, Dr. Frieman was awarded a National Science Foundation Senior Postdoctoral Fellowship in 1964, the John Simon Guggenheim Fellowship in 1970, the Department of Energy Distinguished Service Medal in 1984, and the Richtmyer Award from the American Physical Society in 1984. He has served on numerous science advisory panels and committees, including the Vice President's Space Advisory Board, the President's Committee on the National Medal of Science, the White House Science Council, and the Secretary of Energy Advisory Board. Dr. Frieman has a BS, engineering, Columbia University; MS and PhD, physics, Polytechnic Institute of Brooklyn.

MEMBERS

Lourdes Arizpe is a researcher at the Regional Center for Multidisciplinary Research and former director of the Institute of Anthropological Research of the National University of Mexico. She is vice president of the International Social Science Council and has served as president of the

International Union of Anthropological and Ethnological Sciences (1988-93). She was a Fulbright scholar at Rutgers University in 1978 and received a Guggenheim grant in 1981. She has been on the Steering Committee of Development Alternatives for Women in a New Era (1985-89) and assistant director-general for Culture at UNESCO (1994-98). She holds an MA, National School of Anthropology in Mexico, and PhD, London School of Economics and Political Science.

John Bongaarts is vice president of the Population Council, Research Division, where he has been employed since 1973. His research has focused on a variety of population issues, including the determinants of fertility, population-environment relationships, the demographic impact of the AIDS epidemic, and population policy options in the developing world. He is a member of the Royal Dutch Academy of Sciences and a fellow of the American Association for the Advancement of Science. He has been recognized with the Mindel Sheps Award from the Population Association of America (1986) and the Research Career Development Award from the National Institutes of Health (1980-1985). Dr. Bongaarts holds an MS, systems analysis, Eindhoven Institute of Technology, The Netherlands; and PhD, physiology and biomedical engineering, University of Illinois.

Ralph J. Cicerone is the chancellor of the University of California, Irvine, where he also is Daniel G. Aldrich, Jr. Professor in the Earth System Science Department. He is an atmospheric chemist with research interests in how chemicals in the atmosphere may cause climate change. He is also involved in research on the stratospheric ozone layer, and the sources and sinks of atmospheric methane, nitrous oxide, and methyl bromide. From 1980 until 1989, he was director of the Atmospheric Chemistry Division of the National Center for Atmospheric Research. From 1992 to 1994, he served as the president of the American Geophysical Union (AGU), the world's largest scientific society for earth scientists. He is a past chair of the National Research Council's Board on Global Change. He is a fellow of the American Association for the Advancement of Science, the AGU, and the American Meteorological Society. He is a member of the National Academy of Sciences and the American Academy of Arts and Sciences. He has a SB, Massachusetts Institute of Technology; and an MS and a PhD, engineering and physics, University of Illinois.

William C. Clark is the Harvey Brooks Professor of International Science, Public Policy and Human Development at Harvard University's John F. Kennedy School of Government. He served as director of the school's Center for Science and International Affairs (1993-1994) and also as vice chairman of the University Committee on Environment. Dr. Clark's current research focuses on how societies learn to cope with the policy issues arising through the interactions of environment, development, and security concerns in international affairs. In particular, he has studies under way on the development of fair assessment frameworks for use in the management of climate change and on the comparative histories of social learning in national efforts to deal with global environmental change. Dr. Clark is a member of the Sigma Xi Scientific Research Society and was awarded a MacArthur Prize Fellowship in 1983 for his achievements in environmental policy. He holds a BS, biology, Yale University; and a PhD, ecology, University of British Columbia in Canada. Dr. Clark serves as co-chair of the Sustainability Transition Study.

Robert A. Frosch is a senior research fellow at the Belfer Center for Science and International Affairs of the John F. Kennedy School of Government at Harvard University. After doing research in underwater sound and ocean acoustics, he served for a dozen years in a number of governmental and intergovernmental positions, including deputy director of Advanced Research Projects Agency of the Department of Defense, assistant secretary of the Navy for research and development, assistant executive director of the United Nations Environmental Program, and administrator of the National Aeronautics and Space Administration. In 1989, Frosch revived, redefined, and popularized the term "industrial ecology," and his research has focused on this field in recent years, especially in metals-handling industries. In 1993, he retired as vice president of General Motors Corporation, where he was in charge of the North American Operations Research and Development Center. Dr. Frosch is a member of the National Academy of Engineering. He holds an AB, Columbia College; and an MS and a PhD, theoretical physics, Columbia University.

Malcolm Gillis is the president of Rice University and a professor of economics. Prior to this appointment, Dr. Gillis served as dean of the Faculty of Arts and Sciences and dean of the Graduate School and vice provost for Academic Affairs at Duke University. His research and teaching activities have focused on two broad classes of issues in their national and international dimensions: fiscal reform and environmental policy. He has published more than 70 articles in journals. He is author, co-author, or editor of eight books, including a widely acclaimed 1988 publication, *Public Policies and the Misuse of Forest Resources,* and *Tax Reform in Developing Countries,* published in 1989, as well as the leading textbook in its field, *Economics of Development (4th edition),* now available in five languages. Dr. Gillis holds a BA and MA, University of Florida; and a PhD, University of Illinois.

Richard H. Harwood is C.S. Mott Foundation chair of sustainable agriculture in the Department of Crop and Soil Sciences at Michigan State University. Dr. Harwood worked in Asian farming systems development for 15 years while employed by the Rockefeller Foundation in Thailand and the International Rice Research Institute. He directed the Asian programs of the Winrock International Institute for Agricultural Development from 1985 to 1990. He served as director of the Rodale Research Center in Pennsylvania from 1977 to 1985. Dr. Harwood returned to Michigan State University in 1990 to assume teaching and research responsibilities and continue extension activities in sustainable development. He holds a BS, vegetable crops, Cornell University; and an MA and a PhD, horticulture and plant breeding, Michigan State University.

Robert W. Kates is a geographer, independent scholar, and emeritus director of the Feinstein World Hunger Program at Brown University. His research focuses on the persistence of hunger, climate impact assessment, long-term population dynamics, and the sustainability of the biosphere. A member of the National Academy of Sciences and the American Academy of Arts and Sciences, Dr. Kates serves as an executive editor of *Environment* magazine. He is a recipient of the 1991 National Medal of Science, the MacArthur Prize Fellowship (1981-85), and the honors award of the Association of American Geographers. Dr. Kates has a MA and PhD, geography, University of Chicago, as well as an honorary DSc, Clark University. Dr. Kates serves as the vice chairman of the board and co-chair of the Sustainability Transition Study.

Philip J. Landrigan is the Ethel H. Wise professor and chair of Community Medicine and director of the Environmental and Occupational Medicine at the Mount Sinai School of Medicine. He is responsible for directing research programs, training residents, and teaching medical students. From 1970 to 1985, Dr. Landrigan was a commissioned officer in the United States Public Health Service, where he served as an epidemic intelligence service officer and then as a medical epidemiologist with the Centers for Disease Control. He also established and directed the Environmental Hazards Branch of the Bureau of Epidemiology. From 1979 to 1985, he was director of the Division of Surveillance, Hazard Evaluations and Field Studies of the National Institute for Occupational Safety and Health. Dr. Landrigan holds an AB, Boston College; an MS, occupational medicine, University of London; and an MD, Harvard University Medical School.

Kai N. Lee is the John J. Gibson professor of environmental studies at Williams College, where he teaches environmental studies and public policy. Previously, he taught at the University of Washington (1973-91). His research interests center on institutional arrangements for a sustainability transition, particularly in biodiversity conservation. He is the author of *Compass and Gyroscope* (1993) and a member of the NRC panel that wrote *Upstream: Salmon and Society in the Pacific Northwest* (1996). Dr. Lee has interrupted his academic career twice, as a White House Fellow (1976-77) and as a member of the Northwest Power Planning Council (1983-87). He also serves as a member of the National Research Council's Commission on Geosciences, Environment, and Resources; senior fellow at the World Wildlife Fund US; chair of the environment committee of the Advisory Council of the Calvert Social Investment Fund; and a member of the editorial boards of the journals Ecological Economics and Ecosystems. Dr. Lee holds an AB, physics, Columbia University; and a PhD, physics, Princeton University.

Jerry Mahlman is director of the Geophysical Fluid Dynamics Laboratory of the National Oceanic and Atmospheric Administration and is a lecturer with rank of professor in the Atmospheric and Oceanic Sciences Program at Princeton University. Much of Dr. Mahlman's research career has been directed toward understanding the behavior of the stratosphere and troposphere. This has involved extensive mathematical modeling of the interactive chemical, radiative, dynamical, and transport aspects of the atmosphere, as well as their implications for climate and chemical change. Among his recent commitments, Dr. Mahlman has served on the Joint Scientific Committee of the World Climate Research Program, been a Councilor of the American Meteorological Society, chaired the advisory committee for National Aeronautics and Space Administration's Mission to Planet Earth, and is a member of the Advisory Committee for the Department of Energy's Climate Change Prediction Program. He is a fellow of the American Geophysical Union, was awarded the Presidential Distinguished Rank Award, and received the American Meteorological Society's highest honor, the Carl-Gustaf Rossby Research Medal. Dr. Mahlman holds a PhD, atmospheric sciences, Colorado State University.

Richard Mahoney is the distinguished executive in residence at the Center for the Study of American Business at Washington University in St. Louis. While at the Center, he has written a number of research reports and op-eds for major publications, including *The New York Times*, *Washington Post*, *The Wall Street Journal*, and others. He created "The CEO Series," to which he has contributed many essays, including *The Anatomy of a Public Policy Crisis, Business Must Act for All Its Stakeholders—Before*

"The Feds" Do, Trade Winds or Head Winds?, U.S. Government Export Policy, and *Insights from Business Strategy and Management "Big Ideas" of the Past Three Decades: Are They Fads or Enablers?* Mr. Mahoney joined Monsanto Company in 1962 as a product development specialist. He subsequently held various marketing, technical service, and new product development positions in Plastic Products, Agriculture, and International Operations. He was named executive vice president in 1977, president in 1980, and chief executive officer in 1983. He retired in 1995 as chairman of the board and chief executive officer. Mr. Mahoney holds a BS, chemistry, University of Massachusetts.

Pamela Matson is a professor in the Department of Geological and Environmental Sciences and the Institute of International Studies, Stanford University. Previously, she was a professor of ecosystem ecology at the University of California, Berkeley, and worked for 10 years as a research scientist at NASA/Ames Research Center. Her research has focused on the effects of natural and anthropogenic disturbances on biogeochemical cycling and trace gas exchange in tropical and temperate ecosystems. Other interests include the analysis of consequences of anthropogenic nitrogen on downwind and downstream ecosystems at regional scales. She serves on numerous committees, including the Scientific Committee for the International Geosphere-Biosphere Program, and the National Research Council's U.S. National Committee for the Scientific Committee on Problems of the Environment. She was named NASA-Ames Associate Fellow in 1991 in recognition of research excellence, and is a member of the American Academy of Arts and Sciences and the National Academy of Sciences. In 1995, Dr. Matson was selected as a MacArthur Fellow, and in 1997 was elected a Fellow of the American Association for the Advancement of Science. She holds a BS, biology, University of Wisconsin-Eau Claire; an MS, environmental science, Indiana University; and a PhD, forest ecology, Oregon State University.

William Merrell is the President of the H. John Heinz III Center for Science, Economics, and the Environment. Previously, Dr. Merrill was appointed vice chancellor for Strategic Programs of Texas A&M University where he also assumed the role of professor of oceanography and marine sciences. Immediately preceding this assignment he served as vice president for Research Policy of Texas A&M and was president of Texas A&M at Galveston from 1987 to 1992. He received the Distinguished Member Award for Research Achievement from the Texas A&M University Chapter of Sigma XI, the Distinguished Achievement Award from the Geosciences and Earth Resources Council, and the Distinguished Service Award of the National Science Foundation for "his lasting impact on the course of American science." Dr. Merrell holds a BS and an MA, physics, Sam Houston State University; and a PhD, oceanography, Texas A&M University.

G. William Miller is Chairman of G. Miller & Co., Inc., a merchant banking firm located in Washington D.C. Mr. Miller served as secretary of the US Department of Treasury, from August 1979 to January 1981. Previously he was chairman of the board of governors of the Federal Reserve System; chairman and chief officer of Textron Inc., a diversified manufacturing company; director of the Federal Reserve Board of Boston; and chairman and chief executive officer of Federated Stores, Inc., which operated a chain of department stores and supermarkets. He is currently the non-executive chairman of Home Place of America, Inc., a specialty retail company. Throughout his business career, Mr. Miller has taken an active part in public service, contributing as chairman of the Conference Board, the National Alliance of Business, the President's Committee on HIRE, and the US Industrial Payroll Savings Bond Committee, as well as co-chair of the US-USSR Trade Economics Council and the Polish-US Economic Council. He served as a Coast Guard Officer in the Far East and on the US west coast. He is a member of the Business Council, a trustee of the John H. Heinz III Center for Science, Economics and the Environment, a trustee of the Marine Biological Laboratory, and a member of the Presidents' Circle of the National Academies. Mr. Miller holds a BS, marine engineering, US Coast Guard Academy; and a JD, University of California, Berkeley.

Berrien Moore III is director of the Institute for the Study of Earth, Oceans, and Space at the University of New Hampshire. He has served as chair of the National Aeronautics and Space Administration's (NASA) Space Science and Applications Advisory Committee, for which he received the Distinguished Public Service Medal. He also serves as chair of the Scientific Committee for the International Geosphere-Biosphere Program and its Task Force on Global Analysis, Interpretation, and Modeling. Other boards on which he has been a member include the NASA Advisory Council's Committee on Earth System Science, the National Research Council's Board on Global Change, the Space Science Board's Committee on Earth Science, and the Science Executive Committee for the Earth Observing System. Dr. Moore's computer modeling of the global carbon cycle has received worldwide attention through his publications on the contribution of terrestrial biota to the concentration of atmospheric carbon dioxide and the role of the ocean as a sink for carbon dioxide. He holds a PhD, mathematics, University of Virginia. Dr. Moore served as chair of the Board on Sustainable Development Committee on Global Change Research until December 1998.

M. Granger Morgan is professor and head in the Department of Engineering and Public Policy at Carnegie Mellon University, where he also holds academic appointments in the Department of Electrical and Computer Engineering and the H. John Heinz III School of Public Policy and Management. Dr. Morgan's research involves the treatment of uncertainty in quantitative policy analysis, integrated assessment of global change, and a variety of issues in the assessment and management of risks to health, safety, and the environment. He is also working on the development of methods to perform risk ranking to support decision making in risk management organizations, such as federal agencies. He holds a BS, physics, Harvard College; an MS, astronomy and space science, Cornell University; and a PhD, applied physics and information sciences, University of California, San Diego.

Paul D. Raskin is president of Tellus Institute and director of the Stockholm Environment Institute—Boston, where he directs a comprehensive research program on environmental, resources and developmental policy. He previously was associate professor, Empire State College, State University of New York; assistant professor, State University of New York at Albany; and instructor of physics, City College of New York. Dr. Raskin's current research focuses on the requirements for a transition to sustainability at global, regional, national, and local scales. He conceived and implemented widely used planning tools for these purposes including the Long Range Energy Alternative Policy system, the Water Evaluation and Planning system, and the PoleStar System for integrated sustainable development analysis. He has provided policy assessments for numerous governments and private organizations throughout the world. Dr. Raskin holds a BS, physics, University of California, Berkeley; and a PhD, theoretical physics, Columbia University.

John B. Robinson is director of the Sustainable Development Research Institute and professor in the Department of Geography at the University of British Columbia. Previously, he worked in the Department of Environment and Resource Studies at the University of Waterloo, and as a consultant for federal and provincial departments and several coalitions of environmental groups. His research interests include energy and energy policy, socio-economic modeling and forecasting, scenarios of a sustainable society, sustainable development and resource use, and the history and philosophy of environmental thought. He was a principal lead author of Working Group III of the Intergovernmental Panel on Climate Change, and is a member of the Canadian Committee for the Institute for Applied Systems Analysis, the Canadian National Committee for the Scientific Committee on Problems of the Environment, and the board of directors of the Canadian Global Change Program. Dr. Robinson holds a BA, University of Toronto; an MES, York; and a PhD, University of Toronto.

Vernon W. Ruttan is a regents professor in the Department of Applied Economics at the University of Minnesota. He has authored and co-authored nine books and numerous technical publications, many of which focus on the economies of technical change and agricultural development. He has served on the President's Council of Academic Advisors and assumed the role of Agricultural Economist for the Rockefeller Foundation at the International Rice Research Institute in the Philippines. His non-academic service also includes president of the Agricultural Development Council and positions on advisory committees and boards, including the Research Advisory Committee of the U.S. Agency for International Development. Dr. Ruttan holds a BA, Yale University; and an MS and a PhD, University of Chicago.

Thomas C. Schelling is professor of economics and public affairs at the University of Maryland. Before his current position, he worked in the Executive Office of the President, the Department of Economics, at both Yale and Harvard Universities, and the RAND Corporation. He also has served as a consultant, member, and lecturer to many science- and defense-related organizations such as the Central Intelligence Agency and the Scientific Advisory Board of the U.S. Air Force. Dr. Schelling is a member of the National Academy of Sciences and the Institute of Medicine and has published several books and articles on energy and environmental policy, arms control, military strategy, crime, international economics, and public policy. He holds an AB, economics, University of California, Berkeley; and a PhD, economics, Harvard University.

Marvalee H. Wake is professor and chair of the Department of Integrative Biology at the University of California at Berkeley. Formerly, Dr. Wake was a visiting professor at the Université de Paris VII and the Universitat Bremen, Bremen, Germany. Her research interests include studies of evolutionary morphology, reproductive biology of lower vertebrates, patterns of evolution, and issues in biodiversity science. Her honors include fellow of both the California Academy of Sciences and American Association for the Advancement of Science, and a John Simon Guggenheim Foundation Fellowship. She is the secretary general of the International Union of Biological Sciences and a member of the executive committee of DIVERSITAS, an international biodiversity science program. Dr. Wake holds a BA, an MS and a PhD, University of Southern California.

Warren Washington is a senior scientist in the Climate and Global Dynamics Division at the National Center for Atmospheric Research, Boulder, Colorado. He has been at NCAR since 1963. Dr. Washington's areas of expertise are atmospheric science and climate research, and he specializes in computer modeling of the earth's climate. He has published more than 100 papers in professional journals and his book *An Introduction to Three Dimensional Climate Modeling*, co-authored with Claire Parkinson, is a standard reference on climate modeling. He serves on the National Science Board of the National Science Foundation. He previously served as president of the American Meteorological Society, on the President's National Advisory Committee on Oceans and Atmosphere, on the Secretary of Energy's Advisory Board, and on several National Research Council boards and panels. He is President of the Black Environmental Sciences Trust. He holds a BS, physics, an MS, meteorology, Oregon State University; and a PhD, meteorology, Pennsylvania State University.

M. Gordon Wolman is a professor in the Department of Geography and Environmental Engineering at the Johns Hopkins University, where he has taught since 1968. Previously, Dr. Wolman was a hydrologist for the U.S. Geological Survey. He served as chairman of the National Research Council's Commission on Geosciences, Environment, and Resources for the National Research Council, and president of the Geological Society of America, and president of the American Geophysical Union Section on Hydrology, and the Council of the American Geographical Society. He is a member of the National Academy of Sciences and the Philosophical Society, and a fellow of the American Academy of Arts and Sciences and the American Association for the Advancement of Science. Dr. Wolman holds a BS, Johns Hopkins University; an MS and a PhD, geology, Harvard University.

STAFF

Sherburne B. Abbott joined the Policy Division in January 1997 as the executive director of the Board on Sustainable Development. She has worked with the National Research Council for 13 years, serving previously as the director of the Committee on International Organizations and Programs of the Office of International Affairs and the director of the Polar Research Board of the Commission on Geosciences, Environment, and Resources. Prior to her work with the NRC, she was assistant scientific program director of the U.S. Marine Mammal Commission, a science teacher in a private high school, and a research assistant in cancer research at Tufts University. She has published papers on environmental monitoring in Antarctica, salmonid biology, and polar research. She holds an AB, biological sciences, Goucher College, and an MFS, ecology and natural resource policy, Yale University.

Laura J. Sigman joined the National Research Council as a research associate with the Board on Sustainable Development and the Committee on Global Change Research in February 1997. She holds an A.B. in environmental studies from Dartmouth College.

Appendix B

Acronyms

ARPA	Advanced Research Projects Agency
ASCEND 21	International Conference on an Agenda of Science for Environment and Development into the 21st Century
CFCs	Chlorofluorocarbons
CGIAR	Consultative Group on International Agricultural Research
CITES	Convention on International Trade in Endangered Species of Wild Fauna and Flora
CSD	Commission on Sustainable Development (UN)
EMEP	Geneva Protocol on Long-term Financing of the Cooperative Programme for Monitoring and Evaluation of the Long-range Transmission of Air Pollutants in Europe
ENSO	El Niño-Southern Oscillation
EPA	U.S. Environmental Protection Agency
FAO	UN Food and Agricultural Organization
GDP	Gross Domestic Product
GHCN	Global Historical Climatology Network
GSG	Global Scenarios Group

HCFCs	Hydrochlorofluorocarbons
HFCs	Hydrofluorocarbons
HDI	Human Development Index
IAP	InterAcademy Panel on International Issues
ICSU	International Council for Science
IGBP	International Geosphere-Biosphere Program
IHDP	International Human Dimensions Program
IMF	International Monetary Fund
IPCC	Intergovernmental Panel on Climate Change
ISO	International Organization for Standardization
IUCN	The World Conservation Union
LTER	NSF Long-Term Ecological Research Program
NGO	Nongovernmental organization
NO_x	Nitrogen oxides
NAE	National Academy of Engineering
NAS	National Academy of Sciences
NASA	National Aeronautics and Space Administration
NPPC	Northwest Power Planning Council
NRC	National Research Council
NSF	National Science Foundation
OECD	Organization for Economic Cooperation and Development
PSR	Pressure-State-Response model
RAINS	Regional Air Pollution Information and Simulation Model
SCOPE	Scientific Committee on Problems of the Environment
START	SysTem for Analysis, Research, and Training
UN	United Nations
UNCED	United Nations Conference on Environment and Development (Rio de Janiero, 1992, also known as "the Earth Summit")
UNCLOS	UN Convention on the Law of the Sea
UNCSD	UN Commission on Sustainable Development
UNDP	UN Development Program
UNEP	UN Environment Program

UNESCO	UN Educational, Scientific, and Cultural Organization
UNICEF	UN Children's Fund
VOC	Volatile organic compounds
WGBU	German Advisory Council on Global Change
WCED	World Commission on Environment and Development
WCRP	World Climate Research Program
WHO	World Health Organization
WRI	World Resources Institute
WSC	World Summit for Children

Index